Praise for *Anarchist Cuba*

"A brilliantly written and carefully organized study of anarchism in Cuba during the first decades after the country's independence in 1902. Based on a wide range of documents from archives in Cuba and the United States, Shaffer provides a detailed analysis of political events and ideas of the nation in early twentieth-century Cuba."
—*New West Indian Guide*

"Shaffer considers the different strands and at times internal conflicts that characterized anarchism in Cuba in the early decades of the twentieth century. He does a fine job of showing how Cuban anarchists operated in a larger cultural milieu that extended beyond the workplace and union hall, how they adapted the principal tenets of international anarchism to their own reality and put forth their own version of cubanidad, and, ultimately, how they played a vital yet often overlooked role in the development of the island's revolutionary tradition."
—*The Americas: A Quarterly Review of Inter-American Cultural History*

"Drawing on a wide range of archival materials, Shaffer builds a detailed picture of the anarchist movement's contribution to a leftist revolutionary agenda in republican Cuba, and its part within the complex interaction of different political and social forces that was taking place there at the beginning of the last century."
—*British Bulletin of Publications*

"These essays provide a vivid picture of the transnational nature of the anarcho-syndicalist/anarchist movement."
  —*Anarcho-Syndicalist Review*

"*Anarchist Cuba* is a comprehensive account of a group of people often overlooked in Cuban history, and Shaffer has provided the reader with a sense of what life was like for anarchists."
  —*Journal of Latin American Studies*

ANARCHIST CUBA

Countercultural Politics in the
Early Twentieth Century

Kirwin Shaffer

2019

Anarchist Cuba: Countercultural Politics in the Early Twentieth Century
This edition © 2019 PM Press
All rights reserved

ISBN: 978-1-62963-637-5
Library of Congress Control Number: 2018949074

Cover by John Yates/stealworks.com

PM Press
PO Box 23912
Oakland, CA 94623
www.pmpress.org

10 9 8 7 6 5 4 3 2 1

Dedicated to Kilian, Zeno, Lucía, Harper
. . . and all future grandchildren

Contents

Tables

Acknowledgments

I am grateful for the help, support, and critical advice from many different individuals and institutions in three countries. In Cuba, the staffs at the Museo Municipal de Regla, the Biblioteca Nacional José Martí, the Instituto de Literatura y Lingüística, and the Instituto de Historia de Cuba in Havana were efficient in their professionalism and generous in their tea breaks. I continue to offer my deepest gratitude to Professor Alejandro García Álvarez, who, among other things, introduced me to the wonders of the Instituto de Literatura y Lingüística in Havana.

I owe a special debt to the staff at the International Institute for Social History in Amsterdam who over the years have brought me hundreds of sources. I especially continue to thank and hold dear the institute's former Information Officer Mieke IJzermans for her effortless generosity and friendship over these many years. She also brought material that she thought I would find interesting during the workday and offered numerous sumptuous meals many evenings. There's nobody like her, as anyone who knows her will attest.

In the United States, I am indebted to the staffs at the National Archives in College Park, M.D., as well as the interlibrary loan staffs at the University of Kansas, DeSales University (Pennsylvania), and Penn State University–Berks College. These institutions also provided financial assistance that complemented two Tinker Field Research Grants, a U.S. Department of Education Foreign language and Areas Studies Fellowship, and a James B. Pearson Fellowship for Graduate Study Abroad from the Kansas Board of Regents.

Over the decades, many people have helped me think through the issues emerging in this history. I wish to thank Tony Rosenthal, Betsy Kuznesof, Marc Becker, Frank Fernández, Robert Whitney, Jorge Chinea, K. Lynn Stoner,

Luis Martínez-Fernández, Kenyon Zimmer, David Struthers, Davide Turcato, Mark Leier, Geoffroy de Laforcade, Bert Altena, Constance Bantman, Lucien van der Walt, Steven Hirsch, Evan Daniel, and Barry Carr—along with multiple others big and small who have offered reviews and encouragement over the years. I am especially thankful for the support of my original University Press of Florida editor Amy Gorelick as well as Craig, Ramsey, and Jonathan at PM Press for their immediate interest and assistance in bringing out this paperback edition.

I remain most appreciative of my family and friends who have been with me over the years on a variety of journeys (physical and emotional), especially Ken and Betsy; Dorian and Sarah; Nathaniel, Hannah, Sarra, Imane and Malick; and especially my muse who also keeps me grounded, Zohra. Cheers!

Preface to the PM Press Edition

I began to work on this book over two decades ago. Its original publication in 2005 as *Anarchism and Countercultural Politics in Early Twentieth-Century Cuba* was part of an early wave of renewed interest in the history of global anarchism generally and an emerging interest in anarchist history beyond the traditional European focus specifically. The book also appeared at a time when people began to rediscover non-state socialist alternatives such as the Seattle WTO protests, growing interest in the Zapatistas in Mexico, the World Social Forum, and horizontalism in places like Argentina. These movements and events challenged and confronted a rampant global neoliberalism following the disappearance of the Soviet Bloc. This specific moment in history likewise witnessed a growth and consolidation of the American Empire as wars in Afghanistan and Iraq were four and two years old respectively when the book first appeared.

Since the book's first publication, interest in the history of anarchism in Cuba (and throughout the Caribbean) has grown and evolved. The Spain-based historian Amparo Sánchez Cobos published *Sembrando ideales*, a splendid history that focuses on the important role of Spanish anarchists in shaping the anarchist movement in Cuba. Evan Daniel has written about the role of anarchism leading to the Cuban Independence War from 1895–1898, and—along with historians such as Chris Castañeda—illustrates the important role of Spanish-speaking anarchists in the United States during the 1880s and 1890s who launched early anarchist newspapers in Florida and New York. With these newspapers, they engaged in a global dialogue with anarchists in Spain and Cuba. When we couple this transnational press with the importance of anarchist migrants across the Atlantic and along the U.S. East Coast, we've been able to paint a picture of early anarchist networks linking Spain, the U.S., and the Caribbean.

Havana was a hub of these overlapping networks. From the 1890s to the 1920s, Cuba was the home of the largest number of anarchist groups, the largest number of newspapers, the most activists, several anarchist-oriented alternative health projects, and a few vegetarian restaurants. The newspaper *¡Tierra!* was not only the most important and longest-running newspaper published in Cuba (late 1902 to early 1915) but also the most important newspaper for anarchists throughout the Caribbean Basin from Panama to the Yucatán to South Florida to Puerto Rico. In fact, though published in Havana, it was essentially a "Caribbean" anarchist newspaper. This newspaper and others, coupled with an array of anarchist poets, short story writers, and novelists, shaped anarchist culture in the region.

But it was in Cuba where this anarchist cultural politics was strongest. The paperback edition of this book, now available to a wider audience, will hopefully help a larger number of interested people, activists, and just generally good people to appreciate these radical men and women. These were activists who embedded their trust in each other and devoted the few resources they had to challenge an expanding agri-industrial capitalist system, an emerging Cuban government, and its U.S. neocolonial overlords on issues such as national identity, the meaning of history, immigration, race, gender, education, the environment, and health.

Introduction

It is necessary to turn toward new directions, to purify the environment. In a phrase: it is necessary to constantly agitate among the workers, in every sense of the word if we do not want the workers to continue being exploited by opportunistic politicians and crafty monks.

Antonio Penichet (1918)

A telephone repairman who wrote poetry, a librarian who wrote short stories and advice on health, a printer who wrote novels and helped to start schools, vegetarian restaurant managers, health clinic coordinators for fellow workers, cigar rollers, full-time teachers, housewives, clerks, waiters, bookstore managers, sugarcane cutters, and railroad workers: these were Cuba's anarchists in the three decades following independence from Spain in 1898. While some published fiction or verse, others staged plays and recited poems in front of audiences. Others put their children on stage to demonstrate the power of an anarchist education. Many more listened; no doubt some of them were bored, wondering when the "real" action would begin. Thousands more read the books or saw the plays or perused the newspapers. Even a few rejected civilization and experimented with nudism. In early twentieth-century Cuba, anarchist culture flourished in many different forms.

Previous study of anarchism in Cuba has mirrored the traditional approach to anarchism throughout Latin America by examining the system primarily as a branch of a country's labor movement. However, by seeing anarchism more broadly as a social movement that engaged in a series of political and cultural conflicts with the larger Cuban society, a fuller picture of these diverse people emerges. By taking a sociocultural approach—an approach detailed later in this introduction and in chapter 1—this book arrives at three overarching conclusions. First, when anarchists challenged the cultural, economic, political, and religious institutions, they did so not only during the eight- to fourteen-hour workday in the workplace but also through their writings, rallies, and alternative health and educational initiatives; anarchists challenged Cuba's power holders throughout the rest of the day outside the workplace and inside the daily cultural milieu.[1] Second, this anarchist challenge reflected how the international anarchist movement operated within the context of a unique national situation in which Cuba's political culture was shaped by the wars for independence, the U.S. occupations following independence, and the foreign domination of the economy. As anarchists engaged and criticized the larger hegemonic culture and created their own counterculture (see chapter 1), anarchists modified the larger impulses and issues of international anarchism to fit the specific cultural, ethnic, and political realities on the island; thus, they "Cubanized" anarchism. As a result, one becomes aware of how anarchists, via their cultural critiques and initiatives, struggled to create their own specific sense of *cubanidad* (Cubanness). Third, this study sheds light on Cuba's leftist revolutionary heritage by illustrating an important but largely ignored early chapter of that heritage. In the early twentieth century, Cuba's anarchists played important roles in shaping the Cuban Left by agitating for not only labor reforms but also socialist internationalism, worker-initiated health reforms, radical education, revolutionary motherhood, and gender equity while rejecting the political system, capitalism, and religion.

Anarchism is a philosophy of freedom. As historian Peter Marshall puts it, anarchism "holds up the bewitching ideal of personal and social freedom, both in the negative sense of being free from all external restraint and imposed authority, and in the positive sense of being free to celebrate the full harmony of being."[2] One of the world's best-known and celebrated anarchists, Emma Goldman, defined anarchism as "the philosophy of a new social order based on the liberty unrestricted by man-made law; the theory that all the forms of government rest on violence, and are therefore wrong and harmful, as well as unnecessary."[3] I prefer a broader definition of the term along the lines of what Murray Bookchin calls *social anarchism*: a philosophy that "celebrates the thinking human mind without in any way denying passion, ecstasy, imagination, play, and art. Yet rather than reify them into hazy categories, it tries to incorporate them into everyday life. It is committed to rationality while opposing the rationalization of experience; to technology, while opposing the 'megamachine'; to social institutionalization, while opposing class rule and hierarchy; to genuine politics based on the confederal coordination of municipalities or communes by the people in direct face-to-face democracy, while opposing parliamentarianism and the state."[4] While most anarchists agreed with these sentiments, anarcho-communists, syndicalists, and naturists often disagreed on the best ways to bring forth a state of anarchy.

Anarcho-communists followed the ideas of Russian anarchist Peter Kropotkin, who believed in the communist principle of "from each according to his ability to each according to his need." In this way, anarcho-communists argued that, because humans are by nature social and cooperative beings, then society should be nonhierarchical and everyone should be equally rewarded for their labor contributions. The anarchist "commune" would be composed of free and equal people who were both consumers and producers. There was no single, agreed-upon route to achieve this ideal community; rather, some followed the "propaganda of the deed" belief and engaged in violence, others mobilized workers in labor actions, and still others created social and cultural institutions designed to foster that commune. In Cuba, anarcho-communists mostly organized their own groups independent of labor unions in order to propagandize for their cause, publish newspapers, and at times start schools. The anarchist advance to communism differed from that of the Marxists: the former rejected political parties, engagement with the political system, and the Marxist concept of a socialist state that would make a transition from capitalism to socialism and ultimately to communism. Anarcho-communists distrusted all governments, including dictatorships of the proletariat.

Anarcho-syndicalists evolved from the collectivist ideals of Russian anarchist Mikhail Bakunin and tended to follow a socialist line of "from each according to his ability to each according to his work." To this end, anarcho-syndicalists created revolutionary labor unions and worker-based organizations while the communists focused mainly on creating their autonomous groups. Anarcho-syndicalists hoped that their revolutionary unions would stage a worker-led revolution after which workers would control the industrial means of production. However, the considerable overlap between anarcho-communists and anarcho-syndicalists focused on a general belief in "mutual aid" and the possibility of a cooperative labor organization that operated without state intrusion. Anarcho-syndicalists also took the view that the revolutionary unions had to be concerned with more than just wages. Consequently, they took on educational, cultural, and social functions, like their communist brethren. The central difference between the two groups tended to revolve around the role of the group and the role of the union, which led to different emphases on creating cooperative communes or egalitarian factories and shops. Organizational differences often led to tactical differences when syndicalists used strategies of resistance that targeted workplaces with boycotts, strikes, and other forms of "direct action."[5]

A third strand within the island's anarchist movement was anarcho-naturism. Naturism was a global alternative health and lifestyle movement. Naturists focused on redefining one's life to live simply, eat cheap but nutritious vegetarian diets, and raise one's own food if possible. The countryside was posited as a romantic alternative to urban living, and some naturists even promoted what they saw as the healthful benefits of nudism. Globally, the naturist movement counted anarchists, liberals, and socialists as its followers. However, in Cuba a particular "anarchist" dimension evolved led by people like Adrián del Valle, who spearheaded the Cuban effort to shift naturism's focus away from only individual health to naturism having a "social emancipatory" function.[6]

Although these definitions are rather fixed, people's ideas tended to be more fluid. People were certainly free to change their ideas, and followers often breeched these delineations. For instance, nothing inherently prevented an anarcho-syndicalist in the Havana restaurant workers' union from supporting the alternative health care programs of the anarcho-naturists and seeing those alternative practices as "revolutionary." For this reason, at times throughout this book such terminological delineations, for all their specificity, actually cloud the truth. Thus, when such specific categorization is not necessary, I use the word *anarchist*, as Peter DeShazo did in his labor study of Chile: "a person who has expressed by work or deed a commitment to any of the various strains of libertarian thought."[7] Furthermore, the use of *anarchist* throughout this book reflects the usage of the term during the time period covered in this study, from 1898 to 1925. It was rare for anarchist newspapers, columnists, or fiction writers of the time to break down the terms; rather, *anarchist*, *anarchism*, and *anarchy* became the umbrella terms used by the movement and its various strands. Where it is necessary to highlight divisions in this book, such distinctions are noted.

The exact arrival of anarchist ideas on the island is uncertain. By 1857 followers of French anarchist Pierre-Joseph Proudhon had established the first mutual aid society in Cuba, and a form of reformist populism, influenced in part by socialist ideas, emerged.[8] In the 1860s, the young tobacco worker Saturnino Martínez founded *La Aurora*, the first weekly newspaper devoted to workers' issues. Through his paper, Martínez, though not an anarchist, provided the springboard for educating workers on the need for cooperative, working-class organizations.[9] In 1872, the same year that Bakunin and his followers were expelled from the Hague Congress of the International Workingmen's Association, anarchist cigar makers Enrique Roig San Martín and Enrique Messonier established the Instruction and Recreation Center (Centro de Instrucción y Recreo) in Santiago de las Vegas, Cuba, and started the newspaper *El Obrero*.

In the 1880s, anarchism became a force on the Cuban labor scene. Messonier served as secretary of the anarchist-dominated Workers Circle (Círculo de Trabajadores), and Enrique Creci became secretary of the Central Board of Havana Artisans (Junta Central de Artesanos de la Habana) by 1885. In 1887, Roig San Martín launched the anarchist weekly *El Productor*, which became the island's dominant labor newspaper until it was closed in 1890. *El Productor* and the labor organizations were coordinated through the Workers Alliance (Alianza Obrera), an anarchist-based organization that supported better wages and working conditions for Cuban workers as part of a larger revolutionary agenda. By organizing workers in the far-flung tobacco industry that stretched from Havana to Key West and Tampa, the Alianza became quite possibly the first international workers organization in the Americas.[10]

During the 1890s, anarchists played important, though sometimes conflictive, roles in the struggle for Cuban independence. Some anarchists doubted the efficacy of aligning with a largely nationalistic independence movement led by middle- and upper-class exiles. Others saw the war as a means to liberate the island from monarchy and imperialism.[11] These latter anarchists, who fought with the liberation forces, hoped that independence would lead to a social revolution where anarchist ideals of social equality would find fertile soil in a newly freed people. Yet, independence brought a new imperial power, the United States, and the return of a Cuban, Spanish, and North American economic elite.

During the first decade of political independence, anarchists published a series of newspapers beginning with *El Nuevo Ideal* (1899–1901)—a paper that first appeared the same month that the United States took formal control of the island. While continuing their propaganda via the press, anarchists remained committed to social change, especially through the labor movement, which after independence had split into two competing organizations: the more reformist General League of Cuban Workers (Liga General de Trabajadores), led by the more moderate Enrique Messonier, and the anarchist-supported Workers Circle (Círculo de Trabajadores). Initially rooted heavily in the urban tobacco trades, restaurants, and skilled occupations, anarchists began to reach out to rural sugar workers shortly after independence. Anarcho-syndicalists made contacts through their activities in the Círculo, and anarcho-communists did likewise through their own independent organizations. Both communists and syndicalists supported the major labor actions seeking better wages and workplace conditions in the first decade of independence, especially the Apprentice Strike of 1902. This was important for anarchists because strikers protested employers' preference for hiring Spanish immigrant workers. Because Spaniards were so prominent in the anarchist movement, this support became an important symbolic action linking anarchists with the larger concerns of the Cuban-born workforce.[12]

By 1909, anarchists were publishing three weekly newspapers in Cuba: *La Voz del Dependiente*, *Rebelión!*, and *¡Tierra!*. The latter even became a daily paper for a brief stint. By the 1910s, anarchist activity among workers was profound. Havana's food industry employees, radicalized by anarcho-syndicalism in particular, published their own long-running weekly newspaper *El Dependiente* and called attention to government and employer failures to provide safe workplace conditions; in addition, the paper offered a means through which workers could organize a revolutionary party. As sugar again became the leading sector of the Cuban economy, dominated by foreign capital, anarcho-syndicalists stepped up their radicalism in the rural zones. Successful alliances between Havana-based anarchists and labor organizers in the economically crucial sugar zones of central Cuba led the government to crack down on all anarchists at the end of 1914 and throughout 1915, a repression that temporarily crippled anarchist unions, organizations, and educational initiatives. With sugar prices soaring during World War I, the government responded to not only sugar capitalists' interests but also the fears that a radical labor movement could usher in another U.S. intervention. Officials shut down the long-running *¡Tierra!*, deported anarchists as "pernicious foreigners," and suppressed strike activity until 1917 when strikes again swept the island. General strikes in Havana, coupled with a string of bombings that authorities attributed to anarchists, led the government to again repress anarchists in 1918 and 1919.

By the early 1920s, the war-era economic boom—the famous "Dance of the Millions"—came to an end. Led by anarcho-syndicalists like Antonio Penichet, Alfredo López, Marcelo Salinas, and others and inspired by the Russian Revolution, Cuban workers began to form new labor organizations. Anarchists dominated the Havana Workers Federation (Federación Obrera de La Habana [FOH]), founded in 1921. The FOH renewed attempts to unite workers in the cities and rural zones into one labor organization strong enough to fight for better wages and conditions. The FOH also put resources into building and staffing schools for workers and their children. These schools were modeled after schools that anarchists had created since the early 1900s on the island. Then in 1925 workers created the first nationwide labor federation, the Cuban National Workers Confederation (Confederación Nacional Obrera de Cuba [CNOC]). Led by anarcho-syndicalists, Marxists, and immigrant labor leaders the CNOC was structured to prevent the creation of a highly centralized, non-democratic bureaucracy.

By 1925, anarchists enjoyed their greatest success in the labor movement since the 1880s and early 1890s. But the inauguration of President Gerardo Machado in 1925 undermined this success in Cuba. President Machado believed that he had to pacify an increasingly powerful labor movement in order to protect Cuban nationalism. Fearing that increased labor militancy could serve as a pretext for U.S. intervention, Machado, never a friend of organized labor, launched an all-out repression against anarchists and communists by closing anarchist-dominated unions, deporting striking workers, and colluding in the assassinations of several prominent anarchists, especially Enrique Varona of the railway union (1925), Alfredo López (1926), and Margarito Iglesias of the manufacturers union (1927). Many surviving anarchists went underground or fled the island. Others, forming militant groups to struggle against Machado, ultimately led to the 1933 Revolution that brought down the dictator but paved the way for Cuba's next political strongman, Fulgencio Batista. Although Machado failed to completely destroy the anarchists, the movement never regained the stature and influence that it had in those first three decades following independence.

Anarchists were one of many groups struggling to shape Cuba in the thirty years following independence from Spain. Along with black activists, feminists, and socialists, anarchists struggled to define Cuba's future; in the process they challenged the institutions of the Cuban state, national and international capital, the Catholic Church, and periodic rule by the U.S. military. I acknowledge the importance of these other social groups by noting the anarchists' criticism of or cooperation with them; moreover, the other groups provide context by which to better understand anarchist ideas and actions. This book, however, remains dedicated to exploring and analyzing anarchists from the far left wing of Cuban society and politics. Their views reflect understudied viewpoints and perspectives on issues of national identity formation, immigration, race, health, education, and gender relations at the beginning of the twentieth century. In short, anarchist critiques and initiatives shed new light on the cultural and political struggles occurring in and shaping Cuba from 1898 to the 1920s.

Cuban and International Anarchism: A Historiography

In Cuba's rich history of social conflict, Cuban anarchism has been pushed into relative obscurity. This is not because the movement was minuscule. Although it is impossible to say how many anarchist activists and followers existed at any one time, intelligence reports and the anarchists' own propaganda put the numbers in the thousands by the end of the first decade of independence. These figures grew by the early 1920s when anarcho-syndicalists dominated the thriving labor organizations on the island. For a country whose labor history was a key factor in developing the island and in particular the island's leftist heritage, and in a country where anarchism played a contentious role in that heritage, little has been written on the anarchist movement. In fact, except for a handful of rather polemical works, some of which I discuss in later chapters, one has to read the scattered secondary literature focused on Cuban labor history to find the anarchists. In addition, because most of these histories have been published since the 1959 Cuban Revolution, historians have tended to analyze the anarchists through the lens of the Revolution with often ideologically driven results.

Until the end of the twentieth century, one's view of anarchists generally resulted from how one felt about the Cuban Revolution. Cuban authors on the island have tended to focus on finding the "socialist" (that is, Marxist or proto-Marxist) roots of the 1959 revolution; in so doing they either denied an important role for anarchism in those roots, downplayed the anarchist beliefs of many people by describing them in studies as "socialist" and "Marxist," or labeled anarchists as misguided or naïve. The varying degrees of negative treatment of anarchism in Cuba can be found in works by Mariana Serra García, José Antonio Portuondo, Joaquín Ordoqui, Olga Cabrera, José Cantón Navarro, José Rivero Múñiz, Gaspar Jorge García Gallo, and various official publications. At the same time, writers in exile and writers abroad, sympathetic to anarchism, have tended to overrepresent the accomplishments of anarchists by portraying them as unsung heroes and heroines who were betrayed by the Communists. We see this especially in proanarchist works by Frank Fernández and Sam Dolgoff, as well as in Peter Marshall's history of anarchism where even Che Guevara's "anarchism" is noted.

Two examples illustrate these ideological interpretations of anarchism and their service to larger political objectives: Carlos Baliño and Alfredo López were key figures in Cuban labor history from the early 1900s. Writers on the island have portrayed Baliño as a "Marxist." Carlos del Toro, Cabrera, Cantón Navarro, García Gallo, and others focus on Baliño's role in founding the Cuban Communist Party in 1925; they ignore or downplay his history as an anarchist at the beginning of the century. Meanwhile, Dolgoff, Fernández, and Marshall stress his anarchist activities but neglect his role in founding the Communist Party. Thus, neither perspective is entirely correct. Carlos Baliño was a leftist typical of his time. In the early 1900s, he followed anarchism and gradually converted to socialism. *Socialism*, an undoubtedly vague term in the first decade of the twentieth century, could have meant anything from a parliamentary socialist to the most radical of anarchists. Like many "socialists" during the era, he became a Communist following the Bolshevik Revolution of 1917. Even though he became a Communist, he continued to work closely with anarcho-syndicalists in an anarchist-Marxist alliance that dominated Cuba's main labor organizations in the early 1920s.

A second example is a leading anarcho-syndicalist printer in the 1920s, Alfredo López. Sympathetic and scholarly literature from outside Cuba clearly portrays López as a key anarcho-syndicalist in the island's labor movement. However, in Cuba, Alfredo López plays a different role. For instance, in her insightful biography of López, Olga Cabrera places the man squarely within the larger social dynamics impacting the Cuban labor movement, which portrays him as the "teacher of the Cuban proletariat," but his anarchist ideas are downplayed. This portrayal of him as a labor leader, while dismissing his anarchism, is reflected further in the Museum of the Revolution in Havana—the official post-1959 shrine and interpretation of Cuban history. In the museum's wing dedicated to the island's pre-1959 history, one can see a portrait of López with a brief discussion of his accomplishments; however, his anarchism is never mentioned. In her sweeping history of Cuban labor history, *Los que viven por sus manos*, Cabrera treats anarchists more fairly than earlier historians; yet, her argument is that only a truly national labor movement was possible after, among other things, anarchist leaders in the 1920s came to see the "truth" of Marxism-Leninism. This is the light into which López and other anarchists are cast: the anarchist-Marxist alliances of the 1920s were not mutual meetings of the mind; instead, anarchists "saw the light" of Marxism and joined the Communists.

Other international scholars have helped to chart a better analysis of anarchists, though still tied explicitly to a labor history perspective and mostly rooted in the nineteenth century. For instance, Gary Mormino and George

Pozzetta analyzed immigrant labor communities in Florida's cigar factories. Though it comprises a small part of their book, they illustrate how Spanish, Cuban, Italian, and American anarchists (as well as other labor radicals) worked and agitated side by side, exposed one another to different cultures and cultural perspectives, and thus helped to educate anarchists on a truly "international" perspective. In his research on Cuban communities in the United States from 1852 to 1898, Gerald Poyo shows the close links between major parts of the Florida émigré community and island anarchist leaders. He illustrates how these links and the strong influence of anarchist ideology posed problems between workers who sought a social revolution and other forces involved in a political nationalist independence movement. He analyzes how José Martí pulled these two strands together into a revolutionary movement in the early 1890s and by extension illustrates the impact of anarchists among Cuban workers in both Florida and Cuba. Jean Stubbs reflects on tobacco workers and the role of anarchists in this important economic sector, again with a focus on the nineteenth-century labor movement. She argues that, far from what is commonly believed, nineteenth-century Cuban anarchism was not a direct by-product of Spanish anarchism, and she notes that some anarchist leaders, like Enrique Roig San Martín, were not Spanish immigrants; in fact, many in the island's anarchist movement did not come from anarchist-dominated regions in Spain. All three studies illustrate the importance of understanding the Cuban anarchist movement as one branch of an international anarchist movement, though with specific local characteristics. In addition, all reflect an agreement that anarchists in Cuba (and Florida) modified the movement to represent the specific realities of Cuban labor. I argue that twentieth-century anarchists continued and expanded this trend beyond the workplace to the larger Cuban culture of politics, ethnicity, health, education, and gender.

Arguably the most important labor study that analyzes anarchism on the island is Joan Casanovas's *Bread, or Bullets!* Casanovas illustrates the central impact of anarchism in Cuba's late nineteenth-century urban labor history. Like Stubbs, he emphasizes the Creole, as opposed to Spanish or in particular Catalonian, influences on Cuban labor at this time. And like Poyo, Casanovas excellently portrays the reformist-anarchist split in the labor movement and its translation into a general, though not unanimous, anarchist support for the Cuban independence movement. Casanovas's especially valuable study describes thoroughly the role of urban labor, and ultimately urban-based anarchists, in shaping the evolution of Spanish colonial Cuba. Thus, Casanovas shows how the island's workers played a key role in challenging Spanish colonial rule and providing the backbone (both figuratively and literally) for independence forces.

In short, these works have helped students of the region understand the interactions between anarchists and the larger nineteenth-century workers' movements on the island without the polemical undertones. However, even these historians have studied anarchism as part of a larger analysis of Cuban labor history. Thus, students of Cuba now know far more about nineteenth-century labor history than early twentieth-century labor history. But there is little known about anarchists beyond their roles in the labor movement. Consequently, this study takes a more focused analysis of the men, women, and sometimes even children who took part in all facets of Cuban anarchism both inside and outside the workplace. As a result of this more thorough description of anarchism, the larger Cuban political culture, with which the anarchists regularly engaged, emerges in new ways.

To this end, I have followed broader global trends in the study of international anarchism. Beginning in the 1980s, historians moved away from institutional and biographical approaches and toward a focus on anarchist culture. Significant in this trend are studies reassessing anarchism in the United States, Latin America, and Spain. For instance, through an examination of rank-and-file newspapers and anarchist art forms, Salvatore Salerno shows how the Industrial Workers of the World (IWW) in the United States was a hybrid creation of rank-and-file attitudes and foreign-born intellectual impulses. In this same vein of international influences on anarchist movements, Mormino and Pozzetta looked at the role of anarchists and immigrant labor in radical unions in the United States. Research has focused on the sometimes contradictory challenges that U.S. anarchists faced, such as how to uphold revolutionary idealism while making a living in capitalist America. For instance, Blaine McKinley examines whether anarchists believed one could be a lawyer or merchant and still be an anarchist. On other fronts, McKinley and Donald Winters have discussed the seeming contradiction in U.S. anarchist anticlericalism by showing the repeated use of Christian symbolism in anarchist writings. Bruce Nelson's examination of "movement culture" illustrates how anarchists drew together different ethnicities and traditions to challenge American power brokers and influence American workers in one of the few social spaces that remained open to agitation: culture.

The study of Latin American and Spanish anarchism also received renewed life as scholars shifted to a focus on cultural issues and conflicts. Dora Barrancos reflects this shift in the study of Argentine anarchism in her analyses of anarchist education and cultural issues like health and sexuality. Other studies by Barrancos and Maxine Molyneux illustrate the complex nature of Argentine anarchism by focusing on anarcho-feminism and the impact of female anarchists in a mostly male movement. The research by Barry Carr and Donald Hodges on anarchism in Mexico has shed light on the lingering impact of anarchism on Mexican politics, especially in the formation of the Mexican Communist Party. Anton Rosenthal's study of turn-of-the-century Montevideo, Uruguay, illustrates how anarchists and the city's leaders each used the streetcar to define their own ideas of progress. Scholars in Spain likewise have moved away from an institutional focus to emphasize culture, such as Lily Litvak's examinations of anarchist art and aesthetics. In addition, lesser-known cultural dimensions of anarchism like the anarcho-naturists and their approaches to health and population issues have become topics of new interest, as pursued by Eduard Masjuan. Consequently, to study Cuban anarchism, one has to move beyond the workplace and labor disputes (though by no means forsaking them entirely) to explore and understand the cultural creations of anarchists, how they used their culture to put forth their own ideas and initiatives, and how they challenged those who ran Cuba.

Cuban Anarchism

The chapters that follow provide a cultural and political history of anarchism that unfolds in layers. Readers who expect a traditional chronological account of the anarchists in Cuba will not find it here. For that one may consult the often polemical but nevertheless useful accounts of Sam Dolgoff (*The Cuban Revolution: A Critical Perspective*, 1977) and Frank Fernández (*Cuban Anarchism: The History of a Movement*, 2001). Both focus primarily on the labor struggles involving anarchists from the 1800s to the Castro era. Rather, by building on trends in anarchist historiography since the 1980s, this book explores the cultural history of the anarchist movement topically. Each new topic adds another layer to our understanding of the complexity of anarchism in Cuba. The following chapters concentrate on three important aspects of anarchist cultural politics in Cuba following 1898, what I see as "three sites of cultural conflict": nationalism and internationalism; health and nature; and education and gender. Each topic has its own section in this study. The first chapter of each section

follows a chronological overview of how anarchists addressed each site of conflict. Subsequent chapters in each section turn to anarchist culture, especially
fiction, for a more thematic analysis of the topic.

Following chapter 1, which looks at the larger theoretical concerns guiding
this study, I turn to part 1 to focus on the relationship between anarchism,
nationalist politics, and issues of immigration and race. Chapter 2 addresses the
anarchist critique of Cuban nationalism and how anarchists "Cubanized" anarchist internationalism after independence. Chapter 3 examines independence symbolism in Cuban anarchism by illustrating how anarchists avoided
becoming "nationalists" themselves, yet still used the symbols of national independence to localize the international movement to fit Cuban reality. In particular, they interpreted important images of the island's political culture—the
war itself and José Martí—into their critiques of postwar social relations. Chapter 4 explores how anarchists addressed issues of Spanish and Antillean immigration to Cuba. While anarchists described workers of all countries in noble
terms, they attacked other "foreign" immigrants like international businessmen. These latter were portrayed as the immigrants that workers of all nationalities should see as their enemies. Chapter 5 examines how anarchists dealt
with the particularly thorny issue of race in Cuba. This proved to be another
means of localizing anarchist internationalism to meet the specific racial realities of the island. By addressing immigration and race, anarchists tried to overcome attempts by employers, politicians, and nationalistic labor unions to divide Cuban workers from Spanish, Haitian, and Jamaican workers.

Part 2 demonstrates how anarchists dealt with "real life" health and safety
concerns of the popular classes. Chapter 6 shows how U.S. occupation forces
from 1898 to 1902 and from 1906 to 1909 helped to control yellow fever and to
develop improvements in sewers and sanitation. However, anarchists charged
that such reforms did not go far enough and that rural and urban workers still
suffered from unsanitary conditions both at home and in the workplace. Chapter 7 illustrates how anarcho-naturists helped to create health institutes that
utilized alternative medicine and treatment, urged people to grow their own
food and eat vegetarian diets, and at times promoted alternative lifestyles like
nudism. These anarchists promoted such lifestyles as forms of preventative
health care, but anarcho-naturists added a "social liberating" dimension to
naturismo. Chapter 8 reflects the debate between anarchists over the impact of
"Civilization" and its relationship to "Nature" by examining the role of Nature
in anarchist statements and fiction. Anarcho-naturists promoted a rural ideal,

simple living, and being in harmony with Nature as ways to save the laborers from the increasingly industrialized character of Cuba. Besides promoting an early twentieth-century "back-to-the-land" movement, they used these romantic images of Nature to illustrate how far removed a capitalist industrialized Cuba had departed from an anarchist view of natural harmony.

In addition to making people healthy, anarchists believed that Cubans needed an appropriate education. Part 3 addresses the anarchist critique of Cuban educational systems and anarchist educational initiatives, particularly as they impacted women and children. Chapter 9 describes how anarchists rejected state- and church-run schools and developed their own coeducational institutions. During the day, schools operated for the workers' children. At night, schools taught the workers themselves. Anarchists recognized that formal schools could reach only a small number of people, so, as explained in chapter 10, they broadened their educational audience by utilizing their cultural meetings, newspapers, fiction, and theater to teach anarchist theories of freedom, egalitarianism, internationalism, and progress. These experiments in popular education also stressed the importance of avoiding greed, politics, and vice within the larger culture. Finally, chapter 11 analyzes how anarchist culture functioned as "texts" when directed particularly at women. Because anarchists saw the family as the seed from which to grow a cooperative society, they believed that women in particular needed to be targeted. Anarchist plays and stories served as educational tools that could instruct women and children on how to behave in an anarchist, egalitarian fashion while waiting for that revolutionary society to materialize.

Notes on Sources

In the fluid situation of Cuban cultural, political, and social life in the thirty years after independence, anarchists and most radicals on the Cuban political left understood that a social revolution was a long time away. Consequently, anarchists of all delineations believed that cultural work in the present was necessary not only to lay the groundwork for the future revolution but also to help people live better, healthier, more enlightened lives in the meantime. It was also essential to help Cubans imagine a reality and a future conducive to the anarchist agenda. To unlock this cultural history of Cuban anarchism, I have focused primarily on the printed cultural sources produced by anarchists themselves. These sources serve as the best surviving record of the movement, its actions, and its ideas and visions. Thus, to understand the anarchist critique and cultural vision, this book is based largely around three types of sources: anarchist ideological books and pamphlets, anarchist newspapers, and anarchist cultural productions like novels, plays, and short stories. When relevant, I have incorporated archival material such as intelligence reports on anarchist activity. I have also relied on censuses, other official governmental reports, and publications from the anarchists' rivals and friends to provide context to understand just what the anarchists were challenging. Most of this book's insights were gleaned from anarchists' own political and cultural creations uncovered in institutes and libraries in Havana, Cuba, and Amsterdam, The Netherlands.

Although I pay considerable attention to the men, women, and children whose names and activities emerge, disappear, and sometimes reappear throughout the record, I pay special attention to the literary works and activities of the two most prominent of these anarchists, Adrián del Valle (aka Palmiro de Lidia) and Antonio Penichet. Del Valle was a core personality in Cuban anarchism from his first step in Cuba in 1895 to his death on the island fifty years later. He was born in Barcelona, Spain, in 1872, and came of age in the politically charged atmosphere of late nineteenth-century Catalonia. By 1890, he wrote for and collaborated with the Spanish anarchist newspaper *El Productor*, for which he occasionally wrote under the pen names "Palmiro de Lidia" and "Fructidor." In 1892, while living in New York City, he immersed himself in the city's radical politics. He quickly became the manager of the Spanish-language anarchist newspaper *El Despertar* where he was exposed to the numerous Spanish and Cuban anarchists who passed through the city. As tensions between Spain and Cuba increased in the early 1890s, Spanish-speaking anarchists in the United States began to agitate for Cuban independence. In February 1895, Del Valle left New York and arrived in Havana, just as the island began to explode in its final war for independence. Soon, he befriended the leading anarchists in Havana, but, unable to get from Havana to the separatist-dominated sections of Cuba, Del Valle returned to New York where he wrote in support of the war in *El Rebelde* under the name "Palmiro de Lidia." Following Spain's defeat, Del Valle immediately returned to Cuba, where, in the first month of the U.S. occupation of the island (January 1899), he founded the anarchist newspaper *El Nuevo Ideal*.[13]

Over the following decades, Del Valle became a constant presence in not only the anarchist press that proliferated in Cuba but also mainstream literary publications. He regularly contributed columns for the leading anarchist newspapers *¡Tierra!*, *Rebelión!*, and *Nueva Luz*. From 1912 to 1913 he edited the free-thinking journal *El Audaz*. Then he began his largest publishing job by helping to found and edit the monthly alternative health magazine that followed the anarcho-naturist line *Pro-Vida*. While a mainstay in the anarchist press, Del Valle's prolific pieces of social commentary won him a seat at the more mainstream table of Cuban journalism. He served a fifteen-year stint as an editor for the periodical *Cuba y América* before he became an editor of the highly regarded journal *Revista Bimestre Cubana*, published by the Sociedad Económica de Amigos del País in Havana. During his years at the Sociedad Económica he served as a librarian, and in that role he became a leading force in reorganizing the society's extensive library holdings. This rather erudite existence isolated him from the day-to-day realities of physical labor in Cuba's expanding rural agri-industrial complexes and urban shops. But it afforded him considerable time to interact with the leading authors of his day as well as write for newspapers and magazines. Immersed in the atmosphere of revolutionary politics, labor radicalism, and literary dynamism, Del Valle wrote a series of novels, plays, and short stories, which today serve as key sources in understanding the cultural vision laid forth by the anarchist movement's leading artist. This cultural vision, which I describe throughout this book, was recognized by more than the anarchists who read and published his essays or fiction, staged his plays, and followed his advice on seeking alternative health regimens. In fact, he was recognized by Cuba's literary elite; in 1927 he was the subject of a prestigious public reception at the National Academy of Arts and Letters in which the Cuban Socialist and novelist Carlos Loveira—author of important social novels like *Los Inmorales*, *Juan Criollo*, and *Los Ciegos*—gave the honorary speech praising Del Valle's literary and social career. Del Valle remained a constant presence in Cuban anarchism until his death in February 1945.

Antonio Penichet was Del Valle's contemporary, who likewise produced anarchist fiction and short plays. Whereas the latter's world mainly revolved around intellectual circles, Penichet's world was that of a skilled laborer. As a young man, he arrived in Havana from the Cuban town of Güines after Spanish forces drove out rural Cubans in their infamous "reconcentration" policy during the war in the 1890s. Upon arriving in Havana, Penichet stayed at the home of Manuel Comas Seguí, who not only taught Penichet the printer's trade but also urged him to study anarchist ideas.[14] Penichet helped to edit the printers' *Memorándum Tipográfico* from 1913 to 1916, but during these years he shied away from openly supporting anarchism in the pages of the newspaper. This changed by 1918 when Penichet became a leading anarcho-syndicalist figure in a Cuban labor movement that rapidly recovered from several years of repression during World War I by staging a broad array of strikes. In 1919, Penichet and other anarchists were arrested for their involvement in the strikes. In June, while hiding from authorities, he managed to publish the novel *La vida de un pernicioso* and a short story "El soldado Rafael." Coming on the heels of the Bolshevik Revolution, which Penichet supported, "El soldado Rafael" was suppressed by authorities who feared its call for a military-worker alliance to overthrow the state. He landed in more trouble in 1920 when authorities accused him and other anarchists of inciting workers to engage in bombings throughout Havana.[15]

During the first half of the 1920s, when the labor movement surged in power, Penichet became one of anarchism's leading voices. In 1922, he founded and became editor of the anarcho-syndicalist newspaper *Nueva Luz*, to which he contributed frequent columns on education, the historical and social importance of different inventions and technology, and the overall status of the labor movement. At the same time, Penichet became intricately linked with the FOH school for children. From this experience, he helped to found the CNOC in 1925 and led the organization's Education Committee. To illustrate his prominence in the labor movement, he had to publicly reject efforts by delegates to name a special honor for him during the CNOC's founding convention because Penichet believed such honors were inappropriate. Following the crackdown by the Machado government beginning in 1925, Penichet found himself on the run. He fled to Mexico for a time but returned to Cuba in the 1930s. His involvement in anarchist activities declined after that as he became a historian, an advocate for liberal education, and a librarian like Del Valle. He died in Cuba in 1964.[16]

Del Valle's and Penichet's works are worthy of study in and of themselves, but I focus on their literary works as primary sources that illuminate the anarchists' cultural challenges. As outlined in the next chapter, their fiction and actions served as important cultural frames for the anarchist movement—frames that gave ideational shape to anarchist interpretations of Cuban reality and anarchist goals for the island's future. At the same time these two men themselves were key actors in the movement's educational and health initiatives. I do not argue that all anarchists agreed with everything written by these two key literary and political figures. In fact, many found Del Valle a little too "bourgeois," especially considering his accolades from the larger culture and his life removed from hard labor. In addition, Penichet and Del Valle did not always agree; for instance, in the 1920s anarchists of all stripes debated whether or not to align with Marxists. Penichet and most anarcho-syndicalists thought it a good idea but Del Valle and the anarcho-communists kept their distance. Thus, in this regard, both their individual lives and their ideas, expressed in their plays and fiction, represented a cross-segment of the anarchist community at any given time on the island: some agreed completely with one, the other, or both, while people could easily sympathize or take issue with, say, Del Valle's romantic rural landscapes or Penichet's creation of heroines out of Havana's prostitutes. However, to undertake a cultural history of a social movement, one must rely heavily (though not exclusively) on the leading cultural creators of that movement. In Cuba, many people staged plays, wrote columns, ran schools, and more; but among these activists, Del Valle and Penichet were the two most prolific, widely read, and widely heard cultural figures in Cuban anarchism.

Alan West has noted that "the artistic realm offers us a distinctive way of understanding both present and latent meanings of Cuban reality and history. The greater freedom in the aesthetic realm means that fiction, myth, folktales, popular music, and poetry can be brought to bear on the historical as a 'dialogue between intentional subjects,' as originating thought. And . . . I agree that 'a philosophy of history may well lie buried in the arts of the imagination.'"[17] West's "arts of the imagination" become central to understanding anarchism and anarchist culture in Cuba. West calls Cuban history and culture a *manigua*, a Taíno word referring to a dense, lush landscape—practically a jungle, a "natural profusion of confusion, a locus of escape from oppression and a new spot from which to begin a life of freedom."[18]

We require our own arts of imagination to slice through the dense layers of Cuban history and culture to make sense of the past. At the same time, we must recognize the arts of imagination used by history's actors to understand the historical images they used to describe their present and shape a picture of Cuba's potential future. Again, to this end, I draw heavily on the anarchists' arts of imagination, especially their cultural creations. Literature can help us understand the values and attitudes of historical actors. As E. Bradford Burns once noted, "on one level the novel reflects the writer's points of view ['world view'] on a topic. On another level, it is a document of, a mirror to, a period."[19] Fiction helps us to understand what the anarchists were seeing, interpreting, and imagining. By the same notion, it helps us understand how anarchists tried to get their readers and viewers to imagine Cuba's past, present, and potential future.

After all, anarchist culture was meant to be not only descriptive but also prescriptive; it was designed as a useful way to raise the consciousness of their audiences. In addition, people like Del Valle and Penichet tapped into the larger Cuban culture to write their fiction in their efforts to Cubanize the movement. Consequently, from a rarely heard viewpoint, literature and the arts can tell us a great deal about Cuba's anarchists, their vision for the island, and the island itself.

For thirty years after Cuban independence from Spain, the island's anarchists provided alternatives to the directions promoted by Cuba's economic, political, and cultural leaders. At times, when their agendas overlapped, they cooperated with reformist groups. Sometimes they disagreed among themselves. However, anarchists of all stripes believed that over time, as the social environment became purified of injustice, oppression, and vice, the imagined anarchist New Dawn of individuals—free, thinking, healthy, and equal—working in a spirit of cooperation and mutual aid would evolve until a day, which they hoped would not be too distant, of a social revolution. Against a wide array of political, economic, and cultural forces, Cuban anarchists struggled to keep that hope alive in the unions, the health clinics, the shops, the schools, the literary world, and even the stage.

1

Anarchism, *Cubanía*, Culture, and Power

Cuban society and culture were in a state of flux following independence from Spain. As noted in the introduction, numerous social actors competed to shape a free Cuba. Anarchists were one segment in this multigroup-contested terrain in which people from across the political spectrum and from all classes took to the streets, workplaces, newspapers, halls of government, the stage, and the page to debate what it meant to be Cuban and what path a free Cuba should take. In this context, both Cuban- and foreign-born anarchists acted as one component in the cultural and political struggles to define and create *cubanidad*, that is, what it means to be Cuban.

In recent decades, historians have become interested in the cultural and political struggles to define *cubanidad* in the early republic. Increasingly, scholars examine the conflicts and different ideologies that shaped Cuban political culture during those years. As Antoni Kapcia notes, a dominant feature in Cuban political culture is "the obsession with identity, which dominated politics and dissidence from late in the colonial period until the present day." In the minds of Cubans, and even much of the world, Cuba has been, as Kapcia puts it, an "island of dreams" where people of all political persuasions have been "mixing illusions with teleological visions, and creating 'real' plans on the basis of long-postponed but still believed 'dreams' of utopia."[1] Anarchists were one such group of dreamers.

It is useful to explore Kapcia's ideas on *cubanidad* and *cubanía* ("the political belief in *cubanidad*") to understand the broader cultural and political Cuban contexts in which anarchists found themselves and which they sought to shape. Kapcia builds off Benedict Anderson's path-breaking book *Imagined Communities: Reflections on the Origin and Spread of Nationalism* (1991). Anderson began to reformulate how historians think about nationalism and national identity with his concept of "imagined communities." In the nineteenth century, newly independent countries throughout the hemisphere had to construct what it meant to be Argentine, Chilean, and so on. Following independence from Spain, leaders tried to create a sense of "nation." To this end, nationalism was not "awakened" in people within manmade borders; rather, nationalism was imagined and then constructed. Nations really had no clear identifiable birth, but, through the construction of national histories and identities, restricted political zones were imbued with a sense of creation, development, and tradition. Although it seems that a revolutionary war for independence and the signing of a document granting independence might mark such a national birth, these events are only part of larger processes that themselves often may have no more intrinsic importance than what later leaders or historians choose to give them. Following independence throughout Latin America in the first half of the nineteenth century, political borders were often reconfigured and new nations came into being even after separation from Spain. The creation of the Central American republics and the Dominican Republic illustrate the point. Thus, in such an environment, when can one say the new nation was "born"? It is easy to identify the birth of "national boundaries," but it is not nearly as easy to identify the birth of the "nation" or what it meant to be a citizen of that nation.

At first glance, Cuba seems to offer a different perspective. Not only was there a definable war for independence (1895–1898) from Spain, but also Cuba, as an island, would not have to construct new borders to separate it from its neighbors. Nature had taken care of that. Still, a number of events complicated this seemingly easy identification of the republic's birth. Cuba occupied a unique position in the world system of politics and economics at the beginning of the twentieth century. Central to this uniqueness was Cuba's geographical proximity to the United States and the role of sugar and tobacco in the island's economy. In the decades following the war, foreign, primarily North American, capital dominated Cuba's economy. This economic reality was coupled with the political reality of repeated, constitutionally sanctioned U.S. military interventions. Besides the occupation of 1898–1902, the United States returned under the provisions of the Platt Amendment to the Cuban Constitution first from 1906 to 1909, again in 1912, and then again from 1917 to 1922. In addition to these military, political, and economic impediments to a realization of the birth of nationhood, Cubans encountered large waves of immigration from Spain, Haiti, and the British West Indies. Also strong Spanish and African traditions, derived during the four hundred years of colonial rule and slavery, continued to influence the island's cultural environment; simultaneously, a new school system, modeled on a U.S. system, was being implemented, and cultural imports from the "Colossus of the North" increasingly found waiting customers. Within this context of diverse international influences, Cubans of different political persuasions struggled to imagine and forge a national identity. They attempted to define and construct what it meant to be "Cuban."

Not all agreed on this sense of community or national identity. Kapcia identifies three distinct competing *cubanías*: a "hegemonic *cubanía*" that sought closer formal political and economic ties with the United States; a "*cubanía cultural*" of primarily white, Eurocentric intellectuals seeking some vague regeneration of national values; and, a "*cubanía rebelde*" that, through the formal political system, sought "sovereignty" rather than "independence." The first and third are most critical. Hegemonic *cubanía* included the political and economic leaders in Cuba who saw the island's future (and their personal fortunes) tied to ever-closer relations with the United States. Some, looking beyond the economic motivations to cultural issues, believed that Cuba's adoption of North American notions of progress that contrasted with a perceived Spanish backwardness and African barbarity would elevate Cuba to become a modern country. Consequently, after independence, Cubans "borrowed freely and adopted unabashedly," as Louis Pérez puts it, those North American notions of progress upon which to build a Cuban identity. In this sense, to be Cuban was to be more, look more, and act more like progressive-era, capitalist North America.[2]

As Kapcia notes, *cubanía rebelde* was more hidden; it appeared in Cuban unions, Afro-Cuban religion, the Liberal Party, the Independent Party of Color (Partido Independiente de Color [PIC]), and the Anti-Plattist League.[3] When considering the history and importance of groups challenging the Cuban government throughout the first half of the twentieth century, "rebelliousness" in the name of national sovereignty becomes a central driving force in how these groups defined *cubanidad*. Kapcia argues that *cubanía rebelde* was "a broader ideology of dissent . . . that underpinned much of radical dissidence from the late nineteenth century to the 1950s."[4] Some historians have focused on the role of racial issues in this *cubanía rebelde*. For instance, Aline Helg describes how a decade after the defeat of Spain, Afro-Cubans created the PIC, whereby they pushed to gain full citizenship rights that they believed had been denied them following independence. In essence, the PIC sought a "rightful share" of the spoils of war and citizenship as Cubans. The fact that Afro-Cubans had been denied full Cuban identity and felt the need to create a race-based political party challenged the island's postindependence cultural myth that Cuba was a racial democracy. Like other social actors in Cuba, the PIC utilized the words and images of José Martí to justify that a Cuba for all meant just that: a Cuba for both whites and blacks. The PIC suggested that the idea of a "racial democracy" as a central aspect of *cubanidad* was only a myth defined by the white elite, and they suggested that the idea flew in the face of the reality of racial discrimination. Political elites in Cuba came to see the PIC as a threat to Cuban nationalism for making such claims.

Others have challenged this by suggesting that Cuba's cultural myth of a racial democracy was in fact more than myth. Rather, the ideas of "racial democracy" had taken on ideological overtones that symbolized the incorporation of Martí's ideas of a "Cuba for all." Consequently, when the PIC organized as a race-based political party, it violated the central belief. "Rather," as Alejandro de la Fuente notes, "cross-racial mobilization characterized Cuban political life and the emerging labor movement."[5] The Cuban labor movement endeavored to create such a cross-racial and cross-ethnic mobilization to shape postindependence Cuba and thus create a worker-defined *cubanidad*. As a result, unions and other labor-based organizations struggled to bridge racial and ethnic divisions by incorporating white Cubans, blacks, and Spaniards into their ranks. By stressing a class identity removed from racial considerations, labor leaders helped to bring "class" into the forefront of Cuban politics. This contributed to an imagined postindependence Cuba characterized by not only its "racial democracy" but also its working-class unity.[6]

Kapcia's categories help to break down and identify the interest groups that competed to define *cubanidad* and shape Cuban culture. Unfortunately, Kapcia does not include anarchists in his definition of *cubanía rebelde*. He does note that Spanish anarchists who migrated to Cuba were "seedbeds of radicalism and bases for trade union activity, for these migrants formed, fostered, led and radicalized the existing trade unions" in the late nineteenth century.[7] Yet, he does not include anarchists in the postindependence struggles under the *cubanía rebelde* label. This omission is understandable when one considers his definition for the label because anarchists rejected participation in formal politics.

Despite this omission and its rationale, I argue that anarchists need to be seen as part of this tradition of *cubanía rebelde*—though certainly occupying its far left wing. As I illustrate throughout this book, anarchists partook in the "broader ideology of dissent" that shaped the postindependence years. They consistently challenged hegemonic *cubanía* while offering a radical agenda for a future Cuba whose sovereignty would be preserved from the likes of religious, political, and economic elites, as well as foreign powers. At the same time, anarchists believed that they spoke for the working people and that their critiques and initiatives would best support the interests of the popular classes. While anarchist antipathy for formal politics prevented them from jumping on the nationalist bandwagon so frequently associated with Cuban political parties, they nevertheless were part of a larger political struggle that Cuban radicals would engage in throughout the 1920s. These radicals, as Robert Whitney argues, were involved in the "project of nation-building" that involved "imagining a national community" and then engaging in "acts of political struggle to make these images real."[8] While populists, Marxists, followers of Antonio Guiteras, and other radical nationalists struggled along these fronts in the 1920s, they were part of a larger tradition of *cubanía rebelde* in general who joined a radical leftist strategy pursued by anarchists since the late nineteenth century in Cuba. Thus, even though anarchists functioned outside the realm of formal politics, anarchist actions in the streets and union halls, on the stage, in alternative health institutes and schools, and in their fiction place anarchists squarely on the side of nonanarchists in the *cubanía rebelde* tradition. They were another voice for the voiceless and another voice for the popular classes. This is not to argue that anarchists, no matter the strand, were *crucial* contributors to the development of Cubanness or Cuban national culture. Rather, they were *active* players in the debates *to define* those contested concepts; moreover, they proposed an internationalist vision for the island. Meanwhile, their views on politics, health, education, and gender were important in the development of the island's early leftist politics and leftist *cubanía* with its own notions of an imagined Cuban community.

Power, Hegemonic Culture, and Anarchist Resistance

Anarchists did not overthrow the state; they did not dismantle industrial capitalism; they failed, though not for want of trying, to root out Catholicism and all religion. Their schools did not become the national norm, and their health institutes did not reach the hoped-for multitudes. Even their fiction did not become our modern-day equivalent of bestsellers. Anarchists never had real power in Cuba. That is, they never had what Eric Wolf describes as structural power: "power manifest in relationships that not only operates within settings and domains but also organizes and orchestrates the settings themselves."[9] Despite taking lead positions in the island's labor movement, anarchists were never in a position to "orchestrate the settings" of structural power.

Yet, as Wolf points out, power and ideas in a society connect through culture. Consequently, in times of crisis, ideological responses to the crises tend to draw upon and are exhibited through certain historically rooted cultural understandings. This concept of structural power and its relationship to ideas and culture is complicated by the Cuban case after independence. There was no single "dominant culture" in Cuba, as Kapcia illustrates. Rather, structural power was wielded by an assortment of political and economic leaders. These included national and international owners or managers of the growing industries in sugar, tobacco, utilities, and transportation; middle-class owners of small-scale establishments like print shops, dressmaking shops, restaurants, and cafés; publishers and editors of the mainstream press, especially *Diario de la Marina*; the Catholic Church and growing Protestant churches (the latter intimately linked to the expansion of agribusiness concerns, especially in eastern Cuba); Cuban politicians (mostly middle- to upper-class men, frequently successful in business, and mostly white though sometimes black or of mixed race); the institutions of state power—for instance, the police, rural guard, and the military—as well as what may appear as benign governmental agencies—for example, the health and education departments—important in shaping laws and regulations that impacted both consumer and laborer.

These diverse leading sectors did not always agree on the best direction for Cuba. Some wanted ever-closer ties to the United States; some appealed to their Iberian heritage as the *raza latina*. Others may have seen U.S. intervention as a distinct threat to Cuban independence, but most wanted to expand commercial ties to the north. Some preferred the traditional Catholicism, while others attended Protestant churches and sent their children to Protestant private schools. Occasionally, they fought each other; during the 1906 Civil War, conflict between Liberals and Conservatives ushered in the second U.S. military intervention. Thus, Cuba was ruled by different groups who had different *preferences*. But when challenged by various social sectors like blacks, labor radicals, and leftists in general, they mostly cooperated with each other because, although they might have had different preferences regarding how Cuba was run or the future direction Cuba would take, they almost universally agreed on the central foundations of what should constitute this *cubanidad*: Christianity, capitalist economics, and a more-or-less republican political system based on electoral politics. As a result, few people in this diverse group questioned the basic form of structural power, the central political-economic-religious ideas linked to it, or the relative hegemony that this group held against challenges from the popular classes. Thus, building off Wolf's discussion of how power and ideas are channeled through culture, these agreed-upon concerns reflected what can be called a "hegemonic culture" in Cuba.

Although these different groups held structural power and fashioned a hegemonic culture rooted in the three pillars of politics, religion, and economics, early republican Cuba nevertheless was repeatedly rocked by an assortment of challengers who precipitated a series of culture wars. Although we can locate the leading players who ruled and held power in Cuba and understand the power that they waged, we should remember that the new political culture of the island had not yet been solidified—even if those in positions of power had wished otherwise. The island was in a state of political and cultural transition after 1898. Such a fluid environment gave rise to numerous interest groups who put forth their own ideas and tested the ideological, institutional, and imagination waters. The culture wars that emerged were fought primarily between the hegemonic culture and different interest groups, be they socialists, feminists, blacks, unions, or veterans. Anarchists were one of these subaltern groups in the battle to define Cuba.

The notion of a culture war against hegemonic powers dates to the ideas of Gramsci, who delineated between the different groups holding hegemonic power and those countering it. I use the concept of a "culture war" to mean the "war" between competing paradigms. This war took the form of different struggles: institutional struggles (the political, educational, and health institutions), ideological struggles (different concepts of how to organize societal institutions and who should control them), and struggles of imagination (different visions not only for the future, but also for how the contemporary and historical settings are envisioned and thus how they serve larger goals in the ideological struggles). Anarchists questioned all three of the hegemonic culture's agreed-upon institutional and ideological principles: electoral politics, capitalism, and Christianity. By attacking these principles, anarchists challenged the hegemonic culture's concepts of *cubanidad* in hopes of creating their own anarchist vision for the island.

To explore the anarchist challenge in the culture wars of the early twentieth century, I follow the line of argument laid forth by John Gledhill, who suggested that one needs to look at "the context of such popular 'practices of resistance' in order to see what *kind* of impact they have on power relations, accepting that they do not pose an immediate threat to the stability of existing forms of social and political domination."[10] Thus, I return to the point with which I began this section: anarchists never had real power, but they challenged the power of those who did. By exploring this contested cultural terrain and thinking of anarchists in their multiple roles as labor activists, health reformers, education radicals, fiction writers, vegetarians, and stage actors, we gain insight into various forces shaping the early decades of independent Cuba. We also begin to understand how a counterhegemonic resistance movement used its various weapons against the hegemonic culture "to *transform* who they are through social action and thus do gain a voice and in some ways change history."[11]

Anarchism as a Countercultural Social Movement

As noted in the introduction, studies that focus on the culture of anarchism provide a more balanced view of anarchists, their relationships, and their missions than traditional institutional approaches. In addition, those studies that examine the interactions of anarchists within and against a hegemonic culture help us better understand the social and cultural discourses surrounding the evolution of a larger society's culture and cultural forms. In his examination of late nineteenth-century French anarchist culture, Richard Sonn defines culture as the moral, social, intellectual, and aesthetic bonds within society. Sidney Mintz adds that culture is "a kind of resource" that "is *used*; and any analysis of its use immediately brings into view the arrangements of persons in societal groups for whom cultural forms confirm, reinforce, maintain, change, or deny particular arrangements of status, power, and identity."[12] Eric Wolf reminds us that we cannot "imagine cultures as integrated totalities in which each part contributes to the maintenance of an organized, autonomous whole. There are only cultural sets of priorities and ideas put into play by determinate historical actors under determinate historical circumstances. In the course of action, these cultural sets are forever assembled, dismantled, and reassembled, conveying in varying accents the divergent paths of groups and classes."[13]

In the sense of these writers, cultures are not static entities. Rather, culture includes those aspects of a collective's lives that link or bond a society together through social interactions, intellectual inquiry, morality, and aesthetics at any given time. Because people and thus societies change over time, such bonds, priorities, ideas, and aesthetics, instituted by these societies, likewise change; because historical actors and their historical societies change, the culture likewise changes. Daniel Levine adds that any study of culture should also examine the "creativity and autonomous, self-moved change within a given system." To this end he calls for locating "critical social spaces . . . (that) provide arenas in which important events are remembered and, in some form, reproduced: parades, meetings, commemorations. This is where abstractions of 'human agency' take on concrete form in the work by men and women who, by their actions, make and remake culture: real people, not 'the people.'"[14] This becomes particularly relevant for understanding the anarchists who rejected participating in politics and thus the "formal political space." Meetings, commemorations, schools, health clinics, plays, literature—all became appropriate and useful cultural arenas for anarchists to challenge Cuba's hegemonic forces.

As Sonn notes, anarchists worked extensively in the cultural environment where they found themselves "spreading the word by all possible means: by words, songs, and the personal example of a superior life, as well as by deeds."[15] Because anarchists throughout the international movement refrained from organizing mass political parties or even attacking the state by force of arms (or the ballot), cultural work was crucial. Sonn and Lily Litvak describe this work among French and Spanish anarchists, respectively. Wobblies of the IWW were working in a similar vein in the United States at this same time. "The effort to link art to revolutionary struggle, as a means of disseminating political ideology and creating a worker's culture that challenged the definition of American life imposed by the government and business elites, defined the major motif which emerged from the practice of Wobbly artists," according to Salvatore Salerno.[16] In all three settings, fiction and theater became important tools not only to entertain but also to educate. The creation of anarchist schools and health institutes offered real alternatives to state and church institutions. As Sonn further points out, sometimes "anarchist culture was a substitute for formal organization. Anarchists expressed their solidarity at a grassroots level, in the cafés and union halls, in anarchist libraries and schools, and through the anarchist press. In fact they were sometimes suspected of being more involved in living the revolution than in making one."[17] Like other social challengers of the period, including socialists and feminists, Cuba's leading anarchist activists believed that one had to live and work in the here and now to prepare the masses for that future revolution. Cultural work was central to their preparation.

It is one thing to discuss culture and the cultural impulses of various social groups like Kapcia does. But what do you do when the social group under examination rejects both the class origins and the cultural assumptions that are central to the hegemonic culture's ideology and power? In a time when the country debated and experimented with what it meant to be Cuban, the hegemonic culture consented that Cuba should be a Christian, capitalist republic.

Some interest groups that challenged Cuba's leaders may have questioned one aspect or another of this triad. For instance, the Socialist Party questioned the Christian and capitalist dimensions but nevertheless worked with and in the government. Feminists, while often celebrating the secular, still fell short of calling for the destruction of the Church, capitalism, or the state. In fact, many women's rights activists urged the government to put women in charge of certain "family-oriented" state institutions, as Lynn Stoner has illustrated. "Radical" race-based political parties like the PIC might have questioned the premise that Cuba was a racial democracy, but they chose the established political system as their route to reform. Anarchists, however, condemned all three pillars. Rather than seeking a piecemeal change to the hegemonic culture, anarchists called for the complete rejection of its ideas, institutions, leaders, and symbols. Thus, I suggest that to understand the anarchist challenge in its appropriate context, we should see the anarchist movement as a "counter-cultural social movement." This concept requires some explaining.

Countercultures

In his classic book *The Making of a Counter Culture* (1969), Theodore Roszak examined the then-evolving youth counterculture. Roszak based his definition of a counterculture on how the rest of society tended to view it. A counterculture is "a culture so radically disaffiliated from the mainstream assumptions of our society that it scarcely looks to many as a culture at all, but takes on the alarming appearance of a barbaric intrusion."[18] However, Roszak saw this "barbaric intrusion" as "a brave (and hopefully humane) perversity" to challenge technocratic society. Rather than engaging in revolutionary struggle with the goal of overthrowing the state, ruling class, and economic system and then "merely redesigning the turrets and towers of the technocratic citadel," Roszak saw the counterculture of the 1960s as working on the foundations of society. "It is the foundations of the edifice that must be sought. And those foundations lie among the ruins of the visionary imagination and the sense of human community."[19]

More concerned with the wider aspects of countercultural movements and how they differ from aberrant or deviant behavior, in the 1980s J. Milton Yinger argued that the "term counterculture is appropriately used whenever the normative system of a group contains, as a primary element, a theme of conflict with the dominant values of society, where the tendencies, needs, and perceptions of the members of that group are directly involved in the development and maintenance of its values, and wherever its norms can be understood only by reference to the relationship of the group to the surrounding dominant society and its culture."[20] To Yinger, countercultural movements are both symbolic and behavioral, growing out of a combination of "contra social" actions and criticisms of the society in which the two "streams" (behavioral and symbolic) merge to form a counterculture. Thus, someone or a group performs what society labels "deviant behavior"; the person or group proclaims their nonconformity and then affirms with others that the "deviations" are good. This behavior stream is accompanied by a symbolic stream whereby the person or group criticizes society for failing to live up to its highest values. This evolves into a more general critique of societal values and performance until the "deviant" group creates a set of oppositional values. Yinger argues that the development of a movement containing various groups emerges when the two streams grow closer, that is, when theory and practice begin to join.[21] Similar concepts of an anarchist counterculture have appeared in studies of Argentine anarchism, where the focus has been on anarchist literary and artistic productions. As one writer notes, "Against the established hegemonic culture, the libertarian [anarchist] counter culture formulated a series of critical proposals that are integral and coherent elements of their general political strategy to educate the world's workers and subvert the so-called 'bourgeois order' in the name of the Social Revolution."[22]

This is not to say, however, that subaltern groups, including countercultural movements, are completely separated from the hegemonic culture. Although they may reject its core values and beliefs, their engagement with the hegemonic culture is central to their group identity. "The confrontation of culture and counterculture is a vital aspect of the process of social evolution. Antithetical groups do not escape each other's influence," Yinger concludes.[23] As a result, a counterculture derives from one segment of the larger society and is influenced by the larger society. To reinforce this point, Gledhill notes how "the evolving strategies of subaltern strata are shaped by the structures created by the dominant to implement their hegemony."[24] After all, to note Wolf's point about power, the hegemonic culture "organizes and orchestrates the settings." It is difficult to see "social movements as something entirely separate from the rest of the political domain, immune from the influence of the state," notes Gledhill.[25] Rather, a "focus on social movements encourages us to look at the politics of culture as a process by which groups in 'society' construct or reconstruct identities for themselves in their struggles and negotiations with dominant groups and the state. . . . Even if practices of domination never eliminate the spaces within which counter-hegemonic discourses and practices emerge, they still influence the forms taken by counter-hegemonic movements and their capacity to articulate together to mount a challenge to existing power-holders."[26]

Social Movements

Anarchists thus achieve status as countercultural, but it is also beneficial to see the anarchists as a "social movement," which Charles Tilly defined usefully as a movement that "consists of a sustained challenge to power holders in the name of a population living under the jurisdiction of those power holders by means of repeated public displays of that population's numbers, commitment, unity, and worthiness."[27] Besides recognizing the linkages between challengers and rulers, social movement scholars increasingly have emphasized the importance of recognizing the "ambiguity and contradictions within the movements themselves."[28] To this end, it is essential to identify not only the larger hegemonic culture and thus social, cultural, and political arenas in which the "culture wars" took place, but also to note that anarchists had their own internal squabbles and differing points of view. As Gledhill warns, "What we should avoid doing is transforming social movements into unitary 'actors' devoid of internal contradictions and contradictory tendencies, and isolating them from the larger social, cultural and political fields within which they experience their ebbs and flows."[29] The goal is to avoid portraying the conflicts as two-dimensional, in which there is some amorphous collection of repressors and the challengers are all united as one happy unitary resistance movement. To wit, this book is not a story about the dominators versus the dominated; rather, it is a look at how an array of labor activists, health workers, educators, and writers challenged a multifaceted hegemonic culture, but they—being human—didn't always get along or agree with each other or even necessarily agree on the tactics. They did agree, though, that what they saw as the hegemonic culture's "unholy trinity" of electoral politics, Christianity, and industrial capitalism had to be dismantled, or shy of dismantlement, then these had to be rejected and avoided.

Social movement theory has undergone important shifts since the 1980s. Earlier theories examined how movements emerged and developed as part of the opportunities that give rise to any political opposition. Later theories built on this opportunities-for-opposition approach and focused on movements as "mobilizing structures" whereby researchers concentrated their attentions on how movements mobilized resources. Both sets of theories have cast light on important structural aspects of social movements.

Since the 1980s, scholars have turned their attentions to how social movements "frame" their activities and agendas; or, put another way, how they assign meaning to and interpret themselves, their actions, and the worlds in which they operate and seek to make change. Taking from David Snow's definition of "framing processes," Doug McAdam and his colleagues refer to this process as "the *conscious strategic efforts by groups of people to fashion shared understandings of the world and of themselves that legitimate and motivate collective action.*"[30] The culture of social movements plays a key role in this approach because culture links "social construction and dissemination of new ideas"; thus, framing of social movements fits into general calls to "bring culture back in" to social and political analysis.[31] In this sense, how a movement and the movement's larger social context are framed is key to understanding the vision that movement leaders have of the present and their goal-oriented future. As McAdam adds, "The point is, all that any of the facilitating circumstances noted can do is create a certain structural potential for collective action. Whether or not that potential is realized depends on the actions of insurgents. And those actions are, in turn, shaped by and reflect the understandings of the actors involved. 'Mediating between opportunity and action are people and the . . . meanings they attach to their situations.'"[32] But McAdam also warns that too much "framing" analysis of social movements has been "ideational." That is, there has been too much focus on "ideas and their formal expression by movement actors" and not enough examination of the linkage between ideas and actions. After all, the actions in which a movement engages also speak to how a movement "frames" itself. McAdam continues, "Actions *do* speak louder than words."[33] Thus both the ideas and actions signify the work of the movement. The chapters that follow acknowledge this interaction of ideas and actions in reflecting how anarchists framed their world and their movement. Organizing strikes and boycotts, building health institutes and restaurants, staging plays, and founding schools illustrate the anarchist belief in the necessity to perform constructive work with visible results in the present and thus draw supporters' and potential supporters' attentions to the issues that most interested anarchists. At the same time, this book examines the ideational dimensions of framing by focusing on anarchists' public statements and literary sources. In a sense, ideas shaped the anarchist vision while actions provided the substance.

One other dimension to framing theory that must be addressed connects directly to the specific writings of Adrián del Valle and Antonio Penichet, whose works are important for this study. A central component of framing process analysis concerns the roles of popular intellectuals like Del Valle and Penichet. Framing analysis envisions such popular intellectuals as "Collective Action Framers." While framing implies interpretation and a movement-defined construction of reality, mostly individuals are responsible for putting forth these central frames. In Cuba, Penichet and Del Valle were the main framers through their leadership of different strands of the movement, their roles as leading editors of major movement newspapers, and their preeminent positions as the leading literary figures of the movement. The visions they constructed were the main "collective action frames" that shaped anarchist views of reality and anarchist goals. These frames not only cast an anarchist vision on the cultural, political, and social conditions of early twentieth-century Cuba, but also these frames, both "diagnostic" and "prognostic," gave readers and viewers ways to explain what they saw in their lives and suggestions about rectifying those conditions. Consequently, I return again to the importance of these two men in Cuba's anarchist movement and the special attention they deserve.

Anarchist Counterculture and Revolutionary Imagination

Any social movement hoping to initiate change has embedded in it and its culture a crucial, life-affirming ingredient: imagination. Thus, how anarchists "imagined" Cuba's past, present, and future is closely associated with how their ideas and actions framed the movement. Anarchists envisioned their own identity and future for Cuba that differed greatly from that of the hegemonic culture. To this end, the anarchists appropriated symbols, developed schools, and organized cultural activities to begin constructing their own imagined future Cuba. These symbols had their origins in the international anarchist movement, and especially in Spain where many Cuban anarchists were born and raised. Yet these international symbols were placed in and given a specific Cuban context. Other times these symbols were Cuban in origin and had to be modified to fit a larger anarchist agenda.

To better understand this process of adaptation, fluidity, and imagination, I draw upon one more important theoretical perspective that is directly linked to the theoretical concerns on Cuban culture, power, and social movements. William Rowe and Vivian Schelling show that no culture can be taken as a whole from one context and relocated unchanged. Rather, when cultural forms are separated from their original intention and recombined with new forms into new practices, "hybridization" takes place. When these new cultural forms are lifted from one space and reestablished in a new space, then "deterritorialization" takes place, and the "deterritorialized" culture becomes a new hybrid in its new location. Thus cultural forms may superficially seem the same from place to place, time to time, but they are in fact hybrids adapting to different environments. Rowe and Schelling urge us to see popular culture not as an "object" but as a "site" where various cultural forms interact in new settings. Popular culture thus mixes old and new. Traditions from the past and present and from the country and elsewhere intermingle at a new site.[34]

I suggest that such an understanding of how popular culture arises can be used to understand how the anarchist counterculture emerged and adjusted to the changing realities of Cuba's early republican era. Thus, Cuban anarchist counterculture exemplifies how a hybrid cultural form was shaped over time and space—a hybrid appearing in international anarchist symbols, education, health issues, and fiction that took on a specific Cuban relevance. By way of illustration for what the reader finds throughout this book, consider the case of Adrián del Valle. Drawing on Spanish anarchist themes and writings, Del Valle blended these with his own experiences as a Spanish immigrant in Cuba. Then, he merged his international anarchist beliefs, his immigrant experiences, and Cuban culture to write novels, short stories, and plays often rooted in Cuban settings and for both a Cuban and an international audience. His fiction reflected not only the interaction between international influences and the daily life experiences of anarchists and their followers in Cuba but also certain anarchist visions of progress and development in Cuba, while signaling a larger universal form of anarchist internationalism on the island. Ultimately, a hybridization approach is perfectly suited to unraveling the transnational and transcultural dimensions of Cuban anarchism and the movement's culture because such an approach illustrates how local and national forces responded to, sometimes adopted, and constantly adapted these global forces to reflect local conditions.

At this point we see the convergence of Rowe and Schelling's concepts of popular culture formation and distribution with Kapcia's and Anderson's concepts of *cubanía* and the imagined community respectively. Culture as a symbol of identity merges the past with the present in a "site" of confrontation between different visions of reality and the imagined future. In Cuba, leaders of the hegemonic culture appropriated historic events, people, and national symbols to construct a version of *cubanidad* and even tried to adapt Spanish and U.S. cultural forms into something distinctly "Cuban." Similarly, through their countercultural efforts, anarchists adopted, adapted, and merged their Spanish, anarchist, and island traditions into an anarchist version of *cubanidad*. Just as Cuba's politicians, religious leaders, and businessmen constructed their own national identity and imagined national future, anarchists aimed to create an international identity and imagined anarchist future, in short, a rebellious *cubanía*.

Ultimately, as the following study illustrates, anarchists drew on the everyday lives, habits, and reality of Cubans and Cuban history. This process broadened, even "democratized," the revolutionary dimensions of anarchism by rooting the international movement to the island. By incorporating "Cuban" symbols, anarchists (like other interest groups) not only sought more followers but also attempted to wrestle away from the hegemonic culture certain symbols of the wars for independence and concepts of Cuban identity.

Although it is tempting to "showcase" the anarchists as romantic figures of the past who, if only their ideas had been more widely adopted, could have saved Cuba from a century of neocolonialism on both the left and the right, this is simply ridiculous. These men and women (and sometimes their children) were average people, mostly working all day and trying to do what they could the other twelve to sixteen hours of the day to improve their lives and the lives of the people about whom they cared. The anarchists never significantly threatened the power of those who ran Cuba, though they must have scared them at times; anarchists were constantly harassed and deported, and some were even assassinated. Yet, for all of their idealistic talk about a "social revolution," most anarchists were realists who established schools, cultural events, and health institutes to improve their lives in the here and now. Still, anarchists—whether communists, syndicalists, or naturists—always kept visions of their idealized future front and center. They were but one of many social groups competing for influence and reform in the first decades of the twentieth century; however, given consideration of their platforms, they were arguably one of the most rebellious social movements on the island and the most radical influence shaping the early twentieth-century Cuban Left.

Part I

Anarchism, Nationalism, and Internationalism

2

Cuba for All

Anarchist Internationalism and the Politics of Cuban Independence

Maceo was right when he said: "I'm leaving. In this country one cannot live as a free man."
And he left, but returned as a warrior. The Warrior Liberator knew that Freedom had to be
conquered with the edge of a machete. His memory and the Freedom of the People is today
dishonored with the expulsion of the Anarchists. But, we will be Maceo, and like Maceo we
say: "In this country one cannot live as a free man." But also like Maceo we will pick up the
machete and gain our Freedom. The Freedom to live, the Freedom to struggle against
exploiters and conquer the oppressors. This is our motto and our motto is action.

Anonymous (November 1914)

In late 1914, anarchists around Cuba felt the noose tightening around them.
After years of open conflict with the government both in the press and on the
strike line, authorities were initiating a new wave of repression against radical
workers in order to pacify the country for Cuba's role in World War I. As the
government began to make arrests at the end of the year, those anarchists still
free took to their newspapers to defend themselves like the anonymous author
above. Writer after writer denounced the government abuse and proclaimed
that they were innocent, free men who were unjustly being arrested and deported. However, this plea was more interesting than a simple proclamation of
their right to free speech and association. Anarchist writers, no matter where
they were born, appealed to the 1895–1898 war for independence to condemn
the actions of the authorities. Some appealed to the ideals and heroics of independence heroes José Martí and Antonio Maceo. Others remembered how they
themselves had fought for Cuba's independence by supporting the social revolutionary goals of the masses that took arms against their colonizers. In short,
to defend themselves and their actions, anarchists appealed to independence-
era symbols that were becoming central to Cuba's emerging political culture. At
the same time, they condemned Cuba's leaders, whom they believed had tar-
nished those symbols by perpetrating abuses against average men and women.

Most anarchists had supported Cuba's revolt against Spain from 1895 to

1898. They pushed an "anti-imperialist" and "internationalist" agenda in the island's war for independence; they saw the struggle not as a "nationalist" revolt, but as one link in the chain of an international anarchist revolution against all states, capital, and religion. Following independence, anarchists adopted popular symbols of the war in their struggle to free the island from what they saw as a coercive state apparatus that had replaced Spanish rule but not altered power relations throughout society. To anarchists, the new Cuban state promoted concepts of "patriotic nationalism" that served the ideological purposes of the elite. Meanwhile, anarchists charged, this same Cuban state subverted the independence movement's broader goals of social and economic revolution—postwar goals promised by independence leader José Martí as well as the anarchists.

Anarchists and the War for Independence

On November 26, 1891, José Martí addressed a crowd of Cuban migrant workers at the Liceo Cubano in Tampa, Florida. Martí approached the gathering to help salvage the fledgling independence movement in exile. Middle-class leaders based in New York struggled for some dimension of autonomy from Spain; the leaders feared that a full-fledged war on the island could undermine their economic futures by destroying Cuba's infrastructure. In their nationalist rhetoric, rarely did these leaders discuss concerns important to the popular classes.[1] Meanwhile, Cuban workers in the tobacco factories of Tampa and Key West increasingly challenged Cuban nationalists who failed to include social and economic programs in any independence scheme for the island.

Acting as representatives of the Havana-based Alianza Obrera, anarchists Enrique Creci and Enrique Messonier had helped to form the Local Federation of Tobacco Workers (Federación Local de Tabaqueros) in Key West in 1888. The Florida federation competed directly with the New York–based exile leadership for the allegiance of migrant workers. This drove a wedge in the exile community's attempt to unify the struggle against Spanish colonial rule. Most Florida-based laborers began to demand a "popular nationalism" that held up workers' social concerns as central goals for independence. As long as nationalist leaders refused to acknowledge workers' socioeconomic interests, workers remained reluctant to support an armed struggle to free Cuba.[2]

By the 1890s, Cubans already had waged two unsuccessful wars for independence. The Pact of Zanjón ended the Ten Years War (1868–1878); Cubans failed to gain their two primary objectives of independence and immediate abolition.

In 1879 the Guerra Chiquita (1879–1880) erupted in eastern Cuba when popular black leaders refused to submit to the 1878 peace treaty and return to the plantations. Many Afro-Cubans, who continued to fight the Spaniards under black leaders Guillermo Moncada and Antonio Maceo, believed that a peace that excluded the abolition of slavery and independence was hollow.[3] Owing to continued widespread Afro-Cuban resistance, Spanish authorities cast the revolt in terms of a race war and thus attempted to drain white support.[4] While the Guerra Chiquita ultimately failed to liberate the island, these freed and enslaved Afro-Cubans helped to transform the anticolonial struggle in Cuba from what historian Ada Ferrer calls "a limited political-military uprising to a popular movement for social change."[5] In essence, Afro-Cuban participation in this second war for independence complemented the growing dimensions of popular nationalism. The nationalist struggle to throw off Spain came to include demands for broad social and economic transformation. Thousands of former slaves entered the Cuban wage-labor force during the gradual ending of slavery, which was formally abolished by royal decree in 1886. This growing free wage-labor force was exposed to radicalizing working-class demands within the Cuban independence movement. Just as important, these workers brought their own social demands to help transform the struggle for independence into more than just a limited political fight against Spanish rule.

The Cuban anarchist Enrique Roig San Martín tapped into this evolving sociopolitical dimension in his newspaper *El Productor*. In the 1889 column "La patria y los obreros" [The homeland and the workers], Roig San Martín converted the image of slavery into a critique of a purely political independence movement devoid of a social and economic revolution. He asked how one could have a free country without changes in societal power relations? Or, how could one be free when he served at the mercy of those who controlled the economy? "It is in vain that one speaks of our homeland and our freedom, if one does not begin to secure our individual independence; that we are not for redeeming the homeland while remaining slaves. The degree of independence for the homeland we measure by the amount of independence that its children enjoy, and we have said that there is no free homeland with children as slaves."[6] For Roig San Martín, slavery had not been eliminated but just transformed beyond the exploitation of blacks. Now there were slaves of all colors.

The influence of Havana anarchists could be found not only in Cuba but also across the Florida Straits in Key West and Tampa. In addition to their roles in the establishment of the Federation, anarchists helped to organize a series of strikes throughout the Florida tobacco factories in 1889. Anarchists called on strikers to leave Key West during one such strike, with the Alianza going so far as to send a steamer to bring workers back to Cuba. That the Spanish government did the same, however, enabled the leading Key West patriot newspaper *El Yara* to cast anarchists as "pro-Spanish"—an association that most anarchists would labor hard to overcome.[7]

Through his sympathetic observations of labor movements in the United States as well as his witness to the strong influence of Havana's anarchists on workers in Florida, Martí came to understand the important social concerns of Cuba's workers. He realized that these concerns had to be incorporated into the independence cause to gain broader popular support. This led Martí to Tampa in 1891 to broaden the nationalist struggle to include a socioeconomic agenda, not just political independence. Although Martí embraced issues of social justice, racial equality, and independence, he also stressed the need for class cooperation. He saw continued middle-class support against Spain as a necessary measure to weaken the anarchists' influence with workers.[8] Martí's speech before the Liceo Cubano blended the language of social justice and nationalism and drew the workers into the nationalist camp. In his appeal to the interests of the working class, Martí assured his audience that social concerns would remain part of the independence ideal. However, he rejected open class struggle as counterproductive to the immediate aim of the island's liberation. This stance offered the nonworking class patriot leaders in exile some breathing room. Martí's speech became the basis for his Cuban Revolutionary Party (Partido Revolucionario Cubano [PRC]). The PRC called for a "just and open republic, united in territory, in rights, in work and cordiality, constructed with all and for the good of all."[9]

While Martí preached class alliance as a means, in part, to undermine anarchist strength in the labor unions, many leading anarchists like Creci and Messonier came to accept the need to make cross-class alliances in order to achieve the immediate goal of independence.[10] In January 1892, two months after Martí's Liceo Cubano speech, the anarchist-led Junta Central de Trabajadores de la Región Cubana held a labor congress on the island. The delegates issued their "Manifiesto del Congreso Obrero de 1892," which recognized that revolutionary socialism (anarchism) and Cuba's independence were not mutually exclusive. The manifesto famously argued that the fight for anarchy in Cuba would not be "an obstacle to the triumph of the aspirations of emancipation of this people, for it would be absurd if the man who aspired to individual freedom would oppose the collective freedom of the people."[11] They believed that the island would have to be liberated from its colonial oppressor before the individual socioeconomic rights of all could be achieved.

Still, not all anarchists were convinced that they should support the war or collude with the PRC. Cuba posed a real ideological and practical dilemma for anarchists. Never before had the international movement been faced with how to rectify its "internationalism" with a clear war for national independence. Many anarchist leaders in Cuba continued to work within the unions rather than openly support the PRC. Meanwhile, their Spanish-speaking anarchist comrades in the United States were divided. In 1894 the New York–based anarchist newspaper El Despertar distanced itself from the PRC. This prompted proseparatist anarchists in Tampa to publish the newspaper El Esclavo, which openly called on anarchists to support Cuban independence.[12] Enrique Creci, by now also based in Tampa, clearly backed anarchist support for the war and the 1892 manifesto. By 1895, Creci was publishing the anarchist journal Archivo Social in which he supported calls for independence, particularly Martí's call for a "Cuba libre con todos y para todos."[13] He engaged in a newspaper article debate with Cristóbal Fuente in Havana and Pedro Esteve in New York. Fuente and Esteve refused to see how anarchist support could benefit the larger anarchist cause, for they feared that such support would lead to further repression.[14] Creci responded by joining the rebel army and achieved the rank of captain before his capture and execution by Spanish forces.[15]

Beyond Spanish-speaking anarchists in the United States and Cuba, the international anarchist community also was divided on whether to support the independence struggle. French anarchists who made up the bulk of the Paris-based French Committee for a Free Cuba supported the fight for independence; their support followed the lines of the 1892 Worker's Congress Manifesto. Leading anarchist intellectuals and organizers like Peter Kropotkin in London and Emma Goldman in the United States remained neutral; they understood how anarchists could see this as a great opportunity to cast off colonial rule, but they remained unconvinced that anarchists could thwart the nationalists. In other words, Kropotkin and others feared that anarchists would merely trade a colonial tyranny for a national tyranny.[16] Meanwhile, anarchists in Spain generally supported Cuba's struggles. Beginning with the wars of the 1870s, Spanish anarchists irreverently suggested that if Spain was so endangered by Cuba's struggles, then why were the children of the elite, who asserted this danger, not going to defend the homeland? It followed that, if the sons of the gentry were not going, then neither were the sons of the poor and disinherited.[17] Articles in the Spanish anarchist press expressed sadness at seeing sons shipped off to defend the monarchy, while other articles described the poor state of Spanish soldiers on the field. To justify the anarchist support for independence, Spanish anarchists portrayed Cuba's three uprisings against the Crown as "anti-colonial wars." Anarchist writers in Spain usually distinguished between what they saw as the futility of "political revolutions" and the vitality of independence wars against imperial rulers. Even a leading Spanish anarchist like Pedro Esteve, who earlier had opposed the war, eventually came to work with other Spanish and Cuban anarchists in Florida and New York in support of Cuba's anticolonial struggle. Esteve suggested that Cuba's liberty could be channeled into a social revolution, which then would become an inspiration for all.[18]

Ultimately, anarchist communities in Florida and Cuba, as well as their Iberian *compañeros* generally, came to support the call for independence. When war finally erupted in 1895, anarchists on the island played important roles. They organized and ran supplies for the rebel army, collected funds, and created underground communications networks. Along with other labor activists, anarchists urged Spanish troops to abandon their posts and join the separatists. In addition, they tried to create an anarchist network, mainly in western Cuba, to arm workers. One of the most audacious anarchist roles was an 1896 plot by Havana-based anarchists—working with the PRC in the United States—to set off bombs in the capital in an effort to assassinate General Weyler.[19]

From their particular internationalist perspective, Cuba's anticolonial war was a struggle against injustice and imperialism, which required freedom-loving individuals to fight to sever the links with its colonial master. This process of de-linking also had to include the firm understanding (now also expressed by the nationalist camp under Martí) that a full-scale social revolution would take place after independence. As one leading organizational force of Cuba's workers by the 1890s, the anarchist choice to forego politics and engage directly in the struggle for independence was crucial. This "no politics" approach helped to broaden the anarchists' appeal, both on the island and in Florida. In fact by the 1890s, "the anarchist-led labor movement succeeded in fostering class ties among people of diverse race, political sympathy, and origin (*peninsular* or creole)."[20] Anarchists hoped that Enrique Roig San Martín's slaves of all colors would have their day, and then Cuba would be the launching pad for a domestic and later international social revolution.

Anarchism, Patriotism, and Independence

But that proved to be wishful thinking among the anarchists. In the summer of 1898, U.S. intervention in the war effectively deprived the Cuban liberation army of its own victory against Spanish forces. On January 1, 1899, the United States began its formal military occupation of Cuba, thereby thwarting the broad coalition of Cubans and internationalists who fought for the island's liberation from Spanish colonialism. At the same time that the United States decided to stay in Cuba, the Spanish-born anarchist intellectual and supporter of independence, Adrián del Valle, returned to the island. Del Valle had agitated in Cuba during the early 1890s, but he left to continue his activities and writing in New York at the war's onset. In January 1899 he returned to Havana, and, with other anarchists like Luis Barcia, Del Valle set to work organizing the first post-independence anarchist newspaper *El Nuevo Ideal*. Just weeks after the formal U.S. military occupation began, they published the first edition. From 1899 to 1901, this newspaper led the anarchist critique on the meaning of independence and challenged the island's foreign and domestic leaders, who, to anarchists and other groups on the island, seemed to have abandoned the popular sentiment for broad social change.

Through their press, anarchists joined other social actors in pushing for solutions to the island's problems. An immediate concern involved helping Cubans trapped in the cities. During the war, Spanish military policies led to the forced relocation of people from rural areas to the cities. This allowed Spanish forces to wage an intensive campaign throughout rural Cuba. At war's end, most of these *reconcentrados* were still in the cities. In February 1899, Barcia claimed that 400,000 *reconcentrados* were slowly dying from starvation. With the war over, families should have been able to return to their lands and cultivate them, but the rich and the government appeared unconcerned, claimed Barcia. In trumpeting a rural-urban "national" unity he called on workers in the cities to help their rural comrades.[21] Anarchists saw such unity as key to continuing the revolution and addressing the social questions of the island. To do this, they urged workers to unite on the social front as a class but avoid forming working-class political parties. This latter point was in direct response to the newspaper *Memorándum Tipográfico*'s calls for creation of a workers party to contest future elections. However, Del Valle (writing as Palmiro de Lidia) appealed to his readers' sense of history by claiming that if workers had made politics instead of revolution in the 1890s, they would still be under Spanish rule.[22] Thus the anarchist "no politics" position before the war remained a central component of their doctrine after independence, even as the anarchists tried to unite Cubans across the island.

That anarchism and Cuban independence were crucially joined in the minds of many Cubans is apparent when studying the events in November 1899: anarchists brought Enrique Creci's remains to Havana for reburial next to Enrique Roig San Martín. Creci had led an armed assault from Key West during the war and was killed shortly afterward. When his remains arrived at the Workers Center in Havana, Creci's friend and fellow anarchist Dr. Federico Falco approached the gathering to speak. However, a police lieutenant stopped Falco. The lieutenant claimed he was acting under direct orders from the government. Suddenly, and without warning, forty police officers charged the crowd. *El Nuevo Ideal* likened the police offensive to one of former Governor General Weyler's brutal assaults on innocent men, women, and children during the war. The police temporarily prevented speakers from addressing the audience, but a crowd soon regrouped. They then accompanied Creci's remains in a silent procession to the cemetery with the newspaper's editors at the forefront.[23]

Creci's funeral was more than just the reburial of a fallen anarchist who fought for the island's collective liberation. The procession, accompanying repression, and association of the repression to Spanish brutality brought to the fore several images. First, Creci was not a well-known liberation army general or public figure. In this sense, then, he represented the average Cuban worker. Likewise, his reburial was more than just an occasion to commemorate his contribution to independence. Rather, *El Nuevo Ideal* called it a "homage to all the workers that had fought and died obscurely for independence. Until now, the bourgeoisie have only remembered the generals; it is just that the workers also remember their own, their brothers, those anonymous heroes of the mountains whose blood watered the Cuban soil."[24] The burial provided a symbol of working-class contributions to independence. At the same time, anarchists portrayed governmental repression during the reburial ceremonies as an example of an authority no better than other countries "where despotism rules."[25] From this perspective, power relations remained unaltered and reconfirmed anarchists' view of how Cuba's leaders had forsaken the social goals of independence.

However, citizens knew well that Cuba's elite was not the only party to blame for subverting the revolution. Bureaucrats and officers of the U.S. occupation were intimately intertwined in this process. In *El Nuevo Ideal*'s second issue,

Barcia attacked what he believed were U.S. designs for annexing the island. In fact, even prior to American John Brooke becoming the new governor-general of Cuba, the McKinley administration seemed determined to annex Cuba. Many in the United States saw the island as an extension of the U.S. East Coast, a country whose people were believed incapable of self-rule. Moreover, U.S. officials believed an independent Cuba also might jeopardize American interests.[26] Barcia and others urged readers to fight against American annexationist designs. Several columns throughout 1899 drew comparisons to the Philippines, where guerrillas were waging war against occupation forces. Barcia noted that in the Philippines the United States controlled only Manila while Filipinos controlled the rest of their country.[27] In August 1899, another writer drew attention to the U.S.'s Monroe Doctrine, which proclaimed the Americas for Americans. Filipino resistance to the U.S. occupation angered the United States, but Barcia noted that Filipino resistance was merely imitating the Monroe principle: "The Philippines are for Filipinos." As such, the Filipino resistance could serve as an example to Cubans of how to deal with the U.S. occupation.[28] Although Barcia and other writers always stopped short of calling for armed insurrection against U.S. forces, resorting to such rhetoric underscored a growing feeling of frustration among anarchists—frustrations echoed in the public at large—that the goals of a social revolution, delayed to fight the war, might now be slipping away forever.

Early in the occupation, the United States changed heart and announced that it eventually would recognize Cuban independence rather than push for annexation. However, some anarchists were skeptical and repeatedly questioned such pronouncements. Frequently, U.S. officials said that Cubans were not ready for self-rule, an assessment that justified the continued occupation of the island. Del Valle recalled that this was the same argument that the Spanish government made throughout the nineteenth century when it said Cuba could not be free because it was not yet ready to govern its own affairs.[29] Still, some anarchists began to question what a future Cuban republic would look like. Barcia claimed in 1899 that Cubans, especially Cuban workers, did not want a republic like that of the United States. Too many Cuban migrant workers who had traveled to Florida were direct witnesses to how North American businessmen and politicians treated their workers. Rather, argued Barcia, Cuban workers wanted democratic votes by referenda, paid return migration of Cubans back to the island, lands for workers, and money to work those lands.[30]

Despite widespread fears, the occupation government did hold municipal elections in Cuba in 1900. U.S. officials sought candidates from the middle and upper classes, those most fearful that their properties could be taken by a truly independent, reformist government that might, if elected, try to redistribute land. In addition, the United States helped to design an electoral code that restricted suffrage to Cuban males with property valued at $250 or more or the ability to read and write. Such restrictions meant that only one-third of Cuba's adult males were eligible to vote.[31] To the dismay of North American observers, candidates from the pro-independence coalition of reformers and nationalists won the majority of victories. Troubled by the strength of the *independentistas* on the island and the growing disfavor of annexation in Washington, the United States turned to other ways to control Cuba's fate. Once again, in the conspiratorial world of Cuban anarchists, these new mechanisms confirmed their suspicions of the United States. The most important of these new controls was the new Cuban constitution. In Washington, Congress deliberated on the island's constitution, which came complete with the terms of the Platt Amendment. Among other issues, the Platt provisions guaranteed the right of the United States to intervene militarily in Cuban affairs to protect Cuban independence and maintain a stable government on the island. Although anarchists lamented this whole process of U.S. approval, they nevertheless found it difficult to sympathize with any emergent Cuban government. One anarchist reminded Cubans that local "Cuban" governments had ordered the military to occupy workplaces during a recent strike, allowed the Creci procession to be attacked, and attempted to prohibit the noted Italian anarchist Errico Malatesta from speaking in Havana during his March 1900 visit. He added that workers must not trust a "Cuban" government or capitalists who sought to divide workers, especially along Spanish-Cuban lines. Just because a new government would be headed by Cubans did not mean that the social goals of the war would be any nearer to fruition.[32]

In the spring of 1901, the Cuban constitutional convention deliberated on ratification of the new constitution. During the deliberations, Del Valle wrote how everyone in Cuba seemed to have an opinion on the Platt provisions. From an anarchist perspective, it was obvious that Platt negated Cuba's sovereignty. However, he continued, it was also a natural, logical consequence of intervention. Del Valle tapped into the island's revolutionary heritage. Cuba needed a miracle. Perhaps a great Cuban liberator like Antonio Maceo could be resuscitated to come save the day. "And yet not even that would be good enough," Del Valle concluded, "because if he were revived and saw what many revolutionaries of yesterday were doing today, it is almost certain that he would die again . . . of shame and indignation."[33] Reflecting divisions within Cuban society, the assembly ratified the constitution with the Platt provisions by one vote, ushering in the birth of a new republic in 1902.

The first year of the Cuban Republic did nothing to allay anarchist concerns that those in power would continue to forsake the social revolutionary goals of independence. As Cubans prepared celebrations to commemorate the republic's first anniversary in 1903, anarchists argued that there was very little to celebrate. The constitution contained no provisions for labor rights. The colonial penal code that allowed authorities to imprison those conspiring to alter existing conditions remained on the books. Several unsuccessful strikes had erupted around the island, the most significant being a general strike in support of the Apprentices' Strike in November 1902. The newly created police attacked strikers. Finally, in the central Cuban town of Cruces two workers were found murdered under mysterious circumstances, a crime that prompted popular outcry from around Cuba.[34]

The week before the first May 20 Independence Day celebrations, the recently launched anarchist weekly ¡Tierra! decried these crimes and shortcomings; they claimed the events were grim reminders of the days of Spanish despotic rule over the island. "The struggle for democracy has been converted into an indignant lie because a minority without conscience control power," wrote an anonymous contributor to the newspaper.[35] In the week following Independence Day, ¡Tierra! alleged that workers had seen through the veil of freedom presented by the island's leaders. The paper claimed that workers did not participate in the celebrations, thus "proving" that the majority of Cuban adults understood that what might have been promoted as a celebration of the people's freedom was in reality "only an official party organized and celebrated by those most determined to prostitute that same freedom." As proof, the newspaper described how the buildings of the government and capitalists were decorated with different colored electric lights. Meanwhile workers wandered about in the dark because they lacked even a spare five centavos to light a small oil lamp; the workforce had been idled without pay for three days to prepare for the celebrations. However, always searching for some noble worker response, whether it existed or not, the writer tried to put a positive spin on these events. According to ¡Tierra!, the workers were satisfied with having no light of their own because it enabled them to see who were the real celebrants (and thus beneficiaries) of independence: the elegantly dressed and bejeweled "*patriotas alcoholizados*," in other words, those drunk on their own patriotism. To anarchists, the celebrations looked no different than nationalistic events in Spain. Thus, the paper asked, what was so special about an independent republic if it only aped the former colonizer?[36]

The question of sovereignty and independence could not be overlooked when a civil war between the Liberal and Conservative parties ushered in a second U.S. occupation of the island in August 1906. Disturbed by the violence, President Theodore Roosevelt ordered Secretary of State William Howard Taft and Assistant Secretary of State Robert Bacon to the island to negotiate a settlement. In the midst of the political turmoil, Roosevelt's emissaries reported on the confusing nature of the conflict in the new country. "The government controls only the coast towns and provincial capitals. Anarchy elsewhere," Taft cabled back.[37] The anarchists could have only wished he were right. In fact the outbreak of violence and intervention postponed a long planned anarchist propaganda tour across the island and also prevented ¡*Tierra!* from publishing on September 8. The following week, however, ¡*Tierra!* returned and once again urged its readers to question the utility of politics and political struggles. To capture this sentiment, Amalio de Castro painted a picture of politics that would remain at the core of anarchist hatred for not only the state but also the republican political process: "politics is the art of deceiving and enslaving the people."[38] In this case politics, political parties, and the violence that followed a challenged election prompted a U.S. military intervention that would last until 1909—deceiving the public of its "independence" and illustrating the "enslavement" of the island under U.S. tutelage. Nothing could have illustrated better the anarchist propaganda of the previous five years regarding the "political filthiness" (*asquerosidad política*) of bourgeois politics, added S. Martínez from the central Cuban city of Sancti-Spíritus.[39]

Just months into the second occupation, anarchists were amused by some of the U.S. government's actions. In December 1906 the government under Charles Magoon dissolved the Cuban House and Senate, an action that terminated the congressmen's monthly salaries.[40] However, this ironic amusement was short-lived when anarchists turned to attacking the Magoon government itself. As they prepared to launch an islandwide propaganda tour in 1907, Cuban anarchists welcomed among themselves two Spanish anarchists who had come to lend their aid and voices to the social gatherings and lectures during the trip. But shortly after their arrival in April 1907 Marcial Lores and Abelardo Saavedra were arrested. Rumors circulated that the two had entered Cuba illegally by having third parties like the Spanish government pay for their transportation. This prompted "Garin" to write in *¡Tierra!* that the Magoon regime closely resembled the military government under General Leonard Wood during the first occupation. In the first era, anarchists held Wood partially responsible for preventing Malatesta from speaking in Havana and then expelling him. Magoon's treatment of Lores and Saavedra was no different. "Mister Wood is revived in Mr. Magoon . . . to the point, the first was responsible for an unjust, undefined expulsion; the second for an arbitrary, boundless imprisonment."[41]

While anarchists criticized rule under Magoon, U.S. officials showed considerable restraint and resisted using their muscle to suppress the radicals. For instance, following the arrests of Lores and Saavedra, the inspector general of jails notified Magoon that Lores actually appeared to have paid for his own passage to Cuba by working on the ship and that Saavedra traveled economically in third class. The official saw "no ground under our existing laws to imprison a person for an alleged violation of a law so long as such a violation is not clearly proven and I do not consider that any action be taken in the matter."[42] This official memo spoke only of the men and made no mention of their anarchist beliefs, but that oversight would soon change.

In December 1907 and January 1908, Chief of Military Information Captain John Furlong sent a flurry of memos to Magoon and the general staff. Furlong described a growing anarchist presence penetrating Havana's working class. The captain feared the consistent and prominent role that anarchists were playing in strike activities, and he voiced concern that the anarchists might be preparing for violence. "Spanish working men always join the strikes in Cuba and are generally found to be anarchists who stick closely together and are fiery in their discussions," noted Furlong. Such a description, feeding into old notions of anarchists as "outsiders," emphasized the idea that Cubans would not participate in such a movement. Furlong reinforced this perception by suggesting that there were three types of workers in Cuba: "genuine Cubans" who were keeping alive Martí's ideas, "degenerates" who lacked education and "are devoid of patriotism," and "anarchists" who "stick together and work with zeal for the Spanish influx, wherever it may wish to go." As if not enough of an insult to anarchists, Furlong finished by suggesting to his superiors that while some real anarchists existed on the island, most of those who called themselves anarchists were merely Spaniards who wanted Cubans' jobs.[43] Ultimately, U.S. occupation troops believed that most anarchists and anarchist sympathizers in Havana, who Furlong conservatively estimated to be one thousand strong, were mainly opportunists who found no affinity with Cuba other than as a means to get jobs at the expense of Cuban workers.[44] Nevertheless, the government continued its surveillance of anarchists during the occupation's duration.

Following the restoration of the republic in 1909, anarchists focused their attacks against patriotism at not only the government but also the leading daily newspaper on the island, *Diario de la Marina,* and its editor, Don Nicolás Rivero. One of the island's oldest newspapers, *Diario de la Marina* had been a Spanish liberal organ and the official paper of the Spanish government in Cuba. As described in a turn-of-the-century travel book for an eagerly awaiting North American tourist crowd, the paper "has always been on the side of good order, and has refrained from the radical views, which some other papers have often advanced, frequently thereby leading the masses to riot and crime."[45] A Spaniard by birth, Rivero epitomized Spanish cultural paternalism, added North American journalist Irene Wright in 1910. In addition, Rivero supported wholeheartedly the Church, Spanish colonial rule (until it was obvious Spain would have to withdraw), the 1898–1902 U.S. occupation, and whoever seemed to be the strongest in the ever-changing world of political struggle between Liberals and Conservatives. Regarding labor, Wright noted that "Don Nicolás through his paper lectures the workingmen as an indulgent parent might an ungrateful son; he tells them a deal of truth, in the detail, and they break his windows in recognition of his services, for they are moderns, and have been known to mention 'the principle of the thing.' They talk of 'rights,' and he of 'concessions.'"[46] In part, because Rivero personified all that the anarchists rejected, his newspaper became a frequent target of their attacks. With Cubans once again running the island and *Diario de la Marina* leading renewed appeals for Cuban patriotism, anarchists jumped at the chance to show what they saw as the ridiculousness and hypocrisy of nationalist sentiment among Cuba's leaders. Writing in *Rebelión!* in March 1909, "Ana Harquia" lampooned Rivero, his leading columnist Joaquín Aramburu, and the paper for their sudden patriotism. "Here everything is *Cuban,* the sky is *Cuban,* the music is *Cuban,* the women are *Cuban,* the dog and the cat are *Cuban,* and, the most laughable: el *Diario de la Marina, Cuban.*"[47]

In fact, by the end of the second U.S. occupation, it had become extremely difficult to define just what was "Cuban" and what it meant to be "Cuban." The occupations, the shifting support of the mainstream press, and the squabbles between Liberals and Conservatives were compounded by the sight of children running around in the streets after school playing war. As one observer described it, children divided themselves into "Liberals" and "Conservatives." They formed gangs with their own flags on poles, shouting slogans like "Long Live the Liberal Party!" and marched around in battle formation. Yet, the writer asked, did anyone care? Just what were these children being taught in school and at home anyway? And what was a "Cuban," when kids played war not as Cubans versus Spaniards, but as Cubans versus Cubans?[48]

Such sentiment accompanied growing anarchist attacks against politicians, elite-controlled political parties and their relations to both U.S. occupation forces, and the encroachment of U.S. economic interests on the island. The terms of the Platt Amendment caught Cuban nationalists in the government in a bind, especially regarding labor issues. As North American investment poured onto the island, the Cuban elite either had to make concessions to labor or pass laws creating mechanisms to repress labor. To repress Cuban workers for the economic bottom line of foreign corporations would expose the hollowness of the government's "nationalism" and the leaders' meaning of independence. However, to give concessions to workers would strengthen the labor movement, show the United States that the Cuban government was weak, and then justify U.S. intervention under the Platt Amendment.

In fact, strikes, work stoppages, and slowdowns occurred throughout the island and in virtually every sector of the economy during the first three decades after the creation of the republic. Workers struck in various sectors of construction, tobacco, sugar, and shipping.[49] Although occasionally successful in terms of getting pay increases or better working conditions, the strikes and their ability to affect other sectors of the economy illustrated an important national issue regarding the labor movement. Labor's assaults threatened to disrupt the economy and particularly the profit margins of foreign-owned business. For the Cuban state, as Louis Pérez illustrates, "the defense of foreign property served as a measure of the republic's capacity to discharge its treaty obligations and thereby guarantee national independence. By directly challenging foreign capital, labor indirectly challenged Cuban sovereignty."[50] In other words, if Cuba could not control its labor, then the United States would. To anarchists, such actions illustrated the state's hypocritical patriotic notions of nationalism while offering proof of collusion between capital and the state against the improved conditions of Cuba's masses. Ultimately, there was no more telling betrayal of the notion of *Cuba para todos*. The conflict between anarchist workers and the government around Cruces would embody this "betrayal."

After the first decade of independence, the island's sugar production was increasingly concentrated around the central Cuban town of Cruces in Santa Clara province. Soon, the sixty-four sugar mills in Santa Clara far outnumbered the forty-six and thirty-four mills in Oriente and Matanzas provinces, respectively.[51] Urban-based anarchists believed that rural workers, who endured the harshest physical labor and some of the worst living conditions on the island, offered a relatively untapped potential revolutionary capacity. But several obstacles existed. Rural workers only congregated in the sugar mills for three to four months of the year. During the rest of the year, workers wandered from field to field or moved to towns and cities as day laborers.[52] Despite these obstacles, anarchists believed that they required a presence in the heart of rural industrial Cuba to give their propaganda and organization a chance. To remain isolated in a western city like Havana undermined anarchists' efforts to build a strong, multilayered movement with appeal to residents across the island. Consequently, as sugar production intensified in the Cruces area, anarchists spread to the region and likewise intensified their efforts.

In 1910, Abelardo Saavedra moved from the Havana-Regla anarchist hub to Cruces, where he published a new version of the newspaper *Rebelión!*. After arriving in Cruces, he organized a Workers Center to disseminate anarchist propaganda and strengthen the coalition between the rural and urban proletariat. Building upon his successful organizing, Saavedra began planning an islandwide workers conference in Cruces for 1912. Concerned about this growing anarchist menace in their midst, authorities arrested and deported Saavedra. Nevertheless, other anarchists, including his wife Enriqueta and the female anarchist Emilia Rodríguez de Lípiz, saw the conference to fruition. Opening in February 1912, conference delegates called for creation of an islandwide labor federation to establish schools, push for a workplace accident law, agitate for an eight-hour day, abolish piecework, and establish a minimum wage. Clearly these were more than just anarchist demands. Several of these measures required that anarchists petition the state to pass laws in workers' favor. Traditionally, anarchist antistate rhetoric meant that they avoided seeking government redress. However, the conference reflected a maturing of the anarchist movement and a growing presence of anarcho-syndicalists within the movement. This presence led other anarchists to understand that they needed to work for broader working-class concerns, even if at times this meant joining alliances with nonanarchists and directly working for immediate, legal reforms.[53]

While the movement continued to mature, working-class radicalism surged in the summer of 1914. Building off the Cruces Conference goals of broader working-class cooperation, ¡*Tierra!* urged for the first time that workers form themselves into a revolutionary party. This was the outgrowth of years of anarchist agitation to unite different working-class tendencies into an islandwide movement. As the first sugar harvest of World War I approached in late 1914, anarcho-syndicalism was on the rise and calls for revolutionary violence escalated.[54] Politicians reacted to events by trying to undercut working-class support for radicalism generally and anarchism specifically. The government established labor laws, sponsored a government-backed labor congress, and created a governmental commission to look at social issues. Rather than welcome these government actions, though, anarchists saw them as deceptive maneuvers designed more to gain votes and governmental stability than in creating a sense of social justice that was the very ideal of the independence wars. Although anarchists in Cruces had sought government labor reforms, those initiatives had to come from the workers themselves. If they were to be initiated by the government, then anarchists charged they could not be trusted.

Failing to pacify the growing radicalism, the new government of President Mario Menocal launched a national crackdown beginning in late 1914. Menocal, himself a former independence war leader who had profited handsomely from postwar business ventures, set out to crush the anarchists and their Havana-Cruces movement. The army moved on Cruces and destroyed the workers' organization there. Authorities who labeled anarchists across the island as "pernicious foreigners" (*extranjeros perniciosos*) arrested and deported them. To defend themselves against this charge, many anarchists took to the pages of the Havana-based anarcho-syndicalist weekly *El Dependiente* to recall their own and other anarchists' participation in the war for independence. In several issues, writers attempted to harmonize their anarchist activities and beliefs with their commitment to a free Cuba both during the struggle for independence and afterward. For instance, longtime Cruces-area anarchist José García recalled how he and a colleague had traveled throughout eastern Cuba during the war and had worked to convert Spanish soldiers to the cause of independence. "We conducted our propaganda among them; as a consequence, there were many desertions," claimed García.[55] Authorities ignored their appeals as veterans of the independence struggle. To the government, these anarchist veterans were first and foremost "anarchists" (and thus dangerous outsiders), not heroes. The violent repression worked temporarily for the government. No strikes were reported in the central sugar zones in 1916 while strikes elsewhere were settled without military intervention.[56]

From the perspective of Cuban nationalists, governmental repression against anarchists prevented the United States from having to intervene. In fact, during the 1914–1916 crackdown, the government positioned itself well in relation to the United States. With its 1914 efforts at labor laws and a labor congress, the government presented itself, at least on the surface, as sympathetic to addressing social issues and thus harmonizing the government with the social ideals of the war for independence. The government attempted to show that it could be progressive toward all classes and thus truly "nationalistic." In the same vein, by labeling anarchists and other radicals as "pernicious foreigners" before expelling or arresting them, Menocal showed the United States that the Cuban government could control its labor problem. This assurance was especially important at a time when Washington was preparing for the European war and needed stable supplies of sugar.

However, just as the United States teetered on going to war in Europe, worker agitation in Cuba sprang from its forced dormancy. Workers struck the sugar plantations in the central provinces of Santa Clara and Camagüey, including the Cruces region in 1917.[57] From 1918 to 1920 general strikes involving tram workers, railroad workers, typographers, and others erupted throughout the island. As these new labor actions plunged Cuba deeper into class warfare, a new cadre of anarcho-syndicalist leaders based in the trade unions emerged, including the printers Antonio Penichet and Alfredo López.[58] At the same time, Cuban and U.S. government officials feared a larger international anarchist conspiracy was at hand. A U.S. State Department cable in March 1918 warned that according to captured correspondence the previous fall's sugar strikes had been conducted under leadership from the U.S.-based Industrial Workers of the World and Spanish agitators. The IWW connection was new; although Washington waged its own war against the IWW in the United States before, during, and after World War I, this was the first indication that authorities might be facing an international anarchist presence with links to foreign countries other than Spain. These fears continued into 1920: in a letter to Washington from the American Consulate in Cienfuegos the consular staff voiced fears that the increased presence of IWW literature indicated Cienfuegos and Cruces were again becoming international anarchist centers.[59]

The Cuban government responded to these developments with constitutional suspensions and an increase in the size of the military. The government arrested prominent anarcho-syndicalists Alejandro Barreiro, Pablo Guerra, López, Penichet, and Marcelo Salinas and condemned them to death. Although their sentences were commuted, the threat of execution revealed the government's growing fear of anarchism and its increasingly drastic measures to stabilize the labor situation. When anarchist Luis Díaz Blanco was publicly executed, the massive demonstration that followed his funeral procession touched off a series of violent confrontations against the police. In response, the government suspended constitutional guarantees, deported more than seventy workers labeled as anarcho-syndicalists, and prohibited anarchists from publishing their newspapers.[60]

By the early 1920s, a temporary political calm returned to the island. The new president Alfredo Zayas was more conciliatory to workers. This temporary calm provided anarchists and other radicals with a political space to begin organizing what would become the largest labor federations in Cuban history to that point. Although anarchists had always sought an islandwide movement, not until the 1920 National Labor Congress were they able to effectively and solidly pull it off and include non-Spanish speaking as well as non-anarchist members. This panethnic and pansectarian dimension continued in 1921 with the founding of the anarchist-led FOH and the 1925 CNOC.

While building a national labor movement, anarchists continued a strong anti-imperialist tradition, which dated to their early critiques of Spanish colonialism during the war for independence and their critiques of the U.S. occupations of 1898–1902 and 1906–1909. For instance, the anarchist press kept workers informed of the progress of the Sacco and Vanzetti trials in the United States, and anarchist journalists regularly noted that no justice was to be expected from the North American government that waged war against these anarchists. They even applied this anti-imperialist stance to U.S.-based labor organizations. In the 1920 labor congress, representatives debated whether to send a delegation to the Pan-American Workers Congress [Congreso Obrero Pan-Americano (COPA)] in Mexico. López and other leaders saw the COPA as a front for the American Federation of Labor (AFL) in the United States. Traditionally, the AFL did not organize unskilled workers while preaching class conciliation and the desire to negotiate with the government for workers' advances. In fact, in the United States, the anarcho-syndicalist IWW had long rejected the AFL as a form of "business unionism" that ignored the "true" interests of the working class. López, Salinas, and Arturo Juvenet argued against sending a delegation to the COPA, and convention delegates agreed.[61] Apparently, anarchist efforts to form cross-sectarian, working-class alliances had limits.

Anarchists saved their harshest anti-imperialist words for North American economic control over the island. In early 1923, M. Cuervo, a frequent contributor to the anarchist newspapers *El Progreso* and *Nueva Luz*, assailed those in Cuba who shouted "Cuba libre" while the United States controlled the island. Cuervo asserted that the island had been divided into "small States [sic] formed by foreign companies, and that within these fincas are the owners of lives and haciendas, thus constituting new feudalisms."[62] In a 1924 manifesto, the anarcho-communist Federation of Cuban Anarchist Groups urged a concentrated effort to organize sugar workers on these "feudal estates." After describing the exploitation under which Cuban, Haitian, and Jamaican workers suffered, the federation blamed these conditions on collusion between Cuban and American elites. Such collusion resulted when Cuban troops went to defend "the interests of those people, the majority of whom live outside of Cuba, under the pretext of the need to protect Cuban riches, put in danger by striking workers." Ultimately, concluded the manifesto, "the influence of capital is stronger than the sentiment for the homeland and for humanity. . . ."[63] To anarchists the Spanish yoke had been firmly replaced by the yoke of North American capital.

As the labor movement grew, anarchist internationalism, now acquiring a solid "Cuban" identity through anarchist leadership in the labor federations and cooperation with other labor groups, increasingly pitted itself against the Cuban government, which had long proclaimed its "Cubanness" while continuing to suffer under U.S. military and economic influence. However, the ascension of Gerardo Machado to the presidency in 1925 signaled the beginning of a decline of anarchist influence in the Cuban labor movement. Soon after coming to power, Machado unleashed a reign of terror against anarchists and their communist allies. In his earlier years, Machado had served as mayor of Santa Clara. In 1910, he used the power of his office to break up a railroad strike.[64] As president, he continued his antilabor stance through various measures. In 1925 the government attacked labor organizations. The two-year-old strike against the "Polar" brewery ended when the government closed the anarcho-syndicalist dominated Manufacturers Union (Sindicato Fabril) and its newspaper *El Progreso*. Then anarchist leader and railroad man Enrique Varona was assassinated in 1925. Alfredo López was kidnapped in 1926, and it was years later when his mutilated body was found. As the repression intensified, other important radical labor figures like Antonio Penichet fled into exile. Cuban anarchism was fading away as Machado resurrected a Cuban state that effectively preserved the interests of capital from the growing strength of labor, especially anarchist-led labor. By doing so, he undercut the anarchist movement to such a degree that it would never again have the strength it had in the 1880s or the 1920s. Because Machado apparently prevented U.S. intervention, he thus claimed to have preserved "Cuban independence."

Conclusion: Anarchism, Nationality, and Working-Class Internationalism

If one considers the wide array of social movements—socialists, liberals, blacks, feminists, and anarchists—seeking to define the new Cuba at the beginning of the twentieth century, anarchist movements were the most antinationalistic. To anarchists, the state embodied patriotic nationalist sentiment and thus served as the focal point for their hatred. At the end of the nineteenth century, many groups in Cuba—working-, middle-, and upper-class exiles, residents laboring in the fields and factories of the island, socialists and nationalists of every stripe—came to despise the colonial tyranny of the Spanish state. Anarchists, though, had hatred for the state embedded in their institutional and ideological struggles even before independence. Strident opposition to state power had always been a central tenet of international anarchism. Richard Sonn offers an elegant summary: anarchists believed that

> the state outranked the factory as the essence of the modern malaise. Government, with all its forces of coercion—tax collectors, police, courts, schools, compulsory military service—was the greatest single force constraining the freedom of the individual. If Marxism arose in the mid nineteenth century as a protest against the abuses of laissez-faire capitalism, anarchism arose at the same time in opposition to the tremendous currents of nationalism—the rising power of the state. Anarchism conjured criticism of capitalism, industrialism, and nationalism, going much further than Marxist socialism.[65]

As José Álvarez Junco notes, antinationalism became a major component of anarchist internationalism in Spain as early as the 1870s. Consequently, hatred for the Spanish state became a paramount concern for anarchists in both Spain and Cuba. However, late nineteenth-century Spanish anarchists also adopted certain national sentiments of their own. In this sense, some anarchist writers adopted Spanish cultural symbols or the "Spanish soul" and discussed these in a glowing light. Alvarez sees this as contradictory to anarchist antinationalism. "Upon accepting this practice, anarchists not only incurred a doctrinal incongruity, but also helped lay the foundations for theories that led to the development of racism and whose inevitable practical consequence was the justification of authoritarian regimes."[66] However, I argue that anarchist writers who adopted "Spanish" cultural forms in their writings were adapting anarchist internationalism to make it particularly relevant to Spanish workers and potential supporters. Such local harmonization was aimed to serve, not the state, but rather the international proletariat against all states.

Mikhail Bakunin was the leading anarchist intellectual influence on Spanish anarchism. Bakunin recognized the importance of "nationality" and "locality" to anarchism. "Nationality, like individuality, is a natural fact," he wrote. "It denotes the inalienable right of individuals, groups, associations and regions to their own way of life. And this way of life is the product of a long historical development. And this is why I will always champion the cause of oppressed nationalities struggling to liberate themselves from the domination of the state." He added that "social union is a true, fecund union. But political union, the state, not only foments discord, but obliterates the natural living unity of society." Additionally, Bakunin noted that "the material, intellectual and moral interests have created between all parts of a nation and even different nations, a real and solid unity, and this unity will survive all states."[67] He distinguished between "nationality" on one hand and "patriotism" or "nationalism" on the other. The former symbolized "one's natural love for the place and the people with whom one is reared and indissolubly connected" while the latter symbolized "the absolute power of the state over its native subjects and conquered national minorities."[68]

Ultimately, anarchists adopted Bakunin's ideas. Like Bakunin, most anarchists in Cuba believed in supporting nationalities in their quests to liberate themselves from centralized state tyranny. Generally they supported Cuba's fight for independence and saw the struggle as one where Cuba, a locality/nationality, fought for freedom against Spain, a centralized, imperial tyranny. Beyond this, there was no "naturally occurring" local identity to which they could appeal. After independence Cuba's nationalist leaders sought to establish a new state where the forces of imperialism and capital held privilege. Anarchists rejected this new state and sought to establish their own internationalist vision in Cuba. To achieve this independence, nationalist states and their international economic partners had to be challenged. In the final analysis, then, "anarchist internationalism" and "Cuban nationalism" were not compatible. However, a latent form of nationalism, "Cuban nationality" (the island's local symbols, ideas, and history) did complement the anarchist struggle in Cuba. To this end, anarchists represented a form of *cubanía rebelde* in which they emerged as one of the most radical movements (largely owing to their agitation and refusal to participate in a political system that they distrusted) of the rebellious social groups to challenge the hegemonic culture and seek to create a radical Cuban nationality on the island.

Working-class movements can create both a sense of national and international consciousness simultaneously. "It was through internationalist movements which operated on a nationwide or state-wide scale that national consciousness first developed for many a proletarian," argues Eric Hobsbawm.[69] In Cuba, Cuban- and Spanish-born anarchists led the efforts to create islandwide labor federations in the 1910s and 1920s, launched national propaganda tours, and reported on conditions around the island through the anarchist press. These initiatives illustrated the anarchist drive to spread out from their base in Havana to incorporate the island as a whole into the movement. In addition, the anarchists brought the island closer to the Havana-based leadership and rank-and-file by awakening in the capital city the larger social reality and anarchist organization occurring throughout Cuba.

In the following chapters, I discuss how conflicts over cultural symbols, immigration, and race reflected this anarchist-defined Cuban nationality so that the conflict between anarchist internationalism and Cuban patriotic nationalism became a struggle over the very meaning of independence itself.

3

Symbolic Freedom

Anarchism and the Cultural Politics of Independence

But why do the Cubans want a government, mamá? So that they can order
Cubans to kill just like the Spaniards?

Rodolfo to his mother in *¡Alma Rebelde!, novela histórica*

The war for independence became a popular political and cultural reference
point throughout Cuba after 1898. Just as nationalists throughout Latin America had used their wars for independence to mark the beginning of a new age
and thus a new "national" identity, Cubans came to see their liberation from
Spain as the central event in the new country's young life. People from diverse
ideological walks of life—feminists, workers of different races, Cuban businessmen, and politicians—all imagined what the war meant for them and their
new nation. Anarchists, reflecting this national interest, also adopted this
central reference point into their cultural works. Adrián del Valle and Antonio
Penichet moved beyond the newspaper editorials and union halls to push the
anarchist cause and the anarchist interpretation of the war through their
fiction. Both men tended to place their novels and short stories in either a
Cuban setting or a fictitious country that was obviously Cuba. Both writers
either centered many of their stories on events and issues in the war or incorporated the war as a lasting theme in larger works. Through their fiction, Del
Valle and Penichet promoted the anarchist view of the war as an "anticolonial"
and an "international" struggle, stripped of its patriotic veneer. To this end,
their writings critiqued Cuba's businessmen and politicians, deemed either
profiteers or exploiters who engaged in the war for purely nationalistic or ego-
istical reasons.

   In addition to the war as a galvanizing issue, other anarchists incorporated
independence hero José Martí into their work. They criticized the Cuban state's
use of Martí to support patriotic nationalism; instead, they sought both to
"liberate" the image of Martí from state control and to give his image and its

anarchical representation back to the Cuban people. Although the anarchists were initially skeptical of promoting Martí as an iconographical figure worthy of incorporation into their propaganda machine, they quickly adopted Martí as a Cuban cultural symbol to embody the spirit of liberation and projected their own anarchist ideals onto the symbol of Martí. Ultimately, anarchist leaders believed that they had to localize international anarchism to make its messages relevant to Cubans and thus attract followers to the cause. Because both the war for independence and the image of Marti were central features in creating a sense of Cuban identity in the broader culture, the anarchists exploited these cultural symbols for their own purpose. They not only pushed for freedom and equality in the streets and at meetings but also generated a symbolic freedom by adopting these Cuban independence images as their own. Thus the debates around political symbolism centered around who controlled and best exploited the war and Martí in their imagined notions of *cubanidad.*

The War for Independence in Cuban Anarchist Culture

Some of the earliest uses of the war for independence in anarchist fiction appeared in Del Valle's 1907 collection of short stories *Por el camino.* In "Amor de padre," a colonel in the Spanish army encounters his son Carlos, a captain in Cuba's revolutionary forces. The father cannot understand why Carlos would forsake the love of his father and country by engaging in such patricide:

I cannot rebel against a country that I do not have, replies Carlos.

—Your country is Spain.

—I was born in Cuba.

The colonel stands up straight, arms folded in front of him.

—Yes, you were born in Cuba, but Cuba is part of Spain and my blood, Spanish blood, runs through your veins.

—Spanish blood! . . . blood has no nationality; it's human, only human. If I struggle against Spain, it is not because I hate her, but because I love freedom for the place where I was born. Nor will I let patriotism kill me, because patriotism is always exclusionary. I fight for Cuba's freedom just as I would fight for the freedom of any oppressed people.[1]

The story clearly draws from the 1892 "Manifiesto del Congreso Obrero" where delegates concluded that anarchism and Cuban independence were compatible. Freedom from oppression for one's home and surroundings as opposed to hatred for the fatherland was an internationalist goal.

However, support for the war was offered with reservation. In Del Valle's later fiction, which incorporated the war for independence into the plots, he was careful to glorify neither the struggle for independence nor war in general. Such cautions often involved mothers in the story line. In his short story "El fin de un marinero," Del Valle focused on the aftermath of the Battle of Santiago de Cuba after the United States entered the war. The narrator describes a young Spanish soldier, José Rodríguez, who lay wounded in a U.S. army hospital bed. José soon dies, "villainously murdered by that insatiable monster called national honor!"[2] Yet, just as bad as being murdered by nationalism is the fact that the boy's mother will never see him again as she sits "waiting in vain in some ignorant Spanish village." Here Del Valle, a Spaniard by birth, clearly drew the line between a state's egoistic nationalist pride and a mother's natural love of her son, where the former deprives the latter. Patriotism had brought not only national disgrace but also human heartache.[3]

The symbolic use of motherhood to criticize nationalistic militarism and imperialism appears again in Del Valle's novella *Tiberianos*. Miguelillo is a Spaniard who flees to New York in the 1890s because his political beliefs support Cuban independence. While in New York, he and a friend begin to sell Virginia cigars as though they were true *habanos*. The two convince their buyers that the cigars come straight from the island via Spanish soldiers who dock in New York. However, the war between Spain and the United States meant that Spanish ships would no longer dock in New York; consequently, the men's enterprise would dry up. One evening, sitting in a tavern trying to figure out a new scheme, Miguelillo converses with some Cubans on the growing conflict in Cuba. When the conversation turns to issues of patriotism, Miguelillo tells them that he sympathizes with their desires for freedom, but not as patriots. Once Cuba is free and democratic, he exclaims, it should have the potential to satisfy people's natural aspirations for self-rule. "However, conscientious Cubans will come to understand that they have not yet conquered the true ideal of freedom, equality and social solidarity," adds Miguelillo. "Far from the nationalist ideal of the oppressed people is the human ideal of those who aspire for a society of truly free and equal men, united by ties of solidarity."[4] By the story's end, the war is over. As with "El fin de un marinero," Del Valle reminded the reader—through the character Miguelillo—that he was happy that Spain had lost. "In this struggle, the people who have the most right for our sympathy are the Cubans, who were inspired by an ideal of independence."[5] Nevertheless, Miguelillo laments that the true losers were the mothers in Cuba, Spain, and North America, for they paid the awful price of militarism in the service of patriotism.

Thus, Del Valle, writing on behalf of the Cuban anarchist cause, regarded the war for independence as bittersweet. Cuba gained freedom from colonial rule, but at the expense of very real pain and motherly grief. By raising the issue of motherly loss in Spain, Cuba, and the United States, Del Valle emphasized an important element in anarchist internationalism: motherhood as a universal good suffers when states war for nationalistic pride and gain. Antimilitarism, motherhood, and freedom—three central elements in anarchist thought— were woven into one grand sense of internationalism by drawing on the popular symbols of Cuba's war for independence.

In the 1910s and 1920s, Antonio Penichet rose as a leading anarchist figure and union spokesman. He also began to channel his criticisms of the commercial, industrial, and political elite into novels. Written in the heady strike years of the late 1910s and published in 1921 when anarchism in Cuba began to experience a wave of rejuvenation, Penichet's ¡Alma Rebelde!, novela histórica is the most direct anarchist fictional account of Cuban history from the 1898 war for independence to the late 1910s. The novel also proved to be Penichet's most direct literary attack on how Cuba's leaders had betrayed the ideals of independence. The book opens in 1895 as the war begins. Rodolfo, a ten-year-old, Cuban-born boy, expresses confusion about why some Cubans would fight other Cubans. In addition he wonders with concern about his friends who had Spanish fathers and Cuban mothers. Rodolfo had heard stories about José Martí, and in his youthful mind he imagined Martí as being like Jesus, "always suffering, good and generous, giving loving counsel to all. And in a transcendent moment, after some light reflection and thought, he came to believe that effectively Jesus was Martí."[6] Rodolfo's confusions and reflections lead him to ask his mother about the war. His mother surprises Rodolfo by saying that when you grow up, you have to obey the government, even when it tells you to kill. One must follow its orders.

—And who is the government, mamá?

Again his mother looked confused by the question, but answered:

—Son, the government is that which can; that which decrees, which controls the mayors and the judges and the soldiers and the police . . .

—OK, then the Spanish government orders them to kill and they have to obey. Right?

—Yes, little one.

—Ah, then we don't have to kill, because we don't have a government. Right, mamá, that the Cubans don't have a government?

—Yes, the Cubans have no government, but that is why the Cubans are fighting now—to have their own government. The Cubans want their own government, but the Spaniards won't let them.

—But why do the Cubans want a government, mamá? So that they can order Cubans to kill just like the Spaniards?

Rodolfo's frustrated mother orders him to go play.[7] It is significant that both *¡Alma Rebelde!* and Penichet's other novel *La vida de un pernicioso*, which I discuss in the next chapter on immigration, begin their stories with the war for independence. Anarchists like Penichet recognized the war for its cultural and historical importance in Cuba. The depiction of the war fought for both questionable intents (*¡Alma Rebelde!*) and noble causes (*La vida de un pernicioso*) reflects the often divided attitude that anarchists took to the war. Anarchists recognized the importance of the war for what they came to see as its just program of independence from imperial rule and thus as a noble anticolonial struggle; however, anarchists had feared that the war would become nothing more than an excuse for certain social segments to gain their own government with which to rule others for their own benefit.

José Martí in Cuban Anarchist Culture

One of the most interesting and controversial Cuban symbols that anarchists used to legitimize their endeavors and Cubanize international anarchism was that of independence figure José Martí. From 1905 to 1924, the anarchist press and novelists made Martí into a symbol for the goals of the anarchists: independence and social equality. Although most anarchists had sided with Martí and his PRC in the 1890s, after the war this incorporation of Martí into anarchist propaganda began on shaky ground. In February 1905, Cubans commemorated the tenth anniversary of the war's beginning. The following week, *¡Tierra!* devoted most of its issue to a critique of postindependence Cuba, especially in light of a new statue of José Martí, which had been erected in Havana's Central

Park. One writer noted how the statue depicted Martí with an outstretched arm. To the writer, the hand symbolically pointed to all the injustices committed in Cuba since independence from Spain: the president resided in the same place as the Spanish captain-generals; politicians made laws that they themselves violated; moreover, in November 1902 from the colonial palace of the Plaza de Armas orders were given to armed guards to shoot urban striking workers and to the Rural Guards to act against workers throughout the island's interior. Such was the work of so-called patriots, who proclaimed Martí their hero. In reality, however, anarchists charged that workers did not enjoy the freedom for which Martí fought.[8] Thus, the editors of ¡Tierra! saw Martí's statue as an accuser of those betraying his revolutionary principles.

Nevertheless, while anarchists could use Martí to criticize the island's officials, writers in this same anniversary issue questioned whether Martí would have been any better than these elite had he survived the war. By 1905 throughout Cuba, Martí, known as the "Apostle" of Cuban independence, acquired almost mythical, religious, and certainly martyrlike status. The writer "Celeste" took this semidivination of Martí and contrasted him with Jesus. Although Martí was a good revolutionary, had he survived he likely would have substituted another government in place of what existed in 1905. Because all governments were tyrannous, Martí's would have been too; however, Jesus was different, wrote "Celeste." Jesus "'the man-god' propagandized for true freedom, equality and fraternity that exist only within anarchy. Jesus Christ was an anarchist." "Celeste" concluded it was better that Martí live on in marble as a statue than sit in the presidency. At least as a statue he could continue as an inspiration for the oppressed.[9]

In the early years of the republic, anarchists were conflicted about his symbolic importance, but José Martí ultimately became a central weapon in the anarchist side of the culture wars. They mostly invoked the name of José Martí as an inspiration for the oppressed and as a symbolic tool to attack the abandonment of the social goals of independence. Yet, some anarchists willingly saw José Martí in an even more "positive," that is, anarchist light. For instance, during the 1907 anarchist propaganda tour throughout the island, speakers offered the name and image of Martí as if he were one of their own. During a stop in Colón on May 30, one speaker told the audience that "if Martí had lived, he would have been an anarchist."[10] It was becoming clear that Martí's image in anarchist propaganda could shift from potential tyrant to liberator, but anarchists would increasingly portray him as the latter.

Anarchists frequently invoked not only the name of Martí, but also his famous phrase a "republic of all and for all." Certainly Martí did not mean to conjure images of an anarchist Cuba with these words. However, as well as any phrase from the war era, these words embodied the notion of anarchist internationalism and anarchist democracy because they suggested that the island should be owned in common by and for everyone without barriers to race, gender, or one's place of birth. However, the elite also used Martí's phrase for their own propaganda, which anarchists regularly criticized. For instance, in the summer of 1911 Eugenio Leante's column in ¡Tierra! praised Martí as a philosopher, revolutionary, and humanitarian. He noted how politicians also invoked Martí's words but repeatedly misinterpreted his "*la República de todos y para todos*" phrase. Leante interpreted Martí's words as a critique of imperialism, hence a critique of a growing foreign capitalist presence in Cuba. He concluded that politicians gave lip service to Martí while they allowed the island to be converted into a foreign enclave, the antithesis of Cuba as fertile ground to benefit all.[11]

Just as he incorporated the war for independence into his critiques of nationalism, Antonio Penichet exploited Martí's image to denounce Cuba's leaders. In ¡Alma Rebelde! Penichet used Martí and fellow revolutionary Antonio Maceo to attack not only the state but also the growing perception that the elite and the middle class were living off the state's treasury. For instance, the character Rodolfo, involved in Cuban politics, thought that his anarchist ideas could be instituted through the government. However, Rodolfo despairs at the evolving political and social climate following the restoration of Cuban rule after the U.S. pullout in 1909. He decides to leave political work and return to his shoe shop. As the narrator laments, the state and its treasury had become merely a means to make a living, not an instrument to wield social change for the better, as Martí had intended.[12]

Frequently anarchists used the symbol of Martí to attack the government in its repeated efforts to infiltrate anarchist groups and expel radicals. As noted in the preceding chapter, a wave of repression against anarchists in 1911 included the expulsion from the island of many anarchist leaders like Abelardo Saavedra, editor of Rebelión!. The government, which justified such actions by invoking Martí, claimed that the anarchists were actually working to undermine Martí's dream. Paulino Ferreiro rejected this view: he contended that Martí had neither sympathy for government agents who pretended to befriend a group before denouncing it to the government nor support for deportations. The use of such informants merely demonstrated the lack of real democracy, argued Ferreiro, who added that "Cuba's rulers still hold the leash in their hands as if they were yoking together oxen." He concluded that the republic was not yet of all and for all, as authorities would have one believe through their invocations of the Apostle.[13]

In late 1913, anarchists learned that the government was creating a list of radicals' names, particularly those of Spanish-born anarchists in Cuba. Aquilino López, a manager of the anarcho-syndicalist *El Dependiente*, claimed to have spoken with the secret police, who had placed his name on the list. This prompted López to recall that Martí himself had been accused of disloyalty and of being a bandit, an arsonist, and a criminal all because he professed "advanced ideas." Through these ideas, Martí sought to create a society "more in concordance with man's natural sentiments and enjoyments," argued López. He added that anarchists remembered Martí with respect and affection, and "we long to germinate Martí's work, which exalted a Republic of all and for all. Martí was an apostle and has become a martyr; the only ones who have correctly interpreted his work are men of advanced ideas and who know that the current republic was conquered by all for . . . only a few."[14]

Anarchists revived the image of Martí in the second wave of anarchist activity beginning in the late 1910s. As I discussed in chapter 2, beginning in 1914 the government took yet another forceful stance against the anarchists by breaking the movement through arrests and deportations. By the late 1910s and into the early 1920s, when anarcho-syndicalists had recovered to take leadership positions in the FOH and the CNOC, they stressed the same themes as before—elite hypocrisy, the abandonment of Martí's ideals, the notion that the anarchists were the true inheritors of Martí's "communist" and "internationalist" ideal for the island. Workers were urged to recall Martí's words and become revolutionaries by struggling until justice had been achieved.[15] One writer in *El Progreso* went so far as to denounce U.S.-owned sugar estates like the Cuban Cane Company, which he said smelled of feudalism and siphoned bribes and profits to Cuba's elite, thereby creating a privileged class, directly counter to Martí's notion of a republic without privilege.[16]

In addition to using Martí to condemn Cuba's contemporary leaders, anarchists also used him to denounce militarism. In April 1917, the United States declared war on Germany and Cuba immediately followed suit. Just as the United States instituted a national draft, in Cuba an obligatory military service law was also enacted, an action reflecting Cuba's ties, not only economic but also political and military, with its northern neighbor. Workers met the law's passage with strikes and demonstrations. In ¡Alma Rebelde! Penichet condemned the military service law through the main character Rodolfo. Rodolfo responds to the law by recalling his mother's words when he was a boy in the 1890s: "Governments oblige their people to be soldiers. Governments order them to kill."[17] After the war, anarchists continued to attack militarism, explicitly using Martí. For instance, in early 1923, thousands of schoolchildren paraded in honor of Martí. To one commentator in Nueva Luz, the children were obligated by statesmen and teachers alike to march for hours under the hot Havana sun all in the name of patriotism. However, the writer wondered whether the parade was really supposed to "honor" Martí. He suspected it was actually a militaristic exercise designed to honor Marte [Mars], the god of war.[18]

In all, initially one may be puzzled by the anarchist uses of Martí, who anarchists generally saw as a member of the bourgeoisie—a sympathetic member, to be sure, but still bourgeois—and a man who preached national liberation, cross-class alliance, and the postponement of the social dimensions of revolution until the island's liberation from Spain. However, anarchists generally supported Martí and the PRC. To criticize Martí for this dimension of his thought would be to also indict those anarchists who rallied around him after 1891. Instead, as the years fell by and Cuba gradually grew away from the war, anarchists overcame any initial anarchist hesitancy to use the symbolism of Martí in their cultural and political projects. Anarchists increasingly felt justified in using Martí's name and image for their own imagined notions of a past, present, and future Cuba. Yet, this use of Martí was not merely cynical political manipulation by anarchists. Many of their comrades had died in the war, of which Martí was the symbolic head. In addition, anarchists believed that Martí had "popularized" the independence movement by acknowledging the social demands of workers as part of a larger revolution after independence. After all, to some extent, anarchist pressure, especially among Florida workers, was partly responsible for Martí's recognizing these social demands.

Conclusion: Imagining an Anarchist Cubanidad

Cuba's anarchists struggled to create their own sense of cubanidad that incorporated the themes of working-class unity, socialist internationalism, and the Cuban war for independence. This conflict over interpretation evolved into an important struggle over imagination in the culture wars. In their newspapers and fiction, Cuban anarchists, adopting images of independence and José Martí, incorporated these images of Cuba's past into their critique of post-independence Cuba. In so doing, anarchists infused these symbols with the images and meanings they imagined "internationalism" to embody and thus presented the anarchist movement as the embodiment of the true spirit of independence. The anarchists asserted that the 1895–1898 liberation struggles were essentially "internationalist," that the contemporary world must include "international solidarity" and an "international perspective" against capitalists and patriotic nationalist states, and that Cuba's future must thus have a socialist-based "internationalist" identity to uphold the goals of independence. When postindependence Cuban reality failed to meet these imagined goals, anarchists used the images of independence and Martí to condemn Cuba's leaders for betraying independence.

The cultural politics surrounding these all-important Cuban images were central to different efforts to create group-defined *cubanidad*s. In the end, interest groups on the island saw independence as pregnant with possibilities and interpretations to support any one group's larger agenda. The anarchist interpretation of both the war and Martí found little sympathy beyond readers of Penichet, Del Valle, and the anarchist press. Yet, these anarchist interpretations, coupled with their incorporation into anarchist culture, illustrate the fascinating ways that all Cubans could interpret their past and how some Cubans thought they could successfully bring down the pillars of the hegemonic culture by using that culture's increasingly canonized symbols against it. Anarchists challenged the Cuban state's efforts to monopolize and define the meaning of the war for independence in postwar Cuba. In a sense, just as anarchists supported liberating decentralized territories and peoples from centralized state tyranny, they also struggled to liberate these symbols from the control of the hegemonic culture.

4

The Cuban Melting Pot

Anarchism and Immigration

So, let immigration come, and with it the dynamite that purifies
the social environment like the storm purifies the atmosphere.

José García (1904)

They poured into Cuba after independence. Men, women, and children headed
to the growing agribusiness sugar complexes in the countryside, the bustling
cigar factories and shops of the cities, and the ports so important to the island's
export industries. These workers came from all over Europe and the Americas,
but most came from Spain, Haiti, and the British West Indies. They brought
their skills, their customs, and their languages. Many from Spain had been
exposed to and even accepted anarchist beliefs. Haitians and Jamaicans brought
with them cultures and histories of slave and labor uprisings on their islands.
Although most immigrants came to earn an honest living, many brought a
rebellious spirit—rooted in their own cultural traditions and experiences—to
Cuba's fluid, conflictive social environment. In the first decades following Cuban independence, few issues divided the populace more than immigration.
Spanish capital remained on the island, and Spanish laborers continued to
flood into Cuba. Spanish and North American capitalists preferred Spanish
workers to Cuban workers. This in turn hampered labor unions seeking to build
broad working-class alliances. By the 1910s, sugar industrialists were turning to
Haitian and West Indian workers to fill the cane fields, which strengthened the
wedge that impeded islandwide worker solidarity.

Spanish and West Indian Immigration after Independence

In the quarter-century following independence, Cuba's population soared
from almost 1.6 million to nearly 2.9 million people. Immigration alone ac-
counted for some 30 percent of this increase.[1] Between 1882 and 1894, nearly
250,000 Spaniards migrated to Cuba. Following independence, Spaniards on

the island were allowed to stay in Cuba and decide to either keep their Spanish citizenship or become Cuban citizens. Fresh waves of Spanish immigrants bolstered this remaining peninsular population. From 1899 to 1905, approximately 150,000 Spaniards arrived.[2] Between 1902 and 1931, 781,535 Spaniards legally migrated to Cuba. In fact, from 1900 to 1930 only Argentina received a larger percentage of Spanish migrants than Cuba, with 48.36 percent and 33.97 percent, respectively.[3] Until 1922, Spaniards represented more than half of Cuba's annual immigration rate—a rate increasingly diminished by Haitian and Jamaican immigrants working in the expanding sugarcane industry.[4] The vast majority of Spanish immigrants came to Cuba to work. From 1880 to 1930, workers comprised the overwhelming majority of Spanish migrants; 59 percent worked as day laborers, 17 percent were peasants or farm laborers, 16 percent had no stated occupation, and the remaining 8 percent included 3 percent who were merchants.[5]

Cuba's postindependence migration history was unique for Latin America. Following independence throughout Latin America in the early 1800s, Spanish migration to the new republics declined; that was not the case for Cuba. The birth of the Cuban republic occurred within a larger global economic development process that increasingly saw North American and Spanish capital flooding the island, particularly in the sugar economy. From the mid-nineteenth

Table 4.1. Immigration, 1912–1919

Total Number of Immigrants by Country of Final Permanent Residence

	1912	1913	1914	1915	1916	1917	1918	1919
Total	38,296	43,507	25,911	32,795	55,121	57,097	37,321	80,488
Spain	30,660	32,140	17,764	23,183	36,286	33,757	13,378	32,157
Haiti	172	1,422	120	2,416	4,829	9,730	10,860	10,136
Jamaica	1,269	2,716	1,792	1,649	6,005	5,866	7,317	23,754

Total Number of Immigrants by Port of Disembarkation

	1912	1913	1914	1915	1916	1917	1918	1919
Havana	32,631	34,597	20,792	24,568	35,991	31,575	17,134	37,165
Santiago	4,803	7,141	4,229	8,047	18,869	23,520	18,034	38,674

Source: Censo de la República de Cuba. Año de 1919. Havana: Maza, Arroyo y Caso, S. en C. (1919), 173–176.

Note: As Aviva Chomsky points out, the West Indian figures represent only those who came under contract; those without contracts or those who simply arrived illegally are not included. See Chomsky, "The Aftermath of Repression," 15–16.

century until well into the twentieth, sugar production expanded in Cuba at rates far outpacing other Caribbean producers. This development accompanied expansion of railroad construction at the beginning of the century, thereby allowing for more efficient transportation of raw sugar to ports for export. In addition, new sugar technology could process record levels of sugar, growth that required ever-growing numbers of cane cutters and thus the need to import labor.[6]

In 1902, Victor S. Clark reported on Cuba's working conditions for the U.S. Department of Labor. Clark suggested that Cuba's tropical climate contributed to a lack of efficient labor performed by Cubans. "Many country people [when they migrate to the cities] relapse into the *dolce farniente* of peasant life in the Tropics and contribute little to the industrial progress of the country."[7] Although census statistics noted that a significant proportion of the native population was gainfully employed, Clark argued that the Cuban worker, "is, man for man, less efficient" than a North American or European worker. He concluded that "two things are necessary for the industrial development of Cuba —immigration and capital"; he added that Spanish immigrants were crucial not only to fill a perceived labor shortage but also to introduce new ideas and innovations that would create higher standards of living in Cuba.[8]

While the island's North American and Spanish employers likewise generally preferred to hire Spaniards, Cuba's political and intellectual elites wove numerous, and at times competing, rationales for this preference. According to one rationale, some Cuban leaders preferred that Spanish immigrants and their families migrate to Cuba because these Spaniards would probably become permanent residents, with two general effects. First, as Clark had hoped, permanent settlers would identify "with Cuban sentiments and interests and raise the prevailing standard of intelligence and citizenship."[9] Second, some Cuban elite envisioned Cuban nationality as fundamentally integrated with the white race. Consequently, Spanish immigration would contribute to the "whitening" of Cuba.[10] Whether reflecting nationalism or racism (or both), the Agrarian League (Liga Agraria) in 1906 and a broad coalition of *hacendados*, bankers, factory owners, businessmen, and the presidents of the Cuban Senate and House in 1911 pushed for the importation of Spanish workers and their families. These immigration initiatives were designed to force migrants to work agricultural lands, a plan that ran counter to most Spanish immigrants' desires to stay in the cities, particularly Havana, where they concentrated in construction, railroads, and other sectors of infrastructure development.[11]

A second rationale for Spanish immigration, however, challenged the notion of whitening and nationalism. This logic saw the need for "laborers" more than it did the need for potential "resident laborers." Consequently, Spanish, Haitian, and Jamaican immigrants most often arrived on the island alone, worked, sent their wages home, and frequently returned home as well. Although such short-term activity may not have contributed to the development of Cuban sentiments or the long-term whitening of the island, such circular migration did create antagonisms and thus divisions within the Cuban working class. These divisions hampered organization within Cuban labor. Employers regularly reported a preference for hiring Spanish workers, supposedly for their better work skills. In reality, however, the hiring of circular migrants more effectively undermined the creation of a strong labor movement because immigrants often were more interested in receiving their wages and returning home.[12] With labor competition, wages remained depressed, and profits grew—maybe not an ideal situation for building a "national" identity, but to foreign business the hiring of immigrant laborers proved "internationally" wise. The second rationale did, though, have a component that nationalists liked. For these leaders, keeping the labor force divided and the labor movement weak meant less likelihood of labor unrest. With labor controlled, there would be less need for the United States to intervene under the terms of the Platt Amendment.

The preference for Spanish immigrants also reflected a larger Cuban cultural affinity for Spain. Cuba may have waged three wars to free itself from Spanish colonial domination, but that does not mean that Cubans wanted to forsake all things Spanish. The 1899 census reported that only 8 percent of Cuba's population was born on the peninsula, but this figure conceals the strong cultural, ethnic, and familial ties between Cubans and Spaniards around the time of independence. Besides these ties, an important Spanish-born bloc of the Cuban population survived the war with their economic and political influence intact. In 1899 more than half of the island's merchants were Spaniards and remained so through the first decade after independence.[13] It is true that some Cubans celebrated a near xenophobic hatred at times for Spain, including attempts to ban the flying of the Spanish flag anywhere on the island, and hostility for immigrant workers. These hostile sentiments for Spain might have served a certain nationalistic purpose, but they were tempered by Cubans who urged other Cubans and Spaniards to get along. After all, some thought, they were all part of the *raza latina* against Anglo-Saxons and Germanic peoples. Obviously, this attitude played back into the whitening rationale. However, this appeal failed to acknowledge Cuba's African heritage.[14] The racialized concept of the *raza latina* went further. In the late 1800s, government officials, immigration policy makers, and members of the Academy of Medical, Physical and Natural Sciences of Havana (Academia de Ciencias Médicas, Físicas y Naturales de La Habana) developed the notion that black and Asian immigrants tended to bring vice, witchcraft, and disease with them. The Academy argued that white workers were less susceptible to these problems; in addition, whites labored harder, acted more civilized, and contributed to a greater degree to the island's progress. This logic remained central to both U.S. occupation and Cuban government immigration policies throughout the early years of independence.[15]

As noted above, the preference for Spanish migrants resulted in high numbers of Spaniards arriving in Cuba throughout the 1910s. However, the sugar industry boomed, especially during World War I, and sugar capitalists required more hands. The racial logic of bringing in a mostly white labor force gave way to the economic logic of bringing in cheap, non–Spanish-speaking workers from throughout the Caribbean. As a result, Antillean immigrant workers, increasingly arriving in Cuba, found work in the island's expanding sugar industry. The introduction of Haitian and Jamaican workers was motivated by the lure of good wages from the laborers' point of view and accomplished through congressional maneuvering.[16] This congressional maneuvering was a response to early independence-era laws. In one of its last legal actions in 1902, the first U.S. occupation government issued Military Order 155. The order, modeled on U.S. immigration policy at the time, prevented the contracting of laborers in other countries to be brought to Cuba.[17] Upon taking formal control of the island, the Cuban Congress left this order in place until 1913. In January of that year, President José Miguel Gómez issued a decree that partially overturned the restriction on contract labor. The decree allowed three thousand contracted Antillean workers to be imported for the Nipe Bay Company with the understanding that the company would ship out the workers at the end of the year's sugar harvest. In August 1917, President Menocal successfully pushed a law through Congress that codified the importation of contracted laborers. Legally, such contracted labor could come from anywhere, but in reality most workers came from Haiti and Jamaica and were destined primarily for the sugarcane fields of southern and eastern Cuba.[18]

It is significant that by 1918 (the year immediately following the legal introduction of contracted laborers) combined Haitian and Jamaican—that is, Antillean—immigrants surpassed Spanish immigration for the first time. In addition, most Spaniards tended to reside in Havana and the central and western provinces, while most Antilleans worked in eastern Cuba. In fact, 1918 was also the first year that the eastern city of Santiago de Cuba surpassed Havana for disembarking immigrants. Owing to Santiago de Cuba's proximity to both Haiti and Jamaica, this city became the main port of choice for importers of Antillean labor destined for Cuba's expanding cane fields.

Anarchist Reactions to Immigration

Wartime relocations of populations from the rural zones to the cities resulted in urban unemployment. The demobilization of both the Spanish and Cuban armies further worsened the employment picture.[19] In fact, as Cuba's overall population soared, employment levels fell from 64.9 percent of the population (1899) to 61.9 percent (1907) and down to 57.2 percent in 1919. Seasonal unemployment further complicated this situation.[20] On the surface, one is hard pressed to see how a labor shortage existed. Still, this was a period of economic expansion, led by the recovery and growth of the sugar industry. Between 1898 and 1928, sugar production grew at a rate three times faster than population growth.[21] This suggests that the labor market in parts of rural Cuba in fact might have been tight and employers did need more workers through immigration— or at least workers who could stay long enough to cut cane and then leave.

Anarchists had mixed reactions to immigration and its impact on jobs. They sympathized with the plights of fellow workers in other lands who hoped to improve their short-term material lives. Many anarchists on the island were themselves immigrants from Spain. However, they well understood how Cuban workers viewed employers' preference for hiring mostly Spanish immigrants. They also knew that this process drove a wedge in the potential unity of multinational working-class organizations, be they unions in general or the anarchist movement specifically. Ultimately, anarchists publicly refused to point fingers at immigrant workers who boarded steamships bound for Cuba. Rather, they urged Cuba's unions to avoid nationalistic antagonisms that pitted "Cuban" workers against "non-Cuban" workers. At the same time, they condemned Cuba's businessmen and politicians, who they thought deceived workers by luring them to Cuba with promises of good wages and working conditions.

Undoubtedly, Spanish workers did have an advantage in the labor marketplace. In addition to the preference of Spanish businessmen to hire compatriots, Spanish workers could count on hearing about job openings and meeting prospective employers in Havana's many Spanish regional centers. These centers provided extensive networks and connections for Spaniards from which average Cuban workers were excluded. The connections further benefited Spanish workers when one recalls the island's economic devastation at the end of the war. With rural areas struggling to become productive again, jobs in the interior provinces were scarce. As a result, the Spaniards who congregated in the port cities thus fueled competition for urban jobs. As a result, many Cuban workers rightly complained that Spanish workers had unfair advantages.

In the spring of 1899, Cuba's labor leaders attacked the preferential practices of hiring Spaniards in the Clay cigar factories. Immediately, *El Nuevo Ideal* urged worker solidarity. Luis Barcia criticized the leaders for trying to create a "Cuban wall" like the Great Wall of China designed to keep out those they did not like, that is, Spaniards. Such discriminatory actions based solely on one's place of birth ignored the fact that many Spaniards had helped in the liberation of the island, noted Barcia.[22] Yet, not all anarchists supported the newspaper's stand. In September 1899 workers based largely in the tobacco trades formed the General League of Cuban Workers (Liga General de Trabajadores Cubanos). The Liga's leadership was comprised mostly of tobacco workers who had labored in the Florida cigar factories, and many anarchists themselves were active in the Liga. The union's secretary and defender of the attack on Clay's hiring practices was Enrique Messonier, a leading anarchist figure in the Cuban independence struggle. Although Barcia claimed that Cuban workers sought to build a wall to keep out Spanish workers, Messonier denied this. "We are not asking, we will not ask for exclusions; but we can no longer tolerate that we are excluded or banished; and so as occurred in the political sphere when we successfully sacrificed to destroy the exploitation of the ancient metropolis, in the social and economic spheres we are disposed also to cast from the land . . . all that represents preferences or monopoly in employment." The nationalistic undertones of independence continued as Messonier suggested that the Liga's actions were also motivated by a desire to help those Cubans abroad who wished to return to Cuba to help build its future.[23]

This early conflict over national identity and work set the stage for many future conflicts among workers. In 1902 tobacco workers went on strike. They again protested the perceived preferential hiring of Spanish laborers. Leaders of this Strike of the Apprentices sought the inclusion of Cubans as apprentice workers in the factories—a position dominated by Spaniards. As the strike spread, workers in other industries joined the movement, which made this the first general strike of the new republic. The government violently crushed the strike in late November. While supporting demands for better wages and working conditions for all laborers, many anarchists feared that some strike leaders were pitting the workers of one country against another. This fear found its way into the workers' press. In the months following the government repression, the newspaper ¡Alerta! and the Liga claimed that the anarchist weekly ¡Tierra! opposed Cuban workers' rights to enjoy the best jobs. ¡Tierra! reacted with its own accusations. The writer "El Guajiro" pointed out that anarchists were quite prominent in the 1902 General Strike. When the government moved against the strikers, labor leaders were thrown in jail. In fact, noted "El Guajiro," officials jailed four editors of ¡Tierra! because of their strike activities, but none of ¡Alerta!'s editors served jail time. The subtlety of these charges would have been obvious to readers.[24]

Although anarchists criticized Cuban labor leaders for succumbing to nationalism, they leveled most critiques of immigration against the government and employers. Most anarchist attacks centered on the "politics of deception." Fundamental to anarchism, no matter what strand, was a distinct distrust of all governments and capitalists. In particular, anarchists considered all politics, even multiparty democratic politics, as essentially deceptive. Politicians deceived workers to get their votes, for instance. Anarchists believed that when politicians, in conjunction with employers, designed immigration policies, the results were bound to be more acts of deception to divide and confuse workers. For instance, when the island's political and economic elite promoted an image of Cuba as a land with abundant jobs at good wages, the anarchists sprang to the attack and charged deception. In May 1900 El Nuevo Ideal challenged an effort by hacendados for more immigration. According to the newspaper, employers were promising good wages, but in reality workers on the estates only received sixty centavos per day in company store coupons.[25] In the sugar zone around Camagüey in east-central Cuba, activist Manuel Bielsa charged that it was common for workers to go and collect their pay, only to be told that all funds at the moment were in Havana. As a result, workers would have to be paid in otherwise worthless store scrip.[26]

In April 1904, President Estrada Palma and his allies began to formulate a new immigration policy. They hoped to entice Spanish workers to relocate to Cuba with their families.[27] When the mainstream press began reporting in 1904 of these efforts to import more permanent laborers, the editors of ¡Tierra! responded. One writer reemphasized that anarchists were not against immigrant labor, but he believed that the present labor surplus on the island resulted from widespread mechanization and employers' preference for hiring five women and children at the same wages necessary to pay two men.[28] In the fall of 1904, the Cuban Congress further developed Estrada Palma's proposals, again under the pretext of a labor shortage. These efforts became law in 1906. Even before that, though, the government placed advertisements in Spanish newspapers seeking Spanish workers. The ads offered to pay for voyages on comfortable steamships with plenty of food, and then, upon arriving in Cuba, workers would receive excellent wages. Havana-based anarchists held a series of meetings to educate workers on the government's proposal. They explained how immigrant workers arrived in Cuba, after they had been deceived into thinking there was an abundance of jobs. They did not come as "Spaniards" eager to take "Cuban" jobs.[29] One commentator noted that the law to introduce families, particularly to agricultural zones, mentioned nothing about work obligations, low rates of pay, long work hours, or poor treatment.[30]

Anarchists repeatedly described the dismal conditions awaiting immigrants. Upon arrival at Havana's Triscornia immigration station in 1908, noted one writer, immigrants needed thirty pesos worth of American gold for deposit. If they lacked it, then immigrants were forced to stay at the station and pay five *reales* per day for boarding. If the immigrant lacked even this amount, then the immigrant could be shipped to the sugar mills to work it off. According to the writer, Cuban officials colluded in a practice of deception in order to create a reserve labor force and potential strikebreakers.[31] Spanish-born anarcho-syndicalist café and restaurant workers illustrated how this practice was not limited to the sugar industry. In an insert distributed in labor newspapers in 1908, the General Association of Havana Café Workers (Asociación de Obreros en General de los Cafés de la Habana) complained how Spanish newspapers published accounts that Cuban wages were high. The insert blamed Cuba's leaders for helping create the image of a Cuba "swimming in abundance" and thus deceiving Spanish workers into immigrating.[32]

A primary rationale for promoting Spanish immigration was the encouragement of settling white families. Anarchists decried the introduction of families to the island because they saw negative side effects, especially on girls. In 1905 Angel Bermejo described the weekly steamships that brought young families to Triscornia: "One sees young women disembarking, very young, almost girls, who now because their fathers lack work have to offer their services as part of the growing number of prostitutes who pass through the streets and plazas, serving as play things for those who, with their gold, had initiated and defended immigration."[33] Although Bermejo's portrayal of the supposed fates of immigrant girls was somewhat hyperbolic, it also touched on reality. The previous year, a Havana survey found that of 585 prostitutes interviewed, most were Cuban-born, but considerable numbers of prostitutes were women who had migrated from Spain.[34] Considering the hostile climate that some Spaniards faced after independence, many prostitutes were reluctant to concede their Spanish birth; thus, actual numbers of Spanish-born prostitutes in Cuba might have been higher, especially if husbands and fathers found themselves unemployed.

Immigration, thus, became an important issue used by anarchists to frame not only their realities but also the rationale and goals of their social movement. Anarchists designed such descriptions of deceit and misery for two specific audiences, one Spanish and the other Cuban. Anarchist newspapers and columns were sent to Spain for distribution and republishing in the Spanish anarchist press. In this way, anarchists competed with Cuba's national and international employers, politicians, government officials, and the press over control of not only Spanish emigration from the peninsula but also the image of Cuba that was broadcast to Spain. Although the elite described scenes of instant wealth, which were published in mainstream Spanish newspapers, anarchists countered with dismal scenarios of Cuban life for the widely consumed anarchist press. At times anarchists added a critique of Spanish workers who felt compelled to immigrate to Cuba. For instance, Vicente Carreras asked why there was emigration from Spain—a land of potential abundance and fertile soil. His answer: "ignorance, the lack of *compañerismo* and union in order to demand that all land be cultivated for the general benefit of all." To Carreras, Spaniards who left Spain for Cuba apparently preferred to waste away in miserable working conditions like beasts "in a climate in which they are not accustomed." He concluded that many Spanish workers feared struggling to improve their own conditions in Spain and thus opted to leave for Cuba in hopes of finding a better life.[35] Eight years later in 1916, when the island's employers needed more immigrant workers for the war effort, Eleuterio García echoed Carreras's line. In response to a Spanish newspaper column urging Spaniards not to travel to Cuba because of the abuses they would suffer there, García wrote his approval by noting that Spanish workers, like workers in all lands, should fight for their rights at home. In Spain, García added, workers at least had more resources on hand than if they traveled abroad. Although it was true that workers were often jailed in Spain, "in Cuba one is often beaten, jailed, killed in the jungle and, when one of these is not done, one is deported."[36] Ultimately, anarchist writers like Carreras and García urged laborers to work within the realms that they knew best and not suffer the added injuries of being treated as foreigners who lacked rights or resources.

Such descriptions were directed to Spanish readers, but they also were aimed at Cubans. Just as Carreras called attention to the problem of land distribution in Spain, anarchists focused similar attention on Cuba. In a 1908 meeting to protest Cuba's immigration policies, anarchists and socialists united to lament the effects of immigration whose sole beneficiary, they suggested, seemed to be the North American sugar trusts invading the island at the time. As one writer in *La Voz del Dependiente* put it, there should have been plenty of land in Cuba for everyone who wanted it. If Cuba's lands were fairly divided, he argued, then anarchists would gladly extol and support immigrant laborers; however, as things now stood, immigration exacerbated Cuba's problems.[37]

Upon the restoration of the republic in 1909 following the second U.S. military occupation, Cuba's leading newspaper *Diario de la Marina* focused on the immigration issue. The newspaper's leading columnist Joaquín Aramburu noted how Spaniards who had lived in Cuba for years liked to say: "I am as Cuban as anyone else." Aramburu agreed, noting that "it is not the birthplace, a mere accident independent of the will" that mattered, "but one's permanent residence, the voluntary adaptation to the surroundings, that determines the condition of citizenship." Aramburu added that many immigrants had, in fact, done much more for the island than many natives.[38] In a sense, this sentiment echoed Clark's 1902 report that described the preference many employers felt for Spanish immigrant workers. In an ironic twist, anarchists should have agreed with part of this sentiment. After all, they also believed that one's birthplace was of little concern.

However, anarchists argued that Aramburu's sympathetic views did not extend to immigrants who happened to have radical working-class sympathies, as periodic roundups of foreign anarchists clearly demonstrated. In response to the deportations of these "pernicious foreigners," as the press and government labeled labor radicals, anarchists noted for the Cuban public (and possibly Spanish public on the peninsula) that foreigners like the deported Abelardo Saavedra were not the kinds of Spanish contributors to Cuba that Aramburu had in mind. As Gregorio Tejo put it, Saavedra was indeed a Spanish citizen, but not cut from the same cloth as Spanish despots in Cuba's colonial past—the kind of international despots who one found in the North American, Cuban, and Spanish companies that exploited all laborers on the island.[39] Another commentator wrote, working-class foreigners were abused because they did not come as "bankers, merchants, railroad, industrial and land companies"— Aramburu's model foreigners.[40]

Not all leftists agreed on immigration. Socialists and anarchists often saw remedies to immigration and unemployment differently. For instance, in 1913, socialists began cooperating with the government in formulating laws to regulate workplace safety, child and female labor, and immigration. Socialist Party members Juan A. Ruibal, Agustín Fernández, and Miguel Villaret sponsored initiatives in support of an Emigration for Families Law. Anarchists rejected these actions because such laws supported other political parties who had long championed such immigration laws. An anonymous writer questioned the need for such immigration when unemployment was rising, wages were falling, and the number of women resorting to prostitution was increasing daily. The writer added that women had few job opportunities as it were, except in low-paying, twelve-hour-per-day jobs of sewing, hat making, and tobacco leaf stripping occupations.[41]

By the end of World War I, as the Cuban labor movement began to mature, workers increasingly looked past their national sectarian origins to cooperate in labor disputes. In the strike waves that rocked the island from 1917 to 1919, Spanish and Cuban strikers struggled side by side. In 1919 Spanish workers, organized by anarchists, formed the Union of Allied Metalworkers [Gremio de Obreros Metalúrgicos y Anexos (GOMA)]. Both Spanish and Cuban workers employed by the United Fruit Company joined the GOMA.[42] By the 1920s, the FOH and the CNOC led the charge to unite workers of all races and origins. In their statements, anarchists decried hatred of foreign workers by arguing that true hatred should be directed toward foreign capital, not foreign laborers.[43]

Although unions and anarchists dealt with the troubling and often conflictive ramifications of Spanish immigration, by the 1910s black, non-Spanish-speaking immigrant workers began arriving in large numbers from throughout the Caribbean. With the U.S. occupation of Haiti commencing in 1915 and most West Indian migrants working in the U.S.-dominated sugar estates of eastern Cuba, the presence of foreign blacks associated with North American business touched off many nationalist and anti-imperialist feelings. Were Antillean workers "stealing" Cuban jobs? Were foreign businessmen unfairly competing with Cuban businessmen? Perhaps more sinister, for nationalists of all classes, particularly those who wanted a "white" Cuba, the preference given to so many foreign blacks challenged their notions of racial supremacy as well.[44]

Strangely, though, the anarchist press rarely dealt with immigration from the Caribbean. This glaring oversight can be partly explained, though not justified, in at least two ways. First, anarchists themselves tended to be of Cuban or Spanish birth. The island's long historical ties to Spain, augmented by waves of Spanish migration after independence and the ties of Cuban and Spanish anarchists fighting for independence, led to a focus on Spanish immigration. Second, the rise of Antillean immigration did not really become important until midway through the 1910s, just when anarchism had been temporarily repressed for the war effort. Consequently, anarchists only occasionally discussed Antillean immigration.[45] Not until the early 1920s did such discussions become noticeable. For instance, 1923 was the peak year for Cuban sugar production in the three decades after independence. In that year, 5,844 Jamaican and 11,088 Haitian immigrants augmented 46,439 Spanish immigrants. Although this was the first trip to Cuba for 97 percent of Spaniards, fully one-third of Jamaican and Haitian immigrants that year had arrived for their second work stint on the island (34.3 and 35 percent, respectively).[46] Unlike Spanish immigrants, Antillean workers were contracted for short work periods and expected to go home. Then they could and often did return to work in following years.

Some anarchists found this troubling. An anonymous writer commented in 1923 that more immigrant labor, with certainly more circular and return migration, was unnecessary. He then tried to discourage further immigration by describing the filthy trains that carried workers to the island's interior, the shacks that functioned as worker housing, and the daily wage of sixty centavos to one peso that had to be spent at the company store. Although these critiques were nothing new, the writer did address different ethnicities. Spaniards were imported, he wrote, because they were well trained in humility and willing to work without resistance. Supposedly Haitians were also preferred for their submissive attitudes and willingness to work for low wages.[47]

By September 1924, the sugar sector of the Cuban labor force became increasingly unionized. Unions demanded eight-hour days and the end to payment via voucher. Then they went on strike. That fall, waves of strikes radiated outward from Cruces, eastward to Oriente and westward to Havana Province. By December more than thirty sugar mills were on strike.[48] Anarchists supported these actions, but they took advantage of the moment to again attack immigration. At the height of strike activity in November 1924, "Fraile Juan" wrote: "In these moments, the white slaves of the mills who have replaced the black slaves of 1844 are revealing themselves as against such slavery and excessive exploitation. And in order to stifle the human aspirations of those men, the government authorizes señor Molinet, manager of the 'Chaparra' and 'Delicias' sugar *centrales*, to bring in three thousand Antillean immigrants." The writer added that the mainstream press, which had so often labeled such immigrants as "undesirable," was now defending capitalist interests in the effort "to break one of the most important workers movements that has surged forth in Cuba."[49] Again anarchists drew attention to not only the role that immigration could play in undermining worker solidarity but also the deceptive dimensions of the elite, who might either decry black immigration or willingly exploit black immigration for profit.

Nevertheless, anarchists had to step lightly when addressing Antillean labor. They never publicly attacked black workers, just those who imported them. In addition, some Antillean workers were active in union efforts on the island. These efforts, and Antillean confrontations with authorities, led to the expulsion of one Antillean leader in 1919 and the deaths of others in 1920 when they came into conflict with the army.[50] In their leadership roles in the FOH and CNOC, anarchists recognized the efforts of Antillean leaders. For instance, Henry Shackleton, secretary of the Antillean Workers Union of Santiago de Cuba (Unión de Obreros Antillanos de Santiago de Cuba), helped to draft the statutes for the CNOC in 1925. In part due to the prominence of people like Shackleton, and a larger anarchist ethos that condemned the capitalist exploitation of all immigrants, the CNOC began to openly criticize the mistreatment of Haitian and Jamaican laborers. Just as anarchists in previous decades counseled Spaniards about the hazards of migrating to Cuba, the CNOC agreed to describe for potential migrant workers throughout the Antilles the Cuban reality so that the migrants might be better prepared to face the situation in Cuba.[51]

However, in 1925 the CNOC's and the anarchists' efforts to reach out to Antilleans was cut short by Machado's repression. By the mid-1920s, anarchist discussion of immigration was minuscule compared to the first two decades after independence. One wonders how effective an outreach may have been. Nevertheless, through their newspapers and their pronouncements from the CNOC and the FOH, anarchists were unceasing in their support for the laboring migrant in the global struggle of international workers versus international capital. Meanwhile, anarchists continued to stress the threats that immigration posed for worker solidarity. First, immigration might drive down wages and incite a nationalist backlash. Second, anarchists focused on immigrants who came to Cuba, not as laborers, but as men bent on exploiting anyone they could to make a quick fortune. Although the anarchist press had reduced its coverage of immigration by the 1920s, these issues were taken up in the period's anarchist fiction, which began to depict the many possibilities of what an immigrant could represent. In this way, fiction writers used the theme of immigration as another way to frame the culture wars.

Immigration in Anarchist Fiction

Immigration played a small but interesting role in the anarchist literary imagination. Occasionally, both Penichet and Del Valle directly and indirectly addressed Spanish, though never Antillean, immigration. Their depictions of immigrants completely challenged the type of immigrant supported by people like *Diario de la Marina*'s Joaquín Aramburu. Whereas Aramburu and his associates supported the immigrant with money, the anarchists countered, true to their anticapitalist politics, that such immigrants were detrimental to the island. In fact, both Penichet and Del Valle depicted ambitious, capitalistic immigrants or immigrants striving to join the middle class in despicable terms; they simultaneously portrayed average laboring immigrants as noble workers.

During the 1919 general strike, the Cuban government cracked down on the strikers and deported twenty-five labor leaders, including fourteen Spaniards. Penichet avoided arrest and deportation, but he was forced to go into hiding, knowing that the government frequently deported Cuban radicals by calling them "pernicious foreigners." Penichet had no intention of getting caught up in such a dragnet. While in hiding he wrote the novel *La vida de un pernicioso*. In the novel, the central character Joaquín discusses how the state manipulates nationalism to foster a climate of fear and hatred against Spanish workers in Cuba. Such a government not only represses its working majority but also fosters a nationalist hatred for Spanish workers. Joaquín questions what it means to be a "foreigner" when he himself (a Spanish citizen) actually had fought against Spanish colonial rule. Why, he asks his fellow workers, were laborers, many of whom fought for or supported Cuba's independence, being abused? Yet, well-off Spaniards—from Columbus's time to the present when many Spaniards continued to control large amounts of capital and enterprise in Cuba—were still portrayed as heroes. "Those who came with Columbus brought slavery," recalls Joaquín. "Of these Spanish descendants who still remain after independence, many appear to support liberty but have not at all reformed their feelings. However, the new arrivals [anarchist workers] bring with them influences of freedom. They come to help others be free; to help remove the economic yoke that asphyxiates Cubans. It may be that the Spanish flag is no longer flying over Cuba, but the Cuban working class suffers the same rigors as before."[52]

In these lines, Penichet expressed a frequent anarchist criticism against the Cuban state: both old Spanish capital that stayed on the island after independence and even new Spanish entrepreneurs were welcome; however, the Cuban government regularly tried to divide workers between "Cubans" and "Spaniards" by saying that Spanish workers were taking jobs away from Cubans. Penichet asked, which was better for Cuba, a character in his novel like Menéndez the Spaniard who sells contraband, Pérez the Spaniard who runs a North American corporation that exploits workers, Lores the Spanish speculator and businessman, or Spanish workers? In the novel, Lores came to Cuba as a pesoless Spanish soldier. However, he gradually built a fortune, first by being a street vendor and ultimately as the owner of nine pawnshops around Havana. To bolster his influence and power, Lores even had his own daily newspaper with a considerable circulation. "The newspaper is the element that he can use best to adulate or combat, to denounce or to conceal" writes Penichet.[53] When Joaquín leads a strike, Lores and his allies run an article decrying Joaquín for being a foreign anarchist. Joaquín is arrested, convicted, and jailed. Upon release, he is determined to lead a revolution. However, while the noble worker who has come to help lead and preserve Cuba's freedom languished in prison for the cause, Lores has emerged as an embodiment of anarchist-defined "degeneracy." More than just a former soldier who now gets rich off the poor who pawn their few possessions to buy some bread, Lores leaves his wife and settles in at his country home—with another man: "He lived with another man! And in that bed, on that mat, on that sofa, he celebrated repugnant and scandalous orgies.... But he had gold; and gold is the great concealer of moral and material sores of men that inclines them to lose courage through egoism and become blind through ambition."[54] In this anarchist moral universe, homosexuality was both immoral and degenerate because it countered the anarchist-defined "natural" state of a union between man and woman. Not only is Lores a rich exploiter of workers, but also his exploitative nature signals a larger moral degeneracy. Far from the model foreigner, Lores represented to anarchists the type of foreigner to be avoided.

The foreign immigrant who was out to make it rich at any cost proved to be a popular theme in other anarchist literature. For instance, in *Ambición*, Del Valle describes the exploits of José Patiño, who leaves his small village in Galicia to work alongside his Uncle Pablo. Pablo runs a store in the Cuban interior city of Morón, which, by the 1920s when this story was written, had become the site of intense labor struggles and government repression. José hopes to earn enough money working at his uncle's bodega so that he can return to Galicia a prosperous man; however, his dreams are consistently thwarted. After ten years, José's earnings are paltry because he returns half to his mother and his uncle guards the other half. Then, José begins to dream about his uncle's demise so that he may at last receive his earnings. Soon José's dreams appear to come true. His uncle has a heart attack, and he tells José that the shop will be his. First, though, he must promise to send the guarded money to his mother and provide for the shop's black female worker Blasa and her two children. Unfortunately for José, Uncle Pablo recovers, but he soon succumbs to another heart attack. As Pablo lies on the floor, José approaches him. He pulls out a handkerchief and holds it over Pablo's mouth to hasten his death. Over the years José's ambition for success leads him to become a millionaire in Cuba. José takes Lola, the daughter of a sugar mill owner, as his wife. The arranged marriage unites wealth, allows Lola to continue in her ostentatious lifestyle, and affords José (who is interested only in accumulating money) the satisfaction that he is married to a young, pretty upper-class woman. Meanwhile, José, the immigrant-turned-successful-Cuban-businessman, ignores his wife. He is unaware that she is having a very public affair with a longtime lover. As years go by, José becomes even more absorbed with making money, until one day he, like his uncle, succumbs to a heart attack. In the story's closing scene, Lola, as though repeating an earlier scene whereby José presided over his own uncle's death, states emphatically: "¡Al fin!" [At last!].[55] The rich turn on the rich and a perverse form of justice befalls the commercially successful immigrant businessman.

Conclusion

Anarchists did not encourage immigration. Rather than attacking poor workers who search for better lives, anarchists criticized Cuban leaders' use of immigration. Immigration brought unneeded laborers into an already crowded labor market, drove down wages, and pitted immigrants against Cubans. In the anarchist conspiratorial world, this latter conflict was part of a deceptive plot to divide the workers on the island and thus further erode any hopes for the promised social revolutionary goals of the war for independence. Rather than interpreting immigration as threatening the "national" workplace, anarchists believed that immigration undermined the possibility of decent work and wages for everyone already on the island. In addition, rather than seeing immigration as undermining nationalism and national identity, anarchists interpreted immigration as primarily serving the interests of national and international capitalists.

Although commentators challenged the immigration-related issues at meetings, in public forums, and through their newspapers, Adrián del Valle and Antonio Penichet turned to fiction to reinforce these points. In their stories, immigrants frequently played central roles. At times the authors portrayed immigrants as noble laborers, emboldened with the spirit of revolution and sympathizing with Cuba's independence struggles. Other times these authors characterized immigrants as conniving merchants who lacked any sense of the meaning of independence or the spirit of egalitarianism; these immigrants became the enemies of workers of all nationalities. This dichotomy underscores an important dimension to anarchist positions on immigration. When anarchists addressed immigration, they stressed that workers had a closer alliance among international workers than workers had with capitalists within their own nation. Although international businessmen in Cuba preferred to hire Spaniards and sometimes Antilleans over Cubans, anarchists tried to remind Cuban workers of the support for Cuban independence they had received from some Spanish laborers, both in Spain and on the island. Just as important, anarchists urged Cuban workers to believe that when Spanish immigrants arrived in Cuba, they had been duped into believing that Cuba afforded a plethora of good-paying jobs. Thus, the same people who exploited Cuban workers were deceiving immigrant workers as well.

5

Anarchism in Black and White

Race and *Afrocubanismo*

We have said that there is no free country with children as slaves.

Enrique Roig San Martín (1889)

Workers associations . . . will oppose every act or decision that
results in the detriment of blacks because of their color.

"Manifesto of the Workers Congress of 1892"

Just as most anarchists condemned those who sought benefits for "Cuban"
workers at the expense of the island's entire working population, they also
attacked those who tried to exploit race for political gain. Anarchists had to
respond to the unique local situations on the island. In Cuba, that also meant
maneuvering through the delicacies of race and racial conflict. Consequently,
just as anarchists incorporated into their messages the symbols of Cuba's war
for independence and the realities of immigration, anarchists also had to confront race to make the anarchist agenda relevant to all Cubans regardless of
skin color. Although blacks did join the movement—with some as prominent
spokesmen—and some anarchists did address racial realities, anarchists generally failed to win over large portions of the Afro-Cuban population.

Race and the Anarchist Response

With the end of chattel slavery in 1886, the burgeoning Cuban labor movement
had to address race and issues pertinent to Afro-Cuban workers. After the April
1888 creation of the Alianza Obrera by tobacco workers, anarchist leaders in the
Alianza like Enrique Roig San Martín and Enrique Messonier knew that they
needed to mobilize as much of the Cuban workforce as possible to sustain strike
activities and increase workers' bargaining demands. This meant reducing racial barriers, fighting workplace discrimination, and incorporating blacks into

the Alianza. Coupled with growing attacks on racism in Roig San Martín's newspaper *El Productor*, the anarchist-led segment of the labor movement tried to unite workers of all colors against Spanish administrators and businessmen.[1] To reinforce this dedication, delegates to the Workers Congress of 1892 attempted to "de-racialize" slavery. In an important declaration emanating from the pre-independence labor movement, delegates stated that workers of all colors and ethnicities were equal slaves in the factories and shops. The campaign to portray postslavery conditions as a new form of slavery had begun.

By independence, both the Cuban labor force and the labor movement were multiracial. Between 1899 and 1907, nonwhite workers comprised 33 percent and 30 percent of the workforce, respectively. However, this is not to suggest that all racial groups were proportionately represented in all trades. These workers were hardly visible in higher paying or more professional occupations such as lawyers, dentists, and teachers. Nevertheless, they proportionately represented more than one-third of all workers in a wide range of unskilled occupations, including apprentices and day laborers, to more skilled (even if frequently low paid) occupations like carpenters, dressmakers, coopers, masons, shoemakers, and tailors.[2] Meanwhile, Afro-Cuban workers began to play important roles in the labor movement. As early as the first year of independence, the soon to be prominent mason Evaristo Estenoz joined with anarchist and nonanarchist labor leaders in early independence strike activity, including the 1899 Mason's Strike.[3] Black activists represented between 43 and 87 percent of the delegates from different regions to the 1914 Labor Congress. Blacks, including Antillean Henry Shackleton, played key roles in organized labor during the 1920s. In fact, by 1933 eight blacks had served as president of the Stevedores Union of Santiago.[4]

These were hard-won successes, especially considering the legal and political hurdles facing blacks on the island. The 1902 Constitution officially provided equality for all citizens regardless of color, noting that "all Cubans are equal before the law." Legality and reality were two different issues, however, especially regarding racial matters. Not only were Cubans of color victims of hiring discrimination, but they also suffered from higher levels of illiteracy than the white population. In 1899, 72 percent of Afro-Cubans older than age ten were illiterate, compared to 49 percent illiteracy for whites. By 1919, 49 percent of Afro-Cubans remained illiterate, compared with 37 percent of whites. High illiteracy made it difficult to get good-paying jobs. Moreover, because literacy was a voting requirement, large segments of the Afro-Cuban population could not vote.[5] Afro-Cubans, then, were doubly segregated from both the economic and political spheres of postindependence Cuba.

However, widespread economic and political disenfranchisement resulted in some Afro-Cubans mobilizing to better their plight via political activity. By 1907, Estenoz and Ricardo Batrell formed a political organization expressly for Afro-Cubans. In July Batrell and another independence war veteran, Alejandro Neninger, issued the "Manifesto to the People of Cuba and to the Raza de Color." They accused Cuba's white leaders of marginalizing blacks during the first U.S. occupation. The manifesto noted that rather than rise up, blacks waited until the foreign troops had left in 1902 to see if the racial discrimination was really the fault of U.S. occupiers, as Cuban whites had contended. It was not. Under the second occupation, the manifesto continued, white Liberal Party leaders had not recommended blacks for government positions. Although white Liberals supposedly hated Conservatives—as evidenced by engaging in civil war against them—these same Liberals and Conservatives socialized together in all-white clubs. The manifesto also attacked Afro-Cuban leaders for collusion with whites in this discrimination. Ultimately, the manifesto concluded that only a separate political organization would improve Afro-Cubans' freedom and status.[6]

In August 1908, Estenoz and a group of followers founded the Independent Association of Color (Agrupación Independiente de Color) in Havana, which would become the Independent Party of Color (Partido Independiente de Color [PIC]). At the same time they founded the newspaper, *Previsión*. The party's program decried the Platt Amendment and called for, among other things, free and obligatory education from six to fourteen years of age, creation of polytechnical schools in each province, free university instruction, creation of a military and naval academy, elimination of racial worries, representation of Afro-Cubans in the diplomatic corps, abolition of the death penalty, open immigration of all races (but excluding women and children unless as part of an immigrant family), repatriation of all Cubans from abroad who wanted to return but lacked the means, and the eight-hour work day.[7] As historian Aline Helg notes, "pride in being black and Cuban, in sum, was the principal racial message of the *independientes*. They wanted Afro-Cubans to be recognized as a full component of Cuban nationality."[8] Through its proposed reforms, the PIC promoted a positive image of peoples of color and openly countered racist dogma. With their challenge, the PIC brought to the fore the sentiment held by many Cubans that the independence promises of freedom and equality were still far from realized.[9] But large segments of Cuba's population feared the PIC, and the white and black elite rejected a political party based on race. Responding to increased PIC virulence and strength, the government closed *Previsión* and arrested Estenoz in January 1910. With Estenoz in jail for six months, the government moved to outlaw the PIC. In February, the Cuban Senate approved the Morúa Amendment to the electoral law, which prohibited political parties based solely on race and upheld the notion that race-based parties violated the Constitution.[10]

Rumors of a black conspiracy spread throughout the island; as a consequence the government arrested PIC leaders in April 1910. Although all leaders were cleared of any crimes, the accusations of a racial conspiracy led by blacks remained in the white public's mind. The government's repression of the PIC included the final passage of the Morúa Amendment into law in May and curtailed the PIC's structure and membership growth.[11] Restricted growth did not mean death for the PIC, however. In May 1912, still outlawed and marginalized, the PIC played its last hand: it called for protest on May 20—Independence Day; PIC supporters hoped that the show of force would pressure the government to legalize the party. The result was catastrophic for the PIC. Cubans across the island reacted with fear and hatred to the protests. To an all-too-accepting public the press portrayed the protest as a "race war." As racial tensions mounted the government systematically and universally repressed the PIC. Black civilians became cannon fodder as well when Cuban troops bombarded and machine-gunned an alleged PIC encampment that turned out to be peaceful Afro-Cuban peasants; 150 innocent men, women, and children were killed.[12] White citizens organized into militias and lynched innocent blacks in towns throughout the island. Constitutional guarantees were suspended, and mass killings "multiplied."[13] By July, Estenoz and his associate Pedro Ivonnet were dead, constitutional guarantees were reestablished, and Cuba's jails were filled with nearly 900 inmates charged with rebellion. In all, the "race war" of 1912 left from two thousand to six thousand citizens dead.[14]

Historians of Cuban race relations in the early years of the republic have generally condemned anarchist attitudes and reactions to these unsettling events. One historian noted how anarchists "showed little interest in the fate of Afro-Cubans" during the summer of 1912.[15] In a larger sense, this view is echoed by other historians who suggest that anarchist-led unions "turned their backs on the black problem" by not addressing racial segregation within the Cuban labor force.[16] Anarchists did find other issues more important than race, and they are justly criticized for not speaking out more on the wholesale racist repression waged by official and vigilante forces. Nevertheless, anarchists were not silent on race or the repression of 1912.

In fact, outraged by exploitation, critical of all political parties, and accustomed to government abuses themselves, anarchists were troubled by all the events surrounding Cuban racism, the PIC's rise, and its ultimate destruction. Throughout the early years of the republic, anarchists struggled, with mixed success, to mobilize Afro-Cubans into the movement. For instance, nine months before the founding of the Agrupación Independiente de Color, intelligence officers for the U.S. occupation government recorded anarchist attempts to mobilize blacks. Captain John Furlong sent a memo to the chief of staff concerning anarchist meetings with striking black workers. In these meetings, four to six blacks were lectured to by a white anarchist "to practice the doctrines of anarchism in Cuba, considering that they [blacks] are in their own country, whilst if such is done by strangers, it would lose its importance."[17] In a separate 1907 memo that explicitly addressed anarchist activity, Capt. Furlong reported on a plot by a group of "colored men in conjunction with a Spaniard" to buy dynamite. The captain suggested that the Spaniard was a recently arrived anarchist, but he cautioned against alarm because relations between Spanish anarchists and Afro-Cuban strikers were tenuous. According to Furlong, blacks saw white anarchists as good at talk, but these whites also wanted the blacks "to place the bombs" and thus run the risk of jail. Furlong added that anarchists were "not satisfied with their tasks, for they state that the negroes, after attending the conference and agreeing to continue the struggle to a triumphant finish, are the first ones to return to work on the buildings going up, and are contented to earn enough to buy a piece of jerked beef and a cracker."[18] There is no reason to challenge Furlong's description of the Spanish anarchists and black strikers looking at each other with both suspicion and derision. After all, as Alejandro de la Fuente has pointed out, "Afro-Cubans identified Spaniards as one of the leading causes of their displacement from attractive jobs."[19] Certainly, anarchists knew this, and it is easy to believe that black workers would accept a common perception that all anarchists were "Spaniards." Also, it is not hard to believe that some anarchists were racists; they heeded the racism of the day that saw blacks as lazy and untrustworthy. Thus, in this climate, anarchists did not ignore Afro-Cubans, but they did encounter obstacles—some apparently self-inflicted—to mobilizing them to the cause.

Nevertheless, anarchists were adept at bringing together nuanced critiques of politics and race. Responding to the 1910 repression of the PIC, *Rebelión!* praised the PIC newspaper *Previsión* in its support of Afro-Cubans and attacks against the conservative *Diario de la Marina*. However, a March 15, 1910, article in *Previsión* attacked two Italians in Cuba for their "anarchism," a criticism that illustrated the PIC's own mainstream views when it came to using the political system to secure social change. *Rebelión!* responded to *Previsión*'s attack by noting that the Italians in question were not anarchists but politicians. *Previsión* conveniently forgot that one Italian in question, Orestes Ferrara, president of the House of Representatives, had flirted with anarchism at the beginning of century but by 1910 had firmly rejected the doctrine. *Rebelión!* cautioned *Previsión* that, although Cubans of color should have the same rights as whites to be, among other things, president of the republic, all politicians were still social parasites.[20] In this regard, race was unimportant. In fact, while the PIC was often portrayed as "racist" and seeking black advantage by its mainstream detractors, anarchists saw it as one more misguided party in a political system that could be neither fair nor just.

Still, anarchists did not deny that racism existed. The long-time Cuban anarchist Miguel Martínez Abello recognized that whites denigrated blacks in Cuba and that Afro-Cubans' inferior social standards were not a result of "nature" but derived from roadblocks created to retard black development. In fact, Martínez implied in June 1910 that the black contribution to the island's history should be praised. "And if any race that populates this island has the right to claim for itself a prominent place in society, it is, without any doubt, the black race." Anarchists, he continued, needed to recognize that blacks spilled a lot of blood for independence and created great wealth for the island. However, argued Martínez, the majority of blacks were in the same condition as the majority of whites. They were oppressed, suffering exploitation at the hands of their bosses and leaders. For this reason, he concluded, blacks should not look to their own political party. Such a party, like all political parties, would merely become one more component of tyranny over Cubans regardless of skin color. Instead, Martínez urged black and white workers to join forces against capitalism and the state.[21]

Soon, anarchists found that Cuban leaders were beginning to associate the most feared African cultural elements, *ñañiguismo*, with anarchism. The *ñáñigos* were members of an all-male Abakuá secret society dating to the mid-1800s. *Ñáñigos* frequently worked in the dock areas of Cuba's ports. As their activities became more intertwined with radical port workers unions in the late 1800s,

Spanish authorities and white Cubans came to see the *ñáñigos* as threats to society. During the 1890s, Governor Camilo Polavieja deported *ñáñigos* because he said they were anarchists.[22] In 1903, Cuba's new government outlawed *ñáñigo* societies.[23] Lino D'Ou, an occasional contributor to *Previsión*, was a member of Abakuá. Some evidence used against the PIC in 1912 included one of his writings that was "apparently written in the language used by the *ñáñigos*." To Cuban officials, this testified to the lingering threat of *ñáñiguismo*.[24] As a warning in March 1912, the anarchist newspaper *Vía Libre* reprinted a *Diario de la Marina* article concerning the recent creation by Havana Police Chief Charles Aguirre of a special Dangerous Persons Bureau. According to the article, the new police bureau aimed to monitor and round up "groups, sects and individuals dedicated to preaching, propaganda and practices of anarchism and *ñañiguismo*."[25] In a move that mimicked the old Spanish colonial government, current officials once again grouped together blacks and radical whites as threats to the power structure. If the *ñáñigos*, and perhaps all blacks by extension, were equal threats, then from the anarchists' point of view blacks and anarchists should unite.

If the anarchist response to the PIC seemed aloof and rather out of touch in 1910, it became more concerted, focused, and critical of the PIC during the 1912 "race war." The uprising occurred in the midst of a port workers strike, which prompted one commentator in *¡Tierra!* to decry the PIC uprising because it launched violent governmental repression against the strikers. For this writer, racial and political uprisings countered the necessity of cross-racial actions of the anarchists so that workers (no matter their color) suffered.[26] Two weeks into the conflict, an anonymous writer in *¡Tierra!* lambasted the PIC's leaders for what he saw as their own political ambition at the expense of the masses they supposedly represented. Those leaders "intend to take advantage for ambitious and personal ends (as are the ends of all politicians, white and black) of the state of disgust that undoubtedly manifests itself in the colored element by their victimization in political and social life in the republic." Although the PIC might benefit a couple dozen blacks, the writer continued, it would be like all other political parties and lack real benefit for the black masses.[27] Thus, as the massacre of blacks throughout Cuba raged on, anarchists continued to focus their attacks on the party's leaders, just as anarchists attacked all political parties regardless of race.

With few exceptions, though, anarchists said little while the repression was occurring. By the time the PIC had been crushed, some anarchists emerged to rethink the whole series of events and how to keep something like it from happening again. Eugenio Leante and Adrián del Valle (writing under the name Palmiro de Lidia) noted the importance of education, politics, and the resilience of racism on the island. On June 22, 1912, a month after the massacre began, Leante published a column in ¡Tierra!; he lamented the continuation of racism and questioned both blacks and whites who focused on issues of race. Racism in Cuba, he began, was caused "by our religious education" that had created "the dangerous prejudice" of thinking that whites were superior to blacks. This "religious" thinking was supported by the popular pseudoscience of craniology, which held that whites were superior to blacks because the latter supposedly had smaller brains. "This prejudice," he continued, "will disappear when we educate our children in good sense and rational thinking, conscientiously teaching them anthropology, psychology and physiology." Through education, he hoped people would reject craniology and recognize that blacks and whites were first and foremost equal human beings.[28]

In July 1912, Del Valle launched his new journal El Audaz. In the first issue, he addressed the massacre and racism. He reminded readers of the independence war's phrase "Cuba Libre" and recalled the strife: "And Cuba was free . . . and you saw, during four years, hatreds, divisions, struggles, fratricides. What was the cause? Ambition for power." He acknowledged that the PIC's uprising in 1912 responded directly to the Morúa Amendment and that black resentment to white political and social hegemony fueled the uprising. He concluded that the cause of the uprising had been racism, which was the whites' fault based on slavery's legacy of continued discrimination.[29] His commentary was the final anarchist word on the race war of 1912. In fact, the anarchists would not return publicly to the issue of race until the 1920s, when race became a symbol of "Cubanization" in anarchist fiction and a tool designed to attract black followers.

Race in Anarchist Culture

Anarchist fiction in Cuba rarely discussed racial issues. In part this reflects the anarchist notion that the true social antagonisms were between those holding political and economic power versus those without power, that is, a class conflict. However, in Cuba, race could not be ignored as easily as it might be in France, Russia, Spain, or other European and even Latin American bases of anarchism like Argentina or Uruguay. People of color comprised a significant sector of the Cuban population after independence in 1898. In 1899, native-born whites formed 57.8 percent of the island's population; by 1907, this rose to 59.8 percent, and by 1919, native whites comprised 62.8 percent. For the same years, native people of color (excluding Haitian and Jamaican migrant labor-ers, but including people of mixed backgrounds) comprised 32.1 percent, 29.7 percent, and 27.7 percent of the island's population.[30] Although the per-centage of native peoples of color declined slightly over the first two decades of independence, these same figures attest to the large Afro-Cuban and mixed-race population in Cuba. Consequently, if anarchists were to appeal to the entire population, then they had to incorporate blacks into the anarchist movement. In part, this meant portraying blacks in the movement's propaganda and popu-lar culture to reflect Cuban reality. To this end, Del Valle utilized race as a way to lift his nonwhite characters to inspirational status, as is clear in his novel *La mulata Soledad* and his novella *Jubilosa*.

In *La mulata Soledad*, Del Valle used Cuba's racial structures to illustrate how anarchism's ideals sought to rise above racial concerns. For instance, one central character, Carlos, is a white medical student tutored by the anarchist Dr. Anaya. Anaya introduces Carlos to the largely black-dominated, run-down tenement houses of Havana while offering anarchist analyses of Cuba's socioeconomic problems. Later, while discussing race and class with two other medical stu-dents, Carlos's friend Domingo Reparaz suggests that whites have a nationalis-tic duty to have sex with mulattos and blacks—a "patriotic endeavor" to whiten the nonwhite race on the island. When the other medical student Manuel Ramos (an Afro-Cuban) suggests that "men of color should have the right to contribute to this process" of leveling the races too by having sex with white women, Reparaz responds that he cannot go quite so far as that.[31]

The novel quickly moves beyond the white students. *La mulata Soledad*'s heroine is a young mulatto woman whose strength, determination, and ethics are seen when she rejects the practice of "using" white men for social advance-ment and then devotes herself to raising a child as a single mother according to anarchist precepts. Early in the novel, we see Soledad working in a seamstress shop, a common occupation for working-class women.

In fact, in 1907, 9,464 women worked as seamstresses in Cuba (second only to women working as laundresses); however, by 1919, though only 9,317 women worked as seamstresses, this had become the largest single job type for working women. In both cases, the vast majority were women of color like Soledad.[32] Early in the novel, Soledad's fellow black and mulatto workers discuss how they hope to seize the first white man who will take them away from their working-poor lives. Soledad rejects this sentiment by arguing that mulattos have always sold themselves to whites for hopes of social advancement. A coworker responds that linking up with whites is preferable because she could then have a lighter-skinned child and, she believes, advance the black race. Soledad is dumbfounded by this remark. Her anarchist parents have taught her to reject such discussions of race and racial preferences that serve merely to divide rather than unite people.[33]

Soon Carlos and Soledad meet, and, despite her derision toward her shop workers for wanting to sleep with whites, the two begin dating. One evening she tells Carlos that she is pregnant. Confused and increasingly pressured by his family to reject the mulatto Soledad, Carlos abandons her to marry a rich white woman. Soledad eventually has a boy and sews on piecework in her home while raising her son. But by novel's end, Carlos returns to Soledad and begins to work in Dr. Anaya's clinic for the poor. The couple, living together in free union, teaches the child love and equality.

In *Jubilosa*, once again a mulatto female character becomes a vehicle to address anarchist notions of race and class. A young law student, Gonzalo, dreams of giving up his studies to take any job and move in with his girlfriend Jubilosa. Jubilosa responds that Gonzalo's parents would never let him marry the seamstress daughter of a mulatto. One day Jubilosa confesses to Gonzalo that she is pregnant. When Gonzalo offers marriage and claims that Jubilosa could "pass" as white, Jubilosa replies that "mulattos who love whites know how rare it is to find themselves standing before a judge or in a church." Gonzalo claims that she is too fair-skinned to be considered a mulatto. Yet Jubilosa responds, "Neither am I white, even though you say that I appear to be. And I am not going to renounce the African blood that runs through my veins."[34] After rejecting the temptation to pass as Gonzalo's white wife, Jubilosa makes him promise not to marry another woman so that they may at least live together. However, Gonzalo breaks his promise, runs off to marry his wealthy white cousin, and sends money to support his and Jubilosa's child. Jubilosa refuses the money. Meanwhile, a black anarchist, Perucho, has rented a room for ten years in Jubilosa's home. Through daily contact and financial help, Perucho eventually becomes the child's surrogate "grandfather." Then one evening, as Perucho walks to his own room, he passes by Jubilosa's door. He hears a soft voice call his name from inside her room. As he walks through the open door, Perucho feels two arms wrap around him and lips press against his mouth. The forty-three-year-old anarchist "grandfather" becomes the lover of the twenty-one-year-old Jubilosa and the new "father" of the child.

The themes in *Jubilosa* echo those of *La mulata Soledad*. A mulatto woman meets and has a baby with a white man who is studying to enter a profession. In *La mulata Soledad*, the woman is betrayed but her lover eventually returns to her, inspired by the anarchist influences of both his mentor and his mulatto lover. In *Jubilosa* the woman, betrayed by her white lover, finds love and redemption in a black, male anarchist. The short story's use of a black male anarchist is worthy of brief comment. It reflects the rise of prominent Afro-Cubans in the anarchist movement in the 1910s and 1920s, namely people like Rafael Serra, also known as *"el abuelo"* [the grandfather] in anarchist circles, Margarito Iglesias (the black anarchist leader of the Manufacturers Union in the 1920s), and Pablo Guerra (a black printer who is thought to have introduced Alfredo López to anarchism). Serra had been involved in anarchist politics since the first decade of the century. He continued to be involved in the island's anarchist movement in the 1940s, long after it had ceased to be politically potent, and served as a member of the National Committee of the Cuban Libertarian Association (Comité Nacional de la Asociación Libertaria de Cuba).[35] Thus, it appears that Del Valle modeled the character Perucho after his friend and comrade Rafael Serra.

Race is crucial for understanding the dynamics of postindependence Cuba. Slavery had formally been abolished on the island for less than a generation by independence. People of African descent and increasing numbers of Caribbean laborers made up significant portions of the Cuban population. Any social movement that hoped to make inroads into the collective consciousness and imagination of such a racially diverse population would have to appeal to the Afro-Cuban and mixed races on the island and thus frame the movement as open to people of all races. Adrián del Valle clearly recognized this. Yet, Soledad and Jubilosa represented more than just the black and mixed-race populations playing a role in a future anarchist Cuba. Rather, as mulattos, both represent the blending of African and European influences that increasingly characterized what it meant to be Cuban. In fact, Del Valle's Afro-Cuban stories tapped into the emerging *vanguardia* and *negrismo* movements on the island, which began in the mid-1920s. Intellectuals and artists had ignored or downplayed the island's African heritage, especially after the massacre of 1912, but by the 1920s artists began intertwining Afro-Cubanism with national identity. The *vanguardia* literary movement tried to politicize the creative process and argued that art and politics should not be separate. Consequently, it was the artist's duty to examine Cuban culture as it had evolved and been distorted under U.S. neocolonialism. As Francine Masiello notes, the *vanguardistas* imagined a "new vision of the role of the author, both as a leader of political activity and as a guide to an alternative esthetics."[36] They tried to stimulate a civic consciousness in Cuba by creating a new sense of Cuban identity that encompassed Afro-Cuban culture. *Indigenista* movements throughout Latin America sought to create a sense of nationalism to counter neocolonialism in places like Mexico and Peru in the 1920s and 1930s. The *vanguardia* movement, which functioned similarly, believed that their political leaders were selling Cuba to the highest bidder. In response, these writers incorporated Afro-Cubans and Afro-Cuban culture into their writings as a "cultural alternative to North Americanization and as a political vehicle for national integrity and survival."[37] The *negrista* movement of poets coincided with the *vanguardistas*. *Negrismo* placed Afro-Cubanism at the heart of its verse. The *negristas* sought a sociopolitical goal similar to the *vanguardistas* and expressed well by Vera Kutzinski: "In the tradition of José Martí, *poesía negra/mulata* sought to define an ideological space that all Cubans, regardless of color and caste, could presumably inhabit on equal terms."[38]

Ultimately, the awakening of the anarchist racial consciousness in Del Valle's 1920s works coincided with these larger literary movements. Del Valle intimately knew members of both movements in his station as a librarian at Havana's Sociedad Económica de Amigos del País—the largest and most-respected library on the island at the time. Although coinciding with these movements, Del Valle's use of the mulatto imagery was not new to Cuban literature; rather, the symbol of the mulatto had been a staple since the nineteenth century. In fact, the literary and physical image of the mulatto evolved to symbolize various nationalist ideologies from the early nineteenth to the mid-twentieth centuries. By the 1920s, when Alejo Carpentier, Nicolás Guillén, and others were using Afro-Cuban and mulatto symbols in their works as alternatives to North American influences, Del Valle joined them.

However, unlike the *vanguardia* and *negrismo* movements, Del Valle avoided celebrating Afro-Cuban culture. Instead, he wrote about Afro-Cubans and mulattos as individual characters. In fact, he almost never addressed Afro-Cuban cultural issues. Del Valle's only fleeting discussion of Afro-Cuban culture is actually negative. In *La mulata Soledad*, Soledad goes to a festival where *santeros* (practitioners of the religion Santería) play a wide array of African-inspired instruments while couples dance. One particular scene causes Del Valle, the narrator, to lament the blatant sexuality expressed in one couple's performance of the rumba: "However, it was difficult to imagine a more lascivious dance." He then proceeds to describe in a negative tone how the man and woman in the center of the room approach one another seductively throughout the dance.[39] This passage reflects a similar incident described in the anarchist newspaper *El Nuevo Ideal*, which Del Valle founded, in 1899. Then, the writer "Ramiro" took a hostile attitude toward Afro-Cuban culture and Santería. Ramiro called the Santería-based dances immoral. He proclaimed that the buildings that housed dances and ceremonies were really "centers of witchcraft" (*centros de brujería*). Finally, he lamented how blacks willingly spent money at these sites on food and alcohol to give to deities (*orishas*) while their children went hungry and barefoot.[40] Anarchist rejections of Santería were not racist; instead, they fell squarely within their assaults on all religion—what was good for the Catholic Church was equally good for Santería. Sexually, Cuban anarchists were not the free-loving, sexual experimenters of popular imagery. They took a rather prudish attitude toward sexualized dances, homosexuality, and other "vices," as they saw them. Anarchists then condemned Afro-Cuban culture through these associations.

Del Valle's focus on women of color in his stories also allowed him to address another important issue for anarchists: free, consensual unions outside of marriage. Anarchists rejected what they viewed as the institutionalized slavery of marriages sanctioned by the state and Church. They believed that men and women should be free to live together outside of these institutional encroachments on individual freedom. Since independence, the proportion of all Cubans living in what the government classified as illegitimate unions (*uniones ilegítimas*) had declined. For instance, from 1907 to 1919 the proportion of people living together outside of marriage fell from 8.6 percent to 6.1 percent of the island's population, while in 1919 23.1 percent of the population was legally married.[41] However, the overall percentage of unions outside legal sanction may have fallen, but the practice was still particularly widespread among the nonwhite population. In light of Del Valle's focus on nonwhite women in free unions in his 1920s fiction, it is illustrative to consider how popular free unions (the anarchist term) or illegitimate unions (the government term) were among nonwhites. In 1919, 73,020 white adults lived together, but 104,310 nonwhites cohabited. Seen another way, 6.1 percent of the adult population lived in illegitimate unions, but, when the statistic is broken down by racial categories as the 1919 census did, a far larger number of nonwhites than whites lived together outside of legal marriage. In fact, nonwhites comprised nearly 59 percent of all such unions on the island. These numbers tend to mask the overall prevalence of adults who chose to live together instead of becoming legally married. Of every 100 white couples, 13 lived together outside of marriage, but 95 of every 100 nonwhite couples did so.[42] Obviously, nonwhite adults more frequently cohabited without legal sanction, or, in anarchist terms, they more frequently engaged in free union than their white counterparts. In fact, the census figures suggest that nearly as many nonwhites lived together freely as were married in 1919. When broken down by provinces, the census found that in Pinar del Río and Matanzas more nonwhite couples lived together outside of legal sanction than in legal marriage (112 and 172 illegitimate unions per 100 legal unions, respectively). In Oriente there were 95 illegitimate unions for every 100 legal ones.[43]

Consequently, when in the 1920s Del Valle wrote these stories of nonwhite women in free unions, he was acknowledging an obvious fact in Cuba's population and basing his stories on Cuban reality. Although anarchist newspapers and other forms of culture only occasionally addressed the issues and problems facing Afro-Cubans, Adrián del Valle attempted to incorporate these people into his fiction. Black and mixed-race Cubans were depicted as everyday people one could find in all walks of life. He portrayed them as hawkers of wares and lottery tickets, old women languishing in the slums of Havana, single mothers striving to make a living by sewing at home, and workers and veterans who understood the anarchist principles of solidarity. By blending racial and gender realities explicitly into his stories, Del Valle put a Cuban face on the international anarchist movement. Bringing together gender, race, and free union status was a way to appeal for increased black, mulatto, and female participation in the movement because doing so reflected the diversity of Cuban reality. In addition, positive descriptions were essential to appeal to black support and overcome racist attitudes held by white workers or anarchists.

Conclusion

This is not to suggest that anarchists were particularly successful in attracting Afro-Cubans to the movement. To be sure there were successes and failures. The anarchists recognized how important racial issues were in affecting the employment and working climate of Cuba. Along those lines, they condemned workplace discrimination and joined with black workers in strikes. At the same time, some Afro-Cubans became leading voices in the movement, including Rafael Serra, Margarito Iglesias, and Pablo Guerra. Yet, despite these moderate successes, the anarchist message was never as accepted by black Cubans as it was by foreign and native whites. While condemning workplace discrimination and attempting to understand the impact of the legacy of racism and slavery on the island, anarchist criticism of the PIC as well as Afro-Cuban culture undermined the larger efforts to reach out to that one-third of the working population that was important in any attempt to localize international anarchism. Criticism of the PIC revolved around its attempts to enter formal politics. Anarchists agreed that blacks on the island should be treated as equals with whites, but anarchists simultaneously condemned the formation of yet another political party, which they saw as but one more means to deceive Cubans—this time Afro-Cubans. Meanwhile, criticism of Afro-Cuban culture rested on a critique of Afro-Cuban religion and dance. Anarchists rejected religion, whether of African or European derivation, while the openly erotic and sexually provocative dance movements of rumba countered the often puritanical anarchist concepts of sexuality. Thus, when anarchists attacked these cultural dimensions, they did so out of a loyalty to their own larger worldview. Ultimately, that worldview could be localized only so far. For blacks who worshipped Santería, enjoyed dancing the rumba, and found nothing inherently wrong with electoral politics, no amount of inclusion of black characters in a few stories was going to win over large numbers of Afro-Cubans. Still, not all anarchists ignored the central issue of race. Rather, by addressing race, no matter how limited, people like Martínez Abello, Leante, Del Valle, Serra, and others consciously attempted to adapt their movement to deal with real Cuban concerns and reflect Cuban reality. Had movement leaders been less puritanical and rigid in their doctrines, and had other anarchists not practiced the racism endemic throughout the larger white society, anarchists may have been more successful in mobilizing Afro-Cubans into the movement.

¡Tierra! The longest-lived anarchist newspaper in the Caribbean, 1902–1915.

LA NOVELA IDEAL

Número 66 · **AMBICIÓN** · 15 céntimos

Por ADRIÁN DEL VALLE

Adrián Del Valle's *Ambición* (Ambition), in which a Spanish immigrant kills his uncle, becomes wealthy (and thus a "bad" immigrant in anarchist eyes), and in turn is betrayed and killed by his equally unethical bourgeois wife.

Adrián Del Valle's *Tiberianos* (Tiberians) reflects anarchist antipathy with Cuba's war for independence.

El príncipe que no quiso gobernar

Adrián Del Valle's *El príncipe que no quiso gobernar* (The Prince Who Refused to Rule) exemplifies anarchist anti-politics when a prince hears the complaints of his subjects, abandons the throne, and moves to the countryside to live with a peasant woman.

"The New Religion." In the new politically independent country of Cuba, anarchists struggled to keep the masses from meekly giving their allegiance to states.

"January 28, 1909; January 28, 1911." True to their anti-government position, even republican democratic schemes were antithetical to anarchist freedom, with puppet master politicians dangling the promises of prosperity before the election, only to enslave the hapless voter afterward.

ANTES   **DESPUES**

PUEBLO «SOBERANO» CONFIA EN MI «HONRADEZ», YO TE HARÉ DICHOSO, FELIZ . . . TE DARÉ LA LUNA . . .

¡TOMA LA LUNA . . . PUEBLO ESTUPIDO! ¡PUEBLO IMBÉCIL . . . !

"Sovereign' people, put your faith in me and I will make you happy. I will give you the moon." But upon being elected: "Here's your moon, stupid imbeciles."

He aquí los dormitorios españoles de Cuba, defendidos por españoles, habitados por españoles y en los que no mueren más que españoles

Spanish restaurant and café workers in their dungy, unhealthy upstairs living spaces (barbacoas): "Here are the sleeping quarters for Spanish workers in Cuba, defended by Spaniards, inhabited by Spaniards, and where Spaniards die."

La jornada de diez horas para los dependientes de cafés

El patrono.—¡Cantinero de mi vida, no puedo corresponder.....
El cantinero.—...Yo de tu vida y tú... de mi muerte... ¡Canalla!...

The dependientes (restaurant and café workers) demand a ten-hour day.
"The Boss: Barman, source of my life, I can't go along with it.
Barman: I may be the basis for your livelihood but you're the root of my death.
Scoundrel!"

The anarcho-naturist *El Naturista* newspaper.

AÑO II. HABANA Y MARZO DE 1915. NÚMERO 6

PRO-VIDA

PUBLICACION MENSUAL

DEDICADA A LA ENSEÑANZA Y PROPAGACION DE LAS CIENCIAS NATURISTA Y SOCIOLOGICA

INSCRITA COMO CORRESPONDENCIA DE SEGUNDA CLASE EN LA OFICINA DE CORREOS DE LA HABANA Y ACOGIDA A LA FRANQUICIA POSTAL

La alimentación natural de la savia de la vida. La Naturopatía es la ganancia de la salud.

DIRECTOR: PROF. J. ALONSO ALMIRO, D. N. Redacción y Administración: Someruelos 23. EJEMPLAR: 5 CENTAVOS ADMINISTRADOR: A. LOPEZ.

El Naturismo, complemento del Socialismo

La risa

The naturist *Pro-Vida* newspaper, the longest-lived such newspaper in the Caribbean, lasting into the late 1920s.

The naturist restaurant and hotel Pro-Vida in Havana.

LA NOVELA IDEAL

NDA

CERO

Por ADRIÁN DEL VALLE

Núm. 157   15 cénts.

Adrián Del Valle's *Cero* (Zero) portrays the anarcho-naturist belief in the purity of rural life versus the corruption of capitalist urbanization.

Adrián Del Valle's *El tesoro escondido* (The Hidden Treasure) on the anarcho-naturist idea that abandoning the city will lead to one's regeneration.

LA NOVELA IDEAL

Número 15 — **NÁUFRAGOS** — 15 céntimos

Adrián Del Valle's *Náufragos*, a short novel on the benefits of a naturist lifestyle, which are undermined when American religion and capitalism arrive on a Pacific island.

"Long Live the Modern School"—a full-page commemoration in *¡Tierra!* marking the 1909 execution of Francisco Ferrer y Guardia. Rationalist education will lead people away from the tyranny of governments, religion, and capitalism, which are in the dark shadows at the bottom.

The 1913 monument to the martyrs who had fallen in the interests of advancing workers' rights in the port city of Regla—an early site of Cuban anarchism.

The first Modern School in Cuba opened in Regla in 1908.

Nueva Luz, the most important and widely read Havana anarchist newspaper in the early 1920s.

The Banes School, a Modern School in eastern Cuba opened by organized labor in the early 1920s.

The Havana School, a Modern School opened in the capitol city in the 1920s with the cooperation of anarchists, some socialists, and the newspaper *Nueva Luz*.

Madres degeneradas

"Degenerate Mothers," a common theme in anarchist discourse attacked bourgeois women but also working-class women who neglected their own children in order to nourish the children of the rich.

---Te avergüenza que el gran mundo sepa que eres madre, ¿verdad?

"You are ashamed that the whole world knows you're a mother, aren't you?" Here the working-class mother points out the hypocrisy of a rich woman who would abandon an unwanted child.

LA NOVELA IDEAL

D. Ivori

JUBILOSA

Número 10

15 céntimos

Adrián Del Valle's *Jubilosa*, in which a young working-class mother struggles to survive and then decides to live with an older black man as her common-law husband.

Colección VOLUNTAD

PUBLICACIONES DE "LA REVISTA BLANCA"

LA MULATA SOLEDAD

POR

ADRIÁN DEL VALLE

Esta novela es un episodio de la lucha de razas en Cuba, escrito con la maestría habitual en el autor de **Náufragos**. Alrededor de esta lucha se teje y se desarrolla un emocionante drama de amor.

VOLUMEN IV : 1'25 PESETAS

IMPRESOS COSTA : ASALTO, 45 : BARCELONA

Adrián Del Valle's *La mulata Soledad*, the quintessential Cuban anarchist novel of an unmarried, mixed-race Cuban seamstress who teaches a bourgeois doctor about the working class, love, and raising a child with anarchist values.

Part II

Anarchism, Health, and Nature

6

Struggles for a Healthy Cuba
Anarchism, Health, and "White Slavery"

An enormous division existed in the country caused by the desire to rise to power. . . .
The system of extravagant waste had been converted into a fatal cancer that was arising to
devour the Republic. The Republic appeared to be a gigantic tree without flowers or leaves.

Antonio Penichet (1921)

In 1900, Rand, McNally & Company published its first tourist guide to Havana and Cuba. The author, Albert J. Norton, went to great pains to illustrate Havana's deplorable health conditions. He did, though, try to alleviate potential travelers' fears. "There is an astonishingly large number of drug stores in Havana. When one becomes aware of the defective drainage of the city and the unsanitary conditions generally prevailing, it can readily be understood why drug stores should flourish."[1] Anarchists viewed with disdain and scorn Cuba's health conditions and health crises in the first decades following independence. While it was one thing to witness the appalling sanitary conditions and resulting disease, anarchists were mostly angered by what they saw as the lack of appropriate responses from Cuba's political, economic, and medical establishment. They argued in particular that the medical profession was not only incapable of curing the populace or even preventing illness but also interested solely in making money. In the anarchists' eyes, postindependence Cuba was little more than an island inhabited by people living and working under inhuman conditions and an injection-happy medical profession ministering to their needs with needles while questing for profits. Anarchists framed their critique of health around the concepts of individual greed, deception, and the power-starved cravings of the hegemonic culture. To this end, they portrayed employers, doctors, pharmacists, and even funeral parlor directors as primarily guided by money; these professionals were too busy looking after their bank accounts to help the working masses on the island.

Although all strands of anarchism entered the health fray, primarily anarcho-syndicalists (especially in the café and restaurant unions) and anarcho-naturists placed the health debate central to the ideological and institutional struggles in the culture war. By focusing on health-related issues, they once again framed their view of Cuban reality to show that little or no social progress had occurred since independence primarily because the same social relations of power remained in place. To these anarchists, the alliance of businessmen, politicians, and the medical professions merely took piecemeal approaches to solving health problems that disproportionately affected the young and the working poor. Instead, anarchists saw health issues as but one aspect of a larger sociological phenomenon requiring a general overhauling of society in accord with how anarchists understood Nature.[2] Injecting people with a serum or passing a health ordinance was not enough. Rather, eliminating inequality and cut-throat competition, which drove down wages and depressed working and living conditions, was required. Once purged of these "germs," Cuban society could begin its postindependence regenerative work of coming into an anarchist understanding of cooperative, healthy living in accord with Nature. Only then, they believed rather myopically, would Penichet's tree of the republic unfold the flowers and leaves of Cuba's true potential.

U.S. Health Initiatives in the Early Cuban Republic

The end of war in 1898 left much of Cuba's infrastructure destroyed, many of its people concentrated in cities following Spanish wartime relocation policies, and the United States in control of the island. For decades to come, people would endure the miseries of wartime, not the least of which included the prevalence of disease and substandard working and living conditions. In the early twentieth century, the social and political ideas of progressivism came to prominence in the United States. Influenced by these ideas, the U.S. military launched sweeping campaigns to sanitize Cuba during its occupations from 1898 to 1902 and from 1906 to 1909. At the forefront of these health reforms was the widely noted and largely successful campaign to control the spread of yellow fever. U.S. health officials stationed with the occupation armies noted the successes in first identifying the culprit mosquito that carried the disease and then eliminating the mosquitoes' breeding grounds in cisterns and low-lying locales. Adjutant General Major W. C. Gorgas in Havana served as the occupation government's chief sanitary officer. He regularly detailed these eradication measures in his 1901 monthly reports. In one he wrote with utmost certainty "that with present disinfection methods, any infection from yellow fever that may be introduced into the city [Havana] can be stamped out."[3]

But in the fall of 1906, at the same time the island was plunging into a civil war that ushered in the second U.S. occupation, yellow fever epidemics erupted in several rural zones. In his report to Provisional Governor Charles Magoon, Major J. R. Kean, advisor to the Sanitary Department, adopted the spirit of the times. He noted that "the disease has adopted revolutionary tactics and taken to the woods, and this extension to the small towns, villages and plantations brings up new and troublesome problems." To combat this spread, Major Kean noted how the "sanitary forces have pursued the enemy into the country . . . to conduct operations against the enemy." To solve the problem, Major Kean called on the government to pay for sanitary education and services in the affected rural zones.[4]

Yet, yellow fever was not the only serious disease in Cuba. Tuberculosis (TB) was more dangerous. More adults in Cuba died from tuberculosis year after year than from any other single disease. Table 6.1 indicates that yellow fever was not even one of the top ten killers of *habaneros*. In fact, as many people died of hernias (27) as they did from yellow fever, which ranked twentieth. In part, this can be attributed to the successful initial campaigns at identifying the spread of yellow fever and taking appropriate actions. Besides, it took very little capital investment to fight the disease: regularly checking cisterns, draining swampy areas, eliminating standing pools of water, and printing educational fliers. Still, the leading cause of death in Havana in 1901 was not yellow fever, for which every U.S. sanitation report devoted half to three-fourths of its attention. TB was the leading cause. In 1886, 1,187 *habaneros* died from TB. At the close of the

Table 6.1. Ten Leading Causes of Deaths in Havana During 1901

Cause	Deaths	Death Rate/1,000 Pop.
Tuberculosis of lungs	833	145.62
Diarrhea/enteritis (under 2 years)	742	129.70
Organic disease of the heart	447	78.14
Afflictions of the arteries (atheroma, aneurism, etc.)	336	58.74
Diarrhea/enteritis (2 years and older)	304	53.14
Simple meningitis	273	47.72
Bronco-pneumonia	193	33.74
Cerebral congestion/hemorrhage	166	29.02
Tetanus	148	25.87
Intermittent fever and malarial cachexia	135	23.60

Source: Table adapted from the chart "Report of Deaths in the City of Havana During the Year 1901," part of the "Report of W. C. Gorgas," in *Civil Report of Brigadier General Leonard Wood, Military Governor of Cuba, 1901,* 14–17.

war in 1898, these figures escalated. Owing to poor sanitary conditions experienced by the masses of Cubans forced to live in refugee camps during the war, 2,795 people in Havana died of the disease. During the next two decades, decrepit conditions facilitated a continued high occurrence of TB so that by 1919 TB was still a leading cause of death (1,209 deaths in Havana alone).[5]

During the second U.S. occupation, the first national sanitarium for TB was established, as were many new TB wards in local hospitals.[6] However, these were treatments, not preventative measures. To be fair, in his 1907 report to Magoon, Major Kean did acknowledge the severity of TB. Of the six-page report, he devoted one paragraph to the disease. Kean insisted that the "alarming prevalence [of tuberculosis] must be ascribed mainly to the excessive over-crowding which exists among the poorer classes in the cities, which evil is aggravated by their traditional fear of the night air, causing them to cut off ventilation as far as possible in the rooms where they sleep." All observers of the day agreed that living conditions were overcrowded, but Kean ignored a central reason why *habaneros* closed their doors at night: security. Too often city dwellers lived in buildings with one street-side entrance, the door of which led down an alley off of which every twelve feet or so another door led to yet another separate twelve-square-foot "home." These *ciudadelas* or *solares* had no other windows or doors except the front entrance.[7] When people closed up their doors at night, it was not due to some "traditional fear of the night air," as Major Kean asserted; rather, it reflected a matter of safety. His remedy was to construct sanitary, low-rent dwellings.[8] However, nowhere in this report, nor in any other, did Kean mention who should fund the construction of the new housing he recommended. Temporary housing would have to be provided for the displaced while their old dwellings were either destroyed and rebuilt or refitted with better airflow, plumbing, and lighting. Again, neither the governments nor the capitalists opened their bank vaults or wallets.

In no report did Kean or others address the horrendous working conditions in factories, bakeries, and restaurants that also led to high occurrences of tuberculosis. In essence, the workplace was off-limits to forced sanitary reform. The financial costs were too great. Old buildings would have to be destroyed and temporary facilities constructed for continued business while new buildings were erected. Factories and other workplaces would have to be fitted with new plumbing, lighting, and ventilation systems. Neither the American nor the Cuban governments would finance such high capital expenditures, and certainly the owners could not be counted on to do so. All of this makes clear that the fight against tuberculosis meant spending large sums of money to build new, affordable, sanitary homes and workplaces. This could be done through legal mechanisms, through a revolution that would truly alter societal power relationships and lead to committed expenditures, or through workers and the poor doing what they could for themselves. Anarchists rejected the first as impractical (business and government were too interlinked and thus would resist), fought for the second option for the future, and pursued the third option until a revolution could triumph.

Anarchism, Children, and Health

Most cultures view their children and youth as the weakest, most susceptible segments of their populations. Special laws, mores, and regulations to protect children are passed and hopefully enforced. Anarchists believed that children were especially vulnerable to the deteriorated living and working conditions in postindependence Cuba. Consequently, they focused considerable attention on the conditions of Cuba's youth, and with good reason. Children's health suffered greatly after independence, and infant mortality was high. As Table 6.1 illustrated, in 1901 diarrhea and enteritis (inflammation of the intestinal tract) were leading causes of death for Havana's children. Youth less than two years of age died at a rate of 129.70 per 1,000 population, and those two years old and older died at a rate of 53.14 per 1,000. Of 5,720 reported deaths in Havana that same year, more than one-fourth (1,453) were less than one year old, and more than one-third (1,940) of total deaths were children ten years old and younger. Finally, youth less than twenty years of age made up nearly 40 percent of all deaths.[9] Eighteen years later the 1919 islandwide census illustrated an actual slight worsening of these figures, as illustrated in Table 6.2.

Table 6.2. Deaths by Age Group

Age	Population	Number of Deaths	Deaths/1,000 Pop.
<1 year	74,918	11,206	149.6
1–4	335,340	6,400	19.1
5–19	1,110,250	1,705	1.5
20–39	839,666	6,580	7.8
40–59	390,185	6,121	15.7
60+	138,645	8,931	64.4
Total	2,889,004	40,943	14.2

Source: Censo de la República de Cuba. Año de 1919. Havana: Maza, Arroyo, S. En C., 249.

Note: Based on figures and deaths registered in 1916.

These figures merely give an aggregate overview of something truly dismal occurring in Cuba in the decades after independence. In 1903 one commentator suggested that high infant mortality and disease were in large part caused by nutritional problems, a reasonable suggestion considering the high rates of death from enteritis and diarrhea. According to the anonymous author of the column "Por la raza" in the pages of ¡Tierra! it was increasingly rare to see mothers nursing their young. While wealthy and middle-class mothers could and did resort to employing wet nurses, this was not an option for poor mothers, who increasingly bottle-fed their infants, according to the writer. However, "especially in Havana, the milk that was sold generally was impure," and the purest milk available was too expensive. While families living on the outskirts of town could get fresh milk from nearby cattle barns, most families were reduced to buying condensed canned milk imported from the United States. The author concluded that such a practice, besides being expensive and making the poor more dependent on imports (and less so on what was available naturally) led to high infant mortality. Those surviving, he predicted, would be more likely to suffer from tuberculosis later in life.[10]

Anarchists took this concern for children's health and used it to criticize Cuban institutions, including the penal and health care systems. A 1909 article in Rebelión! discussed how girls as young as eleven years old had been ordered to serve time in area jails. These were "sick adolescents who are suffering from what this corrupt society has submitted them to"—a reference to child prostitution, among other things. What future did such girls have but to return to the bordello where their health would continue to erode for society's pleasure, asked the writer.[11] Over the years critics also used children's health to focus on the condition of hospitals and mental institutions in Cuba. In a front-page article in Nueva Luz sarcastically titled "La caridad oficial" [Official Charity], one writer asserted that children were physically abused in the Calixto García Hospital of Havana. Instead of treating patients in the children's ward with tenderness, they were beaten with leather straps.[12] In a long discussion of nervous and mental disorders in the island's children, one of Cuba's leading alternative health practitioners and anarcho-naturists, Julián Magdalena, argued that such disorders were basically hereditary. Magdalena and others argued that these children came from sickly parents who had "polluted" their bodies with toxins by consuming alcohol, meat-based diets, and other "poisons." As a result, such toxins disrupted the digestive and nervous systems and led to neurological and mental conditions. So, he asked, how had the official medical establishment dealt with the issue in children? By mid-1916, Magdalena charged, two thousand children had been thrown into the national asylum, of which "many of these unfortunates, even though merely youths, are brought to the *sanitario presidio* and confined for several years, without having committed a crime worse than losing their health and mental faculties. They remain there, separated from their grieving parents and from those who truly love them."[13] Certainly, Magdalena's hyperbole deserves caution. Nevertheless, a survey in 1907 listed 1,018 youth from infancy to age twenty-four in the island's eleven asylums, with Havana's Casa de Beneficencia y Maternidad housing most.[14] Magdalena's point was not to dwell on numbers, but to create an image of official abuse toward and neglect of poor children.

Beyond an interest in children's health in the larger society, anarchists regularly analyzed children's health in the workplace. Frequently Cuba's cafés, restaurants, and boarding houses employed children. This posed potentially great problems. In his 1902 report for the U.S. Department of Labor, Victor Clark warned that the use of children would "present a serious problem to those interested in the social welfare of the country." At this time, cafés operated from dawn to midnight in the cities. Children, like all workers in these establishments, had to work this entire time with few breaks. From such practices Clark noted the decline in not only children's physical well-being but also their moral health. As he put it, "the young employees are early initiated into a knowledge of all the vice prevalent in a tropical city, and are obliged to live under physical conditions detrimental to their health and bodily development."[15]

Anarchists interpreted child labor in the cafés in their own way. In 1904, one writer chastised the employees themselves for allowing their youth to be placed in these conditions. The writer charged that owners took advantage of the youth's weaknesses. These went beyond physical weaknesses to include "power weaknesses" like not being old enough to unionize or agitate for social change. Besides, owners tended to play on feelings of national identity in hiring Spanish youth and men and then dumped their services later. "Can you not see that by regarding you as *paisanos*, these brutes procure more and more each day, and when you can no longer provide services to them, they throw you into the street like a barrel of trash?"[16] Thus, in this telling passage, the writer blends the anarchist critique of health with the previously discussed issue of Spanish employers preferring Spanish workers, with the result that the workers are doubly abused. By using children to fashion their interpretation of Cuban health and social conditions, anarchists were able to frame, in an almost

Manichean way, the "evil" of contemporary society versus an anarchist ideal. Unequal power relations contributed to poor sanitation, poor housing, poor work conditions, and abuse. Because children were the weakest and most innocent members in society, they tended to be victimized the most by these poor conditions. Such victimization could be seen by their over-representation in mortality statistics. Ultimately, anarchist social critics pitted this society with its trappings of exploitation against the purity and innocence of children—the most helpless sufferers of such "barbarity."

Living and Working Conditions in the Cities and Countryside

Few factors affect people more directly and regularly than where they live and work. Nearly a decade after the war's end, the number of livable dwellings increased around Cuba by one-third (262,794 in 1899 to 350,830 in 1907). Population growth, though, outstripped the increase in places to live. In fact, Havana living conditions declined as the city's population rose to almost 300,000 in 1907.[17] Whereas there were 9.4 people per dwelling in 1899, by 1907 there were 10.3 per dwelling. Seen from another angle, an average of 2.5 families occupied each dwelling in Havana. Other cities were only slightly better.[18]

Ultimately, most commentators of the period (liberals, socialists, anarchists, and U.S. officials) regarded living conditions in turn-of-the-century Cuba as pestilent at best. In his 1907 thesis for a degree in public law, Manuel Román y Moreno argued that while the law of supply and demand ruled the labor market, the state had an obligation to defend workers' interests. The state could do this, he charged, by constructing cheap housing with a modicum of "aesthetic character" and providing loans, lands, and public services.[19] Quoting Benjamin Disraeli, he concluded that "the best guarantee of civilization is the dwelling where one lives: the home, which is the school of domestic virtues."[20] Drs. Ramón Alfonso and Diego Tamayo expressed similar sentiments in their critiques of urban and rural housing and its relationship to public welfare. They noted that in 1904 fully one-third of Havana's population lived in tenement houses. These very crowded housing units permitted little to no light or fresh air from entering. There was no space for drainage so that waste left the area only very slowly, often leaving a residue. It would not be an exaggeration, they claimed, "to affirm that the subsoil of the city is topped off with a layer of excrement."[21] Add to this situation the prevalence of bad drinking water, multiuse bathing facilities, barefoot children, and dead flies and one had optimal breeding grounds for TB and other diseases.[22]

Besides calling for urban housing reforms, Alfonso and Tamayo also recommended that housing in the countryside be replaced in order to be "in harmony with the social progress of their inhabitants and, why not say it one more time?, with our own civilization." Gradually, wood structures could be built for about 750 pesos or brick houses for 1000 pesos, with plans that allowed the owners to pay all at once or in installments.[23] There was no discussion of how people would afford this. The average rural worker earned between 175 and 243 pesos per year from 1901 to 1907, when Alfonso and Tamayo issued their report. Most wages were used to feed an average family of four. Over time this situation worsened as costs for food surpassed rural worker incomes. This situation grew dire after 1917 when the Menocal administration permitted free entry of immigrant labor. More workers in agriculture fed wage competition, and salaries fell. More workers also meant more demand for food; thus, prices increased.[24] Ultimately, after 1917, more workers in Cuba competed for fewer jobs and experienced a higher cost of living. Consequently, rural workers found it increasingly difficult to afford quality housing.

By the 1920s, housing continued to be a concern for social reformers. The Socialist Francisco Carrera y Justiz once again took up the charge for affordable housing. But his justification for more affordable housing differed from other social commentators. While Alfonso and Tamayo had argued earlier that a clean, sanitary home could discourage vice, crime, and other societal immoralities, Carrera y Justiz saw the continuation of poor living conditions as contributing to the degeneration of body and spirit, "undermining the notion of the home as the most solid base of patriotism."[25] Thus, in the midst of growing political and cultural attempts to develop a new sense of Cuban national identity that could thwart a perceived colonial subservience to the United States, Carrera y Justiz helped to politicize housing issues.

Throughout the first three decades of independence, anarchists joined these criticisms of housing conditions and their relationship to health on the island. Even before independence, Manuel Fuentes's 1894 article in the newspaper *Archivo Social* summed up the anarchist approach to housing and health as a broad sociological problem. Workers' housing was little more than shabbily constructed hovels from which owners tried to extract as much rent as possible, he suggested. "This is the end: the rent. There is no other reason or any other law than the rent." Besides the abuse from landlords, stores also abused the working poor by charging high prices for inferior merchandise. However, the small shopkeepers were not necessarily to blame for this, but large-scale merchants sold shoddy merchandise at high cost. "For them [the large-scale merchants] there are no humanitarian sentiments, nor love for one's neighbor, nor sentiments of equity or justice," Fuentes concluded. "For this class of people, there is only business, and to business they render the same kind of worship that sectarians of a religion offer to their idols." Consequently, workers had to labor long hours in poor conditions to pay their debts. Yet, with such bad conditions, workers became sick and then turned to doctors, who were little better than snake oil salesmen, having "bought with their university degrees the right to kill others with impunity."[26] In this single sweeping article, one discovers the foundation for all later anarchist critiques of health: the interrelationships between profit, deception, and the professions, which thus allow more profit through more deception. Anarchists claimed it would be insufficient to tackle only one element; the whole system had to be supplanted.

Immediately following independence, anarchists lamented how in all the discussion about the "regeneration of Cuba" the most important and pressing issue that workers should really be talking about was housing. Housing proved a popular issue that anarchists imbued with remembrances of the war for independence. For instance, in September 1907 Abelardo Saavedra wrote of two men, "Joaquín" and "Vicente," in the Havana suburb of Marianao. Both were veteran pro-independence guerrilla fighters even though both were of Spanish birth. Joaquín, a carpenter with two children, earned $2.50 per day. Vicente had earned his wealth by robbing from battlefield corpses. With his "earnings" after the war, he bought the best lands around Marianao. He offered to build a place on the land of Joaquín's choice and then rent the site to Joaquín. The house was finished in 1902, and Joaquín moved in with his family; they paid ten pesos per month in rent. Ten years later Joaquín confronted Vicente with the fact that it had cost the latter only 500 pesos for the land, lumber, and wages to build the house; Joaquín—sick, hungry, widowed, and unemployed—charged that he had already paid 1,200 pesos in cumulative rent, yet Vicente now threw him out of the house.[27] Such a story, though fictional, must have struck a familiar chord among the readers of ¡Tierra!, which printed Saavedra's story. It illustrated, as well as any real life event, how the underlying social imbalances had not changed since the war, and how even working-class war veterans could see their homes taken away if conditions prevented them from meeting rents.

Anarchists also believed that Cuba's dismal housing situation and wealthy landlords undermined the family and an individual's freedom to live as one chose. For instance, in 1913 one writer to El Dependiente remarked about the growing number of signs outside Havana's boarding houses and other places for rent. Such signs read "Rooms for rent to single men or married couples without children." S. Martín claimed that such signs forbidding married men or families might just as well suggest "Sterilization, citizens!" Under legal protection tenement house owners could restrict who they wanted living in their buildings. But anarchists saw this "property right" differently; it enabled owners to threaten workers' natural rights to have children and families. Such property-based social coercion was antithetical to the natural rights of free individuals, argued Martín. "Who told these usurious gentlemen that they are so intelligent as to mitigate the laws of Nature?"[28] Consequently, it was bad enough that the property-owning class, with government backing, had failed to clean up, lighten, and expand affordable housing for workers and thus improve the health of the island's population, but now this same property-owning class wanted to control the social and living arrangements of its workers.

Although coercive, substandard, and unhealthy living arrangements existed for most of Cuba's workers, anarchists also portrayed the workplaces as reservoirs of danger, filth, and disease. In the rural zones of the island, especially around Santa Clara, José García began suggesting in 1904 that rural working conditions were possibly worse than in the days of chattel slavery and Spanish colonialism. In the past, he charged, "the black-skinned slave was one hundred times better off than the wage-earners of all colors today. The black slave had food, clothing, housing, doctors and medicine year-round, and they had a certain guarantee of protection because they represented something of value, like a horse today. The sugar mills then were small sugar plantations (cachimbos) with small productivity. In order to produce 2,000 hogsheads (bocoyes) of sugar, owners needed 2,000–3,000 slaves. Today," García concluded, "they employ a fourth of that number to produce 30,000 bocoyes of sugar, and then the workers are only employed through the grinding period. But there are no guarantees of employment or even of food." While workers in the sugar mills were paid twenty pesos per month, this was rapidly consumed with nine to twelve pesos going for food "that even pigs would reject" and the rest going for cigars, barbers, and laundry. Owners even threatened to withhold food to keep workers from rebelling against these conditions. Finally, García asserted, owners provided no housing for these workers, so most slept at the mill around the machinery.[29] By the 1910s, conditions for rural labor barely had improved. One writer in 1913 argued that rural labor in Cuba was best compared to African slavery; he noted the same criticisms of food, wages, and housing that José García made nine years earlier.[30]

Work conditions in the cities were not much better. Immediately after independence, writers in *El Nuevo Ideal* began to criticize conditions in the tobacco factories. Dr. M. Delfin wrote that past Spanish indifference to workplace health issues had created a lingering series of problems. He proposed that workers organize themselves into groups with a male delegate representing every hundred men and a female delegate every hundred women in the factories. The resulting organization would see that a doctor and an engineer accompanied them as part of a sanitary delegation to improve the factories' conditions. One of the first places to start was a simple rescheduling of when the factory floor was swept. Workers in the Villar y Villar tobacco factory had complained that they suffered breathing difficulties because the sweeping of the floor occurred during work hours, which caused workers to breathe in the dust and particles.[31]

Female tobacco factory workers had specific dilemmas to overcome. The female stemmers of tobacco leaf (*despalilladoras*) suffered from some of the lowest wages in the tobacco industry.[32] Beyond this economic issue was an important health issue. From six in the morning to five in the afternoon, these women stooped over a barrel of tobacco leaves with little rest, fresh air, or sunlight. Women suffered from bad digestion as well as intestinal and uterine problems due to a combination of poor diet, eating in filthy workplace surroundings, and constantly working while bent over. Critics charged that the youngest female stemmers were particularly vulnerable. Quoting an unnamed health practitioner, the writer Adriano Lorenzo suggested that the girls "who have not begun to menstruate, usually find their development retarded, her reproductive system corresponding to the overall development of her body. Her chest narrows, her back contorts, her breasts do not develop, her hips narrow—in short: her whole body stops developing."[33] Another writer asked what would happen when these girls, whose bodies were not adequately developed, began to have babies, assuming they could become pregnant or carry a fetus to term?[34] Thus, once again anarchists exposed conditions that Cuba's youth—this time young girls in unhealthy factories—had to endure.

Early twentieth-century labor codes enacted throughout Latin America aimed to keep women out of the production process. These codes were often justified on the grounds that women needed to be protected because their first duty was to bear children. The anarchist concern for female workers' health also focused on protecting girls in their future roles as mothers. However, unlike the labor codes that would be enacted in the Americas, Cuba's anarchists did not want to prohibit women from the workplace. Their concern was improving safety and health in order to protect girls who would become, in essence, working mothers. These mothers-to-be would have to be healthy and strong to rear the next generation of enlightened children and future workers. As anarchists saw it, when health and safety standards in the workplace threatened women of all ages, they threatened the next generation of workers and thus the next generation of potential revolutionaries.

While anarchists focused considerable attention on working conditions in the tobacco industry, other sectors of the economy came under similar scrutiny. Influenced by anarchist printers, hygienic conditions in printing houses received the wrath of the typographers' press in the 1910s. Most print shops were improvised in existing buildings. As a result, these structures often lacked good air flow and sunlight. Beyond this, the typographers noted truly despicable sanitary conditions. Toilets were always filled with paper and water tanks did not work right so that bowls always overflowed. Water faucets where people washed the ink from their hands rarely worked, and when they did there seemed to be no towels around.[35] Consequently, people often ate with ink-covered, dirty hands in foul settings.

As bad as these conditions seemed to be, nothing could prepare one for the filth and slavelike conditions that leftists said existed in the island's bakeries and among their workers. In 1899 anarchists lamented bakers' sixteen-hour workdays. They claimed that most bakers had to sleep at the bakery near the ovens because there were no beds.[36] Twelve years later, the situation was just as bad. In his pamphlet, designed to raise awareness and initiate legislative reform, Socialist Party leader Carrera y Justiz noted how the country's bread supply easily could become contaminated. In 1907 fewer than seven hundred bakers in Havana provided all the bread for the hospitals, jails, army, rural guard, health clinics, and most of the general public. Bakers' arms eventually wore out from rolling dough during a sixteen-hour shift, so they switched to using their bare feet to knead the bread. Because no towels were present, sweat always fell into the dough along with cigar and cigarette ashes from the workers' constant smoking. Insects, spiders, and rats fell into the dough, and workers tended to sleep on the same tables where the dough was rolled out.[37] While one should question whether or not these descriptions bordered on being little more than early twentieth-century urban legends, the important issue at work here is how socialists and anarchists regularly wrote and spoke of these conditions in a way as to frame a particular interpretation of Cuban reality. These descriptions, while not yet offering a prognosis, did offer a particular diagnosis of the health concerns facing Cuba's working poor and the larger societal consequences if not addressed.

Anarcho-Syndicalist Clerks and "White Slavery"

Nowhere did the concepts of health, working conditions, and living conditions so closely intersect than with the café *dependientes*. Through their weekly
anarcho-syndicalist newspapers *La Voz del Dependiente* and *El Dependiente*, the
dependientes challenged the hegemonic culture on economic, political, and
social fronts. In 1910, the North American journalist Irene Wright detailed their
living and working arrangements; she wrote that the *dependientes* "usually
reside in the building where they work" and if the owners were "decent and
agreeable men, this system of 'living in' works well enough, as far as the individual is concerned, for then the 'dependents' are happy and properly fed."
However, *dependientes* received only part of their wages in cash. The rest was
placed toward credit in the business. Consequently, their wages rarely were
sufficient to allow them to marry and thus live outside the establishment. In
fact, were the workers to demand full wages paid in cash, the wages "would not,
even if they held their jobs, suffice for their needs in this city where the poorest
living costs so very dear." Adding to this indignation, Wright noted that these
workers "are not free to leave the store when their work is done, if it is ever done,
unless it be their 'night off.' Instead, they sit in the store doorway and play
dominoes, or, if they are young and ambitious, ask and readily obtain leave to
attend night school at the particular 'regional society' as a member of which
they are inscribed before ever they leave the government immigrant station at
Triscornia."[38]

Wright's description of the *dependientes'* virtual enslavement in their place
of work is depressing, but it ultimately fails to capture the outlandish conditions within these establishments. Since the mid-nineteenth century, *dependientes* worked and lived in semifree conditions. Most were recent Spanish
immigrants, unable to find employment in other shops without first receiving official permission. Even after the abolition of slavery, *dependientes* remained less free than the freed former slaves.[39] The *dependientes* described
their situation as "white slavery" with good reason.[40] Besides questionable
payment schemes and being virtually locked in at night with the doors shut
on them after closing time, one *dependiente* complained about their poor
diets. He claimed that the food of the guests and owners was always of better
quality than that of the workers, and this after workers labored through four-
teen- to sixteen-hour days.[41]

Throughout the day *dependientes* breathed cooking fumes, grease, and smoke from ovens, and tobacco smokers had no time to step outside for fresh air or sunlight. These same fumes and smoke became trapped along the cafés' ceilings and in the upper-level storerooms. At night the employees had to sleep in these same storerooms, again with no ventilation for fresh air.[42] To complicate this environment, few cafés had showers or baths for workers to clean themselves properly. This prompted one unnamed writer to lament that "these young men neglect cleanliness and since 14, 16 and 18 hours of fatiguing labor makes them sweat so much, it results that the *barbacoas* are converted into the poorest dens and which are an outrage committed against health."[43] *Dependientes* placed great attention on the *barbacoas*—lofts above the shops and cafés, used traditionally as in-store warehouses for grains, fruits, and other foodstuffs. In Cuba these lofts also functioned as the *dependientes'* dormitories. The spaces were barely large enough in which to stand. Workers slept on old cots or in hammocks. Besides serving as the employees' dormitories, the *barbacoas* continued to function as storage rooms for the shops, meaning that the foodstuffs stored there attracted cockroaches and rats.[44] Consequently, overworked employees labored and lived among filth, smoke, and germs in unsanitary facilities and slept in pest-infested, claustrophobic dens.

This situation was particularly dangerous not only for workers but also for the general public. This was after all an important food industry within which there existed the conditions for an outbreak of TB or other diseases. This health concern became an important site of contention between employees and owners. *Dependientes* repeatedly warned that unsanitary conditions created the perfect environment for disease. Because employees worked long hours, ate poor-quality food, had little or no access to fresh air and sunlight, and slept among rats carrying potentially disease-plagued fleas, the *dependientes'* bodies were weakened and susceptible to illness. That these same employees then had direct contact with food and people of all classes meant that the *barbacoas* became potential breeding grounds for epidemics.[45]

By 1913, Cuba's Health Department began to make similar observations. The chief health officer in Havana, Antonio López del Valle, told a session of the Academy of Sciences that the *dependientes* were those residents of the city most in danger of tuberculosis. Cuba's tropical climate made working and living in such long, hot days that much more unbearable. The *dependientes* drove home this point themselves by contrasting Cuban conditions with those of English clerks. Their English counterparts, they claimed, worked fewer hours each week and had more time off despite the fact that Cuba was a tropical climate. To make matters worse, Cuba's own state employees worked only six-hour days in the summer—by law.[46]

Dependientes worked sixteen- to eighteen-hour days despite a Closing Law that ordered cafés, pharmacies, and other establishments to close after ten hours of operation. Merchants and the mainstream press opposed the law as an infringement on free enterprise. As a result, most of the island's cafés remained open until the early hours of the morning, which meant that *dependientes* continued working a minimum of sixteen hours. In November 1913, the *dependientes* warned their readers that café owners, led by Manuel G. Arias, were forming a "Centro de Cafés" aimed at repealing the Closing Law. Even though café owners openly ignored the Closing Law, the threat of enforcement—especially considering that the Health Department was now investigating the matter—spurred owners to have the law repealed. *Dependientes* urged their followers to resist this repeal attempt and in the meantime to boycott certain mineral waters distributed by Arias's firm; they argued that the boycott was a fair response against a man who sought to retain white slavery in Cuba.[47] This boycott and resistance to the owners came on the heels of other attempts by owners to resist reforming the living conditions. *Dependientes* warned that owners had too much economic and political clout, and for this reason the Health Department had not forcibly made owners improve or shut down the *barbacoas*.[48] In the midst of the *dependientes'* campaign to end contagious illness among them, the Havana café "El Central" at the corner of the important commercial intersection of Neptuno and Zulueta streets stood as a critical roadblock. The Health Department admitted that the café violated public health ordinances, especially regarding efforts to reform the *barbacoas*, but nothing was being done to correct the problem. As P. Colin put it, the *barbacoas* of El Central had become "the Cuban Bastille" in the health war.[49] To anarchosyndicalists, the café also served as an important symbol of the government's continued support on the side of business.

While the Health Department at times appeared to understand *dependientes'* concerns, little official assistance came the way of these employees. The Health Department printed pamphlets on how to prevent tuberculosis, but it did little else. Even if it had forced owners to close the *barbacoas*, there was no provision suggested to help *dependientes* find other accommodations. Because workers would have to find their own living quarters, they would have to pay rent. These payments would eat away at the *dependientes'* meager salaries, especially considering the high cost of living and the low wages of Havana. Likewise, no provisions were being made to force owners to raise *dependientes'* wages to afford such housing.[50] Consequently, the *dependientes* faced a dilemma: Should they continue living in subhuman accommodations, threatening their own health and that of the public? Should they move out of the *barbacoas* (if allowed to by the owners who could have fired them if they had left) and suffer a drastic loss in real income plus the amount of their salaries invested in the cafés by the owners? Or, was a more radical option possible?

Beginning in 1913, and coming on the heals of the Cruces labor conference in which some anarchists increasingly called for pansectarian alliances and radicalization of the movement, articles in *El Dependiente* called for the creation of a revolutionary syndicalist labor federation. To many, this seemed to be the only effective means to stop the practice of *barbacoas* and white slavery on the island.[51] The call to organize along even more radical anarcho-syndicalist lines reflected the *dependientes'* commitment and frustration. They certainly were not entirely powerless. Beyond the calls for a revolutionary labor federation, they practiced a form of "publicity sabotage" against the café owners. Through public attacks and criticisms in the *dependiente* press, owners and their unhealthy practices were displayed for public scrutiny. Interestingly, *dependiente* actions in Cuba were part of an international anarchist campaign seen in places as far away as Paris and New York. The *dependientes* in Havana openly lambasted health conditions and the café owners at precisely the same time as their international café and restaurant worker compatriots. For instance, responding to "unsettled grievances with their employers," Parisian café cooks in 1912 stood in front of their stoves. When the rush-hour clients swarmed into the dining rooms, the only things found boiling in the pots were stones and the restaurant clock.[52] In the United States, one thousand New York waiters described despicable, unsanitary conditions in the kitchens of the city's eateries.[53] By publicly relating conditions in the cafés and restaurants, workers tried to dissuade customers from eating in the cafés and restaurants. They hoped that public outcry and diminished customer traffic would affect the owners' bottom line and thus force the owners to improve workplace conditions.

In essence, these workers realized that laws might exist, but their application and enforcement depended more on societal relations of power, not equity and justice. Although health laws and ordinances existed on paper, the actual rooting out of the true sources of health problems and disease involved heavy capital expenditure for new buildings. In addition, the dispossessed could find little recourse before the law. Despite all their efforts, *dependientes* and other anarchists achieved little against their employers and the government. Throughout 1914 and 1915, writers still lamented the government failure to look out for the public's health by not enforcing the Closing Law.[54] Then from 1914 to 1917, radicals felt the full-scale assault of government repression discussed earlier, and the *dependientes* abandoned their crusade. Owners of capital and government officials had once again controlled the day.

Conclusion

"Health" became a central institutional and ideological struggle between anarchists and Cuban power holders. When anarchists analyzed health issues, they covered a broad spectrum of issues including children's health, disease eradication, and workers' living and working conditions. Rather than focus on one single issue and its elimination, anarchists tied health issues together and used these topics as venues to criticize the larger social and political establishments of the island's economic and political leaders—doctors, landlords, bosses, or politicians. Until the resurrection of the sugar economy destroyed by the war, the government had neither the resources, the power, nor the will to force property owners to address living and workplace conditions, or to do this itself. However, once sugar money returned to Cuba, some building improvements did begin. North American–based companies built new roads and bridges, railroad beds, and wharfs. But the export-oriented infrastructure did little to improve actual workplace conditions for Cuba's workers. New homes were built with electricity, water, and indoor baths, but these were largely situated in Havana's upscale outlying suburbs.[55] The government did initiate a series of public works projects. From 1907 to 1919, it spent some $19 million to pave Havana's streets and improve the sewer system. But these improvements, in conjunction with new highways, bridges, and upgrading of ports, were not done to improve the lives of the working masses; increasingly the government sought to attract tourists, keep them healthy so they could report back on how wonderful Cuba was, and thus attract more tourists.[56] In essence, the public works projects were about lining the pockets of those with property and power in Cuba.

In their critiques of state-capital negligence, anarchists joined with other social reformers and activists in freely describing the conditions of exploited workers as "white slavery." Considering the housing, working, and wage conditions of both Cuba's rural and urban labor forces, this description may have been more accurate than hyperbolic. Yet, what gave resounding importance and effectiveness to the term *white slavery* was Cuba's late abolition of African slavery in the 1880s. Consequently, when anarchists described the health environment that existed throughout the island and especially among the workers as "white slavery," they tapped into a bitter image of preindependence Spanish exploitation that, by the 1910s, was only two generations removed. When applied particularly to largely Spanish owners of cafés, the term took on a potentially revolutionary connotation. When the Cuban government failed to effectively intervene in this situation, anarchists could claim to the readers of their newspapers that here was "proof" that no real power had changed in Cuba since independence. Capital and the state continued to work for the interests of the wealthy at the expense of the average worker. When applied to health and living conditions, these deadly effects allowed the *dependientes* to call for revolutionary action in the 1910s.

Anarchists longed for a social revolution, and they hoped that such a radical transformation was reserved for a not-so-distant future. Until that day arrived, however, the challenge was living and working in the present in as healthy a manner as possible; such a challenge affected not only individual workers but also the entire family. For this, many anarchists began to follow or support in some way anarcho-naturism, which offered lessons on improving one's health in the present while simultaneously providing the groundwork for the social revolution.

7

Curing Bourgeois Ills

Anarcho-Naturism vs. Cuba's Medical Establishment

When science is truthful and is grounded in the laws of Nature, the predispositions and causes of illnesses in violation of all the precepts of Nature will be known years in advance; then there will be a true science that regenerates the people, and, because they are no longer useful or necessary, reduces the number of hospitals, *casas de salud*, sanatoriums, clinics, asylums, insane asylums, jails and penitentiaries, judges, magistrates, notaries, courts and the whole medley of institutions born and rooted in ignorance. Men healthy in body are healthy in spirit; their bodies and organs work admirably; they are just, good-natured; they analyze everything, they are frank, loyal and caring toward all.

Julián Magdalena (1916)

Workers in the nearby cane fields froze in their tracks. Around them the air filled with the anguished screams of a ten-year-old boy. While loading cut sugarcane into a train car, the car rolled on top of the child, crushing his arm and leg. The spectacle of child labor was enough to rankle anarchists, but the correspondent who sent this account to ¡*Tierra!* emphasized something equally horrific. When workers rushed the boy to local doctors in San Juan de los Yeras, near Santa Clara, they refused to examine him because no one had the means to pay for the needed treatment. While the boy bordered on passing out from the excruciating pain, his fellow workers rushed him to the hospital in Santa Clara where doctors finally ministered to him. To readers of the article in March 1912, the point was all too obvious when the correspondent summed up that "here, you have in the first place this leprosy of doctors" who refused to treat poor workers and their families. The writer concluded that such doctors were little better than the clergy or the military. All, he believed, sought to suppress the working poor.[1]

In the early twentieth century, individuals and groups of mostly socialists and anarchists developed alternative health initiatives to improve people's standard of living. Many of those men and women followed one of several forms of *naturismo*. Naturists emphasized simplifying one's lifestyle and experimenting with "alternative" health care and diets. They believed that people could improve their own health without resorting to costly doctors or state-sanctioned vaccination campaigns. Because they stressed preventative health care, the *naturistas* urged Cubans to strive for better living and working conditions where fresh air, sunlight, and cleanliness were the norm, not some romantic dream. In addition, people needed to grow their own food when possible, adopt simple vegetarian diets, and seek homeopathic therapy for ailments. *Naturistas* also encouraged people to avoid the professional medical establishment: it represented centralization, close ties to the state, persecution of alternative medicine, and profiteering off the poor (except upon occasion when it actually acquiesced to help the poor, like the little boy whose limbs were crushed). Ultimately, in Cuba practicing naturist health surpassed mere health; it provided a legal, political, and ideological issue to highlight the anarchist countercultural agenda on the island and reflected one more battle in the island's culture wars.

Anarchism and Naturism in Cuba

Naturism was first and foremost an early twentieth-century international lifestyle movement. Its followers rejected the growing mass production of the age and what they believed were the antinatural consequences of unchecked industrial development; for example, naturists cited rampant urbanization that created unhealthy living conditions, food adulteration that undermined Nature's bounty and poisoned consumers, and the growing industrialization of work with its unnatural rhythms and dangerous conditions. However, *naturism*, like *socialism*, was an umbrella term that found different expressions and tendencies. The two most important issues in the trans-Atlantic naturist movement revolved around the perceived causes of this "crisis of industrialism": how could one best counter this cause, and for what end did one strive. One individualist tendency focused on the importance of individual regeneration by growing vegetables, eating vegetarian diets, and attending alternative health institutes. Followers of this line of thought cut across all social classes, and this largely explains why no corresponding social analysis critically appraised the encroachment of capitalism and the larger socioeconomic roots of people's afflictions. Thus, followers of this tendency believed that one "got better" on one's own. As Eduard Masjuan clearly illustrates in one of the very few studies of *naturismo*, anarcho-naturists challenged this individualist tendency by adding a social critique to *naturismo* and urging followers to think of their actions as part of a movement for social change.[2]

Beginning in the late 1800s, anarcho-naturism proliferated throughout the

French and Spanish anarchist movements. French anarcho-naturists became important components of not only the anarchist health movement but also the anarchist literary and artistic movements. In the 1890s, French anarcho-naturist poet Adolphe Retté began writing "popular and propagandistic works in the service of the revolution." Retté and his French comrades promoted a commonplace, natural world in their vision against industrial civilization.[3] Likewise in Spain, anarcho-naturists produced a plethora of short stories. These stories centered on themes such as getting close to Nature. Other stories portrayed bourgeois society, the state, and the church as undermining Nature and thus unraveling what anarchists saw as humanity's natural cooperative instincts.[4] Beyond literature, Spanish anarchists closely held to the "concept of living close to nature," as one historian has put it. These radicals experimented broadly with such innovations as "vegetarian diets, often favoring uncooked foods; ecological horticulture; simplicity of dress; a passion for the countryside; even nudism."[5]

Spanish anarcho-naturism emerged around 1903 when the writings of two French anarchists, Henri Zisly and E. Gravelle, began appearing in Spanish anarchist newspapers. Zisly and Gravelle argued that the disappearance of the forests, the contamination of the atmosphere, and a perceived climatic change all resulted from the growing dominance of technology and industrialization. Besides environmental changes, technology and industrialization were forcing people to eat processed food and work at unclean jobs. In short, technological progress was destroying Nature while turning people into slaves.[6] They argued that capitalist organization of society was to blame, and many people listened. Albano Rosell became a leading Spanish proponent of anarcho-naturism. Forced into exile during the 1909 government crackdown against anarchists in Spain, Rosell fled to Latin America, which he described as a "seedbed of naturist centers." Rosell found naturism throughout Latin America, especially Uruguay and Argentina. However, he was disturbed that these naturists mainly followed the individualist tendency and mostly lacked any social critique. This was not the case, though, in Cuba, which had Latin America's most developed anarcho-naturist movement following a social emancipatory agenda.[7]

Still, not all anarchists were comfortable with various aspects of naturism. The more important disagreement, centered on the relationship between *naturismo* and anarchist economic principles, had its roots in another conflict concerning the role of commercialized *naturismo*. In short, what did one eat, how did one live, and what did one do for a living? Masjuan appropriately labels this "capitalist" wing of naturism "*el sector comercialista del naturismo*." This strand of naturism was rooted not in socioeconomic, but in "medical," analysis. Practitioners in Spain and Latin America came from all classes and believed that better health as an individual issue only required healthier eating and more lawful living.[8] As a result, numerous merchants in these countries began selling "health food." It was one thing for a middle-class proprietor to sell such items, but what about when a struggling shopkeeper with anarchist sympathies did this? What was one to think? Could such a person be a "good" anarchist?

No better example of this conflict exists than the controversy swirling around the Havana bookseller and anarcho-naturist José Guardiola. Guardiola ran bookshops that handled works on hydrotherapy, vegetarianism, and other naturist themes, besides selling anarchist newspapers like *¡Tierra!* and *El Dependiente*. In the first decade of the twentieth century, Guardiola regularly contributed money to the printing of *¡Tierra!*, and his name frequently was listed as a financial contributor for various political causes organized by the newspaper. However, in September 1909 a number of anarchists attacked Guardiola for what they viewed as his profiteering from selling *naturista* books. They wondered if Guardiola could really be an anarchist sympathizer while also making profits. In his defense, Guardiola gave his own lessons in the dilemmas of living in a capitalist society while holding convictions for the need of its demise. He wanted to keep prices low in order to have a sufficient customer base, but also needed to earn enough money to stay in business. So what if he made a little profit off of a naturist book, Guardiola asked? He was providing a necessary service at a reasonable price. Guardiola promised that all would come out even in the end: he considered the economic situation of the people who owed him money and, following that assessment, determined how vigorously to pursue collection of the debt.[9]

Responding to charges that he was not always an ideal anarchist, Guardiola admitted having spent more time promoting vegetarianism than anarchism, but he argued that humanity becomes freer as it moves toward anarchism. Still, he warned that one should not ignore how changing to a vegetarian diet could promote better digestion and thus better health. In this way, healthier people could actively fight off what anarchists saw as charlatans who passed as doctors and pharmacists while stealing the pitiful wages of workers. In addition, eating a vegetarian diet could help one become a better anarchist. "I believe that we are what we eat; if what I eat is pure, then pure and hygienic will be my actions as well."[10]

Some anarchists remained skeptical of Guardiola. For instance, in ¡Tierra!'s "Campo Neutral" column reserved for theoretical debates between the island's anarchists, ¡Tierra! published a scathing critique of Guardiola by "Un Guajiro Recalcitrante" (aka Abelardo Saavedra). The column again accused Guardiola of being a speculative merchant who lived off the sweat of laborers by taking their money for questionable books and doing so at a profit. More damning, though, was the author's accusation that Guardiola actually campaigned against anarchism by stating that one could not be a true anarchist "without having first submitted to the rigorous teachings of Louis Khune." A European naturist, Khune proposed a holistic alternative health regimen based on a vegetarian diet, avoidance of tobacco and alcohol, and seeking natural, homeopathic treatments for ailments rather than visiting medical doctors. The writer charged that Guardiola himself was not a good Khunista because he smoked, ate meat on occasion, and was too ready to abandon *naturismo* and seek medical or surgical help when someone in his own family was injured. Saavedra asked what was so wonderful about vegetarianism anyway. Some priests and members of the bourgeoisie were vegetarians, and yet they were still murderers and exploiters. Besides, few if any major anarchist thinkers were vegetarians, he added. Kropotkin, Bakunin, Reclus, Malatesta, Grave, and others were omnivores, but no one would question their commitment to living out the anarchist ideal. It was fine to eat vegetarian and follow other *naturista* practices in regards to health, but "we can never believe that it has anything in common with anarchism." In fact, concluded the writer, for some people vegetarianism bordered dangerously close to being a religion. Like cannibals who believed in acquiring magical powers by eating prisoners, Saavedra charged, Guardiola and other *naturistas* saw almost mystical properties in eating only vegetables.[11]

By late November 1909, the editorial group of ¡Tierra!, feeling the columns had become too personal in their attacks, agreed not to publish any more on the debate between Saavedra and Guardiola.[12] This did not stop La Voz del Dependiente, the leading anarcho-syndicalist newspaper whose writers frequently supported the anarcho-naturist line. The head of the international anarchist school movement in Cuba, Miguel Martínez, had come under attack by Saavedra at this time as well, and in the midst of his own defense in the pages of La Voz del Dependiente, Martínez took the opportunity to defend Guardiola. Martínez viewed Guardiola as not a scoundrel or bourgeois, but "a sensible man" who had actually helped workers by giving them breaks. As Martínez put it, Guardiola was a shopkeeper who sold workers supplies and "gave us food when we would have otherwise gone without." Thus, even though Guardiola and others like him were not workers but merchants, at least they were honorable, sympathetic, and willing to extend credit without interest to help workers survive tough times.[13] In a final defense, an anonymous writer in April 1910 assailed Guardiola's critics for denouncing Guardiola while carrying out their own money-making activities. Siding with Saavedra in the antimerchant debates were Francisco Sola and Emiliano Bajo. According to the writer, Sola and Bajo had their own business where they not only wrote letters for the illiterate but also sold books. "There Sola did what he doesn't want Guardiola to do: he sold books, making commerce—oh, sacrilege!—with the bread of the Ideal. But he sold the books at higher prices than Guardiola." So, while Guardiola's critics were busy harassing him about selling books, they did the same thing while making more money. Who was the real exploiter of workers, the writer wondered.[14]

Although the confrontation between Guardiola and his detractors may have taken on personal undertones, this debate actually illustrated two potentially threatening issues dividing some anarchists and anarcho-naturists: earning a living and still living as a good anarchist. Could one be a merchant and an anarchist? Did one have to eat only vegetables to be a good anarchist? Anarchists and anarcho-naturists agreed that eating vegetables or buying health food was not enough; a social critique and agenda had to exist too. Yet, could you be a good anarchist while eating roast pork (not an extraordinary question considering the Cuban love for such a dish)? Still, the relationship between profit, health, lifestyle, and being a good anarchist was less contentious in Cuba than might be thought from this controversy. Over the years, anarchist newspapers regularly featured pronaturist articles and advertisements for *naturista* newspapers, publications, and health facilities. A commercial component generally was taken for granted among most anarchists. After all, this was capitalist Cuba. However, all anarchist strands rejected a *naturismo* that lacked any larger socio-emancipatory elements.

Del Valle wrote in 1915 that *naturismo* and anarchism should have the same end: "the amplified and happy life of a human being." Socialistic societies without *naturismo*, he argued, would see many causes that produce social ills eliminated. However, without a simultaneous turn to *naturista* practices, "bad individuals and thus social evils would persist" as a threat to an egalitarian society. Neither would nonegalitarian societies allow the free flowering of a *naturista* lifestyle. Contemporary unequal societies, Del Valle added, were infested with high urbanization, specialization of work, unhealthy homes, poor hygiene, vice, the struggle for life, and an overriding quest for wealth, ambition, and power. This "contributes in forcing us to live in an environment that is the total negation of a sane environment. We need to be able to nonviolently submit ourselves to a natural life regimen."[15] All agreed that lifestyle was important, not only for how one lived in a capitalist society, but also in preparing for the social revolution. Many anarchists believed that a *naturista* lifestyle had to simultaneously evolve with a revolution. In other words, vegetarianism and the revolution had to occur together. Not all preached the necessity of eating vegetables, taking steam baths, using electronic devices as curatives, sunbathing, or even running around nude. However, most anarchists understood the precarious state of health and health care on the island and were convinced that healthy living today was crucial for making healthier revolutionaries tomorrow.

Anarcho-Naturists versus the Medical Establishment

In chapter 6, anarchists, particularly the syndicalists in the cafés and restaurants, distrusted the state and private enterprise to improve health conditions. Anarcho-naturists likewise believed that Cuba's professional medical establishment could not be trusted because it had far too many connections to the state, held a rigid medical orthodoxy that discouraged or prevented inexpensive *naturista* health alternatives, and was more interested in enriching itself at the expense of the social good. In the first issue of his newspaper *El Naturista* in 1912, Dr. Luciano Soto explained this to his readers. Somewhat sarcastic in tone, he suggested that the government and medical doctors were colluding partners with a distinct interest in seeing the maintenance of high death and illness rates. If death rates fell, funeral parlors would lose profits. If disease rates declined, pharmacists could not sell drugs. Producers of alcohol did not want laws or hygienic ordinances that prohibited the consumption of alcohol. Finally, he charged, doctors opposed a hygiene that would deprive them of patients. Consequently, in Dr. Soto's conspiratorial world, anyone with power (symbolic, economic, political, and even medical) was an enemy of humanity.[16]

The notion that commerce more than the Hippocratic Oath guided the medical profession was a popular theme in anarcho-naturist critiques. Although writers often made sweeping generalizations against the medical community, they just as often related personal or second-hand stories of dealing with the medical professions. For instance, in 1910, *¡Tierra!* asked for donations to help the old, blind anarchist Adolfo Rodríguez of Esperanza receive treatment that might allow him to regain some vision. Writing in response to this donation campaign, *Rebelión!*'s editor Abelardo Saavedra lamented how typical it was that the poor had to hold fund-raisers to get medical help because they were forced to give all they had just to get well.[17]

Cuban anarcho-naturism was more than just an imported philosophy and course of action. In fact, the ideas and activities embarked on in Cuba were hybrid creations that merged European and Cuban ideas and practices. Although anarchists derived such conclusions about the medical establishment from European anarcho-naturist writings and experiments in Europe, they also found a reception to their ideas because some poorer Cubans held similar perceptions of the medical community. For instance, the former slave Esteban Montejo related his own distrust of doctors. "Doctors today give different names to these diseases. They call them infections or rashes, and it turns out that it takes longer to cure them than before when we had no injections, or x-rays, either." Montejo believed that such treatments were less effective than herbal cures found in Nature. Besides, he argued, "I want to know why doctors don't go to the countryside to experiment with plants. It seems to me that they are such good businessmen that they don't want to just come out and say that such and such a leaf will cure you. Then they fool you with prepared medicines that in the end are very expensive and don't cure anybody. Back then, I couldn't buy those medicines, and therefore I didn't go to a doctor. A man who earned twenty-four pesos a month couldn't spend even a centavo on a bottle of medicine."[18] It is impossible to tell how many average Cubans agreed with Montejo's or the anarchists' descriptions of doctors in the early twentieth century. Clear, however, is that anarchists' portrayals of doctors motivated mainly by profit incentives mirrored the sentiments of Cubans like Montejo.

The anarcho-naturist distrust of doctors extended to their distrust of centralized health and medical institutions as a whole. In his "Crónica naturista" column in the pages of *Pro-Vida*, "Arbusto del Futuro" denounced the codification of medical degrees and practice under central control. He urged his colleagues to "accustom ourselves to decentralization. We have spent long enough submitting to a centralism that has not stopped being as pernicious as it is tyrannical!" Centralization of the medical profession forced doctors to follow and obey official health practices, and thus doctors became obedient to the very state that anarchists by definition hated and despised. Arbusto added that state restrictions actually eliminated freedom of thought, action, and experimentation.[19]

Because of their unorthodox views, anarcho-naturists felt the weight of repression in both an ideological and a judicial sense. They believed that the repression resulted, again, from state-doctor collusion. Because naturist health practices fell outside official centralization, *naturistas* were subject to legal penalties for practicing medicine without a license. Nobody seemed to suffer repression more than Julián Magdalena, perhaps the best-known of the early anarcho-naturist practitioners on the island. In the spring of 1911, authorities in Pinar del Río arrested Magdalena after the city's doctors and pharmacists denounced him for practicing without a license. Magdalena was sentenced to a year in jail.[20] In a series of columns appearing in *La Voz del Dependiente* that same spring, Magdalena described to readers the repression of *naturista* health by the city's medical profession. Magdalena cited the island's high infant mortality rates, high death rates for children less than ten years of age, and growing cancer rates. Then he charged that the official medical community was impotent to solve these health problems; the licensed doctors pumped drugs into these people, but they died anyway. Still, officials did not imprison such doctors. However, someone like himself who had done nothing but "assert with examples that natural water, the sun, exercise, and rest are elements that cure more efficiently than drugs" was thrown in jail simply because he had no official license and operated outside the health hierarchy of power.[21]

In his criticisms of legal and free speech repression against *naturista* health practitioners, Magdalena employed a traditional anarchist tactic by using religious symbols of martyrdom and persecution. While in jail he compared his situation to that of Jesus, who 2,000 years before "dazed with the torch of rebellion all the ignominies, insults, bantering and hypocrisies of those exploiting the people." Magdalena noted that like him, Jesus had worked for the poor and dispossessed, only to be punished for it. "Execution was the only prize obtained by the prophet of Nazareth for his sublime and undying work," Magdalena wrote. "Sad compensation for his love of the working class, the rebelliousness of his soul, his great love for the disinherited! That is the reward generally received by those who rebel against traditions, against customs."[22] In 1914 Magdalena compared the continued repression of *naturismo* with the Spanish Inquisition. Whereas the original Inquisition directed its energies against the spirit, the current "inquisitors" aimed at the body. While an inquisitorial court might no longer exist, "there are others of the same disposition, called clinics, hospitals, *casas de salud,* asylums and insane asylums." Within these inquisitorial walls, medical professionals supposedly derived official medical doctrine. In the fourteenth century, Magdalena added, "everything that was considered reprehensible was removed from texts, and those who had the courage to demonstrate their convictions were punished." Little had changed in the new inquisition where any health ideas "that are not in scientific (?) [sic] texts are reprehensible" and those who challenged the sacred scientific texts were fined, detained, or even arrested.[23] This use of religious symbolism in no way signaled support for Christianity. In fact, a critique of health and the Catholic Church sometimes went hand-in-hand. For instance, *El Nuevo Ideal* reported in 1899 that twenty-four Catholic churches existed in Havana; each had three *pilas* (holy water basins) near their entrances. The newspaper wryly noted that this meant there were "*72 focos de infección*" due to all the hands in them. Thus, the Church could poison not only the mind and spirit but also the body.[24]

Anarchists of all tendencies also sharply rebuked official medicine's growing use of drugs and injections, especially the government's attempts to battle smallpox with obligatory inoculations. Anarchists and anarcho-naturists challenged obligatory inoculations on two fronts: medical science and civil liberties. Writers in the pages of the monthly *Pro-Vida* took great exception to the government's law requiring all minors and some adults to have injections against smallpox. One questioned the whole validity of using injections as preventatives. Such a practice, he suggested, was like saying you need to drink six to eight glasses of gin to fight off alcoholism. Beyond this, injections were seen as "antinatural" because they "violently" introduced foreign matter into a person's bloodstream with uncertain effects. Some charged that doctors who gave inoculations could also prove highly dangerous because they inspired a false notion of security while failing to advise recipients about other preventative measures like changes in diet, hygiene, and lifestyle. To those who argued that nonvaccinated people posed a threat to the general population, one writer asked facetiously why such a nonvaccinated person would be seen as a health threat: after all, wouldn't those vaccinated people necessarily be protected from those nonvaccinated?[25]

Anarchists also considered injections dangerous to women during childbirth. True to what later practitioners would label "natural childbirth," one writer criticized doctors for injecting pain-relieving substances into birthing mothers. Obstetricians could not safely use ethyl-bromide or ethyl-chloride. Chloroform and ether were too dangerous to use except during the final stages of pushing out the baby. Instead, obstetricians increasingly relied on opiates for pain relief, even though the same doctors acknowledged that these drugs were "inconvenient" because they also tended to paralyze the mother's intestines.

Instead of too willingly giving injections to deaden the pain of contractions, the writer suggested a series of hydrotherapy treatments such as hot water and steam baths to relax muscles and ease tensions. To better prepare for childbirth, the mother should adopt a vegetarian diet, which would cause less stress on the digestive and intestinal organs "and effectively prepare the mother to better raise her child."[26]

From a civil liberties critique, writer Solomo A. Riestra argued that the obligatory vaccination law was one more attempt by the medical community, acting through the government, to maintain power. The right to reject being vaccinated "is another freedom that is sacrificed in the holocaust of medical fanaticism—the hardest, the cruelest and most disagreeable of fanaticisms." Riestra claimed that such a law was dangerous because not only did injections add foreign matter into bodies with uncertain effects but also a law requiring such injections violated an individual's freedom of conscience if he or she wished to turn to other health care practices. Riestra anticipated that his opponents would label such claims as fanatical; therefore, he countered that the true fanatics were those in the medical and governmental communities who thought that their dogmas should be imposed on everyone.[27] The anarchist mistrust of inoculations echoed throughout the wider Cuban population. During the second U.S. occupation, Chief Sanitary Officer of Havana Carlos Finlay described the reluctance of people to accept mandatory inoculations. In his report to Provisional Governor Magoon in 1907, Finlay lamented that "the law prescribing obligatory vaccination to all non-immunes is but very imperfectly complied with except in moments of alarm when the Sanitary Department obliges all non-immunes in the neighborhood to submit to it under the penalty prescribed by the law."[28] Whether people mistrusted shot-giving doctors or simply believed, like Esteban Montejo, that injections were ineffective, anarchists added a political spin. Forced inoculations violated individual privacy and freedom.

While anarcho-naturists challenged the medical establishment's vaccination programs, such programs also became the source of biting satire. The medical community argued that inoculations were an effective preventative measure against disease and in protection of the community's health. Their detractors, however, alleged that such measures did not address the real issues that created death by disease, namely underlying social inequality and exploitation, which created breeding grounds for illness. An anonymously written column titled "Injectomanía" sarcastically questioned just how far the increasingly popular belief in injections-as-preventatives would go. "And now we have to inject ourselves with a serum containing rabies for rabies, a serum with smallpox for smallpox, a serum with tetanus for tetanus, a serum with diphtheria for diphtheria and.....ah, MISERY FOR MISERY." Next, the writer feared, there would be an "excitant tonic" and then a "tranquilizer" to keep the people in emotional balance and not agitate for change.[29]

In sum, from the anarcho-naturist perspective, the medical establishment was little more than another expression of the forces of domination, like the state, capital, and the church. This establishment restricted membership to those who could afford its training and who would obey its rules of conduct and practice. Such a class-biased, authoritarian-appearing body likewise had little interest in helping the poor. And when anyone tried to help the popular classes through affordable naturist treatments, these practitioners faced the possibility of punishment by the legal and medical establishments for practicing medicine without a license or without regard to official procedures. Despite this legal, medical, political, and ideological conflict—in short, health battles in the culture wars—naturist practitioners continued to work, naturist health articles continued to appear in the anarchist press, and naturist clinics and facilities began to open around Cuba.

Healthier Living, Healthier Revolutionaries

Although the island's anarchist press promotion of an *anarco-naturista* critique of Cuba's health system began just after independence, several years passed before *naturista* centers existed. By 1905, the Naturist Center was founded in Havana, and in 1910 Ramón Suárez and Dr. Mateo Fiol gave regular lectures on *naturismo* at the Naturist Institute and the Hydrotherapeutic Institute in Havana. The lectures were advertised in the anarchist press, but there is no indication that Suárez and Fiol offered broader social emancipatory dimensions to their talks.[30] Not until the 1910s did the anarcho-naturist movement take off. Two years after the 1912 premiere of Dr. Soto's *El Naturista*, the naturist doctor J. Alonso Aladro began publishing *Pro-Vida*. Over time the anarcho-syndicalist clerk and manager of *El Dependiente*, Aquilino López, regularly wrote for and helped to publish *Pro-Vida*. Then Adrián del Valle took over editorship of the newspaper, solidifying the link between all three strands of anarchism in Cuba.

In January 1915 *Pro-Vida* announced the merger of the Pro-Vida Naturist School and the Institution for Self Improvement with the Naturist Association of Cuba; they established joint offices at Someruelos 23 in Havana. Besides these offices and a vegetarian restaurant, the Someruelos address also housed a gymnasium that offered daily exercise classes from eight to nine in the evenings, which made the program accessible to average daytime workers.[31] By September 1916 the Naturist Association and its Pro-Vida Restaurant had relocated to Neptuno 57, at the heart of working-class Havana, reachable by four different tram lines running throughout the city.[32] By 1917 formal *naturista* groups and institutions had spread throughout Cuba. The Naturist Association claimed branches in Havana, Cienfuegos, Puerto Esperanza in Pinar del Río province, and Placetas near Santa Clara in central Cuba.[33] There was even a vegetarian Pro-Vida Restaurant operating in Tampa, Florida, by mid-1917. Local organizers of these branches were themselves leading *naturista* figures on the island: Aladro, López and Eugenio Leante in Havana, Julián Magdalena in Puerto Esperanza, and Juan Ruiz in Cienfuegos.[34]

While anarcho-naturism required a broader social and political dimension, a vital part of the movement in Cuba took a holistic approach to health that focused primarily on one's diet as a preventative measure and hydrotherapy, solar therapy, and massage as both a prevention of and cure for ailments. Society could not be saved without the individual and vice versa. Food and diet were crucial ingredients to maintaining one's health. Only through healthy eating could one avoid either digestive ailments, which *naturistas* tended to believe were the central causes of bodily ailments requiring treatment by money-grabbing doctors, or death, if one could not afford a doctor.

One of the stranger dietary issues linked to *naturismo* and anarchism revolved around the selling, advertising, and consumption of Coca-Cola. Since the beginning of the century, Havana's restaurants had served Coca-Cola, and in 1902 Cuba had one of the company's few off-shore bottling plants.[35] Anarchists developed a love-hate relationship with the beverage. Advertisements for the popular soft drink regularly appeared in *La Voz del Dependiente* along with other advertisements for beers and even cognacs. In 1911 the newspaper published an article on recent research in New York that suggested how caffeine caused intestinal inflammation and congestion. Because of the new reports of health-related problems associated with the beverage, the author urged readers not to drink it and *dependientes* in the cafés not to serve it.[36] At this time Coca-Cola ads disappeared from the newspaper, only to reemerge in May 1914. Then in 1916 Eleuterio García warned the readers of *El Dependiente* against consuming Coca-Cola because it was bad for the health. "Coca-Cola, as demonstrated by the Health Department, is composed of toxins that are dangerous to people who unknowingly ingest them." Despite this momentary reliance on the word of the government, a Coca-Cola ad still appeared on page three of the same issue.[37]

By 1917, though, anarcho-naturists began promoting the supposed health benefits of Coca-Cola. *Pro-Vida* ran advertisements for Coke that included the phrase "Eliminate anemia" in the ad copy. With no explanation provided, one can deduce that the soft drink was thought to enrich the blood through carbonation because anemia was basically a deficiency in the oxygen-carrying material of the blood.[38] The same year, the paper claimed that certain goods imported from the United States, like Grape Nuts and Post Toasties cereals, contained health benefits. Dr. Aladro, a founder of *Pro-Vida*, sold these cereals in Havana. He offered to advise people on their use in conjunction with eating a vegetable-based diet. As one notice put it, Post Cereals are "in accord with those principles in Dr. J. Alonso Aladro's 'Health Certificate'" and assured readers he would sell the cereals at modest prices.[39]

The apparent contradiction between accepting advertisements for alcohol or imported goods from the United States while promoting lifestyles opposed to alcohol and imperialism is striking. Equally striking is the fact the *La Voz del Dependiente* and *El Dependiente* solidly supported anarcho-syndicalist and anarcho-naturist philosophies yet chose to accept advertisements for local and international products. In short, prominent weekly anarchist newspapers accepted capitalist advertisements. At the same time, *Pro-Vida*, under the editorship of anarcho-communist and naturist Adrián del Valle, also accepted such advertisements. The cynic could argue that this illustrated how poorly committed the editors were to revolution and social reform, or how they might have spoken of social emancipation but were closer to the individual and commercial naturist line than they cared to admit. However, this view ignores an important point that every publisher of every anarchist-leaning newspaper faced. Anarchist papers always teetered on the brink of insolvency. The anarchist weekly ¡Tierra! did not publish advertisements and consequently regularly ran large debts over the course of its decade and a half in print. Nevertheless, the advertisement-filled newspapers of the *dependientes* and *naturistas* remained financially solvent for their entire multiyear runs. Consequently, by accepting advertisements, the newspapers acknowledged the necessity to earn money in order to continue propagating anarchist, *naturista*, and revolutionary viewpoints. To many anarchists, this life in a degenerative capitalistic context reflected the dilemma José Guardiola had faced.[40]

As already suggested, vegetarianism played a central role in the *naturista* philosophy. Anarcho-naturists promoted vegetarianism as a healthy, cost-effective alternative for the poor and working class, and they offered simple, practical advice. The anarcho-syndicalist *Nueva Luz* published a regular column, "Por amor a la tierra (Notas de un campesino)" [Loving the Land (Notes from a Peasant)] in the 1920s. The first article subtitled "El Tomate" praised the tomato for its versatility. Not only could the fruit be used in several dishes, but also its supposedly medicinal values included benefits for curing liver problems. The author urged people to grow tomatoes in any space of the home they could find. Other articles discussed the benefits of homegrown squash and kidney beans. Lemon trees could produce fruit useful to treat scurvy and intestinal worms, and chayotes could be both a diuretic and an aid for pregnant women. Homegrown commodities were more than just a means to eat healthier. They were also a way to lessen dependence on markets and thus capitalism. "Here, in Cuba, what we have to do is lose the habit of going to buy everything at the market or the green grocery," noted one anarchist.[41]

Thus, *naturistas* believed that a vegetarian diet, preferably homegrown and devoid of toxins like alcohol and caffeine, could make Cubans healthy. To complement such a diet, and when people did become ill, *naturistas* recommended a mixture of homeopathic treatments, solar and hydrotherapy treatments (at home and in *naturista* facilities), and occasionally nudism. Acting as president and secretary respectively of the Naturist Association, Vicente Santos and Aquilino López highlighted the need for *naturismo*, especially among the island's children. They noted the high levels of infant mortality in Cuba and urged readers to familiarize themselves with *naturista* practices if they did not want to see their children perish before them. Santos and López presented *naturismo* as a universal health alternative that allowed parents to become "our own doctors for our own children."[42] This included not just eating well and avoiding vice, but also lessons in cleanliness for children. For instance, *naturistas* offered practical advice on giving children daily baths. Noted one writer, bath water should be heated to 20 degrees C. in the winter and left in its natural state in summer. If children were irritable or nervous, parents should bathe them in an infusion of linden-bloom and water. If the child was of a delicate constitution, salt-water baths were recommended. Finally, parents were advised to wash children's eyes with warm water and a few drops of lemon juice to avoid "that terrible childhood disease known as *oftalmía purulenta*" (purulent ophthalmia, a severe inflammation of the eye).[43]

While *naturismo* advised people on how to best care for their families at home, *naturista* practitioners also created their own schools and centers. Here people could receive a wide variety of treatments ranging from saunas, massages, and showers to the more elaborate male and female sun rooms, directed electric heat lamp treatments, and even mild electrotherapy. Prices were reasonable. For one peso per month in 1915, families received unlimited consultations, children's examinations, and access to baths, saunas, and solar facilities at the center run by the Naturist Association in Havana. To encourage members from outside Havana to come occasionally to the city, non-Havana residents were charged half price.[44]

Of the various treatments available, *naturistas* themselves most often discussed solar therapy. *Pro-Vida* outlined the benefits of such a treatment, especially in combating tuberculosis.[45] More generally, though, the benefits of solar therapy were best described in an anonymous column from 1917:

> The sun's light stimulates glandular activity, increases evaporation, stimulates one's metabolism, cleanses blood flow, increases oxidation, alleviates tension of the tissues and thus pain, increases the volume of blood in the arteries, destroys dangerous bacteria, increases phagocytes and renders useless morbid germs, influences marrow, increases perspiration and distributes heat throughout the body. Such are the results that solar light, the fountain of life and energy, is also the best means for the conservation of one's health.[46]

Anarchists believed that the sun held truly beneficial qualities. Before the recognized threat of skin cancer descended upon humanity, these early twentieth-century health practitioners saw in the sun powers not only of prevention and cure but also regeneration. The sun, as an embodiment of Nature, was crucial for good health and purifying the environment of dangerous germs and bacteria. Individuals could tap into this all-powerful energy through sun baths.

At times the *dependiente* Hilario Alonso pushed this *naturista* line beyond normal discussion. If sun bathing in institutes could be beneficial for one's health, then directly frolicking in Nature with no clothes on could be equally advantageous. In short, Alonso advised Cubans to experiment with nudism. He argued that living without clothing brought forth healthy benefits and liberating qualities because it allowed people to become more in touch with Nature.

> You are very wrong to believe that those individuals who practice free cooperation are dependent on clothes and shoes and shelter. Such dependency hurts that cooperation. In order to live, man does not need shoes, or shelter, or clothes because these elements separate man from the air,

from the light, from the sun, and from the water—all with which he should be in contact. And in so doing they enslave the body with illnesses that in the majority of times the individual will pay for with his life.[47]

Ethically from this point of a view, a dependence on clothing and housing—improvements for which anarchists fought via struggles for better wages and living and working conditions—could actually be harmful to individuals. In one sense, such a reliance on these items meant a continued dependence on merchants, markets, and thus capitalism. In another sense, such reliance separated humans from the natural elements, which only made people lose touch with the natural world and thus the harmonious lives they could lead in accordance with Nature.[48] Alonso's promotion of nudism, though, generally fell on deaf ears. Although naturist nudist communities emerged in Spain by the 1920s, apparently none arose in Cuba.

But the symbol of nudity, as opposed to actually going around without clothes, was perhaps more important for Alonso and the brave nude few. The sun was more than just a health instrument for anarcho-naturists. Rather, the sun embodied the essence and power of Nature. To them, the sun symbolized a new dawn and thus a point on the horizon toward which humanity had to strive to live a harmonious life. To live under the sun, to live within the confines and dictates of Nature's physical and moral guides, to come to acknowledge the power and also the harmony of healthy living provided by Nature's guiding light—these would lead one toward better health and better living. When combined with vegetarian diets, hydrotherapy, and the larger ideas of anarchism, solar therapy, and perhaps even nudism could make healthier revolutionaries.

Conclusion

Like their counterparts in Spain or France, many anarchists in Cuba were convinced of the necessity to reorient people's lives not only at the workplace or in society, but also in the individual body itself. By reorienting one's physical appearance and behavior, men, women, and children could more closely align themselves with Nature. In Cuba after 1898 workers increasingly suffered from the rise of industrial capitalism. Anarcho-naturists wanted to reorient people's lifestyles to better cope with these transformations. They urged people to reject the official medical establishment, which they charged was more interested in money-making and power than in preventative care and poor people's health. Injections of serums were considered antinatural and scientifically invalid.

When required by law, such injections were seen as authoritarian. By following a vegetable- and fruit-based diet, growing one's own fresh food, avoiding alcohol and stimulants, taking solar and hydro therapy, and going about in the nude, people could avoid most diseases and ailments. When they did become ill, naturists offered health practices like baths, massages, therapies, homeopathic aids, and the healing power of the sun as cures.

However, anarcho-naturists insisted that these benefits were not enough in and of themselves. Avoiding vice, eating health food, and taking steam baths alone would never challenge the underlying socioeconomic forces that created the poor conditions in the first place. Ultimately, through regeneration and organization, anarcho-naturists sought to liberate people from the misery and ailments they encountered in early twentieth-century Cuba. These revolutionaries offered practical advice about health while contributing affordable health initiatives for all. And in their countercultural minds, these anarchist preventatives and treatments were just what the naturist doctor ordered to combat the ills of bourgeois culture.

8

Rejecting Civilization

Nature, Salvation, and the Rural Ideal in Anarcho-Naturism

What is the city but a dung heap? Every evil of the body and soul accumulates in the city. Here, one cannot think, breathe, nor live healthy.

The character Bertín in *El tesoro escondido*

As we have seen, anarcho-naturist health advocates and practitioners promoted healthy living and health clinics for the island's urban residents within a larger socioeconomic critique that promoted social liberation, not just individual recuperation, as the movement's ultimate goal. The institutes helped people recover, or at least replace, what anarcho-naturists believed modern, urban, capitalist civilization had stolen from them: healthy, spontaneous, happy lives in harmony with Nature. Many further believed that cities represented a modern, industrial civilization founded on and filled with filth and exploitative labor. They were convinced that industrial civilization, as one increasingly encountered in Cuba, had been created by and for a select few on the island, not the average resident who suffered under the weight of disease and exploitation.

To counter these perceptions, several anarcho-naturists believed that one found "true" Nature in rural areas. Ideally, the countryside was the best place to engage the sun, live on the land, breathe fresh air, and do noble labor. Although the countryside might not be unspoiled by the worst of civilization, at least it was believed to be healthier and purer than cities. These anarchists portrayed living the rural ideal as a means for getting back in touch with Nature's laws of equality, harmony, justice, and mutual aid. But of course not everyone could pack up and head to the hills. Consequently, when people like Adrián del Valle promoted a rural ideal, they did more than encourage Cubans to abandon the cities. More important, they offered Cubans an image of a harmonious, tranquil lifestyle that both urban and rural industrial capitalism had supplanted. Del Valle and his associates represented rural life in mostly nostalgic ways, with representations promoting an ideal environment and a code of human conduct for salvation from capitalist industrialization. They designed these images to appeal to both urban and rural audiences. Cubans could read about and imagine these rural ideals, then look around them and see how far removed they were from Nature.

Debating "Civilization" and "Nature"

To say that these "back to nature" anarchists were against civilization is really to say that they opposed modern civilization rooted in industrial capitalism and the consequent socioeconomic as well as environmental transformations that ensued. Philosophically, these anarchists had roots in the philosophies of Paris-based *naturista* Henri Zisly. Zisly described himself and his followers as "anti-scientific libertarians," meaning that they rejected cars, engines, machines, and especially cities. In a letter published in *¡Tierra!* in 1903, Zisly described his anticity sentiments this way: "Naturists combat the conglomeration of many people—such as we find in cities—because from such situations inevitably are born all social evils: diseases, epidemics, unhealthiness, prostitution, authority, excessive work, alcoholism, fictitious necessities." Zisly concluded that *naturistas* preferred to live off the land without cultivating it, but recognized how some cultivation probably was necessary.[1]

This is not to say that anarchists as a whole and anarcho-naturists specifically hated all things "modern" or that all anarchists even rejected the idea of cities. But the critique of the modern city had long been integral to anarchist thinking in Europe. To writers like Kropotkin, Elisée Reclus, and William Morris, modern cities were the direct consequence of industrial development. Without planning, their unchecked expansion spread ever deeper into fertile lands, while workers in the cities' cores increasingly were cut off from the land. These anarchist thinkers sought a new kind of city that was planned with the interests of the residents in mind, and which would exist in balance with the countryside. The Spanish engineer Fernando Tarrida del Mármol's late nineteenth-century articles published in the Spanish anarchist press described a "free anarchist municipality" that rejected unlimited growth and was organized around a mutualist concept of society in which people alternated and cooperated in growing food around the edges of the city as well as producing the population's necessities in the city. The key to creating the "new communitarian urbanism" was balance between agricultural and industrial labor and a harmonization "of all things urban and all things rural."[2] The anarchists saw the surrounding cities, like Havana, falling far short of this harmonious balance. Consequently, to denounce civilization was to denounce the way cities existed at the end of the nineteenth and beginning of the twentieth centuries. Anarchists of all delineations considered these types of cities to be some of the greatest inhibitors of human beings living freely, equally, and harmoniously with the natural world and thus with one another.[3]

However, not all of Cuba's anarchists agreed with their anarcho-naturist brethren who criticized civilization in broad, sweeping strokes. One writer calling himself "Dr. Solagua" challenged the anticivilization streak of many *naturistas*. The "doctor" suggested that human progress resulted from the need to find food and to cure illness. Each step in curing illness was an evolutionary step in human progress, part of a civilizing process. Far from calling for a return to the land and rejection of machinery, the writer argued that planes, ships, and trains more quickly transported food and thus were ultimately beneficial to humans, "in spite of the obstacles that private interests put in the way of this." Civilization was a fine thing once the commercializing tendencies in its midst were purged. Thus, Dr. Solagua concluded, the attacks on "civilization" should stop.[4]

Although the debate over the meaning of "Civilization" continued, another debate on the meaning of "Nature" ensued. Not everyone accepted the quasi-religious and even legalistic overtones often ascribed to the word "Nature." The anarcho-naturist writer Eugenio Leante issued such a warning in 1912. He criticized those who saw and described Nature in religious and legal terms. Leante noted that some people viewed Nature as a "god," the result of "our 'religious education.'" Others spoke of Nature as being "very wise" or "very capricious." Leante condemned such phrases as the equivalent of saying "God is omnipotent"—a blasphemy among atheistic anarchists. To rectify this deification of Nature, Leante urged a solid scientific education. Yet, too often even those who subscribed to scientific views of Nature spoke of Nature's "laws." Leante believed this was equally abhorrent. Some anarchists spoke of Nature in holy terms following years of religious indoctrination in the mainstream culture; similarly, Leante concluded that speaking of Nature's laws reflected life in an environment saturated with lawyers and legislators.[5] Consequently, to speak of Nature was fine. However, in the continuous battle to regenerate the individual as well as the social body and consciousness away from the corrupting influences of the present society, people had to watch their words. One should not ascribe legal, political, or religious connotations to it.[6]

Leante voiced a minority view in Cuba's anarchist circles. His public critique of how some anarcho-naturists described Nature in religious terms was unique for a contemporary. The invocation of a nostalgic and quasi-religious image of Nature was common throughout international anarchist circles because it reflected an imagined ideal state of harmony, equality, and justice where all worked cooperatively. They believed that modern capitalist industrialization and centralizing states denigrated this natural order with their competition, hierarchies, and filth-plagued cities. Leante's attacks against talking about Nature in terms of "laws" also countered the majority anarchist opinion. Kropotkin and other anarchists like Reclus, both professional geographers, popularized the notion that anarchism was not only a labor or social movement but also provided a scientific view of the natural world. In particular, Kropotkin believed that mutual aid, not the struggle for survival, was the primary engine moving evolution. "Happily enough, competition is not the rule either in the animal world or in mankind. It is limited among animals to exceptional periods, and natural selection finds better fields for its activity. Better conditions," Kropotkin concluded, "are created by the *elimination of competition* by means of mutual aid and mutual support. In the great struggle for life—for the greatest possible fullness and intensity of life with the least waste of energy—natural selection continually seeks out the ways precisely for avoiding competition as much as possible."[7] Kropotkin theorized that human cooperation had yet to be totally destroyed by modern competitive society or the state. In fact human society could not have survived had it eliminated this fundamental law of Nature. To believers, this lent considerable weight to the anarchist position that Nature was guided by certain laws of mutualism, harmony, equality, and justice. That these laws may have been hard to observe, noted anarchists who disagreed with Leante, was owing to the unnatural (or even antinatural) forces of capitalism and politics. In short, "political man" was unmaking "natural man."

One central natural image repeatedly expressed in anarchist propaganda was land. Anarcho-naturists and anarcho-communists in particular filled their speeches and literature with romantic notions of the land embodied in phrases like "land and freedom." Not only was the "land" to be held and worked in common, but it was also to be the realm where people regained the natural elements of mutual aid and solidarity. Like Kropotkin, they argued that these natural elements had never been destroyed. Thus, most anarcho-naturists were convinced of the need for land and open spaces to perform worthwhile labor and receive the benefits of the sun and fresh air.

Some Cuban reformers like Socialist Francisco Carrera y Justiz suggested that open spaces in the cities could accomplish this. He proposed that municipal governments provide parks. Basing his estimates on the appropriate number and size of parks on figures from London and Washington, D.C., Carrera y Justiz suggested that one acre of park was required for every 200 people. With Havana's population of 500,000 in 1925, the city would need 2,500 acres of parks.[8] Anarchists liked parks, but they saw them as nice places to offer a brief respite; however, in and of themselves they were inadequate for reorienting one's life. Besides, anarchists found little socio-emancipatory effect resulting from people strolling through a park. Rather, land—that is, living on the land and working on the land—was the necessary element for a regenerative life in harmony with Nature, anarcho-naturists argued. Julián Magdalena, in the religious tones that so riled people like Leante, suggested that the land could even baptize and make reborn those people succumbing to antinatural vices associated with industrialization. Magdalena stressed that people, especially workers, must take responsibility for their own conditions. If people had land and if they were to work it daily for two hours, then so much would be different. No longer would there be a need for war and other unnatural products that result in the exchange of one's labor to a state's military or a capitalist for a mere crumb of bread. Instead, Magdalena concluded, workers could feed and house themselves and disengage from the capitalist (and thus antinatural) world.[9]

Nevertheless, not everyone could move to the country and begin to work with their hands. For this reason, anarcho-naturists urged people residing in cities to live on the cities' edges where they could escape the urban noise, stifling air, and pollution while tending vegetable gardens for nutrition and flower gardens to please the eyes and nose. They advised that a clean home on a city's fringes could be "like a tabernacle that guards the best and most intimate things of your life."[10] However, one huge problem stood in the way of the anarcho-naturists' romantic notion of land, countryside, and escape from civilization: early twentieth-century rural Cuba looked nothing like a place for modeling workers' tabernacles.

The Cuban Countryside

While anarchists conjured images of a bucolic rural environment, Cuba's countryside underwent an industrial transformation rivaling that of the cities. Anarcho-naturists charged that sugar plantations brought the same health and social problems to rural areas that they attributed to urban industrial civilization. In 1912 Dr. Luciano Soto described the irony that in Cuba urban dwellers actually appeared more healthy than rural dwellers, who suffered from an abundance of illnesses like anemia, tuberculosis, yellow fever, malarial fever, and intestinal problems. In framing the anarcho-naturist interpretation of modern Cuba, he argued that in "civilized nations" rural dwellers had large huts with tiled floors, kitchens designed so that smoke could escape, and animals living outside; these same rural residents ate inexpensive, fresh, and abundant food. Yet, this was not the case in Cuba, and especially not on the sugar and tobacco plantations where workers ate what Soto saw as an unhealthy rice-jerked beef-codfish diet and lived in filthy, dirt-floored *bohíos*.[11] In fact, jerked beef and codfish were the main sources of protein for rural workers. Certainly, vegetarians looked with scorn at this diet. But most rural workers found it increasingly difficult to get even this food. Although the rural population increased after independence, its ability to consume basic protein declined through poor wages and high prices. From 1905 to 1929, the consumption of these foodstuffs fell from 52 to 38 pounds per person. These protein sources were not replaced.[12]

Soto and other anarchists blamed unhealthy rural conditions on the expansion of sugar estates throughout the island and thus implicitly condemned the encroachment of North American capitalism. Even before the defeat of Spain in 1898, U.S. investors had begun purchasing Cuban sugar estates devastated by the war.[13] Immediately following the war, North American–based land companies purchased properties across the island. By 1905 these corporations and individuals owned 60 percent of rural Cuba, Spaniards living on the island owned another 15 percent, and Cubans owned an additional 25 percent of the island's rural properties.[14] With the return to Cuban civilian rule following the second occupation from 1906 to 1909, Cuba's Liberal Party promised rural workers that it would seek to improve the workers' plight, which all agreed was rooted in landlessness and dependence on plantation-based wage labor. Liberal President José Miguel Gómez refused to prohibit U.S. companies from any future purchases of Cuban land, but he did portray himself as a populist leader doing something for average Cubans. In an April 1910 address to Congress, he claimed that the solution required the state to acquire land and parcel it out to Cubans. This would help to alleviate rural poverty and slow the expansion of U.S. firms. However, nothing came of such plans.[15]

As demand for sugar in the United States surged, especially during World

War I, more and more Cuban land was transformed into agri-industrial complexes. Sugar production rose from nearly two and a half million tons in 1913 to more than four million tons in 1919.[16] Railroad companies expanded to connect new fields with ports and markets for export. The four largest companies added nearly 6,000 freight cars to their tracks from 1913 to 1920.[17] Between 1900 and 1926, sugar industrialists created seventy-five *centrales*. These were large, modern, mechanized agricultural factories with their own railway networks to quickly transport cane from the fields to the mill and from the mill to the port.[18] These complexes covered vast tracts of productive land, of which part was left uncultivated. As acquisition of extra land caused land prices in general to increase, many small-scale producers were no longer able to afford the purchase price. In addition, corporate *centrales* became major controllers of lands adjacent to them. These smaller "controlled" lands, not owned by the *central* corporation, were leased by the corporation for sugar production and then rented to farmers under contract to the corporation. However, the renters (*colonos*) had no outlets for their cane other than the corporate mill. The only feasible way to get *colono* cane to the corporate mill was along the corporate railway. This *colono* network proved vital to corporate profit. For instance, in 1920 the Manatí Sugar Company owned 25,000 acres of land, but a 1919 contract allowed the company control of another 37,000 acres. Thus, even "independent" farmers under contract were intimately linked to rural Cuba's industrial transformation.[19]

As sugar production expanded eastward, landowners increasingly cleared acres of forested lands that "were considered especially desirable in providing the conditions for productive cane agriculture due to their abundance of organic matter." Owners rejected open savannas for sugar because they "were often deficient in nutrients compared to the forests."[20] Throughout the first quarter of the twentieth century, forests fell at unprecedented rates: producers sought to bring ever larger amounts of acreage under cultivation, and formerly forested land planted in sugarcane actually lost fertility after about five years, which required even more land to be cleared.[21] It is estimated that in 1900 some 35 percent of Cuba was covered in forests; by 1940 this fell to 18 percent. By 1925 sugar industrialists had cleared forests at annual rates of about 100,000 hectares "or at twice as high as in any other historical record."[22]

As industrialists transformed the land, they also transformed the lives of workers. To work these lands, large numbers of laborers were brought in. They not only worked at but also lived close to the mill. Through immigration, natural population growth, and the *colono* system, farmers increasingly became proletarianized. For instance, by 1931, average farm families had 5.8 members. One child might gain his own piece of the family farm, but the other children generally had to work for wages away from the farm. Between 1898 and 1931, more than 73,000 persons older than fourteen years of age, who were born in rural Cuba, were incorporated into rural wage labor.[23] This process of proletarianization and alienation was visible on the Manatí lands. As the company expanded throughout eastern Cuba, owners laid plans to build living quarters for up to 3,000 sugar workers. Consequently, rural workers were herded into company towns and alienated from independent lives away from the *centrales*.[24] Just as this process began, anarchists appeared in the region. By 1914 anarchist supporters had emerged on the Manatí estate.[25]

The tense relationship between capital, land, and labor worsened during and immediately following World War I. Sugar strikes disrupted Cuba from 1917 to 1920. Some reformers blamed the strikes squarely on the social pressures arising from rural conditions and offered possible solutions, such as the one appearing in the pages of *Revista Cuba Contemporánea*. The intellectual Rogelio Pina argued that Cuba needed its own Homestead Act, modeled on the U.S. program. Under such a proposal, rural workers would receive enough land for self-sufficiency and agree to devote the four-month sugar harvest season (*zafra*) to the *centrales*. During the eight-month dead season, these small landowners would work for their own livelihoods. Supposedly, this would undercut any drive to go on strike, pacify the rural workforce, and contribute to nationalizing Cuban lands.[26] Like others plans to solve rural crises, the government ignored this one in favor of using the army to settle rural uprisings.

Obviously, descriptions by contemporaries and historians did not match the rural life envisioned by anarcho-naturists. In reality, rural life was carved up by industrialists and their allies in the government, a direct contradiction to an anarchist-defined rural ideal. The abysmal conditions of Cuba's rural workers reflected this larger economic and environmental transformation.

Yet, despite these conditions, the anarchist vision of a more harmonious rural life full of simplicity, health, and camaraderie could appeal to rural workers. Anarchist strongholds in Cuba existed mainly in Havana, the principal site for anarchist organizing and the anarchist press. However, when one examines weekly anarchist newspapers like *¡Tierra!*, which regularly published the names and locations of contributors to the newspaper, often large percentages of income came from outside Havana. In fact, by examining the weekly contributions to *¡Tierra!* from 1903 to 1914, one discovers that financial support from smaller cities and towns as well as the countryside was crucial to the newspaper's frail bottom line. An analysis of *¡Tierra!*'s balance statements, published on the last page of each issue, reflects a rather surprising conclusion. When broken down annually, contributions from *habaneros* did not exceed those from throughout the country. Considerable amounts arrived to the paper's business office from other working-class cities like Cárdenas, Matanzas, Camagüey, Cienfuegos, and Santiago de Cuba. These frequently were matched by smaller contributions from *centrales* in the sugar zones that spread ever eastward. Presumably, these financial supporters were likewise sympathetic to anarchism. In addition, the person who sent in a few centavos or pesos from Morón, Cienfuegos, Manatí, Holguín, or Cruces also shared his or her copy of the newspaper with others, by either passing it along to others or reading it aloud.[27]

Beyond this, in the decade following independence, Cuba's internal migration patterns contradicted the global norm in that rural populations actually increased more rapidly than urban populations, as illustrated by Table 8.1. Except for the western province of Pinar del Río, the ratio of urban-to-rural inhabitants fell in every Cuban province between 1899 and 1907. In short, while urban populations increased, rural populations, especially in the large agricultural zones of Camagüey, Matanzas, and Santa Clara, grew at faster rates. This was a direct consequence of the growth of a rural industrialized workforce on the *centrales*. Add to this that anarchist organization grew considerably in the

Table 8.1. Percent of Urban Inhabitants by Province, 1899–1907

Province	Population of Cities with at least 1,000 Inhabitants		Percent of Total Population	
	1899	1907	1899	1907
Total	740,283	899,667	47.1	43.0
Camagüey	35,543	43,798	40.1	37.0
Havana	328,947	401,629	77.4	74.7
Matanzas	103,578	109,641	51.2	45.7
Oriente	108,747	133,143	33.2	29.3
Pinar del Río	22,337	43,628	12.9	18.2
Santa Clara	141,131	167,828	39.5	36.7

Source: Cuba: Population, History and Resources, 1907. Washington, D.C.: U.S. Census Bureau, 1909, 136–37.

1910s in central Cuba around Cruces and Santa Clara. The Cruces movement became so strong from 1911 to 1915 that the government had to repress it and deport the movement's organizers.

"Civilization" and the Rural Ideal in Anarchist Fiction

Thus there existed both a growing urban and rural audience for the anarchist message. For thirty years, anarchists described the contrast between Civilization and Nature in newspaper columns and speeches. But by the time the movement hit its zenith in the 1920s, the best expressions of the anarchist rural ideal could be found in Adrián del Valle's fiction. Del Valle placed many of his stories in rural settings to some extent if not entirely. He portrayed rural life as purer than civilization, which is a term that, for Del Valle, encompassed cities, governments, and capitalism. For instance, in the novella *Camelanga*, two political parties, both led by doctors and generals, vie for control of the model republic of Camelanga. A civil war leads to twenty years of dictatorship, and foreigners are invited in to exploit the country's natural resources. The expansion of capitalism brings roads, railroads, telephones, and telegraphs, "but where these haven't yet arrived, things remain as before." Ultimately the dictator's illegitimate son Marcial leads a revolt that topples his father. Marcial reigns as the new president, but quickly becomes disillusioned with politics. As the story ends, Marcial travels to the mountains of Camelanga where he goes to study, farm, and raise chickens. His life is full and content, so much so that when the republic is threatened again and a governmental commission pleads with him to run for public office, he refuses. The disillusioned revolutionary finds harmony in simple living and work in the "natural" countryside, not the "unnatural" political scheming he left behind in the capital city.[28]

The same theme of a political leader abandoning politics and fleeing to a more natural rural life arises again in the novella *El príncipe que no quiso gobernar* [*The Prince Who Didn't Want to Govern*]. Filiberto's first order of business upon becoming ruler is to tour the country clandestinely dressed as a *campesino*. One day on his tour, the incognito prince engages poor *campesinos* in a café. They discuss how society should be organized. The first says that everyone should work for one day per week. When the prince asks who would work the machines or produce the art, the *campesino* responds that most of the actual work is now done so that only a few can enjoy the art or products produced by the many anyway. A second *campesino* advises that the rich and poor take turns working so that all can equally enjoy the fruits of labor. A third *campesino* would issue a decree that "from all for all, and each lives by his work."[29] Frustrated with his governing council's refusal to implement social and economic reforms following his return, Filiberto abandons his reign and leaves the palace. Five years later, his former advisor Ploticus finds Filiberto raising a family in a fertile valley. Filiberto explains to him that here he lives happily by cultivating the land in harmony with Nature.

A true proponent of *naturismo*, Del Valle filled his stories with the redemptive powers of the land and rural life, as seen through both Marcial and Filiberto's characters. This salvation quality of the land comes through clearly again in the novella *Cero*. The title character has fled society to scratch out a humble existence in the Cuban hills. One day Cero encounters a lost, disoriented man who has forgotten his identity, so Cero names him Cero-Cero and takes the man to his modest farm. During the next thirteen years the two men live and work together in solidarity, friendship, and trust. Then one day Cero-Cero regains his memory and recalls that he is Alonso Castillejos, president of the Banco Intercomercial in Havana, who was once worth $10 million. He decides to abandon their rural home and return to Havana. Castillejos's long lost family, friends, and business associates do not warmly receive him, however. After nearly a year of mental depression in Havana, Castillejos writes Cero of his plan to abandon the city and return to the farm. In grand fashion, Castillejos fakes his own suicide and flees back to the countryside. In the end, Cero-Cero lives, but Alonso Castillejos is dead. The former capitalist and member of the elite is "reborn" as a rural peasant.[30]

One of the best examples of anarchist fiction that focuses on the rural ideal and Nature's regenerative powers is Del Valle's novella *El tesoro escondido* [*The Hidden Treasure*]. Not only are the anarcho-naturist issues of land and redemption central, but the story also includes references to Cuban independence, involves issues of race, and takes on the Cuban medical establishment. Set on the island of Bacuya (easily recognized as Cuba, and in fact possibly a play on words: "Cuba, ya" or Cuba now), the story opens with a focus on the white Bertín and the black Bertón—two long-time friends and veterans of the island's three wars for independence. Bertín laments the island's economic dependence on foreign capital, especially the loss of landownership. "The land should be owned in common by the nation, given to those who wish to cultivate it, with the right only to those products derived from his labor," argues Bertín.[31]

One day Bertín and Bertón travel to the capital city to see the sights and visit

Bertín's four grandsons. All four aspire to be or are part of the bourgeoisie. One is in the military, another is a priest, a third is a government lawyer, and the fourth is a medical official. "Four professionals who consume and do not produce," laments Bertín.[32] Although all the grandsons are pleased to see their eighty-four-year-old grandfather, each encounter quickly turns ugly when Bertín criticizes their life choices. For example, Bertín criticizes the lawyer Gonzalo for helping the government betray the ideals of the revolution by turning the country into a land of salaried laborers working for foreign capital. "I am an enemy, today as yesterday, to all those that want to convert Bacuya into a feudal estate," announces Bertín.[33] Finally, Bertín meets his grandson Anselmo, the medical official. Anselmo asks Bertín if he believes in medicine. The grandfather snaps to attention and declares he neither believes in medicine nor doctors but in clean living, sun, fresh air, and exercise. To emphasize the point, and true to the naturist undertones of the story, Bertín claims that he neither takes medicine nor visits doctors. At this point Bertín, noting their unhealthy looking pale faces, tries to get Anselmo to move his family to the countryside. Bertín asks, "What is the city but a dung heap? Every evil of the body and soul accumulates in the city. Here, one cannot think, breathe, nor live healthy." When Anselmo tries to point out that cities represent a certain level of civilization with beneficial inventions like automobiles, Bertín responds that "the cities are social tumors whose disintegration would be most convenient for the health of human society."[34]

Five years pass after this meeting. There is no contact between the grandsons and Bertín except for a few letters written between the grandfather and Anselmo. Bertín dies, and, per his request, Bertón sends letters to all four grandchildren. The letters claim that Bertín has hidden a treasure behind his house. To get it the four grandsons must come to the countryside to dig up the land in order to find it. After several days of hard work, the brothers unearth a box buried on Bertín's land. Inside they discover a letter telling the four that the land now belongs to them, but the owners must agree to cultivate it. If no one accepts these terms, then the land becomes the possession of the city of Coabá. However, the letter warns that the land cannot be used as a means of exploitation and gaining wealth. Rather, it must serve "as a natural source of life." Only the frustrated doctor Anselmo accepts the "treasure." As the story concludes, Anselmo turns to Bertón, tells him of his decision to move to the countryside and work the land, and adds "you will teach me to cultivate the land. You will be my *compañero*."[35]

Adrián del Valle's fiction often played around the edges of the anticivilization theme; yet, his novel *Náufragos* [*Castaways*] takes the theme to a new level in comparison with that of other anarchist writers or even his other works. In this novel, the character of Alvar is a Cuban doctor disenchanted with his life and in particular the medical profession that he recently has abandoned. Fed up with civilization, he travels the world searching for a harmonious life. As the novel opens, Alvar is sailing on the steamer *Sirius* from San Francisco to Hawai'i. In the opening dialogue between himself and a Chilean engineer named Beltrán, Alvar lays out his opposition to professional medicine and his growing advocacy of *naturista* health ideas; he notes that "my professional practice has made me doubt the effectiveness of current curative methods. I believe that, instead of making the sick better with drugs, what we do is adapt them to a morbid state that pretends to be their normal constitution, but in reality restricts their human lives." Thus, this former medical doctor implicates the medical profession for merely treating patients' symptoms and in so doing relegating patients to continue their lives in misery. Ultimately, he notes, "with each passing day, civilization deviates away from the natural life."[36]

Midway to Hawai'i, a Chilean tycoon's yacht pulls alongside the *Sirius* in a medical emergency. The yacht's doctor is dying, and the owner Don Pedro asks Alvar to sail with them to Hawai'i. During the journey Alvar helps heal a Chilean Indian servant suffering from tuberculosis. He also offers naturist advice to cure Don Pedro's rheumatism and the captain's ulcer. However, shortly after his arrival the yacht explodes, sending seven people to a lifeboat suddenly cast adrift in the vastness of the Pacific Ocean. The seven (Alvar, a sailor, a female servant, and four aristocrats) land on a deserted island they name Carolina. The castaways are stranded on the island for two years. In that time, Alvar sees how healthy eating, robust work, sunshine, and fresh air have improved the health of all the castaways, particularly the aristocrats. All begin contributing to make life better, and as they do so the class differences between them begin to fade. Alvar is convinced that the reason lies in having escaped civilization. "Observing all of this, he [Alvar] smiled delightedly, thinking that there, with neither the conventionalities nor the egoisms imposed by civilized society, the survivors were demonstrating their individual natural and spontaneous inclinations."[37]

This setting, which Alvar finds idyllic, is enhanced when he and the sailor Oliver discover a nearby, inhabited Polynesian island. Here the natives seem to live in a savage paradise where the word "savage" has positive connotations compared to "civilization." The islanders' religion has no priests and their leader is more a figurehead than an autocrat. Men, women, and children frolic much of the day and swim nude together with no pretensions of social division or moral repugnance to the naked body among them. When Oliver asks whether the islanders are happier than they are, Alvar says yes, because civilized people have lost touch with this natural harmony based on being in contact with the land and its surroundings. "Civilized people cannot enjoy that state. We have believed too much in necessities. We are slaves of too many interests."[38] He adds that "civilized" people work harder than these "savages," obtaining fewer useful products from their labor and all while seeing themselves and their children brutalized by those in power—a message that Cuban workers could doubtlessly appreciate.

The islanders tell the castaways not to expect a rescue ship any time soon. It had been 20 years since a ship had passed by their island of Maruba. To this Alvar proposed that the castaways begin to have children to populate their little slice of paradise. The idea repulses some because they would do so outside of a civilization-defined concept of civil and religious wedlock. Others do not want to believe that they will spend the rest of their lives on the island. Still, Alvar wonders, could a truly regenerative people be organized on this island? After all, his building blocks were not the most socially redeeming of people; they were vice-filled, vice-driven capitalists and aristocrats. While "bad social traits" would not necessarily be passed on to any children, the fact that the children's parents were afflicted by vice had to have a negative effect on their bodies and thus on any resulting children. However, if the parents were to convert fully to a naturist lifestyle and any children were raised from birth this way, then perhaps through good diet, fresh air, and vice-free living the next generation on Carolina could be the basis for a regenerated humanity. "The true organizational labor had to begin with the next generation—labor that was primarily educational, of which Alvar would be in charge. He had to cultivate the sentiments of self-worth, solidarity and mutual aid in the children. The land for all, the products of labor for all, with each having the same rights and no more than anyone else. A placid and tranquil life with plenty of room for games, diversions, and all other individual inclinations."[39] But Alvar's dream is short-lived.

Soon a Protestant missionary ship arrives and rescues the castaways, but Alvar remains with his native lover Nureya.[40] The missionaries return to Maruba and change the peaceful "savages" into "Christians." As Alvar feared would happen, a nitrate company arrives to mine the island's rich guano beds, changing the islanders into miserable, poorly paid wage laborers. Owing to a supposed shortage of workers, the New York–based Maruba Phosphate Company imports Chinese laborers. All workers now live in filthy huts and shacks, while the island's new white residents enjoy spacious, clean, electric homes. The workers increasingly succumb to civilization's vices like crime, theft, prostitution, and especially alcohol. The new clothes they wear restrict their health and spontaneity. They eat less fruit and more canned goods imported from the United States. Days previously filled with games, dancing, and song, now are filled with hard, dangerous toil, and enjoyment is restricted to Sunday afternoons. Lastly, these conditions spur a rise in previously unknown ailments, especially tuberculosis and suicide.[41] While anarchists and naturists saw their long-running critiques reflected in *Náufragos*, Del Valle's wider working-class Cuban audience also surely recognized these same predicaments in their own lives: the encroachment of international corporations, shifting diets, fewer hours of the day for enjoyment, increases in working-class immigration to labor in the expanding rural economy, and of course the transformation and exploitation of everyone's Nature for the profit of a few.

This transformation of the "primitive" island equally impacts Alvar's thinking on civilization and primitivism. Alvar comes to see that one cannot return to a precivilized life. "How chimerical it was to think of returning to a primitive state. The virginity of the people, like that of maidens, cannot be recovered after it is lost. The happy island had been converted into a disgraced island; paradise into hell." With the departure of his fellow inhabitants on Carolina, Alvar had lost his hopes of creating a new society there. The arrival of missionaries and capitalists on Maruba had spoiled his dream of living in a primitive state of Nature. Now, Alvar decides to act for the present. He begins secretly organizing the workers for a strike. A march to the company director's office, however, results in workers being shot at and forcibly returned to work. Like many of Del Valle's real colleagues in Cuba, Alvar is arrested and deported as a pernicious foreigner.

Upon returning to the U.S. mainland, Alvar makes his way to New York City, which he sees embodying all that is wrong with civilization. Through a series of coincidences, Alvar meets up again with Don Pedro and his former fellow castaways. Don Pedro, back to form in a capitalist environment and corresponding mentality, demands that Alvar accept a payment of 30,000 pesos for Alvar's medical service over the two years they were together on Carolina. Alvar reluctantly accepts the money, and then he devises a plan. He will return to Cuba and buy a plot of fertile land. There he will found a colony for men and women to live equally, freely, naturally, and in a spirit of mutual aid. "In sum, at least here could be a tentative effort to create a small social Utopia in order to observe how far it was possible for the animal-man to transform himself into the rational man." But before Alvar can return to Cuba, he is run over by a New York streetcar. Technology and urban civilization finally do him in.[42]

Adrián del Valle's fiction became a primary vehicle for the anarcho-naturist "back to the land" message that portrayed the benefits of rural life and work. In a sense, anarchists and naturists offered an imagined rural ideal as a source of salvation for both urban and rural workers—an ideal that challenged the effects of industrial civilization in both the cities and countryside. Ultimately, anarchist fiction offered utopian hopes for a revolutionary alternative to their contemporary lives. Yet, at the same time, this fiction portrayed rural settings that were disappearing from Cuba, thus reflecting how far the capitalist industrialization of the countryside was transforming rural Cuba.

It may be telling that this idyllic vision of what could be and what had been was written by a man who did not labor with his hands and who lived in cities his whole life. Undoubtedly, these stories appear to be out of touch with reality. But describing reality was only a part of Del Valle's agenda. In a larger sense, Del Valle was partly a realist and partly a dreamer. Thus, one must read these stories as he intended his audience to read them—as a combination of social realism and what scholars of utopian studies Lyman Tower Sargent and Kenneth Roemer call "social dreaming." That is, from a social realist perspective, Del Valle's stories portrayed (if not altogether accurately described) the everyday conditions of the poor, while criticizing the hegemonic culture that maintained those conditions. Meanwhile, the stories also portrayed situations "that encourage readers to experience vicariously a culture that represents a prescriptive, normative alternative to their own culture," that is, social dreaming.[43] The combination of social realism and social dreaming were defining frameworks in Del Valle's fiction. He attempted to both diagnose the Cuban situation and prescribe a solution from an anarcho-naturist perspective.

In the end, then, anarcho-naturists like Del Valle believed that the land and people's return to the land would redeem humanity. Yet, many barriers existed. As his character Alvar discovered, the escape from civilization originally had failed. Then trying to work for its redemption through aiding the dispossessed had resulted in his deportation, with no change to the islanders' conditions. Now, it was back to escaping from civilization. Buying a piece of land in order to build a rural anarcho-naturist utopia would, in a sense, "liberate" the land from capitalist control. Such liberation would at least allow some people to acknowledge and enhance Nature's natural moral and biological guides of mutual aid. Although no such anarcho-naturist commune appears to have been created in the first thirty years after Cuban independence, Del Valle nevertheless knew about such communes that were arising in Spain.[44] In part, his social dreaming of creating an escape was conditioned on what his international comrades were implementing in reality.

Conclusion

Anarchist authors, especially in Spain, had long incorporated Nature and rural images. As Lily Litvak has illustrated, "Nature permitted anarchists to promote their basic idea: anarchy did not intend to annul order and impose disorder, but instead to form a natural society without regulations or laws, because these are unnecessary. In such an environment, solidarity and mutual aid between mankind would develop spontaneously. Superimposed regulations and laws do nothing more than asphyxiate those instinctual and natural phenomenon [sic]. The essential base of anarchism is natural man, earlier and more fundamental historically than political man. It is the capitalist structure that has deformed mankind by dividing people into owners and slaves. From Nature, on the contrary, emerges the principle of equality among mankind."[45]

The return to a "natural" state was more than just a return to some "primitive natural harmony"; it was really a resurrection of what anarcho-naturists understood and put forward as a "true life," that which had been corrupted by capitalism and the modern state. This resurrection offered readers and listeners to these stories an imagined future that could save them from exploitation by capitalists, politicians, and priests—representatives of the hegemonic culture's "unholy trinity," as anarchists saw them. Yet, these images also suggested that people could take hold of their lives and, if not move to the country, then at least pursue lifestyles in harmony with simpler rural lifestyles described in these fictionalized images.

Del Valle took these concepts that were long a staple of Spanish anarchism and Cubanized them by putting them in Cuba, in places that were obviously Cuba, or in rural settings that experienced social processes similar to those faced in Cuba. When plotting a story in a rural setting, he appealed to both urban and rural workers. The former were shown multiple examples of healthy rural characters, free from the debilitating effects of tuberculosis, unhealthy skin, industrial labor systems, and urban vice. At the same time, this urban audience saw urban characters fleeing cities to the more natural, healthy, and regenerative environment of the countryside. The rural audience saw these same characters, too. However, they rarely saw the exploited Cuban *guajiro* or immigrant sugarcane cutter who would have been a part of the expanding agri-industrial sugar complex in Cuba during the decades following independence. Rather, Del Valle's characters were people who had disentangled themselves from capitalism as much as possible by rejecting the push of industrial civilization and living in the natural world of the countryside.

Del Valle was a dreamer. There is no record of how many people's imagination he touched. Certainly his nostalgic ideal did not exist, especially as international sugar interests dissected the island. To readers and listeners of his stories Del Valle presented a Cuba that, although corrupt, could escape the trials and hardships that most people on the island lived every day. In these stories, a type of civilization that promoted competition, hierarchy, and abuse of power infected people's lives. Del Valle hoped to instill in readers the possibility of finding elements of cooperation, mutual aid, and simple living in their present lives. Beyond this, the use of these fictional ideals presented readers a stark contrast with what they found around them. Just as Alvar witnessed the transformation of a peaceful, natural people after the arrival of religion and capitalism, readers witnessed a similar transformation in Cuba's recent history. From Del Valle's perspective, he hoped readers would ask questions: Must our lives be so miserable? Was this truly "progress"? And just how far removed from Nature were leaders taking the island?

Part III

Anarchism, Education, and the Family

9

Freedom Teaching

Anarchism and Education

Many individuals say to me: "those ideas that you profess are very good, but, who straightens men out? Who is capable of convincing an egoist that he ought to give up his egoism?" To this one can answer: in the same way that a religious person has convinced him to sacrifice himself for religious beliefs, and in the same way that the patriot has taught him to die defending his flag. For men to be able to live in a state of anarchy, they must be educated and this is precisely the work that has been done by those generous people who have been educators throughout the ages. . . . Without these athletes of thought, progress would be in its infancy.

Julián Sánchez (1925)

Anarchists directed their revolutionary programs specifically to help workers and their families not only live a better life in the present but also prepare them for a social revolution sometime in the future. To accomplish this, they led strike activities, helped create alternative health institutes, and championed the cause of a working class united across racial, national, and gender lines. Yet, anarchists believed all these efforts would be, if not useless, then at least less effective if the people were uneducated. Consequently, anarchists saw education as an essential revolutionary tool to raise the consciousness of Cubans. To this end, Cuba's anarchists devoted considerable time and scarce resources to develop schools during the first decades of independence when education was a hotly debated issue across the island.

This chapter focuses on two distinct eras of Cuban anarchist education (1898–1912 and 1922–1925) within the context of Cuban education generally and the island's anarchist movement specifically. Anarchist schools were one of many educational options for Cubans following independence from Spain. Like Cuban nationalists and proponents of public education, anarchists believed that religious schools, especially Catholic institutions, increasingly educated only the rich and thus countered ideals of equality and freedom from religious indoctrination. However, anarchists also disliked public schools, which they believed taught a blind form of patriotic nationalism. Anarchists believed that this patriotic education countered socialist working-class internationalism and stifled children's individual thought.

The schools' periodic successes (measured by growth in the numbers of students as well as the continuation of established schools and the opening of new ones) generally coincided with the ups and downs of the anarchist cause within the Cuban labor movement. From 1898 to 1912, with worker organizations divided and in disarray, anarchist educational experiments foundered due to a combination of personality conflicts, shortages of funds, lack of worker interest, and governmental repression.

During the next decade, anarchists and other labor radicals reorganized and focused their attention away from education. In the 1920s, the Cuban working class created the largest labor organizations on the island since the late nineteenth century. As before independence, anarchists occupied central leadership positions in these organizations. Anarchists, in conjunction with Marxists, then used their leadership positions in these organizations to create a new wave of schools. Better organization, larger membership, pansectarian alliances, and increased resources provided more funds to open schools across the island. Still, while the island's labor organization was as strong as ever in the mid-1920s, and the schools created by anarchist-led groups and union organizations expanded, Cuba's labor radicals could not escape the impending governmental crackdown against radicals and foreigners. By 1925, anarchist-based rationalist schools, now squarely adopted by not only anarchists but also other Cuban leftists, came to an abrupt end under President Machado.

Cuban Education Before and After Independence

By 1842, Spanish authorities had established a general plan for public instruction in Cuba under joint government and Church control. In 1871 the government issued a new public instruction decree whose preamble highlighted the political orientation of educational reforms. Coming in the midst of Cuba's first war for independence (1868–1878), the Spanish government sought to create schools that not only would educate but also hispanicize Cubans "to the end that the dominion of Spain in the Antilles may be permanently assured," as the new decree stated.[1] The resulting system focused less on providing a well-rounded education for the Cuban masses and more on indoctrinating Cubans to be loyal servants of Spain.[2] The 1871 decree further suggested that earlier reforms emphasizing liberal arts studies over religious instruction were fatally flawed, and, if not corrected soon, the result would be a continual downward spiral to moral and social decay: "As intelligence has gradually become disseminated the number of offences against person and property, of criminal assaults, of illegitimate unions, of foundlings, of cases of mental aberration, of suicides, have palpably increased, in proportion not alone to the extension, but also to the higher degree, of education."[3] In essence, Spanish officials now feared that widespread liberal education eroded social order, debilitated the minds of colonists, and caused revolt. Officials began to reemphasize religious instruction and passed a new law in 1880 that made elementary school compulsory, with clergy maintaining strict supervision. In addition, although all races were to have equal access to education, the Church continued to prohibit coeducational classrooms.[4] When war erupted in 1895, education played an important rhetorical role. Revolutionaries criticized the colonial educational system as one more repressive tool of imperialism. José Martí drew upon his own liberal inclinations in attacking Catholic education, which he saw as designed to preach loyalty to the Spanish Crown and Rome.[5]

At war's end in 1898, the state of education was, by most contemporary accounts, dismal. Such assessments, made by Cuban liberals and North American occupiers alike, undoubtedly reflected a level of anti-Spanish bias designed to justify completely overhauling the educational system that virtually lay in ruins following the war. Whatever the bias, the system was in fact in total disarray and did not meet the standards expected for a new nation that was to be founded on liberal republican values. Following Spain's defeat, U.S. occupation authorities concluded that compulsory education rarely had been enforced given insufficient public expenditures, insufficient numbers of schools, wealthy families choosing to send their children abroad, and Spanish Captain-General Valeriano Weyler closing most schools except in provincial capitals and garrisoned towns occupied by Spanish forces during the war.[6]

From 1898 to 1902, U.S. occupiers and Cuban officials transformed the island's education system. Administrators appointed the respected Cuban intellectual Enrique José Varona as secretary of public instruction. Varona and Commissioner of Public Schools Matthew E. Hanna redesigned Cuban public education to follow models in vogue in the United States at the turn of the century. The new educational system stressed a mix of formal classroom instruction in the liberal arts as well as manual instruction. Manual instruction would help a child learn real-life skills, especially in agriculture.[7] Instruction also had a specific civics-oriented purpose that would be reinforced by creating the "School City," a model first tested in New York City schools in 1897 by its creator, Wilson L. Gill. The School City, chartered in Havana by Gill in the spring of 1901, aimed to teach the rights and obligations of living in a republican democracy. Gill and Hanna argued that to educate students without some specific training in republicanism would invite disaster for the society. In Cuba, students without this instruction were believed to be especially at risk. As Hanna wrote in his 1901 annual report, the Cuban student now "lives in a democratic country, under a free flag, where he is told that the will of the people is supreme, but in the schoolroom he is surrounded by the influences of a monarchy, where authority is wielded with the rod and the will of the teacher is supreme." According to Hanna, these "impressions made on the mind of the child by constant association are indelible, and if in the schoolroom he lives in an atmosphere of republicanism, feels that he has certain duties towards his playmates and certain rights in his relations with them, and that he is a part of the government, as well as one of the governed, the foundations will have been laid for a good citizen when this boy of to-day becomes the man of to-morrow."[8] Thus, an education for Cubans should both teach trades and instill a love of democracy.

This process to "republicanize" Cuban children not only emulated the U.S. model but also included teaching English in Cuban classrooms, sending nearly 3,000 Cubans to the United States for teacher training, and introducing U.S. textbooks in Spanish translation.[9] Just as the School City promoted acquisition of North American political and cultural values, language training would encourage further acculturation. Those gaining proficiency in English could look forward to individual mobility as trade relations were sure to intensify between the United States and Cuba. Ultimately, in the immediate postindependence years, public schools increasingly exposed Cuban children to a secular, liberal education. Throughout the first occupation, a rapidly expanding number of children learned the arts, civics, and trades. Although only 30,000 students attended classes in 1899, two years later 177,000 students were enrolled in public education, with an average attendance of 138,000 of those students.[10]

However, this is not to say that Cuban education after independence was entirely a North American construct. Beginning in 1909, the administration of President José Miguel Gómez began to implement new education laws that superseded those created during the military occupations of 1898–1902 and 1906–1909. For instance, these laws created daily and weekly curriculum guides and restructured the curriculum to meet the different needs of rural and urban students. By 1914, Enrique José Varona had become Cuba's vice president, which created a climate of heightened expectations for educational reform. These expectations were partially met by new Secretary of Education and the Arts Dr. Ezequiel García Enseñal, who further reformed the curriculum by emphasizing the need to stimulate children's imagination, decreasing rote memorization, raising the importance of nature and natural history study, and promoting pride in self, home, and country.[11] Despite some fifteen years of educational reforms since independence, however, many shortcomings remained: education funds siphoned off via corruption, insufficient numbers of school buildings under construction, overcrowded schools, shortages of books, and an "unhygienic" school environment in which most schools lacked playgrounds, running water or bathroom facilities, clean air (locations were too close to factories), and adequate natural surroundings (for example, few shade trees). The last two factors caused teachers to close windows and curtains, moves that further deprived overcrowded classrooms of fresh air.[12]

For those parents seeking an alternative to overcrowded public education, Cuba offered a plethora of private school options. For instance, in 1909 there were 316 private schools in Cuba; by 1925 there were 606.[13] Religious organizations dominated private education, and both Catholic and Protestant schools generally received praise from U.S. officials and Cuban leaders for their levels of instruction and moral discipline.[14] The variety of private schools had similar curricula but different goals. For instance, Jason Yaremko has shown how North America–based Protestant schools developed throughout the island, especially in eastern Cuba. Besides offering an arts and sciences curriculum, the schools' ultimate goal was "a 'Christian education' oriented toward conversion and salvation" in which students were taught to be "good Christians" and "useful citizens." To this end, Protestant schools taught ideals central to an expanding North American capitalist economy by training students from the lower classes to be efficient workers, housekeepers, and secretaries while emphasizing skills for middle- and upper-class students that would help them to become foremen and managers of the expanding sugar interests.[15] Not only religious institutions offered education. Feminists played a role, too. Although Cuba's public school system was coeducational, Cuban feminists had long argued that girls and women needed special educational opportunities. For instance, K. Lynn Stoner shows that in the late 1800s María Luisa Dolz, the "first woman to link educational reform with nationalism and feminism," believed education of women was key to righting social injustices. Although Dolz's schools aimed at the upper class in Cuba, twentieth-century feminists expanded this notion to working-class women by creating night schools and free classes, by which they hoped to educate women on how "to become men's companions" and thus temper men's inclination to violence.[16]

Consequently, in the first decades following independence, Cuba was awash in schools. The public schools were free, coeducational, and racially integrated. Gross enrollment levels rose, and some new school construction ensued. By the 1910s, educational theorists were promoting innovative ideas about creative learning and the need for clean, safe, hygienic schools. Private schools competed for students, especially those from the more privileged classes who could afford tuitions. In these schools, children could learn the basic arts and sciences, but for families seeking boys- or girls-only education with heavy doses of moral teaching, the Catholic schools were available. Those seeking to align themselves with the growing export economy linked to North American capital found Protestant schools to be an important option.

Anarchists and Cuba's Postindependence Educational System

Anarchists hated the Cuban school system after 1898. Even though the public schools were secular and tried to be pragmatic by teaching skills and trades, anarchists were never comfortable with larger political and ideological forces surrounding public education. They criticized everything from the conditions of schools and pedagogy to what they saw as outright patriotic indoctrination. Anarchist Vicente Carreras complained that he often saw children leaving schoolrooms with an almost savage joy, as though leaving captivity. And what did they do upon release from "captivity"? They would fling stones at old transients, place rocks on tram rails "for the thrill of seeing them derail," and torment birds and animals. Carreras did not blame the children. Rather, the fault lay with the larger social environment in which they were raised and schooled, especially "the false instruction they receive, the routines which they repeatedly faced."[17]

While the claustrophobic conditions of the public schools raised their ire, anarchists reserved their sharpest attacks for what they perceived as questionable political education and patriotic indoctrination of students. In his 1906 article "La imbecilidad triunfante" [Triumphant Stupidity], Tomás S. Gutiérrez complained that recent public school graduates merely had gone through the motions of mimicking their teachers' words about the government. When one asked these students about the "rights" and "obligations" they had supposedly studied, not a student could explain what a right or duty was. In essence, charged Gutiérrez, the public schools had created a mindless herd of youth who provided cannon fodder a few months later during the 1906 uprising.[18] Following the U.S. withdrawal in 1909, officials throughout Cuba began to emphasize the link between "patriotism" and "education." This was not entirely new on the island. In the first half of the nineteenth century, Cuban educational thinkers had linked nationalism and patriotism to education.[19] After 1909, both the Liberal government under Gómez and then the Conservative government under Mario G. Menocal supported using the schools to develop a sense of Cuban identity in children. For instance, in 1910 the government decreed that at the beginning of every day, students should say a pledge of allegiance to the Cuban flag. A 1914 regulation from the secretary of public instruction explicitly called for patriotic education in the classroom in order to develop "love of country" and "to form habits in children that facilitate the carrying out of their political and civil duties." To accomplish this, students were taught to love flag and country, study Cuban history and Cuban poets, and sing the National Anthem.[20] The irony is that such "nationalist" educational sentiments occurred exactly as the island plunged ever deeper into economic dependency on the United States.

Anarchists wasted little time in attacking these patriotic reforms. For instance, in April 1909, M. Moros related a day's lesson that his son had learned. According to Moros, the teacher told the children they should love the Cuban flag because it was a symbol of *la patria* and the children should respect the laws of *la patria* whether they were good or bad. Moros shamed teachers for creating and fostering what he saw as the artificial and unnatural sentiment of patriotism. He added that these self-proclaimed patriots professed that "*la patria* is territory where all individuals live under the same flag. I say that *la patria* is where all villains take refuge."[21] ¡*Tierra!* regularly echoed these anti-patriotic sentiments in anonymously written columns. In September 1910, the paper decried a recent decision by the secretary of public instruction to have schools regularly pledge and honor the Cuban flag. Referring to themselves as "*antibanderistas*" [those against saluting the flag], the editors urged readers to talk to their children and encourage them to reject paying allegiance to a "rag on the end of a pole" that symbolized closed mindedness and divisiveness.[22]

As discussed in chapter 2, anarchists detested patriotic nationalism because it artificially divided people who otherwise could be united around class interests. As was common in the global socialist and anarchist movements of the time, Cuban anarchists believed in socialist internationalism. They hoped to unite workers across all trades, skill levels, genders, races, and nationalities to fight not only what they viewed as the surge and scourge of international capitalism but also those who would promote isolation and insular pride, that is, nationalists. In the first decades following independence, anarchists had seen how "nationalist" elites regularly pitted Cuban workers against Spanish workers to break strikes, cause dissension in the island's labor movement, and thus undermine a strong, united labor force that was ineffective in pushing for higher wages and better conditions. Thus, when anarchists saw young Cubans being taught "Cuban" pride and other patriotic notions in the public schools, they viewed this as one more trick by the state to undermine international worker solidarity.

As noted above, the Catholic Church played a key role in colonial educational affairs in Cuba. The first U.S. occupation effectively ended outright Church interference in public affairs and likewise public schools. In fact, as Stoner points out, unmarried women were considered to be the best teachers in these new public schools. As she puts it, "Righteous women made appropriate replacements for the Religious who had been teachers. . . . In a sense, mother nationalists replaced the Mother Church as the guardians of Cuba's morality and the teachers of the young."[23] However, after the United States concluded its first occupation, anarchists expressed alarm at efforts to weld the church once again to public education. Apparently, the church had willing accomplices in the Department of Public Instruction. In his report to Governor Magoon, Acting Secretary of Public Instruction Lincoln de Zayas worried about what he saw as the overall failure of Cuba's public education system. He particularly lamented that many Cubans from the middle and upper classes chose to send their own children to private schools. The acting secretary argued this was not about keeping their sons and daughters from being educated in the company of blacks or the poor. Rather, he found a religious explanation. Elite families, he wrote, considered teaching religion to their children to be of primary importance, so they crowded their children into private religious boarding and day schools on the island. Many in the elite objected to coeducational instruction as well, preferring that their daughters be sent to sex-segregated Catholic schools. To stem this, Zayas proposed teaching about God in the classroom. "This is the cause which keeps the sons and daughters of our best families from public school: and unless something be done to introduce God, not within the limits of any sect, but in His grand and glorious concept of Our Father in Heaven, the public schools of Cuba will not attract the children of our most distinguished families."[24] As Cubans took over administration of Cuba in 1909, Zayas continued this theme in talks at Havana's prestigious Belén Jesuit academy.[25]

Anarchists were worried. The freethinking, anticlericalist magazine *El Audaz*, edited by Adrián del Valle, attacked the rise of religious education. In an April 1913 article "Los resultados de la enseñanza religiosa" (Results of Religious Education), an anonymous author offered "proof" on the effects of religious instruction in France. Of criminals less than twenty-one years of age, 95 percent had received religious instruction, and of these 90 percent were Catholics of whom 85 percent received religious instruction after their first communion. The author then alluded to the same results for Cuba if religious instruction were not curtailed. "It is an eloquent answer to those who insist on discrediting secular and rationalist education."[26] Not only did anarchists equate religious schools with subservience to Rome and increased crime, but also they alleged that religious education failed to teach courteous behavior. In one anecdotal story, the author told of a Jesuit teacher lecturing to an audience of women from well-to-do families. He urged mothers to prevent their children from using obscenity. After the talk, one mother approached the Jesuit and told him that her children used profanity; what could she do? The teacher told her to send them to a Jesuit school like the Belén Academy for religious and spiritual education. Confused, the mother looked at the priest and said her sons already attended Belén.[27]

When taken as a whole, Cuba's anarchists implied that the same types of patriotic and Catholic forces that had ruled the island for more than four hundred years had not been removed at the time of independence. They had merely been replaced by more localized elite, who had no intention of creating a social democracy full of enlightened, free individuals. This was further proof, anarchists charged, that Cuba's independence from Spain had been subverted. To this end, they claimed that new schools emphasizing individualized, rationalist instruction were necessary to break these forces' hold on Cuba. Only through the free, individual pursuits of knowledge with the teacher serving as a guide could children come to see the truth of the anarchist ideal and Nature's harmonious plan for humanity. For inspiration they looked to Francisco Ferrer Guardia and his Escuela Moderna, which operated in Barcelona, Spain, from 1901 to 1906.

Francisco Ferrer Guardia and the Escuela Moderna

Francisco Ferrer based his Escuela Moderna system on a larger eighteenth- and nineteenth-century trend in education rooted in the writings of Jean-Jacques Rousseau, Herbert Spencer, Leo Tolstoy, Peter Kropotkin, and others. Intellectually, Ferrer drew most heavily upon William Godwin's 1793 attack against states and state-sponsored education in his "Enquiry Concerning Political Justice." Godwin argued that governments used schools to develop loyal followings, just as churches developed loyal parishioners and manufacturers developed obedient workers. State-run schools then, while professing to be "free," were actually designed to eliminate the threat of novel ideas and promote the status quo, a dual purpose facilitated by the traditional practice of "instruction" in schools. Instruction meant lecturing and reinforcing the teacher's opinions to students. Because the teacher was a state functionary, Godwin believed that the teacher disseminated state-sponsored ideas; education, thus, was really in the hands of the ruling class who controlled the state. This environment, Godwin concluded, not only stifled a student's free inquiry to experiment, experience, and discover, but also assured that no new ideas entered the classroom and challenged authority.[28]

The state of Spanish education in 1901 was as dismal as in its former Caribbean colonies in 1898. Following the loss of Cuba, Puerto Rico, and the Philippines, Spain fell into turmoil. Within this turbulent environment there arose a growing debate about education. In 1901, only about one third—that is, 15,000 of 45,000—of the towns had a school. Not only were these ill-equipped schools, but they also taught and rigidly upheld Catholic dogma, a job made easier because Church officials supervised schools just as they had in Cuba.[29] After inheriting a sizeable amount of money from a student to whom he had taught Spanish, Ferrer traveled to Barcelona and opened the Escuela Moderna in 1901 to offer an educational alternative.[30] The Escuela Moderna presented the most radical challenge to educational orthodoxy during this contentious period of Spanish history. Within the curriculum, Ferrer created a school intended for both sexes and all social classes. Boys and girls together studied math, science, and social studies to develop their mental attributes. They also learned about hygiene and enjoyed large amounts of free playtime to develop healthy bodies and explore their imaginations. The school itself rebuked hierarchy by incorporating a nondogmatic curriculum devoid of strict discipline, tests, or rewards.

Though nondogmatic, political issues did creep into the rationalist curriculum. In his book *La Escuela Moderna*, Ferrer included sections of compositions from children ages 12 to 17, who would have had but a few years of rationalist education at most. A 12-year-old boy wrote, "Poor social organization assigns an unjust separation between men, so that there are two classes of men: those who work and those who don't." Another boy the same age wrote, "Aren't the children of the bourgeoisie and the workers both made of flesh and bone? Then, why in society are they different?" A 13-year-old girl wrote, "Fanaticism is produced by the state of ignorance and backwardness in which women find themselves. Therefore, Catholics don't want women to be instructed, since women are the Church's primary support."[31] Although rationalism was to be rooted in the scientific foundations of human and natural existence, an obvious amount of class-conscious political education found its way into the classroom.

Ferrer also urged that "play" and "education" be more closely intertwined. Allowing a child to engage in free play benefited the child because it created a greater sense of joy. This had direct countercultural consequences, especially versus the Church's notion of childhood. "The idea that life is a cross, a bothersome and weighty burden, which has to be tolerated until providence satiates itself with seeing us suffer, radically disappears," wrote Ferrer. "Life, we are told, is about enjoying life, living it. What torments and produces pain ought to be rejected as a mutilator of life."[32] Thus, allowing children ample opportunities for free play and enjoyment would stimulate not only the body but also the human spirit. Ferrer saw another important lesson from free play. Children's spontaneity often led them to "play as" adults, whether pretending to build houses, tend gardens, be doctors, be teachers, and so on. To Ferrer, this activity was more than imitating adults. Rather, "spontaneous play, which is the child's preference, indicates his occupation or natural dispositions. The child plays as a man, and when he reaches adulthood he does seriously that which he enjoyed as a child."[33] In essence, allowing for free, spontaneous activity permitted a child to develop his or her own interests and talents. Thus, play itself was useful preparation for life.

Another issue regarding freedom underlay the Escuela Moderna's program. Students should be neither coerced and disciplined by teachers, nor should students be rewarded and punished through examinations or grades. Discipline, reward, and punishment created a hierarchy or even a "class" system within the schoolroom. In this environment the teacher served as authoritarian. Ferrer found this completely unacceptable, especially when he recalled how the Escuela Moderna was dedicated to undermining a stratified social order. In

Ferrer's school, students could come and go from the classroom as they liked. Students could approach the chalkboard, read, or engage in an activity of their choice, not because a schedule designated the timing but because the student either felt compelled to act or just became bored with the current activity.[34] Free children had to have the liberty to enjoy themselves and find their own proclivities without being forced or disciplined by some overbearing, self-important teacher.

The success of Ferrer's initiatives can be seen in the rapid spread of schools, literature, and ultimately ruling-class repression. By 1904, thirty-two schools in Spain, including nine in Barcelona, received pamphlets and books printed by the Escuela Moderna publishing house.[35] But this early success came to a sudden halt in June 1906 when a would-be assassin tried to kill the king, a threat that prompted the government to launch a crackdown on Spanish radicals. On June 15, in the midst of this repression, Spanish authorities closed the Escuela Moderna, and Ferrer fled into exile. But in April 1908, he returned to Barcelona and started the International League for Children's Rational Education (Liga Internacional para la Educación Racional de la Infancia). The Liga coordinated establishment of rationalist schools in Europe and the Americas.[36] Soon, however, politics and militarism again intruded on Ferrer's efforts. In 1909 Spain attempted to ignite a sense of nationalist, patriotic fervor by going to war against Morocco. Anarchists led the resistance to this war, prompting the government to unleash yet another wave of repression in the summer of 1909. In this repressive atmosphere, authorities arrested Ferrer and accused him of fomenting popular resistance. He was found guilty and went before the firing squad on October 13, 1909.[37] However, Ferrer's efforts and his martyrdom stimulated rationalist education experiments throughout the Americas, especially in the United States, Argentina, Uruguay, and Cuba.

The Rationalist Schools in Cuba to 1912

During the first thirty years after independence, anarchists struggled to create rationalist schools that effectively challenged Cuba's public and religious schools. The actual drive for worker-based, but not necessarily anarchist-based, education predated independence. In the 1850s and 1860s, elite-run cultural centers (*liceos*) offered classes and activities for workers, but the lessons lacked a revolutionary content. Beginning in 1865, *lectores* appeared in cigar factories. These men or women read newspapers, political ideas, histories, and fiction aloud from an elevated platform while workers rolled cigars. The practice quickly spread from the Havana cigar factories to most of the large factories and workshops in Cuba and eventually to the cigar factories in Florida. In 1866, inspired by the success of the *lector*, Havana-based artisans established the first evening school for workers. As anarchists came to dominate the labor movement in the 1880s, they too pushed for worker-based education. In the late 1880s, the anarchist-led Círculo de Trabajadores began to focus on education by funding a library, a periodicals reading room open to the public, speakers, and a school. In 1889 the school taught more than one hundred men at night plus some eight hundred boys and girls during the day. This success led to the opening of new schools around the island.[38]

From 1899 to 1912, anarchists began dozens of schools on their own. Workers in the San Lázaro barrio of Havana initiated a school in 1899, and the first calls for a Social Studies Center (Centro de Estudios Sociales [CES]) in Havana were heard in September 1900. In 1903 a CES was organized in Guanabacoa, across the bay from Havana. However, the major push for children's rationalist schools began in 1905.[39] In 1904 the Spanish priest Eduardo Martínez Balsalobre's *Conferencias sobre el socialismo revolucionario* (Lectures on Revolutionary Socialism) was published in Havana with the Bishop of Havana's seal of approval. Martínez, explicitly criticizing the anarchists for their supreme faith in reason, argued that human reason was neither independent nor infallible; moreover, in trying times one of the greatest errors was to believe in the power of reason.[40] Rationalism itself, he wrote, appeared to be little more than a school of thought that "had as its only mission the defense of the rights of reason."[41]

Incensed by the circulation of Martínez's writings, anarchists renewed their educational efforts. In a two-part column in January and February 1905, J. Fueyo, an early regular contributor to *¡Tierra!*, recalled that several preschools (*planteles*) formerly functioned in Cuba, but these had mostly closed by 1905. In the Havana barrio of San Lázaro, only "La Enseñanza" led by the anarchist Jovino Villar, still remained. To remedy this situation, Fueyo called for the creation of more educational centers.[42] Villar answered this call in November 1905 by opening "Verdad," a coeducational primary and secondary school. Located in the heart of working-class Havana on Calle Neptuno, "Verdad" offered elementary instruction for boys and girls, as well as special and short courses for girls only. The school provided older students with opportunities to learn trades and to become teachers. Besides offering courses in French, English, typewriting, telegraphy, and music, "Verdad" also educated the deaf, mute, and blind.[43]

Having begun with the Círculo de Trabajadores school in the previous century and continuing until 1906, the anarchists' approach to education was not very innovative. As Joan Casanovas points out regarding the Círculo school (and applicable to most schools until 1906), "the rather traditional educational system of the Círculo contrasts with the advanced pedagogical methods of the Spanish anarchist schools at the time." This began to change in 1906. That year in Regla skilled tradesmen and the Ship Caulkers' Guild (Gremio de Calafates) founded their own CES. The *gremio* long had been involved in radical activities. In 1890 members founded the "Flores de Mayo" Mutual Aid Society in memory of the executed Chicago Haymarket anarchists. "The Internationale" was first heard in Cuba in the *calafates'* meetings. The CES school itself was the brainchild of Roberto Carballo, aka El Curro (literally a person displaying a certain freedom of manners). Carballo was a *calafate*, who emigrated from the Canary Islands to Regla in 1875. Known as the "spirit and life of the CES" throughout its four-year existence (1906–1910), he even painted the portrait of Francisco Ferrer Guardia that would hang above the CES door.[44] In the spring of 1908, anarchists formed the group "Educación del Porvenir" in Regla in order to run a Ferrer school out of the CES. In May and June 1908, the group published a manifesto inserted in ¡*Tierra!* and *La Voz del Dependiente*. The manifesto disparaged the government's obligatory educational system, described public school teachers as "teachers and men who aspire to be capitalists" because they taught only to make a living, and leveled criticisms against public and religious schools for undermining children's intelligence through lessons on patriotism and memorized hymns and prayers. The manifesto called for rationalist schools modeled after Ferrer's Escuela Moderna first to take root in Regla and then to spread across the island. Teachers trained in rationalist education would be brought in, and all the publications utilized in the Escuela Moderna and printed by its publishing division would be available at the same cost as in Spain.[45]

Later that year, Miguel Martínez Saavedra arrived in Regla from Spain. Ferrer personally selected Martínez to reorganize the Regla school under the auspices of the recently created Liga.[46] Martínez became the foreign secretary of the Liga's Cuban branch, as well as the Regla school's first full-fledged teacher trained in rationalist pedagogy. The school offered all the methods and programs of the Escuela Moderna in Barcelona, but a noted feature that appealed greatly to the predominantly working-class community of Regla was the school's choir. Every Friday, under the direction of one of Martínez's daughters, also a student, the choir paraded in front of the school on Calle Calixto García behind the Plaza del Mercado singing "The Internationale."[47] Dozens of children parading through the streets and singing the anthem of the international socialist movement directly challenged the patriotic drive to sing the National Anthem and worship the Cuban flag.

From 1908 to mid-1909, anarchists extended the success of the Regla school across the island. They made plans and raised money for schools in Matanzas, San Antonio de los Baños, Havana, and even Cobre in the eastern province of Oriente. In May 1909 Martínez left his teaching post at Regla, resigned his position as foreign secretary of the Liga, and established a night school in the western Havana suburb of Marianao where the anarchist group "Redención Social" had been struggling to found a school since the previous December. Sebastián Aguiar, a Spanish anarchist who had fought for Cuban independence, became the Liga's new foreign secretary.[48] Meanwhile, Ricardo Vera and Tomás Echeverría initiated a rationalist school for illiterate *campesinos* and their nearly ninety children at the "El Corralito" estate in Pinar del Río. Thus, in less than two years, anarchists developed an embryonic rationalist education system from one end of Cuba to the other. Yet, these schools were fragile, developed by individual local anarchist groups and lacking any real organizational strength from the broader labor movement.[49]

A series of internal conflicts and shortages of funds ultimately undermined this initial wave of anarchist schools. By May 1909 controversy enveloped the Regla school. *La Voz del Dependiente* reported that books from the Regla school were being substituted from the private collection of the new teacher Juan Pérez. If this and other rumors such as his dislike for teaching girls were true, then Pérez had to go, urged the paper.[50] Two weeks later, the paper again attacked Pérez for not being a rationalist teacher and for having exalted patriotism by praising both the Cuban and Argentine national flags in the classroom. In addition, *La Voz del Dependiente* accused Pérez of accepting the job while never intending to teach a rationalist curriculum; the paper claimed that he preferred to profit from workers' contributions while betraying those workers' trust.

In response to attacks against its teacher, new CES top officials Abelardo Saavedra and Francisco Sola defended their selection of Pérez as the Regla teacher and asserted their commitment and support. The following week Saavedra had a change of heart: he attacked Pérez as a man who had been expelled from several workers' centers apparently for past collaboration with police. In addition, Saavedra reflected the anarchist movement's general belief that homosexuality was "un-natural" and a sign of degeneracy when he called Pérez a lover "of sodomite practices, according to a comrade who caught him disgustingly living with a mulatto male."[51] Pérez's ouster temporarily quieted the storm.

Unfortunately, the real fireworks of personality conflicts were about to explode, and the timing could not have been worse for the movement. The 1909 revolt in Barcelona and Ferrer's arrest were hot issues in the Cuban anarchist press and important topics at rallies. Revulsion to Ferrer's execution began to fill the long languishing financial coffers of those trying to raise funds for schools. Anarchists pledged to build a school in Havana that would be dedicated to Ferrer, and funds were to be deposited in a bank to earn interest until there were sufficient funds to build the school.[52] However, the tragic events in Spain that could have unified the anarchist movement and initiated a successful building of rationalist schools occurred just as new conflicts erupted between leading anarchist figures in Cuba.

On October 5, 1909, only two weeks before the news of Ferrer's martyrdom reached the island, *Rebelión!* published the article "Algo Injusto" (Something Unjust). The author reported that José Requeña, a frequent contributor to the paper and activist for "free unions" between men and women, was living with a public school teacher in Güira de Melena, a town just west of Havana. Upon discovering that their teacher lived with an anarchist, the town's priest, mayor, and several businessmen forced Requeña's female companion from her job. The author questioned the loyalty and solidarity of anarchists who paid hard-earned money for people like Martínez, Pérez, and "many others who come to Cuba to enrich themselves on the backs of workers, always shouting that we need our own education for our children." These same men shout "solidarity," but they neglect a good woman victimized by repression.[53]

Martínez tried to respond, but of the three weekly anarchist newspapers in Havana and Regla, only *La Voz del Dependiente* published his letters in which he disassociated himself from the Liga. In a not-so-subtle jab at Saavedra and Sola, Martínez warned that the rationalist and anarchist movement was being endangered from within like a virus.[54] By printing the letters, *La Voz del Dependiente* asserted that the paper was not siding with Martínez specifically; rather, the paper argued that in the name of free speech offended parties had the right to defend themselves in the press. The editorial group of *¡Tierra!*, allied with

Saavedra and Sola, was not impressed and broke relations with *La Voz del Dependiente* in January 1910.[55]

However, the conflicts grew deeper, more divisive, and more personal, which resulted in the Regla school's collapse by the late spring of 1910. Throughout 1910, Martínez and his allies maintained a running slander campaign against Sola and Saavedra through the pages of *La Voz del Dependiente*. They labeled Sola a profiteer, an agent provocateur, a heavy drinker, and a purchaser of women's favors. Ultimately, Martínez and *La Voz del Dependiente* blamed Sola and his divisiveness for the collapse of the Regla school, the Regla CES, and the withering away of the Liga. That part of the blame had to rest with Saavedra for his alliance with Sola (and thus the alliance of *Rebelión!* and *¡Tierra!*) was not missed by Martínez, who increasingly referred to Saavedra as "Pope" and Sola as "Caesar."[56]

Yet, despite the internecine divisions that brought down the school, anarchists remained committed to Ferrer's dream. Other rationalist experiments emerged. On the eastern end of Cuba at El Cobre, anarchists collected funds to start a new school.[57] In the Havana suburb of Vedado, anarchists organized the "Enseñanza Mútua" school at Calle 19 y F. This school lasted until 1912, but its relations with the Liga were tenuous, in part because personality conflicts continued (the anarcho-naturist José Guardiola was the school's treasurer and coming under attack by Saavedra, as discussed in chapter 7) and no members from the Liga were elected to the school's board.[58]

By September 1910, Martínez had rejoined the Liga, with the apparent intention of staging a coup of sorts. In an October 1, 1910, manifesto (less than two weeks before anarchists were to commemorate the first anniversary of Ferrer's execution), *¡Tierra!* accused Martínez of stealing control of the Liga. Only a handful of regular members attended a September 13 meeting of the Liga, but Martínez arranged for approximately a dozen of his colleagues to attend and then proceeded to reorganize the committee. The same day, *¡Tierra!* received a request from the Liga for all the money that the newspaper had collected for the new Ferrer school. *¡Tierra!* refused to turn over the money to the new Liga, which Martínez now controlled, and suggested that the money would not be spent on erecting a school if the Liga got hold of it. *¡Tierra!*, seeking time, requested that all past and present members of the Liga should decide the matter. Martínez responded by saying that once you ceased making monthly donations to the Liga your rights also ceased; therefore, old members who had let their dues lapse should not be allowed to decide this issue. To make matters worse, Martínez announced that ¡Tierra! could no longer collect money in the Liga's name. At this point, the newspaper and the Liga broke relations, and the paper asked the donors of the money to decide its fate: forward the funds to the Liga or deposit them in a bank under the paper's account.[59]

Meanwhile, even in the midst of these disputes, anarchists began to create still more schools in Havana's working-class suburbs. By January 1911, a school and supplies to teach thirty students had begun in Sagua la Grande. Even though the school's organizational group "Sociedad Racionalista" had dissolved by April, the school continued to function and began to ask for monetary support.[60] In the Havana suburb of Cerro, members of ¡Tierra! and their allies formed the anarchist group "Agrupación Ferrer," an organization to rival the Liga, with the aim of creating a new school.[61] Both schools needed money. In June, ¡Tierra! announced that it was time to decide what to do with the nearly 145 disputed pesos sitting in a bank account. The amount seemed too small to build an entire school from the ground up, so the paper proposed using the money to aid schools that were already open or on the verge of opening, in particular in Sagua la Grande and Cerro.[62] This infuriated members of the Liga, whose new secretary, Miguel Lozano, demanded that ¡Tierra! send all the money to the Liga by June 11; if the paper refused, then the Liga would take the matter to authorities. This only raised the ire of the newspaper, whose editors asked how anyone who threatens to go to the police could call himself an anarchist and rationalist.[63] It then ignored the Liga, and throughout the coming months the newspaper distributed all its funds to the two schools.

The Cerro school was the most ambitious educational effort since the Regla school folded in 1910. Throughout 1911, funds were raised through individual donations, money collected at weekly meetings and cultural events, and subscription. One by-law of the Cerro CES included a ten-centavo weekly payment for members, part of which went to creating a school.[64] By late 1911, the school was able to operate without the cloud of discord hanging over it as relations between ¡Tierra!, the Liga, and El Dependiente (the successor of La Voz del Dependiente) had mended. Though the record is silent on the issue, one can reasonably speculate on why former adversaries were able to resolve their differences. In part, government repression is the answer. Late in the summer of 1911, the government deported Saavedra, Sola, and other anarchists as they made preparations for the Cruces-based Workers' Congress. Then Martínez disappeared from the pages of the anarchist press when he moved to the port city of Cienfuegos to begin translating anarchist books and pamphlets.[65] With three major antagonists gone from the scene, relations improved. It is ironic that government repression allowed anarchists, at least this time, to regroup and consolidate their efforts.

By October, the Cerro school was operating under the teachings of Antonio Juan Torres and J. F. Moncaleano, the latter a former Colombian university professor who greatly admired Ferrer. They soon were educating forty boys and girls, three of whom were Moncaleano's own children.[66] The school operated until the summer of 1912, when Moncaleano, feeling the urge to join the Mexican Revolution, left his family in Cuba to start a rationalist school in Yucatán, Mexico. Buttressed by financial support in the form of cash donations, Moncaleano's wife Blanca tried to keep the school operating and even offered both summer school classes for interested students and a "boarding school" in the building for students who lived too far to comfortably commute. Blanca Moncaleano's appearance in the anarchist educational world was new. In fact, contrary to the Cuban public school system where female teachers dominated the classrooms, women occupied few spots in anarchist educational leadership in general and as teachers specifically. Not until 1911 when Isabel Alvarez sat on a CES board in Cerro, Blanca Moncaleano spoke and taught in the same school from 1911 to 1912, and María Luisa García wrote a column on rationalist education in 1914 did women play significant roles in the educational movement.[67] However, despite Blanca Moncaleano's efforts, the Cerro school withered away; ¡Tierra! ceased publication of the school's financial accounts by late summer 1912.[68]

Ultimately, a combination of internal conflicts and insufficient funds undermined the initial wave of rationalist schools in Cuba. Although personality conflicts were temporary, the constant struggle to get money may have been the movement's Achilles' heel. The schools were financed by subscriptions, fundraising, donations, and minimal tuition. To gather a picture of school finances, one need look no further than the back pages of most issues of ¡Tierra!, which regularly published weekly collections. The figures illustrate how, after the school paid rent and teachers' salaries, there was little to buy supplies. The Cerro school did run surpluses in its first months, but by April 1912 slight deficits caught up with the school.[69] Whereas anarchist schools in places like Argentina had large labor organizations like FORA to help back their schools, no such sweeping labor organizations existed in early republican Cuba.[70] Yet another factor played into the financial instability of rationalist schools: a plethora of demands for contributions. From 1910 to 1912, anarchists in Cuba were beseeched by requests to fund a number of local and international concerns. Not only did sympathizers send money for schools, but they also donated funds to three anarchist newspapers publishing more or less simultaneously: *Rebelión!*, *La Voz del Dependiente* (and its successor *El Dependiente*), and *¡Tierra!*. Supporters also sent money to help families of deported radicals as well as the wives and children of those revolutionaries (like Moncaleano) who voluntarily went abroad and left families behind. Finally, this period marked the beginning of the Mexican Revolution. Anarchists throughout the island regularly contributed funds to be sent to Mexico to finance various revolutionary projects.

Consequently, supporters were potentially substantial sources of revenue. Had there been no Mexican Revolution or no wave of deportations or no multiple newspapers, then perhaps those responsible for creating and running the schools would have been more successful in raising funds. Although the anarchists' internal divisions and constant financial dilemmas weakened the drive to establish schools, the conflicts and problems also illustrated the anarchists' important commitment to education. To these men and women, issues of finance as well as the personal character of teachers and movement operatives mattered a great deal. Some critics argue that the anarchists were more interested in name-calling and petty squabbles; however, a more enlightened view remembers that the squabbles derived from the passion to establish an appropriately correct rationalist school system. The anarchists' divisions helped to undercut the educational movement, but the passion that drove these people toward conflict with each other was the same passion that motivated their repeated efforts to create the rationalist schools in the first place.

The 1920s Resurgence of Anarchism and Rationalist Schools

The governmental repression during the first years of World War I that stymied anarchist agitation also undermined anarchist educational activity. However, as anarchists came to dominate a resurrected labor movement, they used their positions in that movement to renew rationalist education. Central to this expansion was a growing alliance between anarchists (mainly anarcho-syndicalists) and other leftists in the 1920s. This alliance first became obvious in 1922 with the widely distributed pamphlet *Tácticas en uso y tácticas a seguir*. Written by the anarchist printer Antonio Penichet, the forty-five-page pamphlet highlighted and explained different strategies that Cuban revolutionaries might employ. Penichet's final strategy concerned the development of rationalist schools. Penichet argued that, more than ever before, workers had to create schools that served workers' interests and not the interests of the Church or the state. "While we do not have our own schools, we will continue to see our future obstructed. We must save our children from becoming social debris. We must save the future with our cause."[71] Without the schools, Penichet believed, the future was lost.

Although the pamphlet updated traditional anarchist discourse concerning education and Ferrer's educational philosophy, it is significant that Penichet chose the old, respected socialist Carlos Baliño to write a prologue for the pamphlet. From before independence, Baliño had flirted with the whole spectrum of socialism. Originally, he was an anarchist, then a reformist socialist, and by the 1920s a committed Marxist. Baliño, who with University of Havana student Julio Antonio Mella founded the Cuban Communist Party (PCC) in 1925, wrote how he greatly respected Penichet and considered him a comrade and friend.[72] The formal linking of Baliño and Penichet laid the foundation for close ties between anarchists and communists in the development of Cuban rationalist education in the 1920s. However, as with relations between anarchists and communists throughout the world after the 1917 Bolshevik Revolution, not all anarchists were comfortable with this alliance. In particular, anarcho-syndicalists who published the newspaper *El Progreso*, the anarcho-communist and anti-Marxist *Acción Libertaria*, as well as anarcho-naturists questioned this linkage and cooperated only loosely with nonanarchists. Penichet and likeminded anarchists, who occupied positions in the labor movement, worked as ideological brokers between communists and dissenting anarchists.

In August 1922, anarchist labor leader José Peña Vilaboa noted that while the recently formed Workers' Federation of Havana (FOH), the largest labor organization on the island and one in which anarchists held a commanding presence, led the way in uniting Cuban labor organizations, education remained central to creating a strong social movement: "The Federation's most basic objective and which will soon be obtained is Rationalist Education— fundamental to our emancipatory endeavors."[73] A year in the making, the FOH inaugurated its rationalist school and library in the Havana Workers Center on October 4, 1922. José Miguel Pérez, the future first general secretary of the PCC, served as the school's teacher with Carlos Baliño and the Afro-Cuban anarchist Rafael Serra filling in as substitute teachers.[74] The school opened with eleven students, two of whom were the children of FOH head and anarchist leader

Table 9.1. Public Primary School Instruction in Cuba, 1901–1922

	Number of Teachers	Number of Students Enrolled	Percentage of Students Attending School
1901	3,000	177,000	na
1907	3,649	122,214	31.6
1919	5,743	335,000	31.2
1922	6,075	344,331	35.0

Source: Chart constructed from "Annual Report of the Commissioner of Public Schools, June 1901," in Civil Report of Brigadier General Leonard Wood, vol. 7, 184–185; Cuba: Population, History and Resources, 1907, 122–123; Primelles, Crónica Cubana, 104–105, 567.

Alfredo López. Two other girls in the initial class were daughters of FOH Financial Secretary and anarchist Alejandro Barreiro.[75]

Supporters hoped that the school would be the first in a series scheduled to open throughout Havana. In particular, these rationalist advocates thought that the timing was right. Public education had made few inroads into Cuba's unschooled population since independence. Upon first glance, Table 9.1 seems to illustrate a general improvement in Cuba's public schools. Although the figures reflect a gross doubling of the number of teachers and enrolled students from 1901 to 1922, the percentage of children from age five to age seven who actually attended school remained relatively stagnant. Furthermore, in 1920 President Menocal vetoed pay raises for public school teachers, a political move that only discouraged more people from becoming teachers.[76] Such moves, according to anarchists, forced teachers to take on second jobs, a distraction that made it difficult for teachers to properly dedicate themselves to teaching.[77] In addition, public school classroom sizes remained large. From 1920 to 1924, Cuba's public classrooms averaged 108 students each, with a student-teacher ratio of sixty to one, a ratio that had barely improved from the sixty-one to one figure documented nearly twenty years earlier (from 1901 to 1902).[78] Consequently, some basic conditions in public schools were as poor as at independence.

The lingering inadequacy of public education throughout the 1910s had bolstered the popularity of private (mostly religious) education. Private schools remained a source of bitter contention for Cuban nationalists. The school inspector Ismael Clark in 1915 argued that private schools maintained poor educational standards, perpetuated class and racial differences, and undermined nationalist sentiments critical to developing a citizenry rooted in civic virtues.

Because the island's social and economic elite were likely to send their children to such schools, nationalists argued that these people, as Laurie Johnston puts it, "developed a low level of patriotism" that fostered Cuba's dependence on foreign business and accepted the penetration of foreign cultural influences.[79] Proposed legislation in 1915 would have forced private schools to submit to state inspection, use only state-approved texts, hire only Cuban-born individuals as directors, teach civics and Cuban history, and fly the Cuban flag. The measure failed largely because most of Cuba's politicians had received private education, and they continued sending their children to private schools.[80] The irony was not lost on the anarchists: the elite preferred private education, therefore they rejected tough new regulations for private schools, and ultimately protected future rationalist experiments.

Nationalist objection to private education partially revolved around antireligious, in particular, anti-Catholic sentiments. When seen as a holdover of colonial rule, many viewed Catholic education as fostering a sense of antinationalism.[81] Anarchists and supporters of rationalist education, while condemning the public schools in the 1920s, built on this larger anticlericalism in the national education debates. Throughout 1922–1924, rationalist school advocates described both public and private education as antirational because they taught children to worship "gods," one represented by the flag and the other by the cross. In covering the inauguration of the FOH school, *Nueva Luz* described the school as a reaction to the growth in private religious education. The rationalist school "is necessary to prepare the worker and to save the worker's child from the clutches of religion," asserted the writer.[82] An anonymous columnist urged readers to send money and lend support for a rationalist school to save workers' children because all Cuban children, according to the writer, were being beseeched by religious groups to send money to help fund new priests and missionaries.[83] Referring to the growth of Protestant schools, another writer urged the expansion of rationalist schools to counter those of "Catholics, Protestants, Baptists, etc."[84] In fact, antireligious sentiment became especially prominent in the anarchist press; nearly every issue included cartoons lampooning the Catholic clergy for its purported corruption and sexual peccadilloes.[85]

Consequently, anarchists found themselves in a unique position in the Cuban educational debates of the 1910s and 1920s. Anarchists agreed with nationalists on the need to counter religious education because such schools fostered class divisions and even questionable loyalties. Nationalists criticized religious schools for their antinationalism; anarchists criticized religious schools for their antihuman irrational mystical dogma. However, rationalist school supporters continued to condemn simultaneously the government's public education system. To anarchists, public schools failed in pedagogy, erred by emphasizing unwavering patriotism, and condemned workers' children to overcrowded and underfunded classrooms. In fact, true to the antipatriotic sentiments imbedded in rationalist education, rationalist schools during the 1920s would neither display the Cuban flag nor have their students pledge allegiance to it. Continuing their fierce hatred of patriotism, supporters regularly reminded readers why one should not honor the Cuban flag. For instance, in September 1923, one writer in *Nueva Luz* lamented that public school children were being forced to worship a piece of cloth "that only serves to divide humanity," especially Cubans, and that such worship was inhuman and immoral.[86] Such a symbol would have no place among anarchists.

Rationalist schools, spreading quickly after 1922, opened in Cárdenas in western Cuba, Caibarién in central Cuba, and Banes in eastern Cuba.[87] More than one hundred people attended the Banes school opening on July 1, 1923, after nearly six months of planning by the various labor groups in the area. Ultimately organized by the Banes Workers Union and its "Education and Publicity Committee," the school began with seventy-four children and eighty adults in day and night classes respectively—an impressive figure when one considers that anarchists traditionally found their strength in the central and western provinces. Because their classroom held only twenty-five desks with three chairs each, the school was literally full from the start, and the Committee made appeals to the community and surrounding sugar *centrales* for financial support to expand. Such help came in the form of donations collected in small amounts. For instance, workers on the Central "Cieneguita" sent $5 to the school at one time that fall.[88] In September 1923, in the port city of Cárdenas, the Unión de Obreros Industriales organized a rationalist school that grew throughout the next year; ultimately the school moved into its own building, supported by a workers' theatre group.[89] Meanwhile, the anarchist-led Sindicato Fabril opened a second Havana school in the Puentes Grandes neighborhood.[90] Still the longest-running and most successful was the FOH school in Havana. Although only eleven students began in October 1922, by February 1923 fifty-five children attended the day school, and seventy-two adults attended night school. A month later day school attendance climbed to seventy-six children.[91]

The FOH school looked like many public schools in several ways: desks were arranged in rows, a chalkboard hung on the wall, the teacher's podium stood at the front of the classroom, and bookshelves surrounded. The rationalist schoolroom thus offered a physical likeness to its public school counterparts. Even the curriculum had certain similarities. Children attended classes for two hours in the morning and two hours after lunch. They studied arithmetic, geography, grammar, history, natural history, spelling, and basic science. Yet, the rationalist school complemented these topics in ways that distinguished it from the public school. Teachers set aside time for students to explore their artistic inclinations through drawing. In addition, two class periods per week taught physiology and hygiene because rationalists believed that formal education was a means to teach healthy lifestyles to children, whom the teachers hoped would take those lessons home to their parents. Teachers devoted Saturday mornings to educational lectures or trips to either workshops or the countryside. Educators believed that trips to workshops exposed children to their future work environments. Perhaps the visit would awaken an innate interest in a certain trade or heighten awareness of abysmal working conditions. Teachers designed journeys to the countryside to allow students time to frolic freely in Nature. While playing in and exploring the natural world, teachers hoped students would, on their own, come to understand and appreciate what anarchists considered the cooperative natural order that existed outside of the competitive and corrupting influences of the industrial city.[92] In short, education was key to creating future revolutionary generations, a sentiment that Antonio Penichet expressed a few years earlier in *La vida de un pernicioso*. The novel's conclusion features the main character lying on his death bed and urging his fellow activists to start a school, which they call "El Porvenir."

Yet, before schools could create these future revolutionary generations, qualified teachers had to be found. This was not just an anarchist dilemma. Finding appropriately trained teachers, willing to work for low pay, had been a common problem throughout Cuba since independence. After 1909, the government had created teachers examinations, but not until 1916 were there schools and special correspondence courses for teachers. Still, most highly qualified people went into other, better paying fields.[93] Rationalist education had its own unique educational foundations, and not just any teacher would suffice. By heeding the advice of the first wave of anarchist schools, supporters urged school councils to be cautious about whom they hired.[94] Soledad Gustavo noted that after teaching several years in a coeducational academy, she had deduced that the greatest influence of the teacher was as a role model to students. To this end Gustavo proposed founding a school to train teachers in rationalist education.[95] Vicente Canoura, the first manager of *Nueva Luz* and author of several pieces on education, echoed the caution regarding teachers. He questioned whether there were enough qualified teachers to fill the number of rationalist schools springing up around the island. After all, he warned, not just anyone could hop up to the podium or stroll inside a classroom and instruct in rationalism. One had to be trained to know how to recognize individual learning patterns and create appropriate individualized learning programs. Supporters did not immediately solve these problems, but all concerned were pleased with the selections of Alberta Mejías Sánchez and Ramón César in the Banes school as well as the FOH's selection of José Miguel Pérez as that school's teacher. Pérez had taught in private schools in Cuba after he emigrated from the Canary Islands in 1920. However, his activism in social struggles in Spain and his association with radical working-class elements in Havana eased the minds of those who questioned a private school educator in the rationalist schools.[96]

Besides the need to find qualified teachers, rationalist education supporters had to fund the schools, which were to be free to students. Supporters resorted to an old way of financing the bulk of many school expenses: worker donations. Yet, unlike funding concerns from the earlier era of 1908–1912 when rationalist schools primarily were financed on the backs of small, scattered anarchist groups, by the 1920s rationalist education had become a more "mainstream" idea in Cuban labor radicalism and thus the schools drew on a wider resource base for donations. For instance, individuals frequently sent between $.50 and $5.00 to *Nueva Luz*, which distributed the money to the schools. Some unions like the Havana Electric Workers Union decided to take the money that they would normally spend semi-annually on pamphlets and send it to the schools instead.[97] Other workers in places like the "Cieneguita" sugar mill in Abreus, or Havana, or Ciego de Ávila appointed delegates to collect funds from throughout an individual workplace and send the funds to schools.[98] Moreover, as in the earlier era, fundraisers were held.[99]

The FOH school in Havana, however, benefited most from the increased efforts of pansectarian organizing. The FOH drew funds from the various labor unions, including those representing trolley workers, cigarette makers, printers, construction workers, painters, confectioners, and others whose contributions were specifically dedicated to the school. Unions and individuals federated with the FOH paid the school's utility bills and the salaries of three teachers at the school (Pérez, José Peña Vilaboa, and Eloisa Barreiro—the latter the wife of labor leader Alejandro Barreiro).[100] Anarchists and other leftists on the island found a large list of worthy causes toward which to send their money, especially political prisoners in the United States (Sacco and Vanzetti, Enrique Flores Magón) and Cuba and funding designated to keep Havana's *Nueva Luz* in print. Thus, securing enough funding for schools remained a persistent worry.

While rationalist schools for children emerged around the island financed by a wide array of schemes, other developments in radical education were also emerging. A formal alliance between workers and university students led to the creation in November 1923 of the José Martí Popular University (Universidad Popular "José Martí" [UPJM]) for working-class adults. University students and the workers in Cuba rarely cooperated in close alliance after independence, although missed opportunities abounded. In 1904, the anarchist newspaper *Germinal* commented on Spanish university students with anarchist leanings. The paper suggested that the University of Havana might too be a source of future members to swell anarchist ranks.[101] However, U.S. journalist Irene Wright described a certain moral and intellectual poverty of students and student life at the University of Havana around 1909. Still, Wright reminded the reader that there "are serious-minded and well-informed" students who "take a surprising, and, to an American, inexplicable, interest in matters one might imagine would concern them not at all. They frequently lead in demonstrations for or against the government. They stoned the office of an editor who denounced Ferrer. . . ."[102]

The UPJM was the creation of anarcho-syndicalist Alfredo López and the young university student Julio Antonio Mella, who grew up in the radical port city of Regla. In 1923 Mella headed the First Revolutionary Congress of Students (Primer Congreso Revolucionario de Estudiantes) that denounced the Platt Amendment and, by extension, all imperialism. The Congress expressed solidarity with the Russian Revolution and the FOH, while announcing an interest in creating a "popular university." As president of the University Student Federation, Mella maintained his efforts to found a popular university. Meanwhile, Alfredo López worked to develop the UPJM with classes for adult workers.[103] Organizers intended the UPJM to complement the FOH adult night school that was inaugurated in January 1923 and included two hours of courses on weeknights, which focused on mathematics, grammar, spelling, and writing.[104]

Still, potential conflicts abounded. Some anarchists, while greatly approving of the concept of the UPJM, questioned just what was happening in the early stages of the school. In 1924 Pérez wrote a three-part series of critiques in *Nueva Luz* titled "Palabras de un maestro, a J. A. Mella" (Words from a Teacher, to J. A. Mella). Pérez questioned whether university students were truly capable of running such a school: After all, the students of the elite University of Havana came primarily from privileged classes; under pressure these university students might really respond to their class interests and abandon workers.[105] Despite the UPJM's name, Pérez further accused it of being "bourgeois," not "popular" because its student leaders lacked the class understanding, vigor, and drive to advance knowledge to a higher internationalist and rationalist understanding.[106] To this end Pérez urged the UPJM to be more than just a bourgeois mouthpiece that told workers to avoid vice, prostitution, and unhealthy habits, but rather he encouraged university students to actively join in the fight against the roots of these evils. In the same vein, he argued that one could not wall up the sciences in either the academy or the laboratory. The sciences had to be applied to solving real problems of the popular classes.[107] Although it would be overly presumptuous to claim that Pérez's criticisms helped Mella to see the light, by March 1924 both *Nueva Luz* and the Sindicato Fabril's *El Progreso* were praising Mella and the UPJM for acting directly with workers.[108] By early 1925 the UPJM was conducting courses every Tuesday and Thursday evening in Havana, and its own orchestra performed at the May Day celebrations that same year.[109]

A sense of optimism reigned in February 1925, when labor leaders, including the most prominent anarchists of the day, held a national workers congress in Cienfuegos. Like earlier workers' conferences, education was a key plank in the platform. Antonio Penichet headed the congressional education commission, which called on workers to create a worker education commission in every Cuban town, even if no organized unions yet existed. Each commission was charged with purchasing workers' newspapers for the community, creating rationalist schools, collecting small monthly dues to print propaganda and educational pamphlets, organizing popular universities, identifying people who could give public talks, and encouraging the use of phonographs, cinema, and other communications technology to educate people.[110]

However, before these efforts could bear much fruit, the Machado government began its efforts to destroy the strengthening workers movement. In August 1925, Machado closed the Sindicato de la Industrial Fabril and arrested its anarcho-syndicalist leader Margarito Iglesias. The closure cut off a major financial contributor to the FOH and thus the schools. For instance, during the period from October 1, 1923, to the end of December 1924, the Sindicato gave $1,133.95 to the FOH out of a total of $6,280.93 in contributions from all sources; that is, the Sindicato donated nearly 20 percent of its funding.[111] In September, the anarchist railroad union leader Enrique Varona was jailed and then murdered. In October 1925, FOH head Alfredo López was arrested and not released from jail until January 1926. In the meantime, anarchists began to flee the island to Florida and Mexico. Then, in July 1926, López was kidnapped; his remains were not discovered until seven years later.[112] This wave of repression, aimed particularly against anarchists and their allies, resulted in the abandonment of the schools. In fact, this abandonment was precipitated by one of the government's first repressive measures. In August 1925, Pérez, the FOH school teacher, was deported as a "pernicious foreigner." In response, students from the FOH school issued a manifesto. They noted how they had become accustomed to assaults on workers, but taking aim at teachers was something new. This was reminiscent of Spanish repression during the war for independence, they cried. "Just as our parents tell us of the horrors committed by [General] Weyler, with his kidnappings, concentration camp policies, crimes and oppressions, we will tell our own children of the crimes committed against us."[113] Once again, from the anarchist worldview, independence had brought little progress. Pérez's deportation symbolized the government's larger crackdown against radical labor. The repression first unleashed in 1925 precipitated the collapse of the rationalist education movement just as it was reaching new heights of success.

Conclusion

One must be cautious not to overstate the successes of anarchist education. Nevertheless, although generally small and short-lived, the rationalist schools illustrate several important processes at work on the island in the decades following independence from Spain. First, an examination of the schools expands our knowledge of leftist politics in Republican-era Cuba. Educational initiatives reveal how anarchists challenged the state and the Church not only in the workplace and the streets but also in the classrooms. Second, the anarchist conflict with the Cuban educational system reveals how one understudied segment of the population pursued a vision for Cuba that fell squarely outside the bounds of official notions. While government officials struggled to educate the population with high doses of moral and civics training, anarchist education emphasized freedom of thought, the sciences, and rejection of patriotic overtures like saluting the flag, pledging allegiance, and singing the national anthem. Third, just as anarchists condemned public education, they likewise spoke out against religious education and engaged in a long-running cultural debate about the role of religious schools and what they meant to a democratic Cuba. Finally, for all their words and deeds to create an alternative educational system that would offer a new vision of Cuba's future, anarchist education supporters ran into the same problems as the public schools. They both had too few resources and a shortage of qualified teachers. Yet, the schools, first developed by anarchists and then adopted by Cuban leftists in general, must be regarded as nearly forgotten monuments to Cuba's leftist heritage that emphasized education for revolutionary change decades before the rise of communist mass educational reforms after 1959. While anarchists experienced immense hurdles, they nevertheless opened schools in every part of Cuba where they offered educational alternatives to state-operated and religious-affiliated institutions. Ultimately, while never reaching the hoped-for levels of success, anarchist education was on the front lines in the anarchist countercultural struggle in Cuba where it challenged the hegemonic culture's educational institutions, the ideologies that those schools taught, and the process of imagining Cuba's future.

10

Guiding the Masses
Anarchist Culture as Education

The theater, like the school, the book, the pamphlet and the newspaper, is an effective
medium of popular culture and education; and, perhaps with more positive results the
scenic arts can help elevate and ennoble the people's mentality, purging its imagination
of atavistic prejudices, absurd routines, degrading conventionalities, giving refuge
to ideas of humanity and justice, social equality, esteem and self-worth.

Juan Tur (1914)

Anarchists believed that the social revolution could not succeed without having
first prepared people to act in revolutionary harmony. An individual's entire life
had to be reoriented. But to anarchists dedicated to education, learning was not
just for the meeting room or the school. Consequently, anarchists employed a
wide range of cultural events and productions designed to reach beyond just
the workplace. These men and women valued literature and theater for their
consciousness-raising abilities. Their schools arose sporadically, but anarchists complemented the schools with public events, theater, and fiction to
reinforce these teachings and expand their audiences.

Anarchist plays, poetry, songs, and even speeches performed at social gatherings (*veladas*) reinforced the messages and values taught in rationalist schools
for more than thirty years. In particular, this performance culture became a
central medium for women and children to play a role in the social struggle,
and, by example, they appealed directly to women and children in the audiences. Through their performances, anarchists criticized Cuban institutions
and leaders on the central political and social issues of the day. Besides actually
taking to the stage, some anarchists used their press to attack aspects of the
larger Cuban culture that did not fit into the anarchist vision. These cultural
challenges ranged across the whole spectrum of Cuban culture, but focused
particularly on the theater, public monuments, carnival, and even dating practices. Such critiques in the movement's press functioned as a form of cultural

education designed to raise awareness in readers so that they could act accordingly. Thus, cultural practices became legitimate targets in the culture war that anarchists waged for the hearts and minds of potential followers as well as against the hegemonic culture that they so despised. Consequently, to understand anarchist education in its entirety, one must see these radicals' initiatives both within and outside the schoolhouse walls.

Anarchist Social Gatherings and Children

On occasion, such as in 1907, anarchists went on islandwide propaganda tours, but these were expensive, time-consuming, and infrequent. When not on tour, anarchist speakers and performers more regularly held local *veladas*. Frequently, events that directly affected anarchists became the catalysts for holding a *velada*: the assassination of workers in Cruces in 1903, various waves of deportations, the execution of Ferrer in 1909, attempts to launch rationalist schools, the many speaking tours of the Uruguayan female freethinker Belén de Sárraga, and efforts to raise money to underwrite newspapers. Workers and their families came to the events, usually on Sunday evenings, to hear lectures on anarchism, education, health, and family-oriented topics. From a cultural standpoint, anarchist organizers saw the *veladas* as valuable acts of revolutionary culture where men, women, and children also sang revolutionary hymns, performed radical plays, and recited anarchist poetry. These were small events where people who knew each other and each other's children might unite in a spirit of anarchist "community" to reinforce their ideas, rededicate themselves to what must have frequently felt like a hopeless cause, and learn new ideas. These performances offered educational entertainment that anarchists hoped would excite audiences who came to a Sunday meeting after seeing an advertisement in the newspaper. Ultimately, the *veladas* became important, often weekly, educational tools that critiqued Cuban and global politics, suggested an imaginable anarchist future, and reinforced group identity; at the same time *veladas* increased followers.

Speeches may have been important elements of the *veladas*, but the truly invigorating cultural work was found in the songs, poetry, and plays frequently performed by women and children. The attendance of and performances by both women and children caught the attention of military intelligence officers. For instance, in January 1908 U.S. Captain Furlong wrote to Governor Magoon that the "meetings are being attended by women as well as men. The women bring their children and the meetings seem to be part of an educational system established by these anarchists."[1]

Either a speech or a band piece began a typical *velada*. Talks then were interspersed with poems like "Himno al pueblo" (Hymn to the People), "La libertad" (Freedom), "A la anarquía" (To Anarchy), "Los parias" (Homages), "Una limosna" (An Alm), "El sol perdido" (The Lost Sun), and "Las dos grandezas" (The Two Grandees). Children almost always recited the poetry. Most often these children were sons and daughters of anarchists, such as Miguel Martínez Abello's son Augusto who recited poems at *veladas* from 1905 to 1907 or Rafael García's daughter Celia who performed in 1913.[2] In a discussion of his brief 1911 stay with the family of Havana anarchist Jesús López, the noted labor organizer, later government official, and celebrated novelist Carlos Loveira observed how anarchists employed their children in cultural events. For instance, Loveira wrote, López had seven children, one of whom, Jesuito, was a public speaker. All the others had good anarchist names—Germinal, Rebeldía, Aurora, Libertad, Igualdad, and Fraternidad—and they too recited poetry or performed songs at *veladas*.[3]

Some radicals believed it was crucial to use children for cultural events. The children's presence and participation illustrated that the future generations were being prepared for the coming struggles. Also, by memorizing and publicly reciting poetry, children were supposed to gain a sense of a larger social purpose in their lives. However, by the 1920s this use of children in *veladas* came under scrutiny. Zoilo Menéndez, a frequent writer on educational issues for *Nueva Luz*, criticized the practice on two levels. First, the process of rote memorization and recitation were antithetical to the rationalist pedagogy of experience over memorization. Second, Menéndez suggested that such a practice was akin to what religions and political parties did. They taught doctrine to children before the children had developed sufficient mental and emotional faculties to understand the issues; that is, adults encouraged fanaticism before children's reason could be developed. Ultimately, this was unnatural and thus not rationalist, argued Menéndez.[4] When viewed through the lens of rationalist pedagogy, Menéndez was right. Yet, other anarchists, particularly those who claimed to be followers of Ferrer, never publicly criticized the use of children for such propaganda; such acceptance causes one to wonder how well versed in pedagogy Cuba's rationalist educators were. That no public criticism was leveled until the 1920s reflects either a dearth of understanding of Ferrer's philosophies or a blatant hypocrisy, but it is important to recall that even preteenage children in Ferrer's own Barcelona school were writing about social issues. Nevertheless, despite Menéndez's objections, children regularly played roles in *veladas* and other anarchist public events. By using children in cultural events, cultural organizers hoped that these childhood roles would instill a lifetime commitment to struggles for social justice.

While children sang songs and recited poetry, anarchist *veladas* were very much musical affairs, too, and often featured their own choirs, quintets, and bands. In 1905 the anarchist group "Germinal," publishers of a paper by the same name in 1904, also had a choir by that name. With guitars in hand, anarchists frequently put to music poems like "Hijos del pueblo" (Children of the People) and "La libertad." Favorites such as "The Internationale" and "La Marseillaise" often concluded *veladas*. Throughout the years, baritones and tenors performed solo pieces of these and other songs with revolutionary spirit. Although socialists and other nonanarchist groups held *veladas* and some of the same songs may have been used in those gatherings, anarchist *veladas*, distinct in material and content, served a specific political and educational function to complement their entertainment value.[5]

Theater, Art, and Social Customs

The modern democratization of the arts, particularly theater, had its origins in the French Revolution. Throughout the nineteenth century, progressive members of the middle classes sought a form of artistic endeavor that could appeal to the greatest mass of society.[6] By the early 1900s, however, what was called the "popular theater" had become an abomination within many different social circles, in not only Cuba but also the world. In 1918, for example, North American theater critic George Jean Nathan lamented that the overall quality of theater in general had been perhaps irreparably harmed by its gross appeals to a mediocre mass audience. "In a word, the discerning critic comes to realize that the place of the theater in the community is infinitely less the place of the university, the studio and the art gallery than the place of the circus, the rathskeller and the harem." The fine, well-educated young man wanted little more than diversion, so little more than diversion was all he got, Nathan held.[7]

Cuba's mainstream conservative press responded similarly, but these reactions exceeded a critique of general mediocrity in theater and art. In January 1909, *Diario de la Marina* began an antipornography campaign against the so-called free theater (*teatro libre*). The paper published several letters from readers decrying what they saw as the "pornographic filth" that inundated the theater. A Jovellanos doctor argued that if allowed to go unchecked, theatrical works such as "pornographic dances and couplets from shameless literature will continue to infiltrate obscenity and lust into the public spirit."[8] The paper's leading editorialist, Joaquín Aramburu, echoed the doctor's caution. He urged women not to let their daughters go near these potential dens of lasciviousness. Then Aramburu took the antipornography message to another level. "If Cuban mothers want, patriotic endeavors will come to fruition. And I have great hope that they will."[9] In essence, Aramburu believed that the demise of "quality theater" threatened to tear apart Cuba's moral and social fabric. If the rip caused by the popular theater continued, then the very basis of Cuban nationalism could come unraveled. Consequently, Aramburu urged readers not to let down their guard against pornography in the theater, art in general, or even the scandalous postcards sold in shops throughout the city. The fate of the republic hung in the balance. Although this appeal to patriotic fervor against pornographic vice might have arisen at any time in the island's history, the timing of these nationalistic cultural pronouncements is significant. They appeared as the United States ended its second occupation of the island in 1909, a time when numerous social groups embarked on campaigns to define *cubanidad* and public schools initiated a flag-saluting patriotic curriculum.

For all of the popular imagery that surrounds anarchists, especially the image of them as wild-eyed sexual libertines who threw out all sexual taboos, Cuba's anarchists were quite the opposite, bordering on the prudish. Anarchist commentators themselves had little use for the popular theater that Aramburu and others criticized. However, while the elite took the critique of popular culture to a nationalistic level, anarchists applied a class analysis. The movement's columnists regularly lamented how workers would seek diversion and waste their money at the theater. One such criticism came on the heels of Aramburu's attack on the *teatro libre*.

As part of its campaign against the *teatro libre*, *Diario de la Marina* focused on the workers who filled the cheap seats of the upper galleries. During the March 4, 1909, performance at the Neptune Theater, these working-class audience members jeered at the ballerina Chelito because she did not take off her clothes and "display her forms." Acracio del Monte and *¡Tierra!* were equally appalled at this behavior, but just as appalled that workers would even show up at such a place. Del Monte complained that workers, who too readily went to these performances, filled the cheap seats and hoped to catch a glimpse of a leg, a breast, or something else. The following day workers went to their jobs where, in front of child apprentices, they described in detail such female body parts so that "the apprentices who are there to learn a trade only end up learning pornography and the most nauseating depravity." Yet, while Aramburu could make a similar point, one had to look out for his class-conscious slant, Del Monte warned. For while Aramburu criticized the upper gallery (that is, workers), he conveniently forgot to mention that the middle and upper classes filled the lower level's higher-priced seats.[10]

Rebelión! joined in the criticism of *Diario de la Marina*'s campaign against the *teatro libre* by describing the high level of obscenity in plays performed at the Alhambra Theater. Yet, *Rebelión!* went further than *Diario de la Marina*'s critique. *Rebelión!*'s editors argued that when *Diario de la Marina* and Aramburu said they feared the *teatro libre*, this was merely a moral cover for the true focus of their attacks. By publicly condemning risqué productions, Aramburu and his allies hoped also to shut down plays that portrayed biting social critiques and featured themes revolving around free love, antimilitarism, and attacks on the Church—what Cuba's leaders might refer to as social pornography. Plays by such writers as Ibsen, the prolific anarchist Joaquín Dicenta, and other anarchists fell squarely into this category.[11]

Even some plays that appeared superficially sympathetic to anarchism could actually be interpretations that undermined the movement, anarchists warned. For instance, *El Dependiente* urged workers not to be misled by what appeared to be the friendly titled play "La semana roja ó el proceso de Ferrer" (The Tragic Week or the Trial of Ferrer) in January 1912. A. Garrido's play, wrote the anonymous reviewer, was but one more bourgeois swipe at the reputation of the noted rationalist school practitioner. According to the reviewer, Garrido misrepresented Ferrer as one who educated his family "in the most abject mysticism" and who was portrayed as an omniscient superior being instead of just a man doing what everyone else could do.[12]

On occasion, reviews of notable nonanarchist plays found their ways into the anarchist press. For instance, Palmiro de Lidia, who reviewed plays for *La Voz del Dependiente* during 1908, recommended pieces that were noble, useful to humanity, and filled with symbols of idealism. In fact, in an introductory note to the 1898 version of his play "Fin de fiesta," De Lidia hoped that art would become useful, respond to the pursuit of idealism and truth but still represent the realism of average people's circumstances.[13] Plays like "Tierra baja" or "El adversario," both performed in the National Theater, exemplified human dignity and showed the betterment of individuals and the collective, while representing hatred for "the master's despotism," he claimed.[14] De Lidia particularly recommended "El adversario" because of its realistic portrayal of the problems of adultery in the current social scheme. He reminded readers that throughout the history of the theater, adulterous women had been punished, killed, or pardoned. But in "El adversario" the husband and wife divorce and go on living separate, dignified, individual lives. This was particularly radical because divorce was illegal in Cuba until passage of a no-fault divorce law in 1918. This play's message, then, in a society where divorce was still illegal was despised by *Diario de la Marina* but praised by the anarchists. As De Lidia wrote, "With divorce, marriage has stopped being an indissoluble religious institution, in order to become a simple contract that can be broken at will. This indicates a well-marked evolution that will lift us toward free love as the only rational union between the sexes."[15]

While anarchist cultural critics busied themselves reviewing plays, some of their comrades staged their own performances. In fact, at times anarchists organized their own theatrical companies in Havana. In May 1911, Dionisio García, known in Havana for writing several plays that were criticized for their pornographic content, actually led a workers' theater movement. To some degree, then, when Aramburu and *Diario de la Marina* associated radicalism with pornography, García's history offered the moral critics ammunition. Despite his background, though, *¡Tierra!* backed García by arguing that he wrote his pornographic pieces solely to earn an income. Besides, the paper concluded, García was recognized for his exceptional ability to write about real life issues for the stage.[16]

In June 1914, the anarchist press was alive with discussion of poet and playwright Ramón Castaño López's play "El loco," which opened at the Regla Theater and soon after was staged in Marianao.[17] The play portrayed the young anarchist Anselmo struggling with the realities of Cuban life and expectations of his father. Anselmo's father cannot believe that his son throws bombs and assassinates children; this boy could not have come from his deceased wife. Of course, part of the play's purpose was to overcome such stereotypical depictions of anarchists as wild-eyed bomb throwers. In the final scene, authorities detain Anselmo. But the people collectively rise up to demand justice and march on the jail to free Anselmo. Anarchists gave Castaño's play mixed reviews. Most appreciated the noble sentiments expressed in the work and found it preferable to mainstream popular theater. However, Marcelino Galán described how he and his friend traveled across the city to see the play. Afterward, Galán's friend lamented that the play lacked psychological profiles of the characters and noted how he hoped "that the theater could be a cathedral of sociology at the same time as being a bulwark of combat. The social theater ought to be the antithesis of the bourgeois theater."[18] Other criticism rested on the not-so-subtle religious undertones of the play's conclusion where Anselmo is portrayed as calling to the heavens with arms raised toward the sky. To reviewer Gumersindo Rodríguez, this was antithetical to anarchism. He complained to the production company about this, especially decrying the company for "invoking that 'god' who directs heaven, without considering that anarchists do not wait for something from heaven, but from their own valiant and conscientious efforts."[19]

At the same time that anarchists gained key positions in the major labor federations in the early 1920s and translated this strength into a new era of rationalist schools, new waves of anarchist theater companies emerged. Pedro Ambrosio, who also wrote a regular column in *Nueva Luz* for anarcho-syndicalist trolley employees under the name "Un Motorista," led the most notable efforts. In August 1922 the Cigarette Makers Guild launched a drive to promote working-class theatrical productions by publishing a pamphlet with three of Ambrosio's plays: "Azul y rojo" (Blue and Red), "La cigarrera" (The Female Cigarette Maker), and "La huérfana" (The Orphan).[20] By the end of 1922, Ambrosio had organized the theatrical group "Pro Obreros." He advertised that the group would perform for anyone as long as nowhere on the program would there be another production number, song, or speech that was at variance with the group's anarchist principles.[21] As was the case with so much anarchist performance culture, Ambrosio's productions were often staged for fund-raisers, including a benefit at the Apollo Cinema in Jesús del Monte for the ill comrade Alberto Gálvez in March 1923, another benefit at the Principal Palace Theater in February 1924, and a benefit for the Workers Center and Rationalist School in March 1924. This latter performance was to be staged by Ambrosio's newest group, the "Cuadro de Obreros de la Havana Electric" doing Isaac Pacheco's play "La idea."[22]

From 1904 until the 1920s, the most frequently performed anarchist play was Palmiro de Lidia's "Fin de fiesta." This brief, seven-scene play captured many of anarchism's central themes: worker solidarity, exploitative capitalists, and attacks on traditional religious or social customs particularly regarding marriage. Elena, the daughter of wealthy factory owner Don Pedro, is in love with the poor, struggling factory worker Julián. However, Don Pedro wants to marry her off to an old friend. When Elena tells her priest about her predicament, the priest reminds her that she must follow the wishes of her father no matter what. By the end of the play, the audience discovers that Don Pedro intends to close his factory. Workers have gone on strike and set fire to the building, a move that prevented Don Pedro from liquidating his assets. In the final scene, with his factory in flames, Don Pedro confronts the strikers with pistol in hand. However, Elena charges between her father and the strikers just as Don Pedro fires the gun, and he kills her. For women in the audience, the play illustrated how anarchists imagined the enslaving confines of marriage. Yet it also offered women a female martyr—someone who was inspired by love and justice, throwing herself between a capitalist and workers to defend the workers, one of whom she loved. But she paid the ultimate price for her heroic sacrifice.[23]

Thus, before and even during the arrival of movie theaters in the 1910s, the stage provided a venue in which to depict the conflict in the culture wars waged by anarchists. Yet, the countercultural challenge surrounding artistic culture went beyond theater to include discussions of sculpture and public art as well. For instance, while walking through Havana, Antonio Penichet asked what effect the proliferation of statues that honored generals had on the island's children. Answering his own question, Penichet believed that the statues reinforced children's public school lessons where they were taught that these were "great men." As a result, children imitated the exploits of these generals by playing war in their free time. Penichet argued that society had to stop training the children in militarism and cease celebrating killers as heroes. If there were to be statues, then let there be more statues to praise men of science who represented Nature's greatness. After all, he argued, a man of science like Gutenberg in particular, "gave humanity the means to free itself. That is much more valuable than 'espadas,'" a term with several meanings, any of which Penichet could have emphasized: swords, swordsmen, and thus warriors or generals, and matadors.[24]

Anarchists also frequently scorned what they saw as backward, bourgeois, and monarchical Spanish cultural traditions that were not easily laid aside after independence. As discussed in chapter 4, Spanish traditions did not disappear with the arrival of independence. In fact, many in the hegemonic culture felt a certain affinity for Spanish culture as part of the *raza latina*. Yet, these Spanish customs posed potential cultural and identity problems for Cuba's leaders. Although some may have practiced them, the diverse members of the elite had to be wary to strike some balance between those lingering traditions, their own patriotic calls for national identity, and the attraction of cultural imports from the United States. Anarchists condemned several of these Iberian traditions, including carnival and courtship practices.

Carnival was a cultural phenomenon they reviled with all of the puritanical wrath that turn-of-the-century anarchism could muster. For instance, with the upcoming 1904 carnival, the writer "Rojo Bueno" bemoaned the Cuban youth who he thought wasted their time and energy in such celebrations, doing "macabre dances and savage contortions." Bueno described how it turned his stomach to see youth filled with what he viewed as ridiculous preoccupations. He claimed that young people spent all of their free time over ten months preparing to dress like animals in order to put smiles on their exploiters' faces. "Justice, love, freedom, peace, solidarity are empty words for them. Carnival, yes. Dancing, masquerades, jumping, laughing—although the following day they will not have one crumb to eat—is all they think about."[25]

Anarchists also expressed concern about the symbolic and specific effects of carnival on workers in general and children in particular. In a full-page article in 1909 entitled "La reina del Carnaval" (Carnival Queen), an anonymous author criticized carnival's monarchical overtones and lamented the impact they had on workers. At carnival time, a king and queen were elected from Havana's workers. In 1909 the queen was Emilia García. Anarchists derisively named her "Emilia I." In addressing his words to García, the author called her an empress of diversions whose actions were intended "to make the proletariat believe that the rich and the powerful were really interested in uplifting the people." Because she came from a family of workers, she was to appear as a symbol of the workers. But the author lamented that Emilia was little more than "a deliciously perfumed executioner, a majestic and graceful tyrant, a crowned head from the people, an AUTHORITY among AUTHORITIES." Still, she had no real power. The proof? Then as the "queen" so legitimized by Cuba's elite, she should try to use her authority. Emilia could stand up during carnival and openly proclaim: "FREEDOM FOR MY BROTHERS IMPRISONED ON SOCIAL QUESTIONS, GIVE HIGHER WAGES TO WORKERS IN THE SUGAR MILLS, DON'T OPPRESS THE CUBAN GUAJIRO, PROTECT NATIONAL INDUSTRY! and you will see your decorations changed." The following day, those elite and police who escorted her in carnival processions would shoot her fellow workers as rebels, anarchists, or pernicious foreigners because they did not want to pay the cost of "your REIGN."[26]

Despite anarchist objections to and criticisms of carnival, the yearly celebrations grew in size and extravagance. Carnival's popularity with the Cuban masses explains part of this growth. However, by the 1920s U.S. and Cuban businessmen colluded with government officials in efforts to expand tourism. As a result, tourism-related events played a major role in carnival's growth. In fact, by mid-decade, spectators outnumbered participating celebrants marching along the two-and-one-half hour parade route in Havana.[27] As the 1925 celebrations approached, the writer "Universo" described how carnival was the one time in the year where "all forms of libertine behavior" were legalized and where "grotesquely dressed people stroll along the boulevards since the mayor permits it and the priest does not censure it." But why would Cuba's rulers allow this? Was it just a safety valve where workers and the dispossessed could blow steam? In part, yes, said "Universo," but there was more. During carnival, people parading through the streets drank their beer and alcohol. Meanwhile, the island's political leaders and businessmen looked down from the balconies, knowing that they were in charge and making great sums of money from the temporary legalization of all forms of vice.[28] Consequently, anarchists could see carnival as more than just a means by which workers of lower consciousness wasted their time. They viewed carnival as a true testament of elite control; acts that were banned throughout the year were temporarily lifted by those same leaders so that they could, among other things, make even more money off poor people and tourists.

The "debilitating monarchical" effects of carnival upon workers was one thing, but anarchists charged that the effects on children—the next generation who needed enlightenment now to wage the struggle in the future—were potentially more damaging. "Ana Harquía" lamented the debauchery and sexual undertones of carnival. The writer described how boys ran after girls, smelling their backsides (*oliéndole las posaderas*) and "whispering into their ears immoral words against their virtue."[29] Amalio del Castro described parks on Sundays during carnival as repugnant places, filled with coaches and cars full of the bourgeoisie coming and going. But the true repugnance was the youth—boys and girls dressed like men and women. The boys made fools of themselves, acting like chimpanzees, while the girls smiled, vibrated, and "rubbed themselves against hard things and coach seats in the same way that cats do when in heat."[30]

While anarchists generally believed that carnival unleashed dangerous effects upon Cuban youth, they saw equal danger in certain traditional courtship and social practices still in vogue after independence. The writer "Celeste" described the "*batalla de las flores*" where on Saturday evenings men and women paraded down the tree-lined boulevard of Havana's Prado to the oceanfront Malecón sea wall. "Celeste" called the couples little better than packs of hounds (*la jauría*) or gilded riff-raff (*la canalla dorada*) who showed off how well dressed they were for all, especially the poor workers and youth, to see. Since the first cars arrived in Cuba in 1899, with dealerships selling expensive cars by 1905, Sundays became popular days to see the well-off set touring Havana in their new automobiles.[31] Car owners would load the family into their pricey Buicks or Oldsmobile touring cars and set off for the city's beautiful boulevards. This too fell to anarchist wrath when writers began to complain how these couples seemed to enjoy flaunting their wealth before the poor by exhibiting their expensive cars from Arroyo Arena to San Cristóbal in Havana.[32]

Finally, pointing out evidence of elitist hypocrisy in certain social practices became a common theme in anarchist cultural critiques. *Diario de la Marina* published a letter that decried a dance held on Palm Sunday in the National Theater. Vicente Carreras responded by chastising the women who were horrified, under the "pretext of professing religion, that a dance is scheduled on Palm Sunday. What incredible hypocrisy!" he charged.[33] Carreras admitted that he was not fond of dances, but he regarded such upper-class criticism of dances as hypocritical: These distinguished women, who lamented a dance held on a holy day, were frequently the same ones he saw regularly "showing off their white or brown bosoms through low-cut dresses and letting their beautiful or ugly breasts be seen"; moreover, these same women, with arms around the waists of unknown but titled or rich men, may have abandoned children born out of wedlock.

Conclusion

Ultimately, anarchists employed a wide arsenal of cultural events and cultural critiques in their struggles. Public events and public spaces became sites of potential contention as *veladas*, plays, carnival processions, or even the public walkways and avenues of the Prado could attest. Anarchist performances and discussions condemned Cuba's leaders and wealthy. Anarchists labeled elite-sanctioned cultural practices as forms of vice that "rationally inspired" men, women, and children should avoid. Just as important, by condemning certain practices and creating alternative visions, anarchists offered examples of what public life in an anarchist-defined Cuba could be like.

"Art is the graphic expression of beauty. The vision of Humanity's future is expressed in the three central figures of Society: the Learned Person, the Artist and the Worker: Science, Work and Art," wrote one radical in 1922.[34] The historian Bruce Nelson illustrated this in what he described as "movement culture" among the anarchists he studied in Chicago. "Culture," he concluded, "remained the social space most open to agitation, a space once radicalized that could function as a reservoir for socialist values and traditions."[35] Like their radical brethren in Chicago and elsewhere, Cuba's anarchists used these cultural spaces not merely for entertainment, but also as political challenges to the wealthy, the business owners, the politicians, and even the playwrights. As part of this challenge, they designed their own performances to be educational tools that taught others while reinforcing ideas and a sense of community in the converted. This dimension of the culture war employed both passive and active forms of education. The former centered on statues, watching plays, and observing carnival or engaging in certain dating practices. Anarchists also engaged in more active battles by staging their own plays with average people (spouses, children, and others) playing the roles. By singing, reciting poetry, performing plays, and challenging the cultural practices around them, ordinary people, no matter how marginalized, participated in the cultural struggles to bring forth an anarchist-envisioned Cuba.

11

Imagining Women

Prostitutes, Bad Seeds, and Revolutionary Mothers

Women slaves of the slave: incite your *compañeros* to shake off the yokes that oppress all of us equally. Reject the lies and falsehoods of your tormenters, throw out all of your relics and your ridiculous figures, and enlarge the ranks of the libertarians united with the rebels who make propaganda with the pen, the word and the rifle or dynamite, destroying the dens where the wolves of power, money and religion live.

Francisco J. de Mendoza (1912)

Although anarchists viewed culture as one important avenue to educate larger audiences than they could reach through rationalist schools, one primary audience they sought was women. As noted, *veladas* and plays offered women not only leisure and entertainment but also the opportunities to participate by acting, singing, or speaking. In Cuba after independence, a majority of women had at least a sufficient ability to read and write as to be labeled literate by census takers. In 1907 nearly 55 percent of females older than five years of age could read and write. This number rose to 61 percent by 1919 and exceeded 70 percent by 1931.[1] Census figures may not record just how well a woman could read—a range that could span anywhere from merely being able to read her name to reading philosophical and legal books—but these figures offer approximate ideas and provide a picture of the island's female population as having the basic ability to read anarchist fiction, which, it has to be noted, was written with neither sophisticated language nor complicated plots. Of course, one need not know how to read in order to watch a play, hear poetry, or sing a song.

With a large potential audience before them, anarchist writers regularly targeted women as recipients of their propaganda by incorporating female characters that embodied anarchist messages. Male and female readers, people who heard works read aloud, and those women who viewed or acted in revolutionary theater received several "educational" lessons via the female images. Some works suggested how anarchist women should behave. Other works portrayed women as allegorical figures that were useful for interpreting international and Cuban history. Sometimes these fictionalized images helped anarchists measure vice and corruption in contemporary Cuba. Other times female characters were prostitutes and thus portrayed as victims of a corrupt Cuban society. Writers also represented women as conniving, scheming mothers or wives and thus perpetrators of this corruption. Yet, often authors portrayed women as noble human beings whose lives were in harmony with Nature. These noble "revolutionary mothers" lived simply, worked hard, and raised their children according to anarchist principles.

The image of the "revolutionary mother," a popular symbol in world history since the time of the French and Russian revolutions until contemporary twentieth-century revolutionary movements, has been particularly fashionable in Latin America. History lessons and books long have provided pictures and descriptions from the Mexican Revolution of female soldiers with bandoleers slung over their shoulders. Revolutionary movements promoted the photographs and images of armed female militias or revolutionary units in Cuba in the 1950s and El Salvador in the 1980s. Likewise, millions of people worldwide viewed the famous image of a young Nicaraguan mother with a weapon hanging from her shoulder while an infant suckles at her breast. These images were not new. Their roots partially rest in early twentieth-century anarchist culture. To anarchists, the ideal woman was an enlightened mother who educated her children in revolutionary ideals of equality, justice, and mutual aid. She also attended and participated in anarchist *veladas* and may have taught in anarchist schools. In short, she was a woman who knew no boundaries between the public and the private spheres.

On the surface, the ideal of woman as "mother" appears to resemble the middle-class ideal of the dutifully homebound wife essential for late nineteenth- and early twentieth-century Latin America middle-class development models. In Latin America, this middle-class ideal reinforced the notion that a woman should be restricted to the private realm of the home where she functioned as educator of her children and cleanser of her husband who daily ventured into the filth and vice of the public sphere.[2] In Cuba, middle-class women both challenged and expanded this construction of motherhood after independence. Middle-class feminist organizations arose from 1902 to 1940, influencing legislation, challenging U.S. occupations, and rejecting the individualist tendencies in North American feminism. In their quests to expand democracy in Cuba, feminists wanted to retain their femininity and roles as mothers. They believed that as Cuban "matriarchs" they could bring forth a fuller notion of democracy. However, these feminists were not revolutionaries. They did not seek to end patriarchy or achieve complete social equality. Rather, Cuban feminists used their femininity to gain recognition of motherhood's importance. Motherhood would then play a role in creating a "feminine space" in government where women could use their roles as "mothers and guardians of morality" to oversee welfare programs for children, women, and families.

Anarchist ideals of motherhood challenged these middle-class notions. The anarchists' "revolutionary mother" represented the working class, reviled middle-class values, and rejected working within the government. Rather, anarchist writers of ideological tracts and fiction held up the working mother as a symbol to which women should aspire. In fact, they portrayed the revolutionary mother as the all-important guiding force of the family unit. Cuban anarchists, while denouncing legal and religious institutions of marriage, held the family in high regard and viewed it as the basis for an anarchist form of communism of which the revolutionary mother was both the leading caretaker and the leading symbol.

Social issues concerning women dominated Cuban anarchist literature. Because these works also expressed an anarchist "curriculum," it is useful to see them as educational "texts" and thus as part of the anarchists' larger educational efforts. Thus, fiction that addressed women's issues actually functioned as educational materials specifically targeting women. In fact, the Spanish-based La Novela Ideal series, which published many of Adrián del Valle's novellas, explicitly aimed "to make women and children's hearts pulsate."[3]

Women, Images, and Anarchism in Latin America

Knowledge of the relational dynamics between anarchists (male and female) and women in Latin America is still evolving. Anarchists both led and responded to their larger social climates in Argentina and Brazil, for example. In the early days of the Argentine movement, the dominant discourse focused on women as companions to men. However, by the 1920s, Argentine anarchists replaced this with growing demands that women be able to control their own bodies. In short, anarchists responded to women's demands and thus the anarchist agenda concerning women evolved to fit the specifics of Argentine reality. Such an evolution in how anarchists dealt with women's issues and imagery is illustrated in Argentine anarcho-feminism. Through their newspaper La Voz de la Mujer, anarcho-feminists discussed the multiple origins of women's oppression, especially male power and marriage. Though opposed to marriage, anarcho-feminists still saw women as the main holders of affection in matters of children and love. While not advocating sexual permissiveness, these anarcho-feminists supported free unions between men and women whereby a woman could, without appealing to legal or religious courts, escape a bad marriage. Finally, they sympathized with prostitutes, seeing them as martyrs created and further victimized by social corruption.[4] Other works on class and women in Brazil illustrate how anarchists there followed the lead of women workers. For instance, during the 1917 General Strike in São Paulo, anarchists neither organized the strike nor exerted much influence on the working class. Rather, women textile workers began the demonstrations. From this, anarchists learned to go beyond their political goals by learning the importance of labor organization from women.[5]

Consequently, anarchists in Latin America featured women and women's issues in their propaganda and organization. They began from the anarchist premise of women as individuals equal with men and evolved into fuller, more complex ideas about women and their specific roles and needs in society. Often, the incorporation of these roles and needs evolved as a response to the conditions of women in the larger social context. But this is just one aspect of the relations between women and anarchists. By focusing on how women were incorporated into anarchist fiction, we can add to the overall portrayal of women in the anarchist imagination. This depiction is not merely a literary game; it has real consequences given the way Cuban anarchists specifically used their fiction as educational, consciousness-raising tools for women. Thus, gender roles became another site of conflict in the struggle for Cuba's imagination and women's role in an anarchist-defined *cubanidad*.

Children, Prostitutes, and Bad Mothers

As I noted in earlier chapters, the exploitation of children was a common theme in anarchist publications; such exploitation revolved around conditions of health and labor or potential victimization through degenerate cultural practices. However, authors used children mostly as foils to lament the destructiveness of the modern family and the prevalence of nonrational mothers and fathers. The family, noted Miguel Martínez Abello, could be the arena for "unnatural" sex, incest, sodomy, and masturbation. Besides being exposed to such "degeneracy," he argued that within the family children also first learned to obey despots and to hate.[6] Consequently, authors frequently portrayed children suffering at the hands of deceitful parents and other adults. In Del Valle's "En el hospital" (In the Hospital), Marta's mother and father die before she becomes a teenager, so she travels to Havana to live with her poor aunt who works as a laundress. While living at the house, Marta's cousin rapes her. When the aunt loses her income due to illness, she and her son arrange to prostitute the girl. After several years of this, Marta leaves the house and enters a bordello where she contracts syphilis, which requires her hospitalization. Del Valle's description of the events leaves little sympathy for the aunt and her son. Still, he argues that they were not entirely to blame. Rather, they acted out of economic necessity.[7] Consequently, the story describes not only the fall of a pure spirit (Marta) but also the larger social environment that drove family members to exploit a young girl for sheer survival.

Prostitution was widespread in Cuba, particularly in the capital city. For instance, from 1912 to 1931, the number of prostitutes in Havana alone rose from 4,000 to 7,400. According to histories and travelogues, a person with disposable income could enjoy a sexual free-for-all.[8] One such "treat" was enjoying youthful female bodies. This prostitution of girls and young women appears in a particularly disturbing scene in Penichet's ¡Alma Rebelde!. The Cuban-born Rodolfo makes his way to Havana near the end of Cuba's war for independence. On his way Rodolfo confronts what he sees as multiple social evils caused by the war and exacerbated by influential people in society. He meets a judge, whose daughter sleeps with a priest; a pharmacist's daughter, who sleeps with two different men; two boys of Don Daniel and Don Domingo who are caught in "a repugnant position"; and Petrona, the madam of a whorehouse where business has slowed in the last days of the war. Petrona hears about a military encampment nearby, and to raise much-needed cash, she entices the soldiers to the bordello where two girls begin to service all of them. After the tenth pair of soldiers, the prostitutes are unable to continue "because the girls were spewing out blood from all over especially from the mouth." Both girls die, but there is no scandal because Petrona lives with the chief of police. Petrona simply finds replacements.[9]

In these stories, the organization of girls into money-making enterprises often resulted in the death of the girl, frequently by suicide. This is visible in two other works by Penichet, the novel La vida de un pernicioso and the short story "La venta de una virgen" (Sale of a Virgin). La vida de un pernicioso tells the story of Joaquín, who, after independence, resumes his trade as a shoemaker and begins anarchist agitation. In a strike aimed at the Havana shoe workshop owned by Rosendo, Joaquín is arrested. While in jail, his live-in companion Natalia dies from tuberculosis. The free union relationship between Joaquín and Natalia is held up as an ideal relationship. It is pitted against the "degenerate" homosexual life of Lores, a leading newspaper editor who helps Rosendo. Penichet also contrasts Joaquín and Natalia's relationship with Rosendo and his young live-in servant, the orphan Rosa María. Rosendo sexually molests Rosa María before arranging her marriage to his friend Gumersindo. Distraught at this arrangement, Rosa María clips a newspaper article titled "Aburrido de vivir" (Bored with Living). The article describes how a girl soaked her clothes in alcohol and then lit them, an act of immolation. Rosa María believes that suicide is the only way out of her past sexual abuse and a future life of misery: "That was her only means of freeing herself," concludes the narrator. "How sad that she found herself in such a situation! To be born, to live, and then in the prime of her life, to have to end her life before Nature had fulfilled its mission." One day Rosendo comes home only to find the girl's charred remains.[10]

Penichet's "La venta de una virgen" is even more sinister by discussing a mother's exploitation of her first child, Lucía. The mother, Jacinta, wants a child but does not care who the father is; the important issue is giving birth so that her breast milk can come in. Then she can sell herself as a wet nurse to a rich couple to nurse their child and make money. She in fact succeeds at both endeavors after giving birth to Lucía, and then she has two sons so that she can continue to make money as a wet nurse. After several years of this, Jacinta recognizes that her body is wearing out and becomes desperate; she begins to think up new money-making schemes. As Lucía approaches puberty, her mother recognizes the young girl's striking European features of beauty, especially her blue eyes and blond hair. Subsequently, Jacinta begins to take Lucía to work with her, hoping that a rich man will lay his eyes upon her and pay handsomely for "the enjoyment of her angelic, tender body."[11] Ultimately Jacinta conspires with Godínez, a wealthy man who has a history of enjoying girls' virginity. He brings presents day and night to Lucía, but she rejects his advances. Frustrated, Jacinta and Godínez entrap Lucía one day, and Godínez rapes the young girl. Fraught with despair, Lucía flees her mother and leaps to her death into the crashing waves along Havana's Malecón sea wall. Jacinta begins to cry upon hearing the news of her daughter's death. Yet, Penichet concludes, Jacinta's tears do not demonstrate the anguish of losing her daughter; rather, she weeps for her lost "business."[12]

Besides portraying some women as exploiters of young girls, anarchists often characterized women as "bad seeds." These women were deceitful and consumed with religious or personal interests rather than dedicated to the well-being of the family, their partner, or social progress in general. The conflict between a right-thinking, rationally inspired husband and the bourgeois or religiously devoted wife occurred frequently in anarchist works. In his short story "Paternidad" (Paternity), Jacinto Benavente describes Ricardo's shock when he discovers that his wife Amalia has been allowing their son Adolfo to take religion classes in preparation for communion. Ultimately, Ricardo laments, this is what happens when a revolutionary spends all of his energies in the streets and neglects revolutionary work at home.[13]

This same message is prominent in Penichet's play "¡Salvemos el hogar!" (We Must Save the Home!) in which Matías is a father in an anarchist-defined dysfunctional family. Matías regularly attends meetings and talks at the Workers Center where he becomes convinced of the workers' radical messages. Meanwhile, his children and wife have completely different interests than their father. His son Daniel is primarily interested in the sporting and gaming scene. Daughter María echoes her mother's religious dogma and the middle-class consumerist trappings, which both strive to emulate. In fact, the whole family views the father with contempt and believes that he is wasting his time at the Workers Center. One day his wife Magdalena wants Matías to accompany her to the baptism of a friend's child. Matías declines because he must go to the Center where an assembly on an upcoming strike is to be held. Matías's friend Domingo arrives to escort him to the assembly and berates Matías for the condition of his family, which is "like a summary of current society, all its prejudices, all its errors and all its fanaticisms." To top it off, Matías's youngest son has joined the Boy Scouts—a youth paramilitary organization, in the anarchist mind. In the play's third and final act, the strike has been violently repressed and fights break out between strikers and strikebreakers. Magdalena, María, and Daniel are conceitedly pleased for having recognized what they see as the foolishness of working-class actions. But Magdalena is bitter, too. She yells at Matías and Domingo that due to the strike and no income "now I will not be able to buy the ribbons and scalloped lace to adorn my dress for the dance!" Ultimately the burden of the opposing values is too much for Matías, and he threatens to abandon the family. But Domingo objects: "No, don't drive yourself to despair, Matías. Calm down. What is happening to you is happening to the majority of workers." Workers must educate the home to save it by bringing home books, pamphlets, and other materials. They must take their families to the Workers Centers to hear talks and see performances. Domingo closes by saying to Matías, and thus all workers and especially their wives or *compañeras*, "In the harmonious home, there must exist an affinity for ideas so that through a clear explanation all family members come to understand the humanity of our propaganda."[14]

Women were special targets of anarchist educational and literary initiatives for two important reasons. First, anarchists regularly commented on the religious inclinations of Cuban women. From this perspective, women were the ones who attended mass and filled the confessionals. Through this interaction with religion, the Church was able to influence the religious, political, and social beliefs of mothers who then indoctrinated their children in mysticism, emphasis on the soul and afterlife, and antirational dogma. Were this to continue, then children and the family could not be properly prepared to lay the groundwork for the coming social revolution. Second, and completely opposite of this first description, was the concept of "woman" who occupied an almost reverential place in the anarchist imagination. Anarchists represented women as liberating beings, who could break the chains of slavery. They showed women leading the light of progress in a dark social climate full of deception, struggle, and vice. Most important, they valued women for their roles as mothers and nurturers of children. As a revolutionary mother a woman could best lay the foundations for not only her children but also social progress.

Anarchism, Family, and Revolutionary Mothers

By promoting the image of revolutionary motherhood, anarchists recognized the importance of the family. "Marriage" and "family" were not synonymous, however. While they belittled marriage as an entrapping institution sanctioned by the state and the Church, anarchists promoted the blood and social bonds of the family. In fact, some anarchists like Antonio Penichet believed the family was the foundation for a future cooperative, equal, and free society. In *Tácticas en uso y tácticas a seguir*, Penichet spent five of his forty-five pages outlining this idea. "First, it is necessary to triumph in the home and then triumph in society," Penichet advocated.[15] However, the home and family were more than just the first battle zones in the larger social struggle. Penichet saw the home as well as familial relationships and obligations as nothing short of a small-scale form of communism.

An individual, who appears to have no obligations toward anyone else, meets someone with whom he wants to enter a conjugal life. And we see that this individual, who did not know this person earlier, comes to share with her all his sadness, all his joy, and the product of his labor. Then from here is born a familiarity with other family members, parents, brothers, uncles, nieces, etc. and a bond forms between all of them—something that indicates the march toward communism.... The home, then, is the most pronounced origin of communism and its best field for experimentation.[16]

Penichet's idea of communism was anarchist in nature. The roots of communism did not derive from a revolutionary state that then imposed communism downward upon the masses. Rather, communism had to arise from people's everyday lives. The family, then, served as the most basic grouping of people and the site for the development of human sentiment and cooperative actions. The expansion of this "natural" process of cooperative relationships was then the seed from which larger forms of communist cooperation would emerge. Ultimately, the family was crucial to this growth, but it required a strong, noble revolutionary mother to guide and serve.

Del Valle and Penichet filled their stories with these strong, noble women and mothers. For instance, in "La eterna lucha" (The Eternal Struggle), Del Valle describes a bar scene where two men are getting drunk. They persuade a beautiful woman to sit with them. One man, a poet, continues drinking and eventually falls asleep at the table. His companion listens intently to the woman talk about struggling for "the ideal." Struggling, she argues, is never in vain when it is for an ideal, but struggling for survival is a truly horrible thing. Still, she notes, the struggle is part of Nature's law; the problem is that humans have misinterpreted it to mean struggling against each other. Drawing clearly upon Kropotkin's *Mutual Aid*, Del Valle has his revolutionary female character describe her ideal. "My ideal, the ideal of all generous hearts is this: To replace the brutal struggle of man against man with mutual aid, with mutual love and to see that the eternal struggle to which Nature condemns us has as its final goal the conquest of a free, beautiful, happy life." At that, the two leave, while the drunken poet rises to protest, only to fall face first onto the table.[17]

In "La flor marchita" (The Withered Flower), Del Valle continues this theme of struggle by describing a conversation between an unnamed man and woman. As the couple walks, she picks up a fallen rose and begins plucking it petal-by-petal. The man asks her, "What is woman but the 'human flower' whom bad and weak men pick for their own adornment and to enjoy the fragrance." When they are done with them, he continues, the woman (like the flower) is tossed out. Still, the man notes, women have a special characteristic. Unlike the flower, women can rebel against the brutal hand that picks them and thus against human brutality. The flower and the woman were not born to suffer. Quite the contrary. "Woman, like the flower, was born to enjoy life."[18]

Although women may have been born to enjoy life, the social environment in which they lived often prevented this. Such simple enjoyment of life was difficult to attain in postindependence Cuba. Female workers suffered from joblessness or from jobs: working long hours as stemmers in tobacco factories, laundresses, and seamstresses in homes and shops. Women, with limited educational opportunities, lived in an environment that anarchists described as deceptive and antirational. Consequently, when some women found the strength to perform noble acts in such a setting, anarchists saw them as embodying a noble revolutionary sentiment that would guide humanity in the future. One such woman appears in Del Valle's "En el mar; Narración de un viaje trágico" (At Sea: Narrative of a Tragic Voyage). Flames engulf a ship at sea, and all but the captain go to the lifeboats. One passenger, Lord Vilton, who clearly represents the wealthy with his diamond-encrusted tooth and pompous affectations, tries to bribe his way onto a lifeboat ahead of the women and children. Once safely away from the burning ship, a young mother becomes hysterical. She jumps overboard with her infant, but another female passenger described only as La Rusa saves the baby. At sea, hunger sets in among the survivors, a fact made unbearable by the continuous cries of the starving infant. In a moment of truly noble revolutionary motherhood, La Rusa bears her virgin breasts and offers her milkless nipples to the child. In contrast, Vilton is so hungry that he offers a sailor five thousand pounds sterling so that Vilton can make a gash in the sailor's arm and suck his blood. After three days at sea, the baby dies from hunger and dehydration. Vilton tries to wrestle the infant from La Rusa's hands in order to eat it. In the ensuing struggle, La Rusa throws Vilton's suitcase full of money into the sea, shouting "Get it.... Buy some shark's blood with it!" Then someone hits Vilton over the head and dumps him into the sea. Upon being rescued some time later, La Rusa is still holding the little corpse.[19]

La Rusa's actions reflect the anarchist notion of the noble woman struggling against the rich and powerful. In addition her unselfishness regarding the starving infant exemplified a quality associated with revolutionary motherhood that

Cuban anarchists praised as an ideal capable of saving society. Society had to stop seeing women as merely furniture, moneymakers, or playthings. Their natural gifts of motherhood and a nurturing instinct had to be rescued from the downward spiral of society and the dogmas of the Church. Women were neither fallen flowers tossed aside like furniture when their sexual charms wore out, nor did they embody original sin and the fallen Eve. Women, when their "true" sentiments and proclivities were recognized and employed, were the guiding forces for steering society back in accord with the dictates of Nature. Women, in fact, had the capacity to be the true revolutionaries in this despoiled age. Only by reasserting their natural, noble gifts could women then teach their children truth and justice as anarchists defined it.

Although some women practiced what anarchists believed to be their true callings, Del Valle and Penichet used their fiction to convince those who did not practice these beliefs or whose commitment was shaky to abandon middle-class ambitions and actions. Along these lines, they urged female readers to look toward more noble sentiments and actions as revolutionary women and mothers. In ¡Alma Rebelde!, Penichet describes Rosa, the mother of Miguel, the main character Rodolfo's best friend. Rosa is a strong widow, raising her sons and continuously thwarting the advances of wealthier men. Midway through the novel, Miguel gets his girlfriend pregnant. While the young woman wants to abort the pregnancy, Miguel says no and Rodolfo agrees. Rosa, too, rejects the abortion; she tells her son that once she too had considered having an abortion, but now she is thankful that she carried the child for that child was Miguel.

Abortion raises an important issue concerning anarchist ideals of women's natural role as mothers. While anarchists supported birth control, terminating a life was unacceptable, as Penichet clearly expresses through his character Rodolfo, who argues that no one has the right "to commit those mysterious murders that frequently occur with impunity. The child ought to be preserved for nobody knows what its designated mission is on the earth. It seemed to be an abomination to destroy the child brought forth from a woman's vital organs, and it was neither reasonable nor humane the excuses that many put forth, namely to do it in order to avoid society's gossip." Ultimately, anarchists believed that Cuban society used abortion and orphanages for similar purposes: to remove evidence of "passionate moments." The unborn child became the victim of an immoral society made up of "traders in consciousness" (traficantes de conciencias) and "authorized murderers" (asesinos autorizados).[20] Anarchists thought children had the same rights as adults; thus, abortion of an unborn child amounted to murder. Abortion also challenged the natural role of mother as nurturer, which anarchists found so fundamental to their belief in woman's true nature.

Perhaps the strongest female character in Cuban anarchist fiction is Del Valle's Soledad in *La mulata Soledad*. As noted in chapter 5, Soledad is a working-class mulatto in Havana who comes from an anarchist household and embodies all the elements of what anarchists saw as a woman's true natural revolutionary calling. The story begins with the young medical student Carlos first encountering Soledad on the long tram ride from the Vedado section of Havana to the city's old town shops and factories. When Soledad begins to date the white Carlos, her family expresses a number of different concerns reflecting the racial attitudes of the day. Her brother and sister distrust whites; the former sees whites as the enemy, while the latter questions the intentions of a white man toward darker women. Her anarchist father Jaime also questions his daughter's actions, not because Carlos is white, but because he is a doctor-to-be and thus not a worker. Still, Jaime leaves the decision to his independent, rationally minded daughter. Carlos and Soledad soon join in free union and establish a home together. However, Carlos represents the ambivalence of the upper middle class in a struggle between societal expectations and what is right. The night after Soledad tells him that she is pregnant, Carlos leaves her so that he can marry Estela, a white woman from his social rank. Carlos soon discovers that his new wife not only likes to flaunt her wealth but is also frigid in bed with him. To make matters worse, Estela begins sneaking around and having affairs; Estela merely wants the legal recognition of a marriage to enjoy social privilege and middle-class materialism, but she rejects the notion of children. In the anarchist worldview, Estela rejects her natural calling of motherhood for the hypocritical, unnatural world of middle-class social graces. Meanwhile, Soledad continues sewing in the home, a common practice for female workers, while never abandoning her principles. She raises a child in the difficult circumstances of single motherhood but with the solid support of her anarchist parents.

When Carlos discovers that his wife has cuckolded him, he returns to Soledad. Meanwhile his family disinherits him, and he suffers the social repudiation of living outside of marriage with a nonwhite woman. After an official divorce from Estela, Carlos and Soledad move in together and raise their son. As the novel concludes, the child calls to both and then puts his arms around their heads. "Look, Carlos, the knot that unites us," calls Soledad. "Stronger than the sacredness and legality of marriage," Carlos responds.[21] Ultimately, *La mulata*

Soledad exemplifies the dual purpose of anarchist fiction: it focuses on a debilitating social environment that shaped people's behavior, and it also illustrates how average people could challenge conventions, raise children, and live in free unions. Thus the novel itself reflects Penichet's ideas on the family: Carlos, Soledad, and their son are the basis for communism.

Conclusion

Cuban anarchist writers created women to be avoided as well as women to be emulated. As such, their novels, plays, and short stories were crucial in countering middle-class and religious notions of a woman's role in society. The focus on both women and their new liberating roles was one part of a larger anarchist critique of Cuban society. In particular, this countercultural critique was a direct challenge to the capitalist development ideology regarding women and the public/private sphere divides. Del Valle and Penichet offered their audiences strong, liberating women and revolutionary mothers who actively combated what anarchists framed as a moral and social degeneracy befalling the island. Anarchists imagined that rebellious women like La Rusa, Rosa, and Soledad were crucial for ushering in an anarchist New Dawn for Cuba.

By freeing the imagination of women's potential roles, anarchist authors sought to free women from existing cultural ideals of women's societal roles. Such ideals saw a woman's final role as that of a wife, who raised children to respect middle-class cultural values. Her husband ventured into the public sphere, only to return home at night and be "cleansed" by his Marian-type wife. In this middle-class development ideology, motherhood became a civic duty designed to protect the family while serving as an ideal to raise the lower classes and protect the greater society. Believers of this ideology saw vice and prostitution as a working-class phenomenon that reflected the supposed moral degeneracy of the working poor. Anarchists, however, rejected such a line of reasoning and argued instead that people of all classes partook of vice. If a poor woman resorted to prostitution, then it was not owing to some "moral degeneracy" but to economic circumstances brought on by capitalism and intensified by the threat of legal sanction from the state as well as moral rebuke from the Church. Thus, anarchists viewed prostitutes with sympathy, not scorn. In addition, whereas middle-class ideology sought to keep the mother in the private sphere of the home where she raised the children, anarchists believed that women had to be active in all spheres of society—as teachers in anarchist schools, actresses in anarchist plays, writers and propagandists in anarchist literature—as well as revolutionary motherhood. In fact, part of being a revolutionary mother was helping to enlighten not only her children but also those around her to the "truths" of anarchism and the need to destroy capital, the Church, and the state. There could be no better example to one's child or to society than to work in both the private and public spheres to bring forth social change.

Undoubtedly these images of women's "true" destinies as noble partners and especially as revolutionary mothers reflected a certain patriarchal bias imbedded in Cuban anarchism. Mostly male authors dominated the Cuban and international movements, and they wrote of idealized women who at times sound almost reactionary to a modern ear. In addition, it is difficult to estimate how many women actively joined in the movement. Certainly some Cuban women rejected the promotion of motherhood as an ultimate destiny, which they had neither desire nor ability to fulfill. Even more women embraced motherhood and believed in its sacred mission, and they preferred to live it within the sanctions of formal marriage and traditional sex roles. Other Cuban women, like socialists and feminists, wanted state support for motherhood and saw women's mothering natures as beneficial reasons for why women should be in the government. In addition, anarchists appealed to some of the most marginalized sectors of Cuba: poor women of all races. These poor women were some of the least politicized people on the island, which limited the numbers of female adherents; their apolitical outlook gave anarchists even more reason to target them with anarchist education through either schools or culture.

Many obstacles blocked the paths of women living and working an anarchist ideal. Poor-quality jobs and unsafe working conditions, inappropriate health care (or complete lack thereof), problems surrounding high infant and child mortality, the world of prostitution, and lack of working-class consciousness all impeded women's development. Also, anarchists competed with feminists, socialists, and trade unionists, all of which had their own programs designed to benefit poor women and liberate them from overbearing men. Women moved in and out of these different groups, and nothing prevented women from participating in any combination of groups at the same time.

Ultimately, though, "woman" was a radical icon of Cuban anarchism. Just as images of Nature and the rural ideal could be used to promote rural living while also serving as a yardstick by which to measure the encroachment of industrial capitalism, the use of female images likewise had its promotional as well as ideological components. Certainly anarchists hoped that their literary as well as performance culture would attract female followers. But anarchists also used female images as symbols for anarchist ideals. These radicals hoped that readers of anarchist newspapers, novels, and short stories or viewers of and actresses in anarchist plays acquired an anarchist consciousness from seeing the way women were treated and victimized in Cuban society. Yet, women also inspired anarchists to put forth an ideal for women and family that could serve as a model for Cuba's popular classes. Those same readers and viewers, who recognized how Cuban reality victimized women, might also observe ideal types of female behavior that could be encouraged in spouses, daughters, and friends. Likewise men were exposed to strong, noble women who deserved their respect as intellectual and emotional equals. Thus, when anarchists portrayed women in their fiction, they chose to use images of women not only to reflect an anarchist interpretation of reality but also to inspire social change, a continued merging of social realism and social dreaming that anarchists applied to many issues.

Conclusion and Epilogue

In the three decades following independence from Spain, the meanings of freedom, equality, identity, and progress became central to the debates surrounding what it meant to be "Cuban." Different segments of the Cuban population read their own interpretations into the cultural, political, and social struggles that rocked the island. This book has discussed how anarchists in Cuba operated in, responded to, and helped to shape the fluid social and political situation during those turbulent three decades after independence. Rather than focusing on anarchists as activists within the labor movement who pushed primarily for labor issues, this study has approached anarchism as a countercultural social movement that sustained a thirty-year challenge to Cuba's power holders in the name of the island's popular classes. This movement—made of men and women, old and young, black and white, Cuban- and foreign-born, skilled and unskilled workers, poets, shopkeepers, playwrights, and librarians —challenged not only those political, economic, and cultural leaders who held power but also the political, economic, and cultural foundations upon which Cuba's postindependence leaders based their rule and their notions of what it meant to be Cuban.

The anarchist struggle against the island's leaders, institutions, and cultural foundations was a culture war. In this culture war, anarchists engaged Cuban leaders in institutional and ideological struggles as well as struggles of imagination. The anarchists' leading cultural creators like Adrián del Valle and Antonio Penichet produced literature that framed Cuban reality and the anarchist movement in particular lights. The ideas that these creators and others laid forth were complemented by an array of actions and initiatives from all three anarchist blocs (communists, syndicalists, and naturists). Their actions offered real alternatives for working people to live their ideals while awaiting a hoped-for revolution. This was, in essence, a war between competing paradigms: anarchists rejected not just certain leaders or their policies but also the very premises upon which Cuba's elite justified their power and influence; moreover, the anarchists rejected the future of Cuba that the establishment paradigm envisioned. Anarchists countered with their own idealized interpretations of the past, present, and future. What anarchists envisioned, and what Cuba's leaders tried to suppress, was a radical form of *cubanidad* that was internationalist in orientation, allowed sympathetic concern for Cuban reality, privileged freedom of speech and action, emphasized decentralized and confederal decision-making, and preached racial, national, and gender equality. Several social forces after independence likewise put forth their own *cubanía* (political beliefs in *cubanidad*), but the most radical came from the anarchists because they not only rejected the hegemonic culture's central foundations for what Cuba was to be (a Christian, capitalist republic) but also rejected taking part in any formal political system to bring about their own goals of social justice. Thus, anarchists occupied the most left-wing positions of *cubanía rebelde*.

Although many anarchists were involved with Cuba's labor movement, especially as anarcho-syndicalists came to hold key positions in the labor federations of the 1920s, anarchists as a whole dealt with more than bread-and-butter concerns. Through their ideas, interactions, initiatives, and literature (broadly defined as "culture"), they condemned the political system, the usefulness of party politics, and governmental reforms, while they continued to debate the meaning of independence. They critiqued cultural practices like carnival, dating, suggestive dancing, and the theater. They challenged social issues regarding health, education, prostitution, gender, the family, and living and working conditions. Ultimately, anarchist ideas and practices were part of a larger cultural debate about the meaning of life on the island and the direction of *cubanidad*.

Cuban anarchism was more than just a variant of Spanish anarchism in the tropics, as its detractors sometimes labeled it. Rather, the international anarchist movement modified itself to fit into the realities of postindependence Cuba, specifically tackling core issues surrounding Cuban history, national identity, immigration, health, education, women, and the family. In doing so, anarchism became Cubanized. However, something more was at work. While contributing to the broader political, social, and cultural debates on the meaning of life and work in postindependence Cuba, anarchists also contributed to the narrower fabric of the island's leftist revolutionary tradition. Since 1959, the history of anarchism and its role in Cuba's leftist heritage has been downplayed or distorted. Anarchist internationalism was an important variant of a broader socialist internationalism emerging around the world at the end of the nineteenth and beginning of the twentieth centuries. People like José García, Rafael Serra, Alfredo López, Antonio Penichet, Adrián del Valle, and countless others were among the most visible to develop this internationalism in Cuba. In the 1890s many anarchists, who joined the war for independence, believed it to be a first step in liberating a people from colonial tyranny and hoped this development would begin a social revolution that promoted freedom and equality for all peoples. The harassment of Spanish workers, the conflicts over immigration, the Cuban government's willingness to use force against workers, and the constant threat of U.S. military intervention if the government let workers radicalize too much—all became important issues to anarchist activists, not the least Del Valle and Penichet, the key "framers" of Cuban anarchism. They used these issues to frame a specific interpretation of postindependence Cuban reality; in the process the anarchists portrayed their movement as the true inheritors of the spirit of independence and even the ideals of José Martí. They used this inherited Cuban rebelliousness to justify their attacks on Cuba's political and economic leaders, who anarchists believed were developing a Cuban identity based on hierarchy and divisive concepts of nationalism. The anarchists' latent nationalism—more accurately defined as Cuban "nationality"—helped them to adapt the international movement to fit the specific Cuban context and, they hoped, to attract more followers by creating an anarchist-defined sense of *cubanidad* that would be egalitarian, nonhierarchical, and committed to the workers of the island.

Social justice has been a central theme in the Cuban Left, especially since the Cuban Revolution. Developments in health, education, and gender relations after 1959 were prominent features of socialist change. While the Castro-led government implemented reforms, post-1959 leftists were not the first to draw attention to these issues. Anarchist promotion of these social justice concerns dates to the era of the war for independence. The first U.S. occupation of the island witnessed remarkable improvements in health and sanitation. Yet anarchists believed that "real" health reforms that focused on the elimination of poverty, poor working conditions, and destitute living environments had to be pursued to save humanity and thus create their vision of an anarchist-defined Cuba. Consequently, health became a prominent issue in framing the ideological, institutional, and imaginative struggles that anarchists waged against Cuba's leaders. They condemned what they saw as owner and state negligence in fixing the unhealthy working conditions in the urban factories, the urban cafés and restaurants, and the expanding rural-based sugar complexes. According to this anarchist interpretation, the owners refused to spend the money necessary to improve lighting, airflow, and all-around quality of conditions. In the same vein, they argued that politicians and state agency functionaries were either powerless or unwilling to force owners to make such improvements; thus, anarchists implied that the social revolution promised by Martí during the war had been hijacked by native and foreign capitalists. Because anarchists stressed the importance of family, women, and children, they portrayed owner and state negligence as harmful to not only male workers but also female and child laborers who would give rise to new generations of unhealthy Cubans should changes not be forthcoming.

While anarcho-syndicalists ultimately came to call for revolutionary parties and union-based direct action like boycotts and sabotage to force health reforms, anarcho-naturists emerged, urging Cuba's working poor to do what they could in the present to make themselves and their loved ones healthier. They promoted simple living, getting in touch with Nature, vegetarianism, and an array of alternative therapies designed to maintain or regain one's health. Although syndicalists and naturists took two different, if complementary paths, both groups of anarchists framed their actions in a way that promoted them as helping Cubans in the present while their "nemeses" in business, government, and religion ignored their earthly travails. At the same time, anarchists portrayed Cuba's leaders as having abandoned a way of life that was in harmony with the natural order of the world, which they saw as based on cooperation, mutual aid, and simple living. To this end, anarcho-naturists, led by the journalistic and literary endeavors of Adrián del Valle, framed an idealistic Cuba that they believed should have existed following independence, if those in power had truly followed Martí's and the anarchists' original goals of social revolution. As a result, Del Valle and his associates created an imagined Cuba for their readers and held it up as a measure by which to judge how far removed from Nature Cuba's leaders had taken the island. Such ideational and action-based framing served anarchists not only in their struggles against Cuba's leaders, but also in the creation of a new idealized *cubanidad*. Thus, while the world has focused on the health successes of the post-1959 socialist revolution, health concerns rooted in a critique of capitalism and a vision of an egalitarian natural order long predate the revolution and were central to the Cuban Left as part of the anarchist agenda.

Education and gender equity, likewise, are issues that have received tremendous attention by scholars and observers of the Cuban Revolution. Yet, like internationalism, national identity, and health concerns, earlier generations of anarchists had addressed and debated these issues and launched initiatives regarding them. After independence, two waves of U.S. occupation stimulated public school reforms, religious schools expanded, and even the Cuban government took a more active and creative role in the public educational system by the 1910s. Nevertheless, anarchists rejected these systems on a number of fronts. While they said relatively little about the U.S. role in designing a school system, anarchists saved their harshest rhetoric for Cuban-run religious and public schools. Founded on their traditional distrust of organized religions, the anarchists attacked religious schools, particularly, though not exclusively, Catholic institutions. Anarchist critics portrayed Catholic schools as the embodiment of mysticism and the institution that most frequently attacked sound, rational, scientific-based education. As a result, they saw such schools as holdovers from the pre-independence era that, if allowed to continue, would merely reinforce an earlier form of educational tyranny. Their attacks against religious education at times actually echoed nationalists, who claimed that private schools undermined Cuban nationalism. However, while anarchists and nationalists may have had similar feelings about religious education, anarchists had no love for public schools either. They portrayed the Cuban state as using public education to indoctrinate students into a particular form of patriotic nationalism, that, according to anarchists, was merely a means to reinforce the rule of the capitalist elite, preserve a hierarchical system inherited from Spanish colonialism, and at the same time fashion in students an elite-defined sense of *cubanidad* reinforced by such symbolic practices as saying the pledge of allegiance and singing the national anthem. Thus, anarchists condemned public education by arguing that schools neither helped children understand their rights nor afforded them effective training.

It was one thing to frame the Cuban educational systems as upholders of an elite agenda for the island, but anarchists went beyond these critiques and promotion of ideas to create their own schools. By doing so their actions helped to frame the ideals for which the movement stood. Building on the worker-initiated schools from before independence and the educational experiments of Francisco Ferrer in Spain, rationalist schools went through two phases: first, a haphazard affair loosely organized by anarcho-communist groups developed small alternative schools; second, a more coordinated and better financed school program reflected the anarcho-syndicalist–influenced labor unions of the 1920s. While the schools struggled for lack of stable funding, they also suffered some of the same problems associated with the larger public school system, especially difficulties in finding appropriately trained teachers. However, the schools did not attract large numbers of children or workers. Consequently, anarchists staged (literally) alternative educational mediums to reinforce the schools' lessons while also reaching larger audiences. This revolutionary culture of novels, plays, poetry recitals, short stories, and songs was designed to put forth the movement's ideals, critique the larger social forces that impacted people's daily lives, and even offer some people the opportunity to perform. In a sense, the actual stage at times became a means for people to "perform" as rebels so that their roles as performers simultaneously meant that they functioned as a form of "teacher" to the audiences that watched them. Because women played a key role in the anarchist imagination, they explicitly targeted women with their literary and performance culture. Anarchist authors portrayed women as victims and victimizers, depending on the particular message of the piece. But most important, authors held up women as "revolutionary mothers" who embodied an anarchist-defined natural harmony. Though questionable as to how successfully anarchists attracted women to the movement, their efforts were designed to portray a working mother who could function strongly and equally with men both inside and outside the home where she would further serve as a symbol of an emancipated humanity.

To anarchists, these revolutionary mothers were springboards to develop an anarchist-defined *cubanidad*. In the 1960s and 1970s, efforts to universalize education and additional efforts to attack machismo while improving the livelihoods of Cuban women emerged on the island. The state sought to educate people to promote a socialist Cuba. At the same time, particularly through state-run cultural productions like cinema, a new "revolutionary" wife and mother was promoted as an ideal necessary for the development of Cuban socialism. One need only think about the classic Cuban movies *Lucía* and *Portrait of Teresa*. This is not to say that the socialist government looked to the anarchists for inspiration or that some lingering residue of anarchist education and gender ideals filtered to the top of the decision-making structure in post-1959 Havana. Rather, it is to draw attention to the fact that anarchists and their allies had introduced these concepts into the island's leftist tradition a half-century earlier.

It is essential to remember that anarchists were never strong enough to bring down the Cuban state. In fact, after independence they never directly tried. Besides lacking the arms (and the will to use arms), they tried to appeal to the most depoliticized segments of Cuba's population. Thus, from the start they found it difficult to involve critical masses of people necessary for a sustained armed challenge. Nor were anarchists interested in working within the state power structure through elections or governmental commissions the way that Socialists did and Communists came to do. This refusal to participate reflects the fundamental mistrust that anarchists had for established political systems and the importance that they placed in decentralized "self-help" initiatives where people acted for themselves. This idea of not wanting to take part in politics has been criticized, not the least of which by post-1959 Cuban historians, as idealistic and impractical.

The anarchists' approach was probably impractical, but from their point of view understandable. After all, anarchists had seen many examples of politicians accepting workers' votes, only to then abandon or neglect workers' needs. In addition, a state that was viewed by anarchists as working hand-in-hand with exploitative industrialists, looking the other way when it came to the health concerns of workers, and creating schools that bred blind patriotic obedience was not an entity to which anarchists wanted to sacrifice their principles to join. They were stubborn. Still, despite their stubbornness, they were willing to work with nonanarchists to achieve immediate goals. They occasionally cooperated with Socialists on immigration as well as on women's issues and *naturismo*. They worked with nonanarchist unions to win benefits as well as to form the first large labor federations in the 1920s. Likewise, they joined with Marxists in the 1920s to create alternative schools. In fact, Cuba's anarchists did not even always agree among themselves. Not all supported the war for independence, nor were all postindependence anarchists convinced that they should promote and celebrate the image of José Martí. And, even though there were alliances between anarcho-syndicalists, Socialists, and Marxists in the 1920s, not all anarchists believed that such pansectarian cooperation was in anarchism's best interest. At times, internal divisions threatened not just ideological consistency, but, more important, they threatened the health and educational initiatives that were central to how the movement as a whole portrayed itself to the public as working for the immediate improvement of the working poor. This was particularly true in debates over vegetarianism, pedagogy, finding trained teachers, and personal conflicts.

At this point, some readers may wonder: if the anarchists were so stubborn, at times divided, and then ultimately effectively repressed by the Machado dictatorship by the late 1920s, then is it safe to say that anarchism in Cuba died at that time too? The answer is a qualified "no." Anarchists continued to agitate throughout the decades between the *machadato* and the eventual exile of most anarchists in the early 1960s. With Machado's repression of the anarchists and the PCC, revolutionaries like Antonio Penichet and Julio Antonio Mella fled into exile. Mella was assassinated in Mexico, but Penichet returned to Cuba. In the meantime, those anarchists who posed the least threat to Cuba's power holders—the anarcho-naturists—continued to operate and publish *Pro-Vida* throughout the Machado years. By 1933, anarchists were again participating in strikes that led to the revolution of that year. In fact, having returned from exile, Penichet was elected to the general strike committee of the FOH.[1] During the 1933 Revolution, workers implemented tactics that reflected the anarchist influence in the workers' movement over the previous decades. Striking sugar workers took over mills throughout the island. In the summer, workers converted many of these occupied mills into soviets. This worker initiative actually preceded the PCC's formal call for such creations. The rapid spread of mill occupations and autonomous development of soviets can be attributed to the fact that anarcho-syndicalist influences of direct action and decentralized community autonomy still proliferated throughout parts of Cuba. Thus, anarcho-syndicalism, though not the only radical doctrine involved in the revolution, still lingered in the hearts, minds, and actions of various sectors of the workforce.[2] This weakened but continued presence in Cuba was further seen in the mid-1930s when anarchists supported republican forces in the Spanish Civil War, with many going to Spain. Following the war, they returned to Cuba with a number of their Spanish anarchist comrades.[3]

In the early 1940s, anarchists continued to operate in Cuba. As fascism raged in Europe, Penichet helped to initiate a campaign to purge the Cuban school system of what he and others saw as corrupting influences. While the movement's detractors tried to cast it as "communist," Penichet responded in the summer of 1941 that the movement was an attempt to protect the liberal and democratic aspects of Cuba from encroachment of the Vatican, fascism, and all politics. Such a stance was in line with Penichet's long-standing anarchist beliefs in a free-thinking, secular education.[4] His continuing interest in schools had manifested itself earlier when he headed the Education Committee of the CNOC in the early 1920s. In fact, in 1938 he had published a chapter on Cuban social history from an anarchist perspective in the widely circulated Cuban history textbook *Curso de introducción a la historia de Cuba*.[5]

Besides involvement in this education campaign, anarchist figures played central roles in Havana's libraries. When Penichet worked on the 1941 education campaign, he was the director of the National Library. His fellow anarchist and literary partner, Adrián del Valle, also served as director of the most important library and intellectual center in the country—the Sociedad Económica de Amigos del País. Del Valle's activities were widely noted in Cuba. However, in the years after the 1920s his anarchist beliefs were less well known. At his death in 1945, following fifty years of anarchist activity and literary output on the island, every newspaper except the Communist *Hoy* published his obituary; however, not a single mainstream newspaper mentioned his anarchism.[6]

In April 1943 anarchists formed the Libertarian Association of Cuba (Asociación Libertaria de Cuba [ALC]). The ALC was comprised of delegations from Regla, Marianao, Santiago de las Vegas, Arroyo Naranjo, Casa Blanca, and other cities.[7] The impetus for the ALC's creation has to be located in the growing alliance between the Batista-led government and the Communists in the 1940s. Independent labor organizations were virtually destroyed, but a growing state control of unions was facilitated by the Communists (known as the Partido Socialista Popular [PSP] from 1944 until the rise to power of Fidel Castro) that, as part of its united front strategy, worked with the government to oust more militant activists from the Communist-dominated Cuban Workers Confederation (CTC) founded in 1939. In response, anarchists created the ALC to challenge the state and the Stalinists while also working to resurrect both independence and autonomy within the labor movement.[8]

Batista returned to power through a coup on March 10, 1952, and in April he closed the anarchist newspaper *El Libertario*. From the coup's very beginning, the ALC sought to unite the island's revolutionary groups in an armed resistance against Batista's troops, but to little avail. While this shift to willingly engage in armed militancy distinguishes the anarchists of the Batista era from their predecessors, there is another major difference. It appears that the countercultural initiatives like health care and education were absent from this generation of the movement. Still, the ALC functioned throughout Cuba by the time that Castro landed in the Sierra Maestras in 1956. ALC groups operated in Havana, Pinar del Río, San Cristóbal, Artemisa, Ciego de Ávila, and Manzanillo. In these cities and elsewhere, anarchists worked in unions of different trades. One of the anarchists' strongest centers of support throughout the century was in the food industry. In Havana, food workers published their monthly newspaper *Solidaridad Gastronómica* uninterrupted for eight years. Similarly, anarchists were prominent in the food workers union in Santiago de Cuba.

In 1957, speaking on behalf of the ALC, the anarchist Isidro Moscú attacked the top-heavy, bureaucratic nature of the CTC and the confederation's perceived conservatism in a speech widely disseminated through the mainstream press. Meanwhile, as Fidel Castro and Che Guevara waged guerrilla war in the mountains, anarchists challenged Batista in the cities by participating in various urban revolutionary movements like the Directorio Revolucionario and the Federation of University Students. Anarchists agitated against Batista through clandestine radio broadcasts, and the ALC meeting hall became a center to distribute anti-Batista propaganda. For these actions and others, including using their hall to train some of Castro's 26th of July Movement members to use firearms and for attempts to lead an armed uprising in Pinar del Río Province, anarchists faced the full force of Batista's clampdown. The government imprisoned, caused to disappear, and/or tortured ALC members.[9]

Immediately following Castro's rise to power in 1959, anarchists, continuing to agitate for social change, hoped that the long awaited social revolution finally had arrived. For two years, they irregularly published *Solidaridad Gastronómica* and the ALC's re-opened *El Libertario*. Although the new government embarked on education and health reforms, the top-heavy, bureaucratic nature of these reforms, coupled with the state socialist aura surrounding them, troubled anarchists. Meanwhile, press censorship and newspaper closings rose; schools became regimented, and children were forced to wear uniforms; the government increasingly centralized its power at the expense of decentralized autonomous actions; and old Communists who had worked with Batista, like Juan Marinello and Blas Roca, returned to prominence. Within this environment, anarchists continued to push for their theme of "Socialism will be free or there will be no socialism." However, it was inevitable that the anarchists and the new government would confront each other.

Solidaridad Gastronómica and *El Libertario* ceased to publish in March 1961, and the ALC folded. Anarchist critics of the regime found themselves where they had always found themselves when they spoke out a little too virulently against whatever government happened to be in power: in prison. For most there was only one recourse. While the Castro-led government labeled the more than 400,000 Cubans who went to the United States between 1959 and 1969 as "counterrevolutionaries," anarchists reversed the charges. They declared the Cuban Revolution itself to be counterrevolutionary and fled into exile. Like most of their fellow Cubans, they went to Miami. There, through the Cuban Anarchist Movement in Exile (Movimiento Libertario Cubano en el Exilio) and its journal *Guángara Libertaria*, the old revolutionaries continued into the 1980s to offer an anarchist critique of capitalism, U.S. imperialism, and Cuban state socialism.[10]

Ultimately, neither Cuba's anarchists nor anarchist influences completely disappeared from the island with the rise of the *machadato* in 1925. Certainly anarchist leadership in the labor movement and anarchist cultural initiatives had peaked, but as these few final pages chronicle, and future scholars will explore more fully, anarchists continued to occupy some of the most radical positions on the Cuban political spectrum. This became especially evident in the two years following the 1959 revolution when the anarchists were even too radical for the revolution.

For anarchists, the aftermath of 1959 was similar to the aftermath of independence in 1898. While political leaders promised a social revolution during and immediately after both years, neither revolutionary outcome proved to be what anarchists had in mind. After 1898, rather than give up, anarchists struggled to "live" the revolution through their cultural initiatives and activities both in and out of the labor movement. They promoted "internationalism" in the face of nationalist agendas and fought for better health conditions while creating alternative health initiatives targeted at the poor. They challenged religious and state education, and offered educational strategies that were decentralized, egalitarian, and fundamentally free. In so doing, these anarchist rebels took part in a long tradition of imagining Cuba as an "island of dreams" where humanity could create a free, healthy, educated, and egalitarian beacon for global liberation.

Notes

Introduction

Epigraph: Penichet, *Del ambiente proletario*, 43–44.

1. See Rosenzweig, *Eight Hours for What We Will*.

2. Marshall, *Demanding the Impossible*, xv.

3. Ibid., 402.

4. Bookchin, *Social Anarchism*, 56–57.

5. Marshall, *Demanding the Impossible*, 8–9.

6. Masjuan, *La ecología humana en el anarquismo ibérico*, 458.

7. DeShazo, *Urban Workers and Labor Unions in Chile*, xxxi.

8. Casanovas, *Bread, or Bullets!*, 77–78; Fernández, *Cuban Anarchism*, 17.

9. Fernández, *Cuban Anarchism*, 17–18. For more on the reformism of Martínez, see José Antonio Portuondo's *"La Aurora" y los comienzos de la prensa y de la organización obrera en Cuba;* Mariana Serra García's *La Aurora y El Productor;* Olga Cabrera's *Los que viven por sus manos;* and Joan Casanovas's *Bread, or Bullets!*

10. For discussions of Roig San Martín, his newspaper, and the development of anarchism in the Cuban labor movement during the 1880s, see the above-cited works as well as Jean Stubbs's *Tobacco on the Periphery: A Case Study in Cuban Labour History, 1860–1958.*

11. I discuss these debates in chapter 2. See Casanovas, *Bread, or Bullets!*, 222–31, and Poyo, "The Anarchist Challenge," 29–42.

12. See the coverage in *¡Tierra!* during late 1902, as well as analyses of the strike from two different ideological perspectives: Cabrera, *Los que viven por sus manos*, 85–91, and Fernández, *Cuban Anarchism*, 45.

13. Loveira, *Adrián del Valle*, 8–9; *Diccionario biográfico cubano*, vol. VII, 76–77.

14. Cabrera, *Alfredo López*, 20; Primelles, *Crónica Cubana*, 92–93.

15. Cabrera, *Los que viven por sus manos*, 256–59.

16. Cabrera, *Alfredo López*, 64.

17. West, *Tropics of History*, 4.

18. Ibid., 176.

19. Burns, "The Novel as History," 355.

Chapter 1. Anarchism, *Cubanía*, Culture, and Power

1. Kapcia, *Cuba: Island of Dreams*, 23–24.

2. Pérez, *On Becoming Cuban*, 83–95.

3. Kapcia, *Cuba: Island of Dreams*, 65.

4. Ibid., 6.

5. De la Fuente, "Myths of Racial Democracy," 67.

6. De la Fuente, "Two Dangers, One Solution," 45.

7. Kapcia, *Cuba: Island of Dreams*, 53.

8. Whitney, *State and Revolution in Cuba*, 54.

9. Wolf, *Envisioning Power*, 5.

10. Gledhill, *Power and Its Disguises*, 81; italics in the original.

11. Ibid., 90; italics in the original.

12. Mintz, "Foreword," 9–10.

13. Wolf, *Europe and the People without History*, 390.

14. Levine, "Constructing Culture and Power," 21–22.

15. Sonn, *Anarchism*, 52.

16. Salerno, *Red November, Black November*, 140. See also Richard Sonn's *Anarchism and Cultural Politics* and Lily Litvak's *La mirada roja* and *Musa Libertaria*.

17. Sonn, *Anarchism*, 52.

18. Roszak, *The Making of a Counter Culture*, 42.

19. Ibid., 55.

20. Yinger, *Countercultures*, 22–23.

21. Ibid., 23–24.

22. Golluscio de Montoya, "Círculos anarquistas y circuitos contraculturales," 58.

23. Yinger, *Countercultures*, 287.

24. Gledhill, *Power and Its Disguises*, 88.

25. Ibid., 185.

26. Ibid., 199–200.

27. Tilly, *Stories, Identities, and Political Change*, 90.

28. Gledhill, *Power and Its Disguises*, 185, 196.

29. Ibid., 196.

30. McAdam, et al., *Comparative Perspectives on Social Movements*, 6; italics in the original.

31. Ibid., 6.

32. McAdam, "The Framing Function of Movement Tactics," 339.

33. Ibid., 340–41; italics in the original.

34. Rowe and Schelling, *Memory and Modernity*, 2–3.

Chapter 2. Cuba for All: Anarchist Internationalism and the Politics of Cuban Independence

Epigraph: *¡Tierra!*, November 26, 1914, p. 1.

1. Poyo, "*With All, and for the Good of All*," 70.

2. Ibid., 91–94.

3. Ferrer, "Social Aspects of Cuban Nationalism," 38.

4. Ibid., 44–45.

5. Ibid., 44.

6. *El movimiento obrero cubano*, 66–69.

7. Poyo, "The Anarchist Challenge," 29–42.

8. Ibid., 40.

9. Poyo, "*With All and for the Good of All*," 104.

10. Ibid., 107; Cabrera, "Enrique Creci," 135–36.

11. *El movimiento obrero cubano*, 81.

12. Casanovas, *Bread, or Bullets!*, 222–23.

13. *Risveglio* (Tampa), June 22, 1913, pp. 2–3; Casanovas, *Bread, or Bullets!*, 227.

14. Fernández, *El anarquismo en Cuba*, 42–45.

15. Cabrera, "Enrique Creci," 148–49; Casanovas, *Bread, or Bullets!*, 227.

16. Fernández, *El anarquismo en Cuba*, 42–45.

17. Álvarez Junco, *La ideología política del anarquismo español*, 263.

18. Ibid., 264. See also Núñez Florencio, "Los anarquistas españoles y americanos," 1077–92.

19. Casanovas, *Bread, or Bullets!*, 229–30.

20. Ibid., 202.

21. *El Nuevo Ideal*, February 4, 1899, p.1.

22. Ibid., February 25, 1899, p. 1; March 11, 1899, pp. 1–2.

23. Ibid., November 2, 1899, p. 2; November 9, 1899, p. 3; November 16, 1899, p. 1; November 23, 1899, pp. 1–3; and *Risveglio* (Tampa), June 22, 1913, pp. 2–3.

24. *El Nuevo Ideal*, November 9, 1899, p. 3.

25. Ibid., November 23, 1899, p. 1.

26. Pérez, *Cuba Between Empires*, 270–72.

27. *El Nuevo Ideal*, February 4, 1899, p. 2.

28. Ibid., August 24, 1899, p. 2.

29. Ibid., March 25, 1899, p. 1.

30. Ibid., February 11, 1899, pp. 1–2.

31. Pérez, *Cuba: Between Reform and Revolution*, 181–83.

32. *El Nuevo Ideal*, February 15, 1901, p. 3.

33. Ibid., May 8, 1901, p. 2.

34. *¡Tierra!*, May 16, 1903, p. 1; Cabrera, *Los que viven por sus manos*, 83; Page, "The Development of Organized Labor in Cuba," 39–40.

35. *¡Tierra!*, May 16, 1903, p. 1.

36. Ibid., May 23, 1903, p. 1.

37. Pérez, *Cuba Under the Platt Amendment*, 99.

38. *¡Tierra!*, September 15, 1906, p. 1.

39. Ibid., November 10, 1906, p. 3.

40. Ibid., December 15, 1906, p. 1.

41. Ibid., June 12, 1907, p. 1.

42. Letter from Inspector General of Jails, Penitentiary & Charitable Institutions to Gov. Magoon on Detention of Marcial Lores García and Abelardo Saavedra, May 5, 1907, Record Group 199, National Archives, Washington, D.C.

43. Memo to the Chief of Staff from Captain John Furlong, December 28, 1907, Record Group 199, National Archives, Washington, D.C.

44. Memo to the Chief of Staff on Havana Strike Conditions from Captain John Furlong, December 20, 1907, Record Group 199, National Archives, Washington, D.C.

45. Norton, *Norton's Complete Hand-book*, 142.

46. Wright, *Cuba*, 139–42.

47. *Rebelión!*, March 4, 1909, p. 2.

48. Ibid., October 10, 1910, p. 2.

49. Cabrera, *Los que viven por sus manos*, 85–134; Córdova, *Clase trabajadora y movimiento sindical en Cuba*, 91–101; Pérez, *Cuba Under the Platt Amendment*, 152–66.

50. Pérez, *Cuba Under the Platt Amendment*, 155.

51. Ibarra, *Cuba: 1898–1921*, 436.

52. Ibarra, *Prologue to Revolution*, 113.

53. Cabrera, *Los que viven por sus manos*, 157–64.

54. Ibid., 187–89.

55. *El Dependiente*, November 26, 1914, p. 2.

56. Cabrera, *Los que viven por sus manos*, 189–93.

57. Carr, "Mill Occupations and Soviets," 114.

58. Cabrera, *Los que viven por sus manos*, 217–23.

59. Cable from American Minister at Havana, March 11, 1918; and Letter from American Consulate in Cienfuegos to Secretary of State, January 10, 1920, Record Group 59, Records of the Department of State Relating to Internal Affairs of Cuba, 1910–1929, National Archives, Washington, D.C.

60. Cabrera, *Los que viven por sus manos*, 176; Fernández, *El anarquismo en Cuba*, 58.

61. Tellería, *Los congresos obreros en Cuba*, 99–107.

62. *Nueva Luz*, February 15, 1923, p. 11.

63. *El Progreso*, November 29, 1924, p. 3; *¡Tierra!*, November 27, 1924, p. 1.

64. Page, "The Development of Organized Labor in Cuba," 62.

65. Sonn, *Anarchism*, 5.

66. Álvarez Junco, *La ideología política del anarquismo español*, 254.

67. Dolgoff, *Bakunin on Anarchism,* 401–2.

68. Ibid., 401.

69. Hobsbawm, "Working-Class Internationalism," 13–14.

Chapter 3. Symbolic Freedom: Anarchism and the Cultural Politics of Independence

Epigraph: Penichet, *¡Alma Rebelde!,* 11.

1. Del Valle, *Por el camino,* 111.

2. Ibid., 67.

3. Ibid., 69.

4. Del Valle, *Tiberianos,* 21.

5. Ibid., 28.

6. Penichet, *¡Alma Rebelde!,* 11.

7. Ibid., 14.

8. *¡Tierra!,* March 4, 1905, p. 1.

9. Ibid., pp. 2–3.

10. Ibid., June 12, 1907, p. 2.

11. Ibid., June 3, 1911, p. 2.

12. Penichet, *¡Alma Rebelde!,* 65–68.

13. *¡Tierra!,* October 9, 1911, p. 4.

14. *El Dependiente,* November 5, 1913, p. 2; November 12, 1913, pp. 1–2.

15. *El Progreso,* March 27, 1924, p. 7.

16. Ibid., May 8, 1924, p. 4.

17. Penichet, *¡Alma Rebelde!,* 85.

18. *Nueva Luz,* February 1, 1923, p. 2.

Chapter 4. The Cuban Melting Pot: Anarchism and Immigration

Epigraph: *¡Tierra!,* October 29, 1904, p. 2.

1. Mesa-Lago, "The Labor Force," 10.

2. Mormino and Pozzetta, *The Immigrant World,* 72–73.

3. Iglesias García, "Características de la inmigración española en Cuba," 87; Naranjo Orovio, "Trabajo libre e inmigración española en Cuba," 770.

4. Iglesias García, "Características de la inmigración española en Cuba," 87.

5. Naranjo Orovio, "Trabajo libre e inmigración española en Cuba," 790.

6. To compare Cuba with its nearest competitor Puerto Rico, see Martínez, *Peripheral Migrants,* 36.

7. Clark, "Labor Conditions in Cuba," 684; De la Fuente, "Two Dangers, One Solution," 30–31.

8. Clark, "Labor Conditions in Cuba," 788–89.

9. Ibid., 685.

10. Naranjo Orovio, "Trabajo libre e inmigración española en Cuba," 751; González, "La política inmigratoria," 126.

11. Naranjo Orovio, "Trabajo libre e inmigración española en Cuba," 760–63; González, "La política inmigratoria," 126.

12. Pérez, *Cuba Under the Platt Amendment*, 82.

13. Pérez, *Cuba: Between Reform and Revolution*, 201.

14. García Álvarez and Naranjo Orovio, "Cubanos y españoles después del 98," 109–14.

15. Naranjo Orovio and García González, *Medicina y racismo en Cuba*, 24–29.

16. Knight, "Jamaican Migrants," 97.

17. González, "La política inmigratoria," 122; Pérez de la Riva, *La República Neocolonial*, vol. 1, 23; Pichardo, *Documentos para la historia de Cuba*, vol. 2, 199–201.

18. Pérez de la Riva, *La República Neocolonial*, vol. 2, 28–29; Pichardo, *Documentos para la historia de Cuba*, vol. 2, 420–22.

19. De la Fuente, "Two Dangers, One Solution," 30; García Alvarez and Naranjo Orovio, "Cubanos y españoles después del 98," 109–14.

20. Mesa-Lago, "The Labor Force," 10–11.

21. Ibarra, *Prologue to Revolution*, 175–78.

22. *El Nuevo Ideal*, April 8, 1899, p. 1; April 29, 1899, p. 1.

23. Rivero Muñiz, *El movimiento obrero*, 206.

24. *¡Tierra!*, June 20, 1903, p. 3; June 27, 1903, p. 4.

25. *El Nuevo Ideal*, May 4, 1900, p. 3.

26. Ibid., October 15, 1900, p. 28.

27. Ibarra, *Cuba: 1898–1921*, 150.

28. *¡Tierra!*, June 25, 1904, p. 1.

29. See José García's descriptions in *¡Tierra!*, October 29, 1904, p. 2, and February 11, 1905, p. 2.

30. Ibid., February 11, 1905, p. 2.

31. Ibid., February 8, 1908, p. 2.

32. Untitled insert from *Asociación de Obreros en General de los Cafés de la Habana* (1908) in Max Nettlau Archive, Latin Amerika Libertaire Drucke, Cuba Portfolio, International Institute for Social History, Amsterdam.

33. *¡Tierra!*, January 21, 1905, p. 2.

34. Pérez, *Cuba: Between Reform and Revolution*, 207.

35. *¡Tierra!*, November 14, 1908, p. 3.

36. *El Dependiente*, May 15, 1916, p. 1.

37. *La Voz del Dependiente*, October 8, 1908, p. 4.

38. *Diario de la Marina*, January 6, 1909, p. 3.

39. *¡Tierra!*, September 12, 1911, pp. 2–3.

40. Ibid., p. 1.

41. *El Dependiente*, May 1, 1913, p. 1.

42. Zanetti and García, *United Fruit Company*, 244.

43. Rosell, *Luchas obreras contra Machado*, 95–98, 108–10; De la Fuente, "Two Dangers, One Solution," 42–43.

44. Chomsky, "The Aftermath of Repression," 17–18.

45. De la Fuente, "Two Dangers, One Solution," 33–37.

46. Knight, "Jamaican Migrants," 104–9.

47. *Nueva Luz*, January 11, 1923, p. 6.

48. Carr, "Mill Occupations and Soviets," 135; Cabrera, *Los que viven por sus manos*, 303–8.

49. *El Progreso*, November 29, 1924, p. 7.

50. Ibarra, *Cuba: 1898–1921*, 157.

51. For more on this role of black migrant labor in Cuba, focusing mostly on the early 1930s, see Carr, "Identity, Class, and Nation," 83–116, and De la Fuente, "Two Dangers, One Solution," 43.

52. Antonio Penichet, *La vida de un pernicioso*, 37.

53. Ibid., 50–53.

54. Ibid., 133.

55. Del Valle, *Ambición*, 30.

Chapter 5. Anarchism in Black and White: Race and *Afrocubanismo*

Epigraph: *El movimiento obrero cubano*, vol. 1, 69; ibid., 82.

1. Casanovas, *Bread, or Bullets!*, 193–95.

2. Ibid., 233; *Report on the Census of Cuba, 1899*, 462–63; *Cuba: Population, History and Resources, 1907*, 255–57.

3. Rivero Muñiz, *El movimiento obrero*, 111–29; Fernández, *Anarchism in Cuba*, 49.

4. De la Fuente, "Two Dangers, One Solution," 38–43.

5. Pérez, *Cuba: Between Reform and Revolution*, 211–12; Fernández Robaina, *El negro en Cuba*, 46–67; Helg, *Our Rightful Share*, 117–60.

6. Helg, *Our Rightful Share*, 143–44; Fernández Robaina, *El negro en Cuba*, 59.

7. Fernández Robaina, *El negro en Cuba*, 65–66.

8. Helg, *Our Rightful Share*, 151.

9. Ibid., 158.

10. Ibid., 164–67.

11. Ibid., 179.

12. Ibid., 211.

13. Ibid., 214–21.

14. Ibid., 225.

15. Ibid., 228.

16. Sarduy and Stubbs, *Afro-Cuba*, 79.

17. Memo to the Chief of Staff on Strike Issues from John Furlong, Captain, General Staff, Chief of Military Information Division, December 23, 1907, Records of the Provisional Government: "Confidential" Correspondence, 1906–1909, Record Group 199, National Archives, Washington, D.C.

18. Memo to the Chief of Staff on Operations of Anarchists among Strikers—Havana from John Furlong, Captain, General Staff, Chief of Military Information Division, December 23, 1907, Records of the Provisional Government: "Confidential Correspondence."

19. De la Fuente, "Two Dangers, One Solution," 37.

20. *Rebelión!*, April 10, 1910, p. 3.

21. *¡Tierra!*, June 4, 1910, p. 3.

22. Barnet, *Biography of a Runaway Slave*, 87.

23. Moore, *Nationalizing Blackness*, 31.

24. Helg, *Our Rightful Share*, 17–18, 107–8, 150, 214.

25. *Vía Libre*, March 9, 1912, p. 3.

26. *¡Tierra!*, June 1, 1912, p. 1.

27. Ibid., June 8, 1912, p. 1.

28. *¡Tierra!*, June 22, 1912, p. 1.

29. *El Audaz*, July 5, 1912, p. 2.

30. *Cuba: Population, History and Resources, 1907*, 143–45; *Censo de la República de Cuba. Año de 1919*, 414.

31. Del Valle, *La mulata Soledad*, 34–37.

32. Stoner, *From the House to the Streets*, 198.

33. Del Valle, *La mulata Soledad*, 50.

34. Del Valle, *Jubilosa*, 6–7.

35. *Bohemia*, September 14, 1947, pp. 20–22, 77–78.

36. Masiello, "Rethinking Neocolonial Esthetics," 7.

37. Kutzinski, *Sugar's Secrets*, 142.

38. Ibid., 154–55.

39. Del Valle, *La mulata Soledad*, 64–65.

40. *El Nuevo Ideal*, July 7, 1899, p. 3.

41. *Censo de la República de Cuba. Año de 1919*, 348–49.

42. Ibid., 353. Censuses taken in Cuba combined all nonwhite populations into the category "de color." Cuban census statistics concerning legal and non-legal cohabitation do not delineate unions between people of different races, e.g., a white and black or a black and mulatto—the two examples from Del Valle's fiction.

43. Ibid., 353.

Chapter 6. Struggles for a Healthy Cuba: Anarchism, Health, and "White Slavery"

Epigraph: Penichet, *¡Alma Rebelde!*, 79.

1. Norton, *Norton's Complete Hand-book*, 172.

2. Throughout this book I capitalize *Nature* not only to reflect the anarchist practice of doing so (*la Naturaleza*) but also to illustrate the almost divine qualities that anarchists ascribed to the word and concept.

3. *Civil Report of Brigadier General Leonard Wood*, vol. 3, 273.

4. *Report of Provisional Administration from October 13th, 1906 to December 1st, 1907*, 457–59.

5. *Censo de la República de Cuba. Año de 1919*, 253.

6. Lockmiller, *Magoon in Cuba*, 114.

7. Clark, "Labor Conditions in Cuba," 745.

8. *Report of Provisional Administration from October 13th, 1906 to December 1st, 1907*, 459.

9. *Civil Report of Brigadier General Leonard Wood*, 17.

10. *¡Tierra!*, October 24, 1903, p. 2.

11. Ibid., June 12, 1909, pp. 3–4.

12. *Nueva Luz*, October 28, 1922, p. 1.

13. *Pro-Vida*, May 1916, p. 3.

14. *Cuba: Population, History and Resources, 1907*, 116.

15. Clark, "Labor Conditions in Cuba," 736.

16. *Luzbel*, July 15, 1904, p. 7.

17. *Cuba: Population, History and Resources, 1907*, 136.

18. Ibid, 226–27.

19. Román y Moreno, *La habitación del obrero*, 8–11.

20. Ibid., 21.

21. Alfonso and Tamayo, *La vivienda en pro-común*, 26.

22. Ibid., 28–29.

23. Alfonso and Tamayo, *Viviendas del campesino pobre en Cuba*, 17–20.

24. Ibarra, *Cuba: 1898–1921*, Table 32, no page number; Zanetti and García, *United Fruit Company*, 242.

25. Carrera y Justiz, *El problema social en Cuba*, 56.

26. *Archivo Social*, 1894 (no individual publishing dates) 19, p. 1. *Archivo Social* was published in 1894 by anarchist and future independence fighter Enrique Creci.

27. *¡Tierra!*, September 14, 1907, p. 2.

28. *El Dependiente*, October 8, 1913, p. 2.

29. *¡Tierra!*, October 29, 1904, p. 2.

30. Ibid., August 8, 1913, p. 1.

31. *El Nuevo Ideal*, February 4, 1899, p. 1.

32. Stubbs, *Tobacco on the Periphery*, 77–78.

33. *El Nuevo Ideal*, February 25, 1899, p. 3.

34. *¡Tierra!*, October 17, 1903, p. 2.

35. *Memorándum Tipográfico*, April 11, 1914, pp. 4–5.

36. *El Nuevo Ideal*, June 23, 1899, p. 4.

37. Carrera y Justiz, *Las panaderías y la salud*, 9–18.

38. Wright, *Cuba*, 135–38.

39. Casanovas, *Bread, or Bullets!*, 61.

40. The term *white slavery* generally refers to female prostitution.

41. *El Dependiente*, July 26, 1911, insert.

42. Ibid., April 17, 1912, p. 2.

43. *La Voz del Dependiente*, May 18, 1911, p. 3.

44. *El Dependiente*, December 17, 1912, p. 1.

45. Ibid., April 17, 1912, p. 2.

46. Ibid., November 5, 1913, insert.

47. Ibid., insert.

48. *El Dependiente*, November 27, 1911, p. 1.

49. Ibid., June 18, 1913, p. 1.

50. Ibid., June 18, 1913, p. 1.

51. For some initial calls for this revolutionary option, see articles in *El Dependiente*, January 22, 1913, p. 1, and April 9, 1913, p. 1.

52. Pouget, *Sabotage*, 55.

53. Flynn, *Sabotage*, 13–16.

54. *El Dependiente*, February 11, 1914, p. 4; *Pro-Vida*, July/August 1915, p. 4.

55. Pérez, *On Becoming Cuban*, 117–19.

56. Schwartz, *Pleasure Island*, 18–19.

Chapter 7. Curing Bourgeois Ills: Anarcho-Naturism vs. Cuba's Medical Establishment

Epigraph: *Pro-Vida*, May 1916, p. 3.

1. *¡Tierra!*, March 14, 1912, p. 2.

2. Masjuan, *La ecología humana*, 430–32.

3. Sonn, *Anarchism and Cultural Politics*, 201–6.

4. See Lily Litvak's *Musa Libertaria*.

5. Bookchin, *The Spanish Anarchists*, 5.

6. Masjuan, *La ecología humana*, 433–34.

7. Ibid., 458.

8. Ibid., 446, 452.

9. *La Voz del Dependiente*, September 30, 1909, p. 3.

10. *¡Tierra!*, October 9, 1909, p. 4.

11. Ibid., October 16, 1909, p. 3.

12. Ibid., November 27, 1909, p. 3.

13. *La Voz del Dependiente*, November, 18, 1909, p. 3.

14. Ibid., April 8, 1910, p. 3. Guardiola continued his *naturista* endeavors after this debate subsided. By December 1912, he edited the magazine *Khune* and was president of the Naturist Society in Havana.

15. *Pro-Vida*, May 1915, p. 1.

16. *El Naturista*, December 15, 1912, pp. 2–3.

17. *Rebelión!*, April 10, 1910, p. 3.

18. Barnet, *Biography of a Runaway Slave*, 98–99.

19. *Pro-Vida*, June 1915, pp. 3–4.

20. *La Voz del Dependiente*, May 11, 1911, p. 1.

21. Ibid., June 1, 1911, pp. 2–3; June 6, 1911, pp. 2–3.

22. Ibid., June 1, 1911, pp. 2–3.

23. *El Dependiente*, June 24, 1911, p. 2.

24. *El Nuevo Ideal*, June 9, 1899, p. 2.

25. *Pro-Vida*, February 1915, pp. 1–2.

26. Ibid., March 1915, pp. 1–2.

27. Ibid., March 1915, p. 4.

28. See the report in *Report of Provisional Administration from October 13th, 1906 to December 1st, 1907*, 465.

29. *Pro-Vida*, March 1915, pp. 1–2.

30. *¡Tierra!*, January 7, 1905, p. 4; *La Voz del Dependiente*, April 8, 1910, p. 2, and June 22, 1910, p. 2.

31. *Pro-Vida*, January 1915, pp. 1–2.

32. Ibid., March 1917, pp. 6–7.

33. Ibid., September 16, 1917, p. 6.

34. Ibid., June 16, 1917, p. 4.

35. Pendergrast, *For God, Country and Coca-Cola*, 70, 108, 115.

36. *La Voz del Dependiente*, April 28, 1911, pp. 2–4.

37. *El Dependiente*, July 29, 1916, pp. 1 and 3.

38. *Pro-Vida*, June 16, 1917, p. 8.

39. *El Dependiente*, June 20, 1917, p. 2; *Pro-Vida*, May 1, 1917, p. 8.

40. See *La Voz del Dependiente*, October 29, 1908, p. 2. On the top of the page is an outline of Havana bakers' attempts to form a united front using direct action, boycotts, and sabotage, while an advertisement for Coca-Cola appears at the bottom of the page.

41. *Nueva Luz*, August 10, 1922, p. 7.

42. *Pro-Vida*, February 1916, p. 3.

43. Ibid., July/August 1915, p. 4.

44. Ibid., June 1915, p. 4.

45. *Pro-Vida*, February 1915, p. 1.

46. Ibid., May 1, 1917, p. 1. Phagocytes are blood, lymph, or tissue cells that attack harmful foreign matter.

47. *El Dependiente*, September 30, 1917, p. 2.

48. By the 1920s Hilario Alonso abandoned any pretensions he once had of being sympathetic to anarchism. In 1924 and 1925, *Nueva Luz* criticized Alonso, who had become employed by the Cuban government. In response, the radical Dependientes de Cafés, of which Alonso had long been associated and even at one time served as editor of the union's *El Dependiente*, expelled Alonso as a traitor. See *Nueva Luz*, January 10, 1924, p. 5.

Chapter 8. Rejecting Civilization: Nature, Salvation, and the Rural Ideal in Anarcho-Naturism

Epigraph: Del Valle, *El tesoro escondido*, 18–19.

1. *¡Tierra!*, October 24, 1903, p. 2.

2. Masjuan, *La ecología humana*, 161–64.

3. Ibid., 166.

4. *Acción Conciente*, January 10, 1923, p. 5. In the 1930s anarchists and communists in Cuba accepted the role of machinery in the hands of workers (as opposed to capitalists). Tractors and machinery were featured implements in an experimental agricultural cooperative near Morón. See Francisco Bretau's *La maquinaria y los trabajadores*, especially Penichet's introduction.

5. *El Audaz*, July 19, 1912, p. 2.

6. Leante, *Vertiendo ideas*, 20.

7. Kropotkin, *Mutual Aid*, 72; italics in the original.

8. Carrera y Justiz, *El problema social*, 57–58.

9. *Pro-Vida*, April 1915, p. 3.

10. Ibid., July/August 1915, p. 2.

11. *El Naturista*, December 15, 1912, pp. 1–2.

12. Ibarra, *Prologue to Revolution*, 121–22.

13. Pérez, *Cuba Between Empires*, 359.

14. Pérez, *Cuba: Between Reform and Revolution*, 197.

15. Ibarra, *Cuba: 1898–1921*, 306–7.

16. Pérez, *Cuba: Between Reform and Revolution*, 225.

17. Zanetti and García, *Sugar and Railroads*, 260.

18. Le Riverend, *Historia económica de Cuba*, 579. This is opposed to a "sugar mill" (ingenio) where actual sugar is produced and of which there could have been numerous mills on one *central*.

19. Ibid., 580–82; Smith, "The Political Economy of Sugar Production," 44–45.

20. Smith, "The Political Economy of Sugar Production," 39.

21. Díaz-Briquets and Pérez-López, *Conquering Nature*, 84.

22. Ibid., 142–43.

23. Ibarra, *Prologue to Revolution*, 109.

24. Smith, "The Political Economy of Sugar Production," 42.

25. *¡Tierra!*, January 10, 1914, p. 3.

26. Le Riverend, *Historia económica de Cuba*, 352.

27. Of the anarchist newspapers in Cuba during the time frame of this study, only *¡Tierra!* published its weekly contributions. This conclusion is drawn from analyzing the newspaper at different times of each year, preferably early in the year, in the middle months, and toward the calendar year's end. Because the newspaper was also in some ways a clearing house in which anarchists from throughout the island and abroad sent money to various causes championed by the newspaper, one can often find the individual contributions to those causes from outside Havana as well.

28. Del Valle, *Camelanga*, 17.

29. Del Valle, *El príncipe que no quiso gobernar*, 19.

30. Del Valle, *Cero*, 1–25.

31. Del Valle, *El tesoro escondido*, 7–8.

32. Ibid., 9.

33. Ibid., 13.

34. Ibid., 18–19.

35. Ibid., 30.

36. Del Valle, *Náufragos*, 4.

37. Ibid., 51.

38. Ibid., 59.

39. Ibid., 73–74.

40. Ibid., 79.

41. Ibid., 96–102.

42. Ibid., 140. Ironically, this was how Adrián del Valle's mother was killed in 1912.

43. Tower Sargent, "The Three Faces of Utopianism Revisited," 1–37; Roemer, "Defining America as Utopia," 1–15.

44. For information on the anarcho-naturist communes and nudist communities in Spain, see Eduard Masjuan's *La ecología humana en el anarquismo ibérico*, 429–64.

45. Litvak, *El cuento anarquista*, 24–25.

Chapter 9. Freedom Teaching: Anarchism and Education

Epigraph: *Nueva Luz*, January 22, 1925, p. 7.

1. Cabrera, *Cuba and the Cubans*, 283.

2. Fitchen, "Primary Education in Colonial Cuba," 112.

3. Cabrera, *Cuba and the Cubans*, 288; Fitchen, "Primary Education in Colonial Cuba," 113.

4. Fitchen, "Primary Education in Colonial Cuba," 113–15.

5. Johnston, "Education and Cuba Libre," 26.

6. Fitchen, "Primary Education in Colonial Cuba," 115–18.

7. *Civil Report of Brigadier General Leonard Wood*, vol. 7, 7–8.

8. Ibid., 128. Louis Pérez argues that while Cubans like Varona may have been involved in reorganizing the educational system, U.S. policy makers in Washington believed an educational system was being devised to acculturate Cubans to U.S. political and cultural values if not to outright annex the island, then to "annexation by acclamation." See Pérez, "The Imperial Design," 6.

9. Pérez, "The Imperial Design," 9; Baxter, "The Cuban Teachers at Harvard University," 780; *Civil Report of Brigadier General Leonard Wood*, vol. 7, 34–35.

10. *Civil Report of Brigadier General Leonard Wood*, vol. 7, 184–85.

11. Cartaya and Joanes Pando, *Raíces de la escuela primaria pública cubana*, 13, 16, 27–29.

12. Ibid., 15–18.

13. De la Fuente, *A Nation for All*, 143–46.

14. *Report of Provisional Administration from October 13th, 1906 to December 1st, 1907*, 342.

15. Yaremko, *U.S. Protestant Missions in Cuba*, 64–75.

16. Stoner, *From the House to the Streets*, 36, 133–35.

17. *Rebelión!*, December 14, 1908, p. 2.

18. *¡Tierra!*, June 30, 1906, p. 1.

19. Cartaya and Joanes Pando, *Raíces de la escuela primaria pública cubana*, 4–5.

20. Ibid., 21, 30; Johnston, "Education and Cuba Libre," 28.

21. *¡Tierra!*, April 3, 1909, p. 1.

22. Ibid., September 24, 1910, p. 1.

23. Stoner, *From the House to the Streets*, 35.

24. *Report of Provisional Administration from October 13th, 1906 to December 1st, 1907*, 328.

25. *Rebelión!*, July 3, 1909, p. 2.

26. *El Audaz*, April 15, 1913, p. 12.

27. *Nueva Luz*, June 7, 1923, p. 6.

28. Krimmerman and Perry, *Patterns of Anarchy*, 434–35; Avrich, *The Modern School Movement*, 1–33.

29. Avrich, *The Modern School Movement*, 6.

30. Ibid., 4–6; Ferrer Guardia, *La Escuela Moderna*, 24–28.

31. Ferrer Guardia, *La Escuela Moderna*, 189–99; Cappelletti, *Francisco Ferrer*, 35–41.

32. Ferrer Guardia, *La Escuela Moderna*, 112.

33. Ibid., 113–14.

34. Ibid., 113–14; Cappelletti, *Francisco Ferrer*, 67–68.

35. Ferrer Guardia, *La Escuela Moderna*, 186–87.

36. Avrich, *The Modern School Movement*, 23–24; Cappelletti, *Francisco Ferrer*, 86–90.

37. Avrich, *The Modern School Movement*, 32.

38. Casanovas, *Bread, or Bullets!*, 72–73, 84–85, 162–63.

39. *El Nuevo Ideal*, June 30, 1899, p. 2; September 15, 1900, p. 2. The Guanabacoa school and a 1905 effort between anarchists and café workers in Havana to form a CES apparently failed after only a few months.

40. Martínez Balsalobre, *Conferencias sobre el socialismo revolucionario*, 37–40.

41. Ibid., 1.

42. *¡Tierra!*, January 28, 1905, p. 2; February 4, 1905, p. 3.

43. Ibid., February 7, 1906, p. 2.

44. Gómez Luaces, "Monografía histórica." This unpublished manuscript is housed in the Museo Municipal de Regla. Pages are not numbered.

45. *¡Tierra!*, May 23, 1908, p. 3; May 30, 1908, p. 3; *La Voz del Dependiente*, June 16, 1908 (insert).

46. *La Voz del Dependiente*, October 8, 1908 (insert); *¡Tierra!*, October 31, 1908, p. 3. In October 1908 "Educación del Porvenir" dissolved itself in order to form the Cuban section of the Liga. The Liga attempted to organize rationalist groups throughout the island, with each group sending a delegate to the section's office in Havana. The Liga secretary would collect monthly dues of twenty centavos from each member of Liga-associated groups to be used for starting more schools.

47. Gómez Luaces, "Monografía histórica," no page number.

48. *¡Tierra!*, November 21, 1908, p. 1; March 13, 1909, p. 4; *La Voz del Dependiente*, May 13, 1909, p. 4.

49. *Rebelión!*, April 8, 1909, p. 3.

50. *La Voz del Dependiente*, June 24, 1909, p. 3.

51. *Rebelión!*, July 16, 1909, pp. 2–3.

52. *¡Tierra!*, December 4, 1909, p. 4; December 11, 1909, p. 4.

53. *Rebelión!*, October 5, 1909, p. 2.

54. *La Voz del Dependiente*, October 28, 1909, p. 3; November 18, 1909, p. 3.

55. Ibid., November 18, 1909, p. 3; *¡Tierra!*, January 15, 1910, p. 1.

56. For complete coverage of the controversy, see *La Voz del Dependiente*, November 18, 1909, p. 3; January 31, 1910, p. 3; February 14, 1910, p. 1; February 24, 1910, pp. 2–3; April 23, 1910, p. 3; March 24, 1910, p. 3.

57. *¡Tierra!*, September 3, 1910, p. 3; October 29, 1910, p. 4.

58. Ibid., March 26, 1910, p. 4; *La Voz del Dependiente*, March 3, 1910, p. 2; September 3, 1910, p. 3.

59. *¡Tierra!*, October 10, 1910, pp. 3–4. The manifesto includes copies of all the letters sent back and forth between the paper and the Liga.

60. *La Voz del Dependiente*, January 20, 1911, p. 3; April 22, 1911, p. 4; June 6, 1911, p. 3.

61. *¡Tierra!*, October 22, 1910, p. 2.

62. Ibid., June 3, 1911, p. 2.

63. Ibid., June 17, 1911, pp. 2–3.

64. *Bases y Reglamento*, no page numbers.

65. Martínez continued his interest in anarchist education, contributing occasional columns about education to anarchist newspapers in Latin America. See particularly his letters to the Uruguayan anarchist education journal *Infancia* from 1912 to 1913.

66. *¡Tierra!*, October 21, 1911, p. 2.

67. *¡Tierra!*, July 18, 1911, p. 3; October 14, 1911, p. 2; October 22, 1914, p. 2.

68. *¡Tierra!*, June 8, 1912, p. 3; January 14, 1913, p. 2.

69. *¡Tierra!*, November 18, 1911, p. 4; November 18, 1911, p. 4; December 2, 1911, p. 3; February 17, 1912, p. 4; March 7, 1912, p. 3; April 6, 1912, p. 4.

70. See Dora Barrancos's *Anarquismo, educación y costumbres en la Argentina*.

71. Penichet, *Tácticas en uso y tácticas a seguir*, 45.

72. Ibid., 3.

73. *Nueva Luz*, August 17, 1922, p. 6; *Educación Obrera*, January 15, 1921, p. 2.

74. *Nueva Luz*, September 7, 1922, p. 8; *Nueva Luz*, November 2, 1922, p. 1.

75. Ibid., October 12, 1922, p. 2.

76. Primelles, *Crónica Cubana, 1919–1922*, 269.

77. *Nueva Luz*, September 14, 1922, p. 1.

78. De la Fuente, *A Nation for All*, 144.

79. Johnston, "Cuban Nationalism and Responses to Private Education in Cuba," 30–31.

80. Ibid., 33; Yaremko, *U.S. Protestant Missions in Cuba*, 72.

81. Johnston, "Cuban Nationalism and Responses to Private Education in Cuba," 30–31.

82. *Nueva Luz*, October 19, 1922, p. 1.

83. Ibid., October 19, 1922, p. 2.

84. Ibid., January 25, 1923, p. 1.

85. For a particularly illuminating front-page visual, see *Nueva Luz*, February 15, 1923, p. 1.

86. Ibid., September 16, 1923, p. 2.

87. Cabrera, *Los que viven por sus manos*, 248; *Nueva Luz*, November 16, 1922, p. 6; September 16, 1923, p. 6.

88. *Nueva Luz*, January 4, 1923, p. 8; July 19, 1923, pp. 1 and 3.

89. Ibid., September 20, 1924, p. 3.

90. Ibid., March 15, 1923 p. 6.

91. Ibid., February 8, 1923, p. 6 and March 15, 1923, p. 7.

92. Ibid., November 2, 1922, p. 7.

93. Cartaya and Joanes Pando, *Raíces de la escuela primaria pública cubana*, 53.

94. *Nueva Luz*, January 25, 1923, p. 6.

95. Ibid., February 22, 1923, p. 2.

96. Ibid., May 3, 1923, p. 3; Cabrera, *Los que viven por sus manos*, 247.

97. *Nueva Luz*, December 21, 1922, p. 8.

98. Ibid., February 1, 1923, p. 5, February 22, 1923, p. 8; May 24, 1923, p. 1.

99. See *Nueva Luz*, December 21, 1922, p. 8 and February 25, 1924, p. 6 for examples.

100. Ibid., April 24, 1925, p. 7.

101. *Germinal*, May 15, 1904, p. 1.

102. Wright, *Cuba*, 36.

103. Cabrera, *Alfredo López*, 116–17; *Los que viven por sus manos*, 329–33; Dumpierre, *Mella*, 49–55; Padrón, *Julio Antonio Mella y el movimiento obrero*, 67–83.

104. *Nueva Luz*, January 25, 1923, p. 7.

105. Ibid., January 20, 1924, p. 2.

106. Ibid., January 31, 1924, p. 2.

107. Ibid., February 15, 1924, p. 2.

108. Ibid., March 19, 1924, p. 10.

109. Ibid., April 24, 1925, pp. 2–3; May 25, 1925, p. 2.

110. Ibid., March 25, 1925, pp. 4–6.

111. *Nueva Luz*, April 24, 1925, p. 7.

112. Fernández, *El anarquismo en Cuba*, 64–65.

113. *Nueva Luz*, September 5, 192?; Rosell, *Luchas obreras contra Machado*, 83–84.

Chapter 10. Guiding the Masses: Anarchist Culture as Education

Epigraph: *¡Tierra!*, June 13, 1914, p. 2.

1. Memo for the Chief of Staff from John W. Furlong, Captain, General Staff, Chief, Military Information Division, January 3, 1908, Records of the Provisional Government, Record Group 199, National Archives, Washington, D.C.

2. *¡Tierra!*, November 11, 1905, p. 4; November 30, 1907, p. 1; August 8, 1913, p. 3; *El Dependiente*, August 20, 1913, p. 1; September 17, 1913, p. 4.

3. Loveira, *De los 26 a los 35*, 78.

4. *Nueva Luz*, December 28, 1922, p. 7.

5. Most anarchist *veladas* are briefly described in anarchist newspapers. See specific descriptions concerning musical selections in *¡Tierra!*, October 24, 1903, p. 4; July 16, 1904, p. 3; May 5, 1905, p. 1; July 1, 1905, p. 4; November 11, 1905, p. 4; November 18, 1905, p. 2; August 8, 1913, p. 3; *Nueva Luz*, February 15, 1923, p. 6 for but a handful of examples.

6. Gutiérrez, *Teatro popular*, 66–67.

7. Nathan, *The Popular Theatre*, 232–33.

8. *Diario de la Marina*, January 16, 1909, p. 1.

9. Ibid., p. 1.

10. *¡Tierra!*, March 13, 1909, p. 3.

11. *Rebelión!*, February 11, 1909, p. 1.

12. *El Dependiente*, January 10, 1912, p. 3.

13. De Lidia, *Fin de fiesta*, 2.

14. *La Voz del Dependiente*, October 8, 1908, p. 3.

15. Ibid., October 15, 1908, pp. 3–4.

16. *¡Tierra!*, May 6, 1911, p. 2. In 1912 García's questionable past emerged in his activities as a teacher at the Escuela Moderna in Matanzas where anarchists publicly condemned García's actions in the school, citing him for never being a true believer in *racionalismo*, having supported President Menocal and having attacked other anarchists. *¡Tierra!*, December 7, 1912, p. 3.

17. Ibid., June 11, 1914, p. 2; June 18, 1914, p. 1.

18. Ibid., July 9, 1914, pp. 3–4.

19. Ibid., July 9, 1914, pp. 2–3.

20. *Nueva Luz*, August 24, 1922, p. 2.

21. Ibid., December 28, 1922, p. 7.

22. Ibid., March 8, 1923, p. 8; January 1, 1924, p. 2; February 25, 1924.

23. De Lidia, *Fin de fiesta*, 5–16.

24. *Nueva Luz*, October 28, 1922, p. 4.

25. *¡Tierra!*, February 27, 1904, p. 3.

26. *Rebelión!*, February 18, 1909, p. 1. Two issues later *Rebelión!* published J. M. Méndez's poem "¡Mi reina de la fiesta!" where the author also laments that workers voted for the queen. *Rebelión!*, March 18, 1909, p. 2.

27. Schwartz, *Pleasure Island*, 83.

28. *¡Tierra!*, March 5, 1925, p. 3.

29. *Rebelión!*, February 18, 1909, p. 2.

30. *¡Tierra!*, March 9, 1907, p. 2.

31. Pérez, *On Becoming Cuban*, 336.

32. *¡Tierra!*, February 18, 1905, p. 1.

33. Ibid., April 13, 1906, p. 2.

34. *Nueva Luz*, September 21, 1922, p. 5.

35. Nelson, *Beyond the Martyrs*, 149.

Chapter 11. Imagining Women: Prostitutes, Bad Seeds, and Revolutionary Mothers

Epigraph: *¡Tierra!*, December 28, 1912, p. 2.

1. Stoner, *From the House to the Streets*, 132.

2. French, "Prostitutes and Guardian Angels," 529–53; McCreery, "This Life of Misery and Shame," 333–53.

3. *¡Tierra!*, June 5, 1925, p. 4.

4. Barrancos, *Anarquismo, educación y costumbres*, 265–94; Molyneux, "No God, No Boss, No Husband," 119–45.

5. Wolfe, "Anarchist Ideology, Worker Practice," 809–46.

6. *¡Tierra!*, June 12, 1907, p. 2; *Vía Libre*, July 1, 1911, p. 2.

7. Del Valle, *Por el camino*, 202.

8. Pérez, *On Becoming Cuban*, 193.

9. Penichet, *¡Alma Rebelde!*, 25.

10. Penichet, *La vida de un pernicioso*, 139.

11. Ibid., 198.

12. Ibid., 210.

13. *Nueva Luz*, August 10, 1922, p. 5.

14. Ibid., April 10, 1925, p. 4–6.

15. Penichet, *Tácticas en uso y tácticas a seguir*, 38.

16. Ibid., 40–41.

17. Del Valle, *Cuentos inverosímiles*, 110.

18. Ibid., 193.

19. Ibid., 163.

20. Penichet, *¡Alma Rebelde!*, 91–92.

21. Del Valle, *La mulata Soledad*, 159.

Conclusion and Epilogue

1. Dolgoff, *The Cuban Revolution*, 48.

2. Carr, "Mill Occupations and Soviets," 156–57.

3. Fernández, *Cuban Anarchism*, 62–63.

4. *Por la escuela cubana en Cuba Libre*, 8, 18–19. In addition, the anarchist group "Rumbos Nuevos," headed by J. Díaz and Abelardo Barroso Martínez, worked with the educational campaign (see page 181).

5. Penichet, "El proceso social," 431–47.

6. Eledé, "Adrián del Valle, hombre y señal," 22–23.

7. *Bohemia*, September 14, 1947, 20–22, 77–78.

8. Dolgoff, *The Cuban Revolution*, 54–55; Rama and Cappelletti, *El anarquismo en América Latina*, 175.

9. Marshall, *Demanding the Impossible*, 516; Dolgoff, *The Cuban Revolution*, 55–61; Fernández, *El anarquismo en Cuba*, 82–86.

10. Fernández, *El anarquismo en Cuba*, 87–122; Dolgoff, *The Cuban Revolution*, 79–117; Marshall, *Demanding the Impossible*, 517.

Bibliography

Anarchist Newspapers from Cuba

Acción Conciente (1922–1924)
Acción Libertaria (1924)
Archivo Social (1894)
El Audaz (1912)
La Batalla (1911)
Campana Misteriosa (1905)
La Defensa (1902)
El Dependiente (1911–1917)
Fiat Lux (1914)
Germinal (1904)
Jóvenes Hijos del Mundo (1892)
Labor Sana (1917)
El Libertario (1905)
Luzbel (1904)
Memorándum Tipográfico (1914–1916)
El Naturista (1910)
Nueva Luz (1922–1925)
El Nuevo Ideal (1899–1901)
El Productor (1887–1890)
El Productor Panadero (1922)
El Progreso (1923–1925)
Pro-Vida (1915–1918, 1923)
Rebelión (1910)
Rebelión! (1908–1909)
El Sembrador (1924)
Los Tiempos Nuevos (1921)
¡Tierra! (1903–1914, 1924–1925)
Vía Libre (1911–1912)
La Voz del Dependiente (1907–1911)

Non-Cuban Anarchist Newspapers

El Despertar (Brooklyn, N.Y., 1896–1897)
El Esclavo (Tampa, Florida, 1894–1898)

Infancia (Montevideo, Uruguay, 1912)
Risveglio (Tampa, Florida, 1913–1914)

Cuban Non-Anarchist Newspapers and Journals

Bohemia (1947)
Diario de la Marina (1909)
Estudios: Mensuario de Cultura (1950)

Documents and Reports

Bases y Reglamento. Centro de Estudios Sociales del Cerro. Havana: Imprenta de Castro, 1911.
Censo de la República de Cuba. Año de 1919. Havana: Maza, Arroyo y Caso, 1919.
Civil Report of Brigadier General Leonard Wood, Military Governor of Cuba, 1901. War Department: Washington, D.C., 1902.
Clark, Victor S. "Labor Conditions in Cuba." *Bulletin of the Department of Labor* 7 (July 1902): 663–793.
Comité Central del Partido Socialista de Cuba. *Carlos Baliño: documentos y artículos.* Havana, 1976.
Cuba: Population, History and Resources, 1907. Compiled by Victor H. Olmsted, Director, and Henry Gannett, Assistant Director. Washington, D.C.: United States Bureau of the Census, 1909.
El movimiento obrero cubano: documentos y artículos. 2 vols. (1865–1925 and 1925–1935). Havana: Editorial de Ciencias Sociales, 1975.
Informe de la administración provisional, desde 1o. de diciembre de 1907 hasta el 1o. de diciembre de 1908. Havana: Rambla y Bouza, 1909.
Padrón Larrazábal, Roberto, ed. *Manifiestos de Cuba.* Seville: Universidad de Savilla, n.d.
Pichardo, Hortensia, ed. *Documentos para la historia de Cuba*, vol. 2. Havana: Editorial de Ciencias Sociales, 1969.
Report on the Census of Cuba, 1899. Washington, D.C.: United States War Department, 1900.
Report of Provisional Administration from October 13th, 1906 to December 1st, 1907 by Charles E. Magoon, Provisional Governor. Havana: Rambla and Bouza, 1908.
Rosell, Mirta, ed. *Luchas obreras contra Machado.* Havana: Editorial de Ciencias Sociales, 1973.

Books, Articles, Plays, and Manuscripts

Ackelsberg, Martha A. *Free Women of Spain: Anarchism and the Struggle for the Emancipation of Women.* Bloomington: Indiana University Press, 1991.
Aguirre, José G. *La verdad sobre la industria del tabaco habano.* Havana: P. Fernández, 1905.
Aguirre, Sergio. "Algunas luchas sociales en Cuba republicana." *Revista de la Biblioteca Nacional José Martí*, no. 2 (May–August 1973): 5–40.
Alba, Victor. *Politics and the Labor Movement in Latin America.* Stanford: Stanford University Press, 1968.

Albro, Ward S. *Always a Rebel: Ricardo Flores Magón and the Mexican Revolution*. Fort Worth: Texas Christian University Press, 1992.

Alfonso, Ramón M., and Diego Tamayo. *La vivienda en pro-común (casa de vecindad)*. Havana: La Moderna Poesía, 1904.

———. *Viviendas del campesino pobre en Cuba*. Havana: La Moderna Poesía, 1904.

Alonso Aladro, José. *Espiritualidad redentora*. Havana: Moreno, 1921.

———. *Materio-Espírita. Obra científico-filosófica moderna sobre materio-espiritismo y la vida universal*. Havana, n.d.

———. *Nueva orden masonica-espírita que se titula "Hermandad Materio-Espírita" o "Masoneria Racionalista."* Havana, 1922.

———. *Prosi-Verso*. Havana: Moreno, 1921.

Álvarez Junco, José. *La ideología política del anarquismo español (1868–1910)*. Madrid: Siglo Veintiuno Editores, SA, 1976.

Los anarquistas y las asociaciones de trabajadores. Havana: "Acción Consciente," 1923. (no author)

Anderson, Benedict. *Imagined Communities: Reflections on the Origin and Spread of Nationalism*. Rev. ed. London: Verso, 1991.

Andreu, Jean, Maurice Fraysse, and Eva Golluscio de Montoya, eds. *Anarkos: Literaturas libertarias de América del Sur 1900*. Buenos Aires: Ediciones Corregidor, 1990.

Archivo Nacional de Cuba. *Guía breve de los fondos procesados del Archivo Nacional*. Havana: Editorial Academia, 1990.

Armus, Diego. *Mundo urbano y cultura popular. Estudios de historia social Argentina*. Buenos Aires: Sudamericana, 1990.

Avrich, Paul. *The Modern School Movement: Anarchism and Education in the United States*. Princeton: Princeton University Press, 1980.

Baer, James A. "Tenant Mobilization and the 1907 Rent Strike in Buenos Aires." *The Americas* 49, no. 3 (January 1993): 343–68.

Barnet, Miguel. *Biography of a Runaway Slave*. W. Nick Hill, trans. Willimantic, Conn.: Curbstone Press, 1994.

Barrancos, Dora. *Anarquismo, educación, y costumbres en la Argentina de principios de siglo*. Buenos Aires: Editorial Contrapunto, 1990.

———. "Anarquismo y sexualidad." *Mundo urbano y cultura popular; Estudios de historia social Argentina*. Diego Armus, ed. Buenos Aires: Editorial Sudamericana, 1990, 15–37.

———. *La escena iluminada: Ciencias para trabajadores, 1890–1930*. Buenos Aires: Editorial Plus Ultra, 1996.

Baxter, Sylvester. "The Cuban Teachers at Harvard University." *The Outlook* 65, no. 14 (August 4, 1900): 773–82.

Bayer, Osvaldo. *Anarchism and Violence: Severino de Giovanni in Argentina, 1922–1931*. London: Refract/Elephant, 1970/1985.

Bedford, Joseph. "Samuel Gompers and the Caribbean: The AFL, Cuba and Puerto Rico, 1898–1906." *Labor's Heritage* 6, no. 4 (1995): 5–25.

Bergquist, Charles, ed. *Labor in the Capitalist World-Economy*. Beverly Hills: Sage, 1984.

Boal, Augusto. *Theater of the Oppressed*. Charles A. and Maria-Odilia Leal McBride, trans. New York: Urizen Books, 1974/1979.

Bookchin, Murray. *Social Anarchism or Lifestyle Anarchism: An Unbridgeable Chasm*. San Francisco and Edinburgh: AK Press and Distribution, 1995.

————. *The Spanish Anarchists: The Heroic Years, 1868–1936.* New York: Free Life Editions, 1977.

Bosch y Martínez, Dr. Antonio, ed. *Tópicos y proyecciones de Regla.* Regla, Cuba, 1946.

Bowdoin, William Goodrich. *A Step Across the Gulf: Cuba.* Florida Gulf Coast Series, No. 2. Savannah, Ga.: The Plant Line, 1899.

Bretau, Francisco. *La maquinaria y los trabajadores.* Havana: Empresa Editora de Publicaciones, 1939.

Brock, Lisa, and Digna Castañeda Fuertes, eds. *Between Race and Empire: African Americans and Cubans before the Cuban Revolution.* Philadelphia: Temple University Press, 1998.

Browne, Ray B. "The Voice of Popular Culture in History." *Perspectives: American Historical Association Newsletter* 35, no. 5 (May/June 1997): 26–28, 38.

Burns, E. Bradford. "The Novel as History: A Reading Guide." *Latin America: A Concise Interpretative History.* Englewood Cliffs, N.J.: Prentice Hall, 1994, 355–62.

Cabrera, Olga. *Alfredo López: maestro del proletariado.* Havana: Editorial de Ciencias Sociales, 1985.

————. *El antiimperialismo en la historia de Cuba.* Havana: Editorial de Ciencias Sociales, 1985.

————. "Enrique Creci: un patriota cubano." *Santiago* 36 (December 1979): 121–50.

————. *El movimiento obrero cubano en 1920.* Havana: Instituto del Libro, 1970.

————. *Los que viven por sus manos.* Havana: Editorial de Ciencias Sociales, 1985.

Cabrera, Raimundo. *Cuba and the Cubans.* Philadelphia: The Levytype Company, 1896.

Calcagno, Francisco. *El aprendiz de zapatero.* Havana: El Pilar, 1891.

Cancela, Elina Miranda, and Amaury Carbón Sierra. "La educación clásica de un joven habanero de la segunda mitad del siglo XIX." *Revista de la Biblioteca Nacional "José Martí"* 27 (September–December 1985): 70–94.

Cantón Navarro, José. *Algunas ideas de José Martí en relación con la clase obrera y el socialismo.* Havana: Instituto Cubano del Libro, 1970.

Cappelletti, Ángel J. *Francisco Ferrer y la pedagogía libertaria.* Madrid: Las Ediciones de la Piqueta, 1980.

Carr, Barry. "Identity, Class, and Nation: Black Immigrant Workers, Cuban Communism, and the Sugar Insurgency, 1925–1934." *The Hispanic American Historical Review* 78, no. 1 (February 1998): 83–116.

————. "Marxism and Anarchism in the Formation of the Mexican Communist Party, 1910–19." *Hispanic American Historical Review* 63, no. 2 (May 1983): 277–306.

————. "Mill Occupations and Soviets: The Mobilisation of Sugar Workers in Cuba 1917–1933." *Journal of Latin American Studies* 28 (1996): 129–58.

Carrera y Justiz, Francisco. *La asociación de dependientes del comercio de la Habana como factor sociológico en la civilización de Cuba.* Havana: La Moderna Poesía, 1905.

————. *El municipio y los extranjeros; los españoles en Cuba.* Havana: La Moderna Poesía, 1904.

————. *Las panaderías y la salud del pueblo. La esclavitud blanca.* Havana: La Moderna Poesía, 1911.

————. *El problema social en Cuba, la función y el órgano.* Havana: La Prueba, 1925.

Cartaya, Perla A., and José A. Joanes Pando. *Raíces de la escuela primaria pública cubana, 1902–1925.* Havana: Editorial Pueblo y Educación, 1996.

Casanovas Codina, Joan. *Bread, or Bullets!: Urban Labor and Spanish Colonialism in Cuba, 1850–1898.* Pittsburgh: University of Pittsburgh Press, 1998.

———. "Movimiento obrero y lucha anticolonial en Cuba después de la abolición de la esclavitud." *Boletín Americanista* (Barcelona) 45 (1995): 23–41.

———. "Slavery, the Labour Movement and Spanish Colonialism in Cuba, 1850–1890." *International Review of Social History* 40 (1995): 367–82.

Chanan, Michael. *The Cuban Image: Cinema and Cultural Politics in Cuba*. Bloomington: Indiana University Press, 1986.

Chomsky, Aviva. "The Aftermath of Repression: Race and Nation in Cuba after 1912." *Journal of Iberian and Latin American Studies* 4, no. 2 (December 1998): 1–40.

Ciafardo, Eduardo O., and Daniel Espesir. "Patología de la acción política anarquista. Criminólogos, psiquiatras y conflicto social en Argentina, 1890–1910." *Siglo XIX*, segundo época, 12 (July–December 1992): 23–40.

Clark, Christopher. *The Communitarian Moment: The Radical Challenge of the Northampton Association*. Ithaca, N.Y.: Cornell University Press, 1995.

Concurso Internacional de la Habana iniciado en el periódico "El Libertario." Havana: El Libertario, 1906.

Córdova, Efrén. *Clase trabajadora y movimiento sindical en Cuba, vol. 1 (1819–1959)*. Miami: Centro de Investigaciones y Asuntos Laborales (CLR&S), Florida International University, 1995.

Cuervo, Manuel F. *Cuestión Agraria y Cuestión Obrera*. Havana: Imprenta Compostela 89, 1908.

De Groot, P. L. "A Survey of Latin American Materials: The International Instituut voor Sociale Geschiedenis in Amsterdam." *Latin American Research Review* (Spring 1977): 205–15.

De la Fuente, Alejandro. "Myths of Racial Democracy: Cuba, 1900–1912." *Latin American Research Review* 34, no. 3 (1999): 39–73.

———. *A Nation for All: Race, Inequality and Politics in Twentieth Century Cuba*. Chapel Hill: University of North Carolina Press, 2001.

———. "Two Dangers, One Solution: Immigration, Race, and Labor in Cuba, 1900–1930." *International Labor and Working-Class History* 51 (Spring 1997): 30–49.

De Lidia, Palmiro. *Ferrer. Recopilación de documentos históricos que immortalizarán al caído*. Havana: La Epoca, 1909.

———. *Fin de fiesta. Cuadro dramático*. New York, 1898.

———. *El ideal del siglo XX*. Havana: El Fígaro, 1900.

DeShazo, Peter. *Urban Workers and Labor Unions in Chile, 1902–1927*. Madison: University of Wisconsin Press, 1983.

Del Valle, Adrián. *Ambición*. Barcelona: La Revista Blanca, n.d.

———. *Aristócratas*. Barcelona: La Revista Blanca, n.d.

———. *Arrayán*. Barcelona: La Revista Blanca, n.d.

———. *Camelanga*. Barcelona: La Revista Blanca, n.d.

———. *Cero*. Barcelona: La Revista Blanca, n.d.

———. *Contrabando*. Barcelona: La Revista Blanca, n.d.

———. *Cuentos inverosímiles*. Havana: Nuevo Ideal, 1903.

———. *Cuentos inverosímiles*. 2d. ed. Havana: Nuevo Ideal, 1921.

———. *De maestro a guerrillero*. Barcelona: La Revista Blanca, n.d.

———. *Jesús en la guerra*. Havana: Escuela de la Casa de Beneficiencia y Maternidad, 1917.

———. *Juan sin pan; novela social*. Buenos Aires: B. Fueyo, 1926.

———. *Jubilosa*. Barcelona: La Revista Blanca, n.d.

———. *Mi amigo Julio*. Barcelona: La Revista Blanca, n.d.

————. *La mulata Soledad.* Barcelona: Impresos Costa, 1929.

————. *El mundo como pluralidad.* Havana: La Universal, 1924.

————. *El naturismo.* Havana: Casa "Pro-Vida," 1926.

————. *Náufragos.* Toulouse, France: Ediciones "Universo," n.d.

————. *Por el camino.* Barcelona: F. Granada, 1907.

————. *El príncipe que no quiso gobernar.* Barcelona: La Revista Blanca, n.d.

————. *El tesoro escondido.* Barcelona: La Revista Blanca, n.d.

————. *Tiberianos.* Barcelona: La Revista Blanca, n.d.

————. *Todo lo vence el amor.* Barcelona: La Revista Blanca, n.d.

Díaz de Villegas, Pablo. *Cartilla Política. Comprende además de la cartilla política un estudio comparativo del Individualismo, Socialismo y Comunismo y nociones de Economía Política.* Cienfuegos, Cuba: Valero, 1899.

Díaz-Briquets, Sergio, and Jorge Pérez-López. *Conquering Nature: The Environmental Legacy of Socialism in Cuba.* Pittsburgh: University of Pittsburgh Press, 2000.

Dolgoff, Sam, ed. *Bakunin on Anarchism.* 1980. Montreal: Black Rose Books, 1990.

————. *The Cuban Revolution: A Critical Perspective.* Montreal: Black Rose Books, 1977.

Domínguez Pérez, F. *Cantos de vida.* Banes, Cuba: Imprenta de "El Liberal," 1913.

Dulles, John W. F. *Anarchists and Communists in Brazil, 1900–1935.* Austin: University of Texas Press, 1973.

Dumoulin, John. "El primer desarrollo del movimiento obrero y la formación del proletariado en el sector azucarero: Cruces, 1886–1902." *Islas* 48 (May-August 1974): 3–66.

————. *Azúcar y lucha de clases 1917.* Havana: Editorial de Ciencias Sociales, 1980.

Dumpierre, Erasmo. *Mella: Esbozo biográfico.* Havana, 1965.

————. *La revolución de octubre y su repercusión en Cuba.* Havana: Editorial de Ciencias Sociales, 1977.

Durwood, Long. "La Resistencia: Tampa's Immigrant Labor Union." *Labor History* 6 (Fall 1965): 193–214.

Eledé. "Adrián del Valle, hombre y señal." *Estudios: Mensuario de Cultura* 1, no. 2 (April 1950): 22–23.

Esenwein, George Richard. *Anarchist Ideology and the Working-Class Movement in Spain, 1868–1898.* Berkeley: University of California Press, 1989.

Estrade, Paul. *La colonia cubana de París, 1895–1898: el combate patriótico de betances y la solidaridad de los revolucionarios franceses.* Havana: Editorial de Ciencias Sociales, 1984.

Fernández, Frank. *El anarquismo en Cuba.* Madrid: Fundación Anselmo Lorenzo, 2000.

————. *Cuban Anarchism: The History of a Movement.* Translated by Charles Bufe. Tucson, Ariz.: Sharp Press, 2001.

Fernández Robaina, Tomás. *El negro en Cuba, 1902–1958: Apuntes para la historia de la lucha contra la discriminación racial.* Havana: Editorial de Ciencias Sociales, 1990.

————. *Recuerdos secretos de dos mujeres públicas.* Havana: Editorial Letras Cubanas, 1984.

Ferrara, Orestes. *Memorias. Una mirada sobre tres siglos.* Madrid: Playor, 1975.

Ferrer, Ada. "Social Aspects of Cuban Nationalism: Race, Slavery, and the Guerra Chiquita, 1879–1880." *Cuban Studies/Estudios Cubanos* 21 (1991): 37–56.

Ferrer Guardia, Francisco. *La Escuela Moderna.* Barcelona: Tusquets Editor, 1976.

Figarola, James Joel. *Cuba 1900–1928: La república dividida contra sí misma.* Havana: Instituto Cubano del Libro, 1974.

Fiol, Mateo I. *Cartilla política elemental.* Matanzas: Galería Literaria, 1899.

Fitchen, Edward. "Primary Education in Colonial Cuba: Spanish Tool for Retaining <<La Isla Siempre Leal?>>." *Caribbean Studies* 14, no. 1 (April 1974): 105–20.

Flynn, Elizabeth Gurley. *Sabotage.* Cleveland: I.W.W. Publishing Bureau, 1915.

Foreman-Peck, James. "Insiders and Outsiders: The Political Economy of International Migration during the Nineteenth and Twentieth Centuries." *The Politics of Immigrant Workers: Labor Activism and Migration in the World Economy since 1830.* Edited by Camille Guerin-Gonzáles and Carl Strikwerda. New York: Holmes & Meier (1993): 297–321.

Franco, Jean. "What's in a Name? Popular Culture Theories and Their Limitations." *Studies in Latin American Popular Culture* 1 (1982): 5–14.

French, William. "Prostitutes and Guardian Angels: Women, Work, and the Family in Porfirian Mexico." *Hispanic American Historical Review* 72, no. 4 (1992): 529–53.

García Álvarez, Alejandro. *Algunos aspectos de la realidad sociocultural cubana en las tres primeras décadas del siglo XX.* Havana: Editorial de Ciencias Sociales, 1991.

García Álvarez, Alejandro, and Consuelo Naranjo Orovio. "Cubanos y españoles después del 98: de la confrontación a la convivencia pacífica." *Revista de Indias* 58, no. 212 (1998): 101–29.

García Gallo, Dr. Gaspar Jorge. *Baliño: Apuntes históricos sobre sus actividades revolucionarias.* Havana, 1967.

García Salvatecci, Hugo. *El anarquismo frente al marxismo y el Perú.* Lima: Mosca Azul Editores, 1972.

Gledhill, John. *Power and Its Disguises. Anthropological Perspectives on Politics.* 2d ed. London: Pluto Press, 2000.

Golluscio de Montoya, Eva. "Círculos anarquistas y circuitos contraculturales en la Argentina del 1900." *Caravelle* 46 (1986): 49–64.

Gómez Luaces, Eduardo. "Monografía histórica del movimiento obrero en Regla (1833–1958)." Manuscript, n.d.

González, Dominga. "La inmigración española en Cuba." *Economía y Desarrollo* (January–February 1988) no. 1: 92–107.

———. "La inmigración negra y la situación socioeconómica de negros y mulatos en el campo." *Economía y Desarrollo* (May–June 1988) no. 3: 104–15.

———. "La política inmigratoria en los inicios de la seudorrepública." *Economía y Desarrollo* (September–October 1988) no. 5: 122–29.

González, Julián. *El tabaquero en Tampa. Impresiones personales.* Havana: Imprenta El Escore, 1907.

Griffin, Susan. "Can Imagination Save Us? Thinking about the Future with a Beginner's Mind." Reprinted in *Utne Reader* (July-August 1996): 42–46.

Grobart, Fabio. "The Cuban Working Class Movement from 1925–1933." *Science and Society* 39, no. 1 (Spring 1975): 73–103.

Gutiérrez, Sonia, ed. *Teatro popular y cambio social en América Latina: Panorama de una experiencia.* Costa Rica: Editorial Universitaria Centro Americana, 1979.

Guy, Donna. *Sex and Danger in Buenos Aires: Prostitution, Family, and Nation in Argentina.* Lincoln: University of Nebraska Press, 1991.

Hall, Stuart. "Culture, Community, Nation." *Cultural Studies* 7, no. 3 (October 1993): 349–63.

Halstead, Murat. *The Story of Cuba: Her Struggles for Liberty . . . the Cause, Crisis and Destiny*. Chicago: Franklin Square Bible House, 1898.

Hart, John H. *Anarchism and the Mexican Working Class, 1860–1931*. Austin: University of Texas Press, 1978.

Hatton, Timothy J., and Jeffrey G. Williamson. "International Migration 1850–1939: An Economic Survey." *Migration and the International Labor Market, 1850–1939*. Edited by Timothy Hatton and Jeffrey Williamson. London: Routledge, 1994, 3–32.

Helg, Aline. "Afro-Cuban Protest: The Partido Independiente de Color, 1908–1912." *Cuban Studies/Estudios Cubanos* 21 (1991): 101–21.

———. *Our Rightful Share: The Afro-Cuban Struggle for Equality, 1886–1912*. Chapel Hill: University of North Carolina Press, 1995.

Heredia M., Luis. *El anarquismo en Chile (1897–1931)*. Mexico: Ediciones Antorcha, 1981.

Hernández, José M. *Cuba and the United States: Intervention and Militarism, 1868–1933*. Austin: University of Texas Press, 1993.

Hobsbawm, E. J. *Primitive Rebels: Studies in Archaic Forms of Social Movement in the 19th and 20th Centuries*. New York: W. W. Norton, 1959.

———. "Working-Class Internationalism." *Internationalism in the Labour Movement, 1830–1940*, vol. 1. Edited by Frits van Holthoon and Marcel van der Linden. Leiden: E. J. Brill, 1988, 3–16.

Hodges, Donald C. *Mexican Anarchism after the Revolution*. Austin: University of Texas Press, 1995.

Hoerder, Dirk, ed. *The Immigrant Labor Press in North America, 1840s-1870s*, vol. 3. New York: Greenwood Press, 1987.

Horowitz, Irving L., ed. *The Anarchists*. New York: Dell Publishing, 1964.

Ibarra, Jorge. *Un análisis psicosocial del cubano: 1898–1925*. Havana: Editorial de Ciencias Sociales, 1985.

———. *Cuba: 1898–1921. Partidos políticos y clases sociales*. Havana: Editorial de Ciencias Sociales, 1992.

———. *Prologue to Revolution: Cuba, 1898–1958*. London: Lynne Rienner, 1998.

Iglesias García, Fe. "Características de la inmigración española en Cuba (1904–1930)." *Economía y Desarrollo* (March-April 1988) no. 2: 76–101.

Johnston, Laurie. "Cuban Nationalism and Responses to Private Education in Cuba, 1902–1958." In *Ideologues and Ideologies in Latin America*. Edited by Will Fowler. Westport, Conn.: Greenwood Publishing, 1997, 27–43.

———. "Education and Cuba Libre, 1898–1959." *History Today* 45, no. 8 (August 1995): 26–32.

Kapcia, Antoni. *Cuba: Island of Dreams*. New York: Oxford University Press, 2000.

Kern, Robert W. *Red Years/Black Years: A Political History of Spanish Anarchism, 1911–1937*. Philadelphia: Institute for the Study of Human Issues, 1978.

Knight, Franklin. "Jamaican Migrants and the Cuban Sugar Industry." In *Between Slavery and Free Labor*, edited by Moreno Fraginals et al. Baltimore: Johns Hopkins University Press, 1985, 94–114.

Krimmerman, Leonard I., and Lewis Perry, eds. *Patterns of Anarchy: A Collection of Writing on the Anarchist Tradition*. Garden City, N.Y.: Double Day, 1966.

Kropotkin, Peter. *Mutual Aid: A Factor of Evolution*. Montreal: Black Rose Books, 1989.

Kutzinski, Vera M. *Sugar's Secrets: Race and the Erotics of Cuban Nationalism*. Charlottes-ville: University Press of Virginia, 1993.

Le Riverend, Julio. *Historia económica de Cuba*. Havana: Instituto Cubano del Libro, 1971.

Leal, Rine. *Breve historia del teatro cubano*. Havana: Editorial Letras Cubanas, 1980.

Leante, Eugenio. *La educación*. Havana: El Siglo XX, 1919.

———. *Vertiendo ideas*. Havana: Hermanos Sardiñas, 1917.

Leighten, Patricia. *Re-Ordering the Universe: Picasso and Anarchism, 1897–1914*. Prince-ton: Princeton University Press, 1989.

Leis, Raúl A. "Contra el baká: Cultura y educación popular, en la tarea común de des-pertar a los durmientes." *Casa de las Américas* 26, no. 153 (November-December 1985): 63–75.

Levine, Daniel H. "Constructing Culture and Power." In *Constructing Culture and Power in Latin America*, edited by Daniel H. Levine. Ann Arbor: University of Michigan Press (1993): 1–39.

Lindlahr, H., M.D. *Nature Cure: Philosophy and Practice Based on the Unity of Disease and Cure*. 15th ed. Chicago: Nature Cure Publishing Company, 1920.

Lindsay, Forbes. *Cuba and Her People of To-Day*. Boston: L. C. Page, 1928.

Liss, Sheldon B. *Roots of Revolution: Radical Thought in Cuba*. Lincoln: University of Ne-braska Press, 1987.

Litvak, Lily. *El cuento anarquista (1880–1911). Antología*. Madrid: Taurus Ediciones, 1982.

———. *La mirada roja: Estética y arte del anarquismo español (1880–1913)*. Barcelona: Ediciones del Serbal, 1988.

———. *Musa Libertaria: Arte, literatura y vida cultural del anarquismo español (1880–1913)*. Barcelona: Imprenta Clarasó, 1981.

Lockmiller, David A. *Magoon in Cuba: A History of the Second Intervention, 1906–1909*. Chapel Hill: University of North Carolina Press, 1938.

López Álvarez, Francisco, Carlos Calvo Alonso, and Armando Fernández Zubizarreta. *Los gráficos en el movimiento obrero cubano, 1865–1961*. Havana: Editorial de Ciencias Sociales, 1991.

López Segrera, Francisco. *Cuba: Cultura y sociedad*. Havana: Editorial Letras Cubanas, 1989.

———. *Sociología de la colonia y neocolonia cubana, 1510–1959*. Havana: Editorial de Ciencias Sociales, 1989.

Loveira, Carlos. *Adrián del Valle: escritor y periodista de Cuba: Conferencia dada por el Sr. Carlos Loveira, el día 13 de febrero de 1927, en la Academia Nacional de Artes y Letras*. Havana: Imprenta "El Siglo XX," 1927.

———. *De los 26 a los 35. Lecciones de la experiencia en la lucha obrera (1908–1917)*. Washington, D.C.: Law Reporter Printing Company, 1917.

MacLachlan, Colin. *Anarchism and the Mexican Revolution: The Political Trials of Ricardo Flores Magón in the United States*. Berkeley: University of California Press, 1991.

McAdam, Doug. "The Framing Function of Movement Tactics: Strategic Dramaturgy in the American Civil Rights Movement." In *Comparative Perspectives on Social Move-ments*, edited by Doug McAdam, et al. London: Cambridge University Press, 1996, 338–56.

McAdam, Doug, John D. McCarthy, and Mayer N. Zald, eds. *Comparative Perspectives on*

Social Movements: Political Opportunities, Mobilizing Structures, and Cultural Framings. London: Cambridge University Press, 1996.

McCreery, David. "'This Life of Misery and Shame': Female Prostitution in Guatemala City, 1880–1920." *Journal of Latin American Studies* 18, no. 2 (November 1986): 333–53.

McKinley, Blaine. "Anarchist Jeremiads: American Anarchists and American History." *Journal of American Culture* 6, no. 2 (1983): 75–84.

———. "'The Quagmires of Necessity': American Anarchists and Dilemmas of Vocation." *American Quarterly* 34, no. 5 (1982): 503–23.

———. "'A Religion of the New Time': Anarchist Memorials to the Haymarket Martyrs, 1888–1917." *Labor History* 28, no. 3 (1987): 386–400.

Marsh, Margaret S. *Anarchist Women, 1870–1920.* Philadelphia: Temple University Press, 1981.

Marshall, Peter, ed. *The Anarchist Writings of William Godwin.* London: Freedom Press, 1986.

Marshall, Peter H. *Demanding the Impossible: A History of Anarchism.* London: Harper Collins, 1992.

Martin, Gerald. *Journeys through the Labyrinth: Latin American Fiction in the Twentieth Century.* London: Verso, 1989.

———. "The Literature, Music and Art of Latin America, 1870–1930." In *The Cambridge History of Latin America, vol. 4,* edited by Leslie Bethell. Cambridge: Cambridge University Press, 1984, 443–526.

Martínez, Juan. *Cuban Art and National Identity: The Vanguardia Painters, 1927–1950.* Gainesville: University Press of Florida, 1994.

Martínez, Miguel. *El dependiente y la emancipación. (Dedicado a la Voz del Dependiente y a la Federación de Dependientes de restaurantes, hoteles, fondas y cocineros de la Habana.).* Havana: Imprenta "Nuevo Ideal," 1908.

———. *Un día de elecciones. Comedia en un acto.* Valencia: Imprenta de Pau, Torrijos y Compañia, 1905.

Martínez, Samuel. *Peripheral Migrants: Haitians and Dominican Republic Sugar Plantations.* Knoxville: University of Tennessee Press, 1995.

Martínez Balsalobre, Eduardo. *Conferencias sobre el socialismo revolucionario, predicadas en el Templo Parroquial de Monserrate. Son 9 conferencias dedicadas a combatir al socialismo y al anarquismo.* Havana: La Moderna Poesía, 1904.

Masiello, Francine. "Rethinking Neocolonial Esthetics: Literature, Politics and Intellectual Community in Cuba's *Revista de Avance.*" *Latin American Research Review* 28, no. 2 (1993): 33–45.

Masjuan, Eduard. *La ecología humana en el anarquismo ibérico: urbanismo <<orgánico>>, neomalthusianismo y naturismo social.* Madrid: Fundación Anselmo Lorenzo, 2000.

Mazarr, Michael J. *Semper Fidel: America & Cuba, 1776–1988.* Baltimore: Nautical & Aviation Publishing Company of America, 1988.

Melgar Bao, Ricardo. *El movimiento obrero latinoamericano: Historia de una clase subalterna.* Madrid: Alianza Editorial, 1988.

Mesa-Lago, Carmelo. "The Labor Force, Employment and Underemployment in Cuba: 1899–1970." In *Sage Professional Papers in International Studies vol. 1, part 3,* edited by Vincent Davis. Beverly Hills: Sage Publications, 1972, 1–72.

Mintz, Sidney. "Foreword." In *Afro-American Anthropology: Contemporary Perspectives,* edited by Norman Whitten and John F. Szwed. New York: Free Press, 1970.

Miranda, Olivia. "Paralelo entre Varela y Martí: el anticlericalismo." *Revista de la Biblioteca Nacional José Martí* no. 3(September-December 1981): 167–204.

Molyneux, Maxine. "No God, No Boss, No Husband: Anarchist Feminism in Nineteenth Century Argentina." *Latin American Perspectives* 13, no. 1 (Winter 1986): 119–45.

Moore, Robin D. *Nationalizing Blackness: Afrocubanismo and Artistic Revolution in Havana, 1920–1940*. Pittsburgh: University of Pittsburgh Press, 1997.

Moreno Fraginals, Manuel, Frank Moya Pons, and Stanley L. Engerman, eds. *Between Slavery and Free Labor*. Baltimore: Johns Hopkins University Press, 1985.

Mormino, Gary R., and George E. Pozzetta. *The Immigrant World of Ybor City: Italians and Their Latin Neighbors in Tampa, 1885–1985*. Chicago: University of Illinois Press, 1987.

———. "Spanish Anarchism in Tampa, Florida, 1886–1931." In *"Struggle a Hard Battle": Essays on Working-Class Immigrants*, edited by Dirk Hoerder. DeKalb, Ill.: Northern Illinois University Press, 1986, 170–98.

Naranjo Orovio, Consuelo. "Trabajo libre e inmigración española en Cuba, 1880–1930." *Revista de Indias* 52, no. 195/196 (May–December 1992): 749–94.

Naranjo Orovio, Consuelo, and Armando García González. *Medicina y racismo en Cuba: La ciencia ante la inmigración canaria en el siglo XX*. La Laguna—Tenerife, Canary Islands: Centro de la Cultura Popular Canaria, 1996.

Naranjo Orovio, Consuelo, and Miguel Ángel Puig Samper Mulero. "El legado hispano y la conciencia nacional en Cuba." *Revista de Indias* 50, no. 190 (September–December 1990): 789–808.

Nathan, George Jean. *The Popular Theatre*. New York: Alfred A. Knopf, 1918.

Nelson, Bruce. *Beyond the Martyrs: A Social History of Chicago's Anarchists, 1870–1900*. New Brunswick: Rutgers University Press, 1988.

Norton, Albert J. *Norton's Complete Hand-book of Havana and Cuba*. New York: Rand, McNally & Company, 1900.

Núñez Florencio, Rafael. "Los anarquistas españoles y americanos ante la guerra de Cuba." *Hispania* 51/3, no. 179 (1991): 1077–92.

Núñez Seixas, Xosé M. "Inmigración y galleguismo en Cuba (1879/1936)." *Revista de Indias* 53, no. 197 (January–April 1993): 53–95.

Olive, E. *La pedagogía obrerista de la imagen*. Barcelona: Palma de Mallorca, 1978.

Ordenamiento cronológico de las publicaciones seriadas cerradas. Havana: Instituto de Historia, n.d.

Ordoqui, Joaquín. *Elementos para la historia del movimiento obrero en Cuba*. Havana: Instituto Superior de Educación, 1961.

Ortiz, Fernando. *Cuban Counterpoint: Tobacco and Sugar*. 1947. Durham: Duke University Press, 1995.

Oved, Iaácov. *El anarquismo y el movimiento obrero en Argentina*. Mexico: Siglo Veintiuno, 1978.

Padrón, Pedro Luis. *Julio Antonio Mella y el movimiento obrero*. Havana: Editorial de Ciencias Sociales, 1980.

Páez, Alexei. *El anarquismo en el Ecuador*. Quito: Corporación Editora Nacional, 1986.

Page, Charles. "The Development of Organized Labor in Cuba." Ph.D. diss., University of California, 1952.

Paniagua, Javier. "Una gran pregunta y varias respuestas: El anarquismo español desde la política a la historiografía." *Historia Social* 12 (Winter 1992): 31–57.

Pareja, Piedad. *Anarquismo y sindicalismo en el Perú*. Lima: Ediciones Rikchay Peru, 1978.

Pedroso, Luis. *Acerca de las tradiciones internacionalistas del proletariado en Regla*. Regla, Cuba: Museo de Regla, 1985.

Pendergrast, Mark. *For God, Country and Coca-Cola: The Unauthorized History of the Great American Soft Drink and the Company That Makes It*. New York: Charles Scribner's Sons, 1993.

Penichet, Antonio. *¡Alma Rebelde!, novela histórica*. Havana: El Ideal, 1921.

———. *Del ambiente proletario*. Havana: Avisador Comercial, 1918.

———. "El proceso social." In *Curso de introducción a la historia de Cuba*, edited by Emilio Roig de Leuchsenring. Havana: Municipio de la Habana (1938): 431–47.

———. *El Soldado Rafael; páginas de la vida real*. Havana: Grupo Germinal, 1919.

———. *Tácticas en uso y tácticas a seguir*. Havana: El Ideal, 1922.

———. *La vida de un pernicioso*. Havana: Avisador Comercial, 1919.

Peraza Sarausa, Dr. Fermin, ed. *Diccionario biográfico cubano*. Havana: Anuario Bibliográfico Cubano, 1951.

Pérez de la Riva, Juan. "La inmigración antillana en Cuba durante el primer tercio del siglo XX." *Revista de la Biblioteca Nacional José Martí* no. 2 (May–August 1975): 75–88.

Pérez de la Riva, Juan, and Blanca Morejón Seijas. "La población de Cuba, la guerra de independencia y la inmigración del siglo xx." *Revista de la Biblioteca Nacional José Martí* no. 2 (May–August 1971): 17–28.

Pérez de la Riva, Juan, et al., eds. *La República Neocolonial; Anuario de Estudios Cubanos*. 1973; Havana: Editorial de Ciencias Sociales, 1979.

Pérez, Louis A., Jr. *Cuba and the United States: Ties of Singular Intimacy*. Athens: University of Georgia Press, 1990.

———. *Cuba Between Empires, 1972–1902*. Pittsburgh: University of Pittsburgh Press, 1983.

———. *Cuba: Between Reform and Revolution*. New York: Oxford University Press, 1988.

———. "Cuba Materials in the Bureau of Insular Affairs Library." *Latin American Research Review* 13, no. 1 (1978): 182–88.

———. *Cuba under the Platt Amendment, 1902–1934*. Pittsburgh: University of Pittsburgh Press, 1986.

———. *Essays on Cuban History: Historiography and Research*. Gainesville: University Press of Florida, 1994.

———. *A Guide to Cuban Collections in the United States*. Westport, Conn.: Greenwood Press, 1991.

———. "The Imperial Design: Politics and Pedagogy in Occupied Cuba, 1899–1902." *Cuban Studies/Estudios Cubanos* 12, no. 2 (July 1982): 1–19.

———. *On Becoming Cuban: Identity, Nationality, and Culture*. Chapel Hill: University of North Carolina Press, 1999.

———. "Record Collections at the Cuban National Archives: A Descriptive Survey." *Latin American Research Review* 19, no. 1 (1984): 142–57.

———, ed. *Slaves, Sugar, & Colonial Society: Travel Accounts of Cuba, 1801–1899*. Wilmington, Del.: Scholarly Resources, 1992.

———. *The War of 1898: The United States & Cuba in History & Historiography*. Chapel Hill: University of North Carolina Press, 1998.

Pichardo, Estéban, ed. *Diccionario provincial casi razonado de vozes y frases cubanas*. 1836. Havana: Editorial de Ciencias Sociales, 1985.

Piga, Domingo. "Problemas del teatro popular." In *Teatro popular y cambio social en*

América Latina: Panorama de una experiencia, edited by Sonia Gutiérrez. San José, Costa Rica: EDUCA, 1979, 66–75.

Plasencia, Aleida, ed. *Artículos publicados en el periódico "El Productor."* Havana: Consejo Nacional de Cultura, 1967.

————. "Historia del movimiento obrero en Cuba." In *Historia del movimiento del obrero en América Latina, vol.1 (México, Cuba, Haití, República Dominicana, Puerto Rico)*, edited by Pablo González Casanova. México: Siglo Veintiuno Editores, Instituto de Investigaciones Sociales de la UNAM, 1984, 88–183.

Ponte Domínguez, Francisco J. *Pensamiento laico de José Martí*. Havana: Editorial "Modas Magazine," 1956.

Por la escuela cubana en Cuba Libre. Trabajos, acuerdos y adhesiones de una campaña cívica y cultural. Havana: Cárdenas, 1941.

Portuondo, Fernándo. *Estudios de historia de Cuba*. Havana: Editorial de Ciencias Sociales, 1986.

Portuondo, José Antonio. *"La Aurora" y los comienzos de la prensa y de la organización obrera en Cuba*. Havana: Imprenta Nacional de Cuba, 1961.

Pouget, Emile. *Sabotage*. A. Giovannitti, trans. Chicago: Charles H. Kerr, 1912.

Poyo, Gerald E. "The Anarchist Challenge to the Cuban Independence Movement, 1885–1890." *Cuban Studies/Estudios Cubanos* 15, no. 1 (1985): 29–42.

————. "Cuban Émigré Communities in the United States and the Independence of Their Homeland." Ph.D. diss., University of Florida, 1983.

————. *"With All, and for the Good of All": The Emergence of Popular Nationalism in the Cuban Communities of the United States, 1848–1898*. Durham: Duke University Press, 1989.

Primelles, León. *Crónica Cubana, 1919–1922*. 2 vols. Havana: Editorial Lex, 1957.

Rama, Carlos M., and Angel J. Cappelletti, eds. *El anarquismo en América Latina*. Caracas: Biblioteca Ayacucho, 1990.

Riera Hernández, Mario. *Historical obrero cubano, 1547–1965. Sindalismo, huelgas, economía*. Miami: Renia Press, 1965.

Rivero Muñiz, José. *El movimiento laboral cubano durante el período 1906–1911*. Santa Clara: Universidad Central de Las Villas, Dirección de Publicaciones, 1962.

————. *El movimiento obrero durante la primera intervención: Apuntes para la historia del proletariado en Cuba*. Santa Clara: Universidad Central de Las Villas, 1961.

Robert, Vincent. "'La protesta universal' contra la ejecución de Ferrer: las manifestaciones de octubre de 1909." *Historia Social* 14 (Fall 1992): 61–82.

Rodríguez, Miguel. *Los tranviarios y el anarquismo en México (1920–1925)*. Puebla, Mexico: Universidad Autónoma de Puebla, 1980.

Roemer, Kenneth. "Defining America as Utopia." In *America as Utopia*, edited by Kenneth Roemer. New York: Burt Franklin, 1981, 1–15.

Román y Moreno, Manuel. *La habitación del obrero*. Havana: Avisador Comercial, 1907.

Rosenthal, Anton. "The Arrival of the Electric Streetcar and the Conflict over Progress in Early Twentieth-Century Montevideo." *Journal of Latin American Studies* 27 (1995): 319–41.

Rosenzweig, Roy. *Eight Hours for What We Will: Workers and Leisure in an Industrial City, 1870–1920*. Cambridge: Cambridge University Press, 1983.

Roszak, Theodore. *The Making of a Counter Culture: Reflections on the Technocratic Society and Its Youthful Opposition*. Garden City, N.Y.: Anchor Books, 1969.

Rowe, William, and Vivian Schelling. *Memory and Modernity: Popular Culture in Latin America.* London: Verso, 1991.

Salerno, Salvatore. *Red November, Black November: Culture and Community in the Industrial Workers of the World.* Albany: State University of New York Press, 1989.

Sandos, James A. *Rebellion in the Borderlands: Anarchism and the Plan of San Diego, 1904–1923.* Norman: University of Oklahoma Press, 1992.

Sarduy, Pedro Pérez, and Jean Stubbs, eds. *Afro-Cuba: An Anthology of Cuban Writing on Race, Politics and Culture.* Australia: Ocean Press, 1993.

Schulman, Ivan A., and Erica Miles. "A Guide to the Location of Nineteenth-Century Cuban Magazines." *Latin American Research Review* 12, no. 2 (1977): 69–102.

Schwartz, Rosalie. *Lawless Liberators: Political Banditry and Cuban Independence.* Durham: Duke University Press, 1988.

———. *Pleasure Island: Tourism & Temptation in Cuba.* Lincoln: University of Nebraska Press, 1997.

Secades y Japón, Manuel. *La justicia en Cuba; los veteranos y los indultos.* 2d ed. Havana: La Prueba, 1908.

Secades y Japón, Manuel, and Horacio Díaz Pardo. *El calvario de los obreros. Proceso de la huelga.* Havana: La Epoca, 1909.

Serra García, Mariana. *La Aurora y El Productor.* Havana: Concurso de Historia, 1978.

Shaffer, Kirwin R. "Cuba para todos: Anarchist Internationalism and the Cultural Politics of Cuban Independence, 1898–1925." *Cuban Studies* 31 (2000): 45–75.

———. "Freedom Teaching: Anarchism and Education in Early Republican Cuba, 1898–1925." *The Americas* 60, no. 2 (October 2003): 151–83.

———. "Prostitutes, Bad Seeds, and Revolutionary Mothers in Cuban Anarchism: Imagining Women in the Fiction of Adrián del Valle and Antonio Penichet, 1898–1930." *Studies in Latin American Popular Culture* 18 (1999): 1–18.

———. "The Radical Muse: Women and Anarchism in Early-Twentieth-Century Cuba." *Cuban Studies* 34 (2003): 130–53.

Siguan Boehmer, Marisa. *Literatura popular libertaria: Trece años de <<La Novela Ideal>> (1925–1938).* Barcelona: Ediciones Península, 1981.

Smith, Mark. "The Political Economy of Sugar Production and the Environment of Eastern Cuba, 1898–1923." *Environmental History Review* 19, no. 4 (Winter 1995): 31–48.

Smith, Robert. *The United States and Cuba: Business and Diplomacy, 1917–1960.* New Haven, Conn.: College and University Press, 1960.

Sonn, Richard. *Anarchism.* New York: Twayne Publishers, 1992.

———. *Anarchism and Cultural Politics in Fin de Siècle France.* Lincoln: University of Nebraska Press, 1989.

Spalding, Hobart A. *Organized Labor in Latin America; Historical Case Studies of Workers in Dependent Societies.* New York: New York University Press, 1977.

Stoner, K. Lynn. *From the House to the Streets: The Cuban Woman's Movement for Legal Reform, 1898–1940.* Durham: Duke University Press, 1991.

Strikwerda, Carl, and Camille Guerin-Gonzáles. "Labor, Migration, and Politics." In *The Politics of Immigrant Workers: Labor Activism and Migration in the World Economy since 1830,* edited by Camille Guerin-Gonzáles and Carl Strikwerda. New York: Holmes & Meier, 1993, 3–45.

Stubbs, Jean. *Tobacco on the Periphery: A Case Study in Cuban Labour History, 1860–1958.* Cambridge: Cambridge University Press, 1985.

Teja, Ada María. "El origen de la nacionalidad y su toma de conciencia en la obra juvenil de José Martí: semantización de Cuba y España." *Revista Iberoamericana* 152-153 (July–December 1990): 793–822.

Tellería, Evelio. *Los congresos obreros en Cuba*. Havana: Editorial de Ciencias Sociales, 1973.

Thompson, Ruth. "The Limitations of Ideology in the Early Argentine Labour Movement: Anarchism in the Trade Unions, 1890–1920." *Journal of Latin American Studies* 16, no. 1 (May 1984): 81–100.

Tilly, Charles. *Stories, Identities, and Political Change*. New York: Rowan & Littlefield, 2003.

Toro González, Carlos del. "La fundación de la primera sindical nacional de los trabajadores cubanos (los congresos obreros de 1892 a 1934)." In *La República Neocolonial*, edited by Juan Pérez de la Riva et al. Havana: Editorial de Ciencias Sociales, 1979, 98–103.

———. *El movimiento obrero cubano en 1914*. Havana: Instituto Cubano del Libro, 1969.

Tower Sargent, Lyman. "The Three Faces of Utopianism Revisited." *Utopian Studies* 5, no. 1 (1994): 1–37.

Van der Linden, Marcel, and Wayne Thorpe. "Auge y decadencia del sindicalismo revolucionario." *Historia Social* 12 (Winter 1992): 3–29.

———, eds. *Revolutionary Syndicalism: An International Perspective*. Aldershot, England: Scholar Press, 1990.

Varona, Enrique José. *De la colonia a la república: Selección de trabajos políticos, ordenada por su autor*. Havana: Sociedad Editorial Cuba Contemporánea, 1919.

Viñas, David. *Anarquistas en América Latina*. Mexico, D.F.: Editorial Katun, 1983.

West, Alan. *Tropics of History: Cuba Imagined*. Westport, Conn.: Bergin & Garvey, 1997.

Whitney, Robert. *State and Revolution in Cuba: Mass Mobilization and Political Change, 1920–1940*. Chapel Hill: University of North Carolina Press, 2001.

Winters, Donald. *The Soul of the Wobblies: The I.W.W., Religion, and American Culture in the Progressive Era, 1905–1917*. Westport: Greenwood Press, 1985.

Wolf, Eric. *Envisioning Power: Ideologies of Dominance and Crisis*. Berkeley: University of California Press, 1999.

———. *Europe and the People without History*. Berkeley: University of California Press, 1982.

Wolfe, Joel. "Anarchist Ideology, Worker Practice: The 1917 General Strike and the Formation of São Paulo's Working Class." *Hispanic American Historical Review* 71, no. 4 (November 1991): 809–46.

Wright, Irene A. *Cuba*. New York: MacMillan Company, 1910.

Yaremko, Jason. *U.S. Protestant Missions in Cuba: From Independence to Castro*. Gainesville: University Press of Florida, 2000.

Yinger, J. Milton. *Countercultures: The Promise and the Peril of a World Turned Upside Down*. New York: Free Press, 1982.

Zanetti Lecuona, Oscar, and Alejandro García Álvarez. *Caminos para el azucar*. Havana: Editorial de Ciencias Sociales, 1987.

———. *Sugar and Railroads: A Cuban History, 1837–1959*. Franklin Knight and Mary Todd, trans. Chapel Hill: University of North Carolina Press, 1998.

———, eds. *United Fruit Company: Un caso del dominio imperialista en Cuba*. Havana: Editorial de Ciencias Sociales, 1976.

Zubillaga, Carlos. "Luchas populares y cultura alternativa en Uruguay. El Centro Internacional de Estudios Sociales." *Siglo XIX* 3, no. 6 (July–December 1988): 11–40.

Index

About the Author

Kirwin Shaffer is professor of Latin American Studies at Pennsylvania State University–Berks College. He has authored or edited several books on anarchist culture and networks in Cuba and the Caribbean Basin from the 1890s to 1920s including *Black Flag Boricuas: Anarchism, Antiauthoritarianism, and the Left in Puerto Rico, 1897–1921* and *In Defiance of Boundaries: Anarchism in Latin American History.*

PM Press was founded at the end of 2007 by a small collection of folks with decades of publishing, media, and organizing experience. PM Press co-conspirators have published and distributed hundreds of books, pamphlets, CDs, and DVDs. Members of PM have founded enduring book fairs, spearheaded victorious tenant organizing campaigns, and worked closely with bookstores, academic conferences, and even rock bands to deliver political and challenging ideas to all walks of life. We're old enough to know what we're doing and young enough to know what's at stake.

We create radical and stimulating fiction and non-fiction books, pamphlets, T-shirts, visual and audio materials to educate, entertain, and inspire you. We aim to distribute these through every available channel with every available technology—whether that means you are seeing anarchist classics at our bookfair stalls; reading our latest vegan cookbook at the café; downloading geeky fiction e-books; or digging new music and timely videos from our website.

PM Press is always on the lookout for talented and skilled volunteers, artists, activists, and writers to work with. If you have a great idea for a project or can contribute in some way, please get in touch.

PM Press
PO Box 23912
Oakland CA 94623
510-658-3906
www.pmpress.org

PM Press in Europe
europe@pmpress.org
www.pmpress.org.uk

FRIENDS OF PM

These are indisputably momentous times—the financial system is melting down globally and the Empire is stumbling. Now more than ever there is a vital need for radical ideas.

In the many years since its founding—and on a mere shoestring—PM Press has risen to the formidable challenge of publishing and distributing knowledge and entertainment for the struggles ahead. With hundreds of releases to date, we have published an impressive and stimulating array of literature, art, music, politics, and culture. Using every available medium, we've succeeded in connecting those hungry for ideas and information to those putting them into practice.

Friends of PM allows you to directly help impact, amplify, and revitalize the discourse and actions of radical writers, filmmakers, and artists. It provides us with a stable foundation from which we can build upon our early successes and provides a much-needed subsidy for the materials that can't necessarily pay their own way. You can help make that happen—and receive every new title automatically delivered to your door once a month—by joining as a Friend of PM Press. And, we'll throw in a free T-shirt when you sign up.

Here are your options:
- $30 a month: Get all books and pamphlets plus 50% discount on all webstore purchases
- $40 a month: Get all PM Press releases (including CDs and DVDs) plus 50% discount on all webstore purchases
- $100 a month: Superstar—Everything plus PM merchandise, free downloads, and 50% discount on all webstore purchases

For those who can't afford $30 or more a month, we have **SUSTAINER RATES** at $15, $10, and $5. Sustainers get a free PM Press T-shirt and a 50% discount on all purchases from our website.

Your Visa or Mastercard will be billed once a month, until you tell us to stop. Or until our efforts succeed in bringing the revolution around. Or the financial meltdown of Capital makes plastic redundant. Whichever comes first.

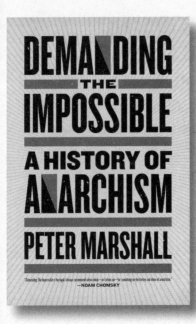

DEMANDING THE IMPOSSIBLE
A History of Anarchism
Peter Marshall
$28.95
ISBN: 978-1-60486-064-1
5.5x8.5 • 840 pages

Navigating the broad "river of anarchy," from Taoism to Situationism, from Ranters to Punk rockers, from individualists to communists, from anarcho-syndicalists to anarcha-feminists, *Demanding the Impossible* is an authoritative and lively study of a widely misunderstood subject. It explores the key anarchist concepts of society and the state, freedom and equality, authority and power, and investigates the successes and failure of the anarchist movements throughout the world. While remaining sympathetic to anarchism, it presents a balanced and critical account. It covers not only the classic anarchist thinkers, such as Godwin, Proudhon, Bakunin, Kropotkin, Reclus and Emma Goldman, but also other libertarian figures, such as Nietzsche, Camus, Gandhi, Foucault and Chomsky. No other book on anarchism covers so much so incisively.

In this updated edition, a new epilogue examines the most recent developments, including "post-anarchism" and "anarcho-primitivism" as well as the anarchist contribution to the peace, green and Global Justice movements.

Demanding the Impossible is essential reading for anyone wishing to understand what anarchists stand for and what they have achieved. It will also appeal to those who want to discover how anarchism offers an inspiring and original body of ideas and practices which is more relevant than ever in the twenty-first century.

> "Demanding the Impossible is the book I always recommend when asked—as I often am—for something on the history and ideas of anarchism."
> —Noam Chomsky

NO GODS, NO MASTERS, NO PERIPHERIES

Global Anarchisms

Edited by Raymond Craib and Barry Maxwell

$27.95
ISBN: 978-1-62963-098-4
6x9 • 408 pages

Was anarchism in areas outside of Europe an import and a script to be mimicked? Was it perpetually at odds with other currents of the Left? The authors in this collection take up these questions of geographical and political peripheries. Building on recent research that has emphasized the plural origins of anarchist thought and practice, they reflect on the histories and cultures of the antistatist mutual aid movements of the last century beyond the boundaries of an artificially coherent Europe. At the same time, they reexamine the historical relationships between anarchism and communism without starting from the position of sectarian difference (Marxism versus anarchism). Rather, they look at how anarchism and communism intersected; how the insurgent Left could appear—and in fact was—much more ecumenical, capacious, and eclectic than frequently portrayed; and reveal that such capaciousness is a hallmark of anarchist practice, which is prefigurative in its politics and antihierarchical and antidogmatic in its ethics.

Copublished the with Institute for Comparative Modernities, this collection includes contributions by Gavin Arnall, Mohammed Bamyeh, Bruno Bosteels, Raymond Craib, Silvia Rivera Cusicanqui, Geoffroy de Laforcade, Silvia Federici, Steven J. Hirsch, Adrienne Carey Hurley, Hilary Klein, Peter Linebaugh, Barry Maxwell, David Porter, Maia Ramnath, Penelope Rosemont, and Bahia Shehab.

"Broad in scope, generously ecumenical in outlook, bold in its attempt to tease apart the many threads and tensions of anarchism, this collection defies borders and category. These illuminating explorations in pan-anarchism provide a much-needed antidote to the myopic characterizations that bedevil the red and black."
—Sasha Lilley, author of *Capital and Its Discontents*

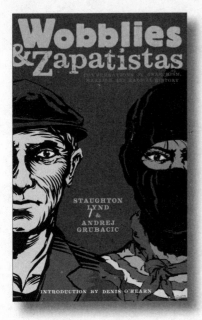

WOBBLIES AND ZAPATISTAS
Conversations on Anarchism, Marxism and Radical History
Staughton Lynd and Andrej Grubacic

$20.00
ISBN: 978-1-60486-041-2
5x8 • 300 pages

Wobblies and Zapatistas offers the reader an encounter between two generations and two traditions. Andrej Grubacic is an anarchist from the Balkans. Staughton Lynd is a lifelong pacifist, influenced by Marxism. They meet in dialogue in an effort to bring together the anarchist and Marxist traditions, to discuss the writing of history by those who make it, and to remind us of the idea that "my country is the world." Encompassing a Left-libertarian perspective and an emphatically activist standpoint, these conversations are meant to be read in the clubs and affinity groups of the new Movement.

The authors accompany us on a journey through modern revolutions, direct actions, antiglobalist counter-summits, Freedom Schools, Zapatista cooperatives, Haymarket and Petrograd, Hanoi and Belgrade, "intentional" communities, wildcat strikes, early Protestant communities, Native American democratic practices, the Workers' Solidarity Club of Youngstown, occupied factories, self-organized councils and soviets, the lives of forgotten revolutionaries, Quaker meetings, antiwar movements, and prison rebellions. Neglected and forgotten moments of interracial self-activity are brought to light. The book invites the attention of readers who believe that a better world, on the other side of capitalism and state bureaucracy, may indeed be possible.

> "There's no doubt that we've lost much of our history. It's also very clear that those in power in this country like it that way. Here's a book that shows us why. It demonstrates not only that another world is possible, but that it already exists, has existed, and shows an endless potential to burst through the artificial walls and divisions that currently imprison us. An exquisite contribution to the literature of human freedom, and coming not a moment too soon."
> —David Graeber, author of *Fragments of an Anarchist Anthropology* and *Direct Action: An Ethnography*

AUTONOMY IS IN OUR HEARTS
Zapatista Autonomous Government through the Lens of the Tsotsil Language
Dylan Eldredge Fitzwater
Foreword by John P. Clark
$19.95
ISBN: 978-1-62963-580-4
6x9 • 224 pages

Following the Zapatista uprising on New Year's Day 1994, the EZLN communities of Chiapas began the slow process of creating a system of autonomous government that would bring their call for freedom, justice, and democracy from word to reality. *Autonomy Is in Our Hearts* analyzes this long and arduous process on its own terms, using the conceptual language of Tsotsil, a Mayan language indigenous to the highland Zapatista communities of Chiapas.

The words "Freedom," "Justice," and "Democracy" emblazoned on the Zapatista flags are only approximations of the aspirations articulated in the six indigenous languages spoken by the Zapatista communities. They are rough translations of concepts such as ichbail ta muk' or "mutual recognition and respect among equal persons or peoples," a'mtel or "collective work done for the good of a community" and lekil kuxlejal or "the life that is good for everyone." *Autonomy Is in Our Hearts* provides a fresh perspective on the Zapatistas and a deep engagement with the daily realities of Zapatista autonomous government. Simultaneously an exposition of Tsotsil philosophy and a detailed account of Zapatista governance structures, this book is an indispensable commentary on the Zapatista movement of today.

> "This is a refreshing book. Written with the humility of the learner, or the absence of the arrogant knower, the Zapatista dictum to 'command obeying' becomes to 'know learning.'"
> —Marisol de la Cadena, author of *Earth Beings: Ecologies of Practice across Andean Worlds*

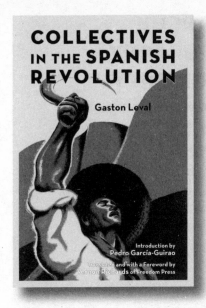

COLLECTIVES IN THE SPANISH REVOLUTION

Gaston Leval

Translation and Foreword by Vernon Richards

Introduction by Pedro García-Guirao

$27.95

ISBN: 978-1-62963-447-0

5.5x8 • 416 pages

Revolutionary Spain came about with an explosion of social change so advanced and sweeping that it remains widely studied as one of the foremost experiments in worker self-management in history. At the heart of this vast foray into toppling entrenched forms of domination and centralised control was the flourishing of an array of worker-run collectives in industry, agriculture, public services, and beyond.

Collectives in the Spanish Revolution is a unique account of this transformative process—a work combining impeccable research and analysis with lucid reportage. Its author, Gaston Leval, was not only a participant in the Revolution and a dedicated anarcho-syndicalist but an especially knowledgeable eyewitness to the many industrial and agrarian collectives. In documenting the collectives' organisation and how they improved working conditions and increased output, Leval also gave voice to the workers who made them, recording their stories and experiences. At the same time, Leval did not shy away from exploring some of the collectives' failings, often ignored in other accounts of the period, opening space for readers today to critically draw lessons from the Spanish experience with self-managed collectives.

The book opens with an insightful examination of pre-revolutionary economic conditions in Spain that gave rise to the worker and peasant initiatives Leval documents and analyses in the bulk of his study. He begins by surveying agrarian collectives in Aragón, Levante, and Castile. Leval then guides the reader through an incredible variety of urban examples of self-organisation, from factories and workshops to medicine, social services, Barcelona's tramway system, and beyond. He concludes with a brief but perceptive consideration of the broader political context in which workers carried out such a far-reaching revolution in social organisation—and a rumination on who and what was responsible for its defeat.

This classic translation of the French original by Vernon Richards is presented in this edition for the first time with an index. A new introduction by Pedro García-Guirao and a preface by Stuart Christie offer a précis of Leval's life and methods, placing his landmark study in the context of more recent writing on the Spanish collectives—eloquently positing that Leval's account of collectivism and his assessments of their achievements and failings still have a great deal to teach us today.

ANARCHY, GEOGRAPHY, MODERNITY

Selected Writings of Elisée Reclus

Elisée Reclus

Edited by John P. Clark and Camille Martin

$22.95

ISBN: 978-1-60486-429-8

6x9 • 304 pages

Anarchy, Geography, Modernity is the first comprehensive introduction to the thought of Elisée Reclus, the great anarchist geographer and political theorist. It shows him to be an extraordinary figure for his age. Not only an anarchist but also a radical feminist, anti-racist, ecologist, animal rights advocate, cultural radical, nudist, and vegetarian. Not only a major social thinker but also a dedicated revolutionary.

The work analyzes Reclus' greatest achievement, a sweeping historical and theoretical synthesis recounting the story of the earth and humanity as an epochal struggle between freedom and domination. It presents his groundbreaking critique of all forms of domination: not only capitalism, the state, and authoritarian religion, but also patriarchy, racism, technological domination, and the domination of nature. His crucial insights on the interrelation between personal and small-group transformation, broader cultural change, and large-scale social organization are explored. Reclus' ideas are presented both through detailed exposition and analysis, and in extensive translations of key texts, most appearing in English for the first time.

"For far too long Elisée Reclus has stood in the shadow of Godwin, Proudhon, Bakunin, Kropotkin, and Emma Goldman. Now John Clark has pulled Reclus forward to stand shoulder to shoulder with Anarchism's cynosures. Reclus' light brought into anarchism's compass not only a focus on ecology, but a struggle against both patriarchy and racism, contributions which can now be fully appreciated thanks to John Clark's exegesis and [his and Camille Martin's] translations of works previously unavailable in English. No serious reader can afford to neglect this book."
—Dana Ward, Pitzer College

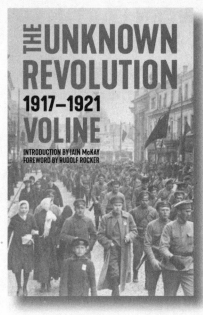

THE UNKNOWN
REVOLUTION
1917–1921
Voline
Introduction bt Iain McKay
Foreword by Rudolf Rocker
$32.95
ISBN: 978-1-62963-577-4
6x9 • 832 pages

This is the untold story of the Russian Revolution: its antecedents, its far-reaching changes, its betrayal by Bolshevik terror, and the massive resistance of non-Bolshevik revolutionaries. This in-depth, eyewitness history written by Voline, an outspoken activist in the Russian Revolution, is accompanied by a biography of the author by Rudolf Rocker and a contemporary introduction by anarchist historian Iain McKay

Significant attention is given to what the author describes as "struggles for the real Social Revolution"; that is, the uprising of the sailors and workers of Kronstadt in 1921, and the peasant movement that Nestor Makhno led in Ukraine. These movements, which sought to defend the social revolution from destruction by the politicians, provide important material for a clearer understanding of both the original objectives of the Russian Revolution and the problems with which all revolutions with far-reaching social objectives have to contend.

Drawing on the revolutionary press of the time, Voline reveals the deep cleavage between the objectives of the libertarians and those of the Bolsheviks, differences which the latter "resolved" by ruthlessly eliminating all who stood in their way in the struggle for power.

This edition is a translation of the full text of *La Révolution inconnue*, originally published in French in 1947. It reinstates material omitted from earlier English-language editions and reproduces the complete text of the original volumes.

"A fascinating and valuable book—a combination of history, eyewitness account, and partisan advocacy—about the Russian revolution of 1917–21."
—Stephen F. Cohen, author of *Bukharin and the Bolshevik Revolution*

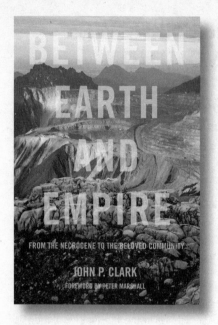

BETWEEN EARTH AND EMPIRE
From the Necrocene to the Beloved Community
John P. Clark
Foreword by Peter Marshall
ISBN: 978-1-62963-648-1
6x9 • 352 pages

Between Earth and Empire focuses on the crucial position of humanity at the present moment in Earth History. We have left the Cenozoic, the "new period of life," and are now in the midst of the Necrocene, a period of mass extinction and reversal of the course of evolution of life on Earth. We are now nearing the end of the long history of Empire and domination, faced with the alternatives of either continuing the path of social and ecological disintegration or initiating a new era of social and ecological regeneration.

The book shows that conventional approaches to global crisis on both the right and the left have succumbed to processes of denial and disavowal, either rejecting the reality of crisis entirely or substituting ineffectual but comforting gestures and images for deep, systemic social transformation. It is argued that an effective response to global crisis requires attention to all major spheres of social determination, including the social institutional structure, the social ideology, the social imaginary, and the social ethos. Large-scale social and ecological regeneration must be rooted in communities of liberation and solidarity, in which personal and group transformation take place in all these spheres, so that a culture of awakening and care can emerge.

Between Earth and Empire explores examples of significant progress in this direction, including the Zapatista movement in Chiapas, the Democratic Autonomy Movement in Rojava, indigenous movements in defense of the commons, the solidarity economy movement, and efforts to create liberated base communities and affinity groups within anarchism and other radical social movements. In the end, the book presents a vision of hope for social and ecological regeneration through the rebirth of a libertarian and communitarian social imaginary, and the flourishing of a free cooperative community globally.

> "Whether in Rojava where women are fighting for their people's survival, or in the loss and terror of New Orleans after the Katrina flood, Clark finds models of communality, care, and hope. Finely reasoned and integrative, tracing the dialectical play of institution and ethos, ideology and imaginary, this book will speak to philosophers and activists alike."
> —Ariel Salleh, author of *Ecofeminism as Politics*